Practice-Based Evidence in the Psychological Therapies

Practice-Based Evidence in the Psychological Therapies

Toward Policy Implications for Research, Training, and Clinical Guidelines

Edited by
LOUIS G. CASTONGUAY
DANA ATZIL-SLONIM
MICHAEL BARKHAM
WOLFGANG LUTZ

OXFORD
UNIVERSITY PRESS

OXFORD
UNIVERSITY PRESS

Oxford University Press is a department of the University of Oxford.
It furthers the University's objective of excellence in research, scholarship,
and education by publishing worldwide. Oxford is a registered trade mark of
Oxford University Press in the UK and in certain other countries.

Published in the United States of America by Oxford University Press
198 Madison Avenue, New York, NY 10016, United States of America.

CIP data is on file at the Library of Congress.

ISBN 9780197748305

DOI: 10.1093/9780197748336.001.0001

Printed by Integrated Books International, United States of America

MIX
Paper
FSC FSC® C183721

The manufacturer's authorized representative in the EU for product safety is
Oxford University Press España S.A. of Parque Empresarial San Fernando de Henares,
Avenida de Castilla, 2 – 28830 Madrid (www.oup.es/en or product.safety@oup.com).
OUP España S.A. also acts as importer into Spain of products made by the manufacturer.

To all practitioners and researchers who take up the challenges but reap the rewards of engaging in practice-based evidence

Contents

SECTION V. INTEGRATION AND DISSEMINATION

CONCLUSION

Preface

This book emerges from a historical context marked by hope, progress, and ongoing challenges. Since the Boulder Conference in 1949, the scientist-practitioner model has served as a foundational framework for integrating research and practice in psychology. While it has inspired significant advancements, its widespread adoption as a fully assimilated philosophy for bridging psychological research and clinical practice remains incomplete. One of the key barriers has been the division between the communities of researchers and clinicians, who often operate within separate spheres of knowledge and action.

There have been exchanges of information between these spheres. Over previous decades, for example, many clinical training programs have emphasized evidence-based practices—practices that are in large part based on empirical results. But while some of these findings, especially those driven by randomized controlled trials (RCTs), are predominantly featured as key components in clinical and policy guidelines, they are viewed by many practitioners as insufficient for, and at times irrelevant to, day-to-day clinical practice.

Although the four of us recognize that RCTs have made crucial contributions to the field and indeed are essential to developing a scientific basis for the psychological therapies, we are also convinced that they are insufficient on their own to act as the gold standard source of findings for the empirical foundations of psychological therapies. Accordingly, we have over many years primarily devoted our respective research endeavors to a complementary research paradigm that yields what is now known as *practice-based evidence*. In contrast to the findings generated by traditional RCTs, as well as other studies conducted in controlled settings, practice-based evidence refers to data collected not only in naturalistic settings but also as part of the clinical routine of these settings. As such, practice-based evidence is based on data derived from clients who are treated in the real world and not restricted to those meeting specific, research-imposed inclusion and exclusion criteria. Hence, it is derived from the actual clinical context, in terms of treatment sites and neighborhoods, within which routine treatments are provided as opposed to clinical environments created and maintained primarily for research purposes. Crucially, research underpinning practice-based evidence is embedded in and/or reflects the process that is taking place ordinarily between therapists and clients and, importantly, represents what therapists do, think, and feel, as well as the impact of their actions and experiences in their daily routine.

In fact, practice-based evidence shifts the place and role of the therapists in research. As opposed to traditional RCTs where the focus is on the effect of specific treatments, in practice-based evidence the role of therapists and the differences between them become the primary focus of this approach rather than factors to be controlled or considered just as noise. In addition, therapists are recognized as primary contributors of data as part of their day-to-day work. In some instances, practitioners are fully involved in the design and implementation of research yielding practice-based evidence, within their own practice and/or in collaboration with other clinicians and researchers (e.g., via practice-research networks). In effect, therapists/practitioners are re-privileged in the paradigm of practice-based evidence, as opposed to treatments alone, and have a central place in the conduct of these investigations.

By allowing such a shift, as well as by reflecting a wide range of clinical realities, practice-based evidence is likely to help research appear more valid and relevant to many clinicians. In our view, encouraging and promoting practice-based evidence can thus be a viable strategy to improve the current state of the scientific-practitioner model. Within this context, the overarching aim of this book is to illustrate how practice-based evidence can complement findings from RCTs and, in doing so, why it should be recognized as an essential component of the scientific basis of mental health care.

To achieve this aim, we invited influential scholars (clinicians and/or researchers) to join us in describing, within the context of their respective professional journeys, practice-oriented studies that they have conducted, as well as in deriving from these studies clinical, training, and policy implications that should be emphasized in the field. By bringing together these scholars, the book offers a window on practice-based evidence collected in different clinical settings (e.g., private practices, outpatient clinics, community-based clinics, national health care systems, hospitals, university counseling centers, training clinics) across several regions of the world (Africa, Australia, Europe, Latin America, the Middle East, and North America).

We want to express our gratitude to these scholars and their coauthors for providing us with such noteworthy chapters—each of which, we believe, offers persuasive arguments for the unique value of practice-based evidence. We are also grateful to many clinical, administrative, and researcher colleagues with whom we have conducted practice-oriented research, as well as to cohorts of graduate students and postdoctoral fellows who for years have allowed our research programs to flourish. In addition to their own research contributions, we thank Emily Beattie, Serena Chen, Katherine Davis, Natalie Pottschmidt, and Hongjun (Michael) Tan for their help in editing all the chapters of this book.

Sarah Harrington, our editor at Oxford University Press, has been extremely helpful and supportive, and we want to express our deep appreciation to her. We are also grateful and touched that Patricia Santoso has agreed to have her beautiful artwork reproduced on the book cover. Finally, we are thankful to the clinicians and clients who have contributed data to the studies presented in this book, as well as other empirical investigations conducted in clinical routine. Without their contribution as primary stakeholders of mental care delivery, there would be no practice-based evidence to guide and support it.

Louis G. Castonguay—State College, PA, USA
Dana Atzil-Slonim—Ramat-Gan, Israel
Michael Barkham—Sheffield, UK
Wolfgang Lutz—Trier, Germany

About the Editors

Louis Georges Castonguay, PhD, is a Liberal Arts professor of psychology at the Pennsylvania State University. He has been involved in the development of practice-research networks aimed at investigating psychotherapy as practice in natural settings. Among his previous 13 co-edited books is the seventh edition of the *Bergin and Garfield's Handbook of Psychotherapy and Behavior Change*, which he co-edited with Michael Barkham and Wolfgang Lutz. He received several awards, including the Distinguished Psychologist Award for his lifetime contributions from the Division of Psychotherapy of the American Psychological Association, as well as the Distinguished Research Career Award and the Lifetime Contribution Award from the Society for Psychotherapy Research (SPR). He served as president for both SPR and its North American chapter.

Dana Atzil-Slonim, PhD, is a professor of clinical psychology at Bar-Ilan University, Israel, where she also serves as the research director of the Community Clinic. At the forefront of integrating clinical science with cutting-edge artificial intelligence (AI), her work harnesses both data-driven and theory-based approaches to uncover the intrapersonal and interpersonal dynamics that drive therapeutic change. Honored with awards such as the Outstanding Early Career Achievement Award from the SPR, she is dedicated to advancing precision in mental health care.

Michael Barkham, PhD, is an emeritus professor of clinical psychology at the University of Sheffield, UK. He has devoted the past 40 years to research comprising the development of client self-report outcome measures to be adopted in routine clinical practice as well as promoting the paradigm of practice-based evidence as a complementary approach to trials methodologies. He was lead editor of the text *Developing and Delivering Practice-Based Evidence: A Guide for the Psychological Therapies* (Wiley, 2010) and, with Wolfgang Lutz and Louis Castonguay, of the seventh edition of *Bergin and Garfield's Handbook of Psychotherapy and Behavior Change* (Wiley, 2021). He has received awards from national and international societies in recognition of his work.

Wolfgang Lutz, PhD, is a professor of clinical psychology and psychotherapy at Trier University, Germany. He is one of the pioneers of patient-focused feedback research and empirically based personalization of psychological treatments and has worked in this area for over 30 years using data from routine clinical practice in several countries. He is co-editor (together with Michael Barkham and Louis Castonguay) of the prestigious *Bergin and Garfield's Handbook of Psychotherapy and Behavior Change* and served as president of the Society for Psychotherapy Research. The Association for Psychological Science has listed him on their Faces and Minds website as a distinguished researcher and leader in the field of psychological science.

Contributors

Dana Atzil-Slonim, PhD Bar-Ilan University, Israel

Robbie Babins-Wagner, PhD Calgary Counselling Centre, Canada

Michael Barkham, PhD University of Sheffield, UK

James F. Boswell, PhD University at Albany, State University of New York, USA

Heidi Brattland, PhD Norwegian University of Science and Technology and Nidelv Mental Health Center, St. Olav's University Hospital, Trondheim, Norway

Ashleigh G. Cameron, BPhil (Hons) University of Western Australia

Louis G. Castonguay, PhD The Pennsylvania State University, USA

Michael J. Constantino, PhD University of Massachusetts Amherst, USA

Alice E. Coyne, PhD American University, USA

Jaime Delgadillo, PhD University of Sheffield, UK

Anne-Katharina Deisenhofer, PhD Trier University, Germany

Susan Douglas, PhD Vanderbilt University, USA

Steffen T. Eberhardt, PhD Trier University, Germany

Paula Errázuriz, PhD Pontificia Universidad Católica de Chile, Millennium Institute for Research on Depression and Personality and PsiConecta Mental Health NGO, Chile

Fredrik Falkenström, PhD Linnaeus University, Sweden

Nick Firth, PhD University of Sheffield, UK

Ann F. Garland, PhD University of California in San Diego and University of San Diego, USA

Caroline J. Harris, BA Oakland Cognitive Behavior Therapy Center, USA

Jeffrey A. Hayes, PhD The Pennsylvania State University, USA

Miriam I. Hehlmann, PhD Trier University, Germany

Geoff R. Hooke, BAppSc (OT) University of Western Australia

Amanda Jensen-Doss, PhD University of Miami, USA

Letian Li, BA Oakland Cognitive Behavior Therapy Center and University of California at Berkeley, USA

Wolfgang Lutz, PhD Trier University, Germany

Andrew A. McAleavey, PhD Helse Førde Hospital Trust, Førde, Norway

Anuj H. P. Mehta, BSc University of Massachusetts Amherst, USA

Yesenia Mejia, PhD University of California in San Diego, USA

Danilo Moggia, PhD Trier University, Germany

Christian Moltu, PhD Helse Førde Hospital Trust and Western Norway University of Applied Sciences, Førde, Norway

Helene A. Nissen-Lie, PhD University of Oslo, Norway

Samuel S. Nordberg, PhD Reliant Medical Group, Worcester, and Atrius Health, Newton, MA, USA

Andrew C. Page, PhD University of Western Australia

Jacqueline B. Persons, PhD Oakland Cognitive Behavior Therapy Center and University of California at Berkeley, USA

Ruby J. Ross, BSc (Hons) University of Western Australia

David Saxon, PhD University of Sheffield, UK

Jana Schaffrath, MSc Trier University, Germany

Brian Schwartz, PhD Trier University, Germany

Ashleigh E. Smith, BS University at Albany, State University of New York, USA

Antonia Vehlen, PhD Trier University, Germany

Garret G. Zieve, PhD Oakland Cognitive Behavior Therapy Center, USA

The authors' affiliation(s) were those at the time of writing.

INTRODUCTION

1

Practice-Based Evidence and Practice-Oriented Research

Setting the Stage for the Expansion of the Scientific Foundations of Psychological Therapies

Louis G. Castonguay, Dana Atzil-Slonim, Michael Barkham, and Wolfgang Lutz

Randomized controlled trials (RCTs), which are aimed at examining and/or comparing the impact of specific forms of psychological therapy for a particular disorder, are frequently identified as the top-ranking input for the delineation of evidence-based practice. However, many of their defining features (e.g., inclusion and exclusion criteria; selection, training, and monitoring of therapist adherence and competence) have limited the extent to which their findings are generalizable to day-to-day clinical work. Concerns regarding internal validity have typically come at the cost of external validity. The investigative reach of RCTs is also limited because various characteristics of the structure and practice of therapy, such as the centers where treatments are delivered, are hardly amenable to randomization. Consequently, many practitioners do not view traditional research as pertinent to their work, both in terms of what is being investigated and how it is being investigated, which in turn has contributed to the schism between research and practice.

Another source of knowledge, practice-based evidence, can and should complement results from RCTs in building a scientific foundation of psychological therapies. Practice-based evidence has been defined as the empirical findings emerging from practice-oriented research (Castonguay et al., 2013, 2021). This type of research is characterized by three major features: the investigation of naturalistic settings (as opposed to clinical contexts created for the sole purpose of research endeavors); the investigation of the clinical

Louis G. Castonguay et al., *Practice-Based Evidence and Practice-Oriented Research*. In: *Practice-Based Evidence in the Psychological Therapies*. Edited by: Louis G. Castonguay et al., Oxford University Press.
 DOI: 10.1093/9780197748336.003.0001

routine in these naturalistic settings (as opposed, for example, to studies aimed at examining the effectiveness of therapies that have been empirically supported in controlled settings); and the investigation of clinical routine without drastic changes imposed in the delivery of care (e.g., the prescription or proscription of interventions).

The primary goals of practice-oriented research are threefold: (1) to describe factors that are involved in the accessibility and implementation of mental health services; (2) to understand if, how, for whom, and by whom these services might work (or not); and (3) to provide ways to improve practice, whether locally, nationally, and/or internationally. By collecting data as part of day-to-day clinical work, and at times by improving care as care itself is being investigated, practice-oriented research provides opportunities for a seamless integration of research and practice. In fostering such integration, some practice-oriented research also involves the active engagement of clinicians in the design, implementation, and dissemination of studies. At its core, practice-oriented research represents a vision borne out of the view that the function of each clinical setting is to be responsive to the needs of client populations in the context of locally available resources for mental health care, that each and every therapist and patient matters, and that the wealth of their data delivers empirical evidence that warrants equal footing to that derived from clinical trials.

A major turning point in practice-oriented research history began to take place in the 1980s with the emergence of patient-focused research. Led by Ken Howard and colleagues, this research program represented a shift from a primary emphasis on aggregate analyses of therapeutic approaches (focusing on which treatments work and/or are better than others) to the investigation of individual client change (focusing on profiling the trajectory of change). This shift rapidly broadened to include a wide range of clinically relevant issues such as the role played by practitioners in fostering outcome, the effectiveness of routine care provided in various clinical settings, as well as the delivery of feedback about treatment progress to clinicians. The desire to better understand and improve care in real-life environments also led to the development of a variety of partnerships, best captured in the form of practice-research networks aimed at fostering active collaboration between numerous stakeholders (e.g., researchers, clinicians, administrators) in the selection, design, implementation, and dissemination of psychological therapies research.

At the present time, after decades of innovations and contributions to empirical knowledge, practice-oriented research has risen as an alternate paradigm to the traditional research paradigm such that there is now a substantial body of literature attesting to the feasibility and yield of practice-oriented research (see Castonguay et al., 2013, 2021). Practice-oriented research and traditional research, however, should not be viewed as antagonists but, rather, conceived as complementary, derived from different sources of knowledge, that together provide a more robust and relevant scientific foundation for the psychological therapies. The two types of knowledge they provide (evidence-based practice and practice-based evidence), with their respective strengths and limitations, should be viewed from a position of equipoise. Unfortunately, as yet, this is not the case, and a primary goal of the following chapters is to make the case that practice-based evidence is a different but equally valuable source of science.

Accordingly, therefore, our view is that scientifically, practice-oriented research rests on solid foundations. The hallmarks of this paradigm, as well as the methods, measures, clinical tools, and organizational infrastructures that facilitated the generation and implementation of practice-based evidence, have been described previously (see Barkham et al., 2010). In addition, practice-oriented research has yielded a substantial body of clinically relevant information, as reviewed in three chapters of successive editions of *Bergin and Garfield's Handbook of Psychotherapy and Behavior Change* (Castonguay et al., 2013, 2021; Lutz et al., 2021). However, practice-oriented research has failed to have the broad and significant impact it deserves on clinical guidelines and public policies. For example, findings emerging from clinical practice in England, let alone from other regions in the world, have not been recognized as a legitimate source of knowledge in the development of their treatment guidelines (the National Institute for Health and Care Excellence [NICE] guidelines).

The goal of this book is to promote the recognition and implementation of practice-based evidence by building on and extending previous reviews. It attempts to do so, first by presenting some the most impactful practice-oriented research programs conducted in a variety of clinical settings around the world. And second, by offering research, training, clinical, and public policy lessons that can be derived from practice-based evidence emerging from these programs.

Structure and Focus of the Book

Following this chapter, the book is divided into five sections. The first section illustrates major approaches of practice-oriented research and their applications in different clinical settings: the collection of practice-based evidence related to various aspects of care delivery, as well as the embedding of RCTs in the clinical routine in the English National Health System (Barkham & colleagues); the measurement and enhancement of individualized client change, or patient-focused research, via routine outcome monitoring (ROM) and clinical feedback in an outpatient training clinic in Germany (Lutz & colleagues); and the development of research networks in different clinical settings (training clinic, private practice) in the United States (Castonguay). This initial section provides a platform for the remainder of the book by focusing on key aspects of subsequent chapters, namely, (1) developing, assessing, and improving clinical services in routine settings; (2) privileging the investigation of variables other than specific treatment approaches; (3) training; and (4) fostering partnership of clinicians, researchers, and other stakeholders of mental health services.

The second section is devoted to the people who contribute to treatment and who have been both the focus and the users of practice-based evidence, namely, therapists and patients. Studies conducted in Norway on practitioners' differential levels of effectiveness, contribution to the alliance, and emotional burden are presented (Nissen-Lie), as are investigations in the United States that have led to the identification of specific domains of therapist effectiveness and the matching between such expertise and clients' clinical problems (Constantino & colleagues). Also described is a research program conducted in Norway that has been aimed at developing and improving a broad monitoring and feedback system for clinical routine, based on a collaboration of patients, therapists, and other mental health care stakeholders (Moltu & colleagues).

The third section focuses on research programs that have examined different facets of the process of change, such as clients' emotional and cognitive experiences, therapists' interventions, therapeutic relationship, and complex dyadic processes between client and therapist. The chapters describe studies conducted in a training clinic in Israel (Atzil-Slonim), as well as in Swedish outpatient clinics and African hospitals (Falkenström).

The fourth section presents research programs conducted with and for specific populations: youth treated in community-based care settings

(Garland & Mejia), US college students (Hayes & Castonguay), and patients in a psychiatric hospital in Australia (Page & colleagues). The chapters describe the collaboration of multiple stakeholders (e.g., therapists, nursing staff, client families, administrators, technical experts, researchers) in conducting studies on various topics such as the assessment of and feedback on clients' difficulties, treatment effectiveness, dropout, therapist interventions, client therapeutic-interfering behaviors, therapeutic alliance, dyadic processes, client variables, clinical supervision, as well as therapist and center effects.

The fifth section aims at pushing forward the implementation and dissemination of practice-based evidence. Included are chapters demonstrating how US practitioners in private practice can collect data to investigate questions such as treatment effectiveness, clients who do not respond to treatment, homework compliance, and sudden gains—enabling them to embrace and contribute to practice-based evidence (Persons & colleagues); how the implementation of ROM in daily practice can lead to the improvement in services provided in a Canadian counseling center, as well as the examination of crucial questions such as supervisor effects (Babins-Wagner); and how clinically relevant and scientifically rigorous studies can be conducted in regions of the world, in this instance in Chile, with great needs but limited resources for mental health care (Errázuriz). This section also includes a chapter presenting a conceptual model to guide the integration and dissemination of practice-based evidence through the challenges of everyday practice—a model based on decades of research (Douglas & Jensen-Doss).

Writing Guidelines for the Authors

When we invited the lead author of each chapter to join us in this collaborative project, we asked them to adopt, in ways that would fit their own style of writing and the idiosyncratic nature of their work, three guidelines. First, we told them to frame their chapter within a personal narrative, highlighting what led them to create and maintain their practice-oriented research program, as well of the meaningful steps that have defined this professional journey. As a result, each chapter presents a story, a story that brings psychotherapy research to life and demonstrates that practice-oriented research / practice-based evidence is a dynamic paradigm that is both evolving and capturing vast areas of research activity.

Second, we asked them to be selective in the studies that they reported, focusing on what they considered as best examples of their work. As a result, the book illustrates how several practice-oriented investigations are at the cutting edge of research, relying on large samples of clients and therapists, innovative and rigorous designs, as well as advanced statistical analyses, to capture the complex nature of psychotherapy. It also illustrates how practice-oriented studies vary in terms of core dimensions of practice-based evidence, such as how the collection of data involves modifications to clinical practice, is actionable, and is transportable to other similar settings.

Third, we asked the authors to derive implications from findings of the studies they presented. As a result, each chapter offers recommendations about how to improve the day-to-day implementation and effectiveness of psychotherapy—locally, nationally, and internationally.

Because these recommendations represent unique contributions of practice-oriented research and practice-based evidence, they are the focus of the concluding chapter of this book (authored by the editors and Boswell). In particular, public policy implications are emphasized to make the argument for the value of this paradigm in informing the delivery of care in the psychological therapies.

References

Barkham, M., Hardy, G. E., & Mellor-Clark, J. (Eds.). (2010). *Developing and delivering practice-based evidence. A guide for the psychological therapies*. John Wiley & Sons.

Castonguay, L. G., Barkham, M., Lutz, W., & McAleavey, A. A. (2013). Practice-oriented research: Approaches and applications. In M. J. Lambert (Ed.), *Handbook of psychotherapy and behavior change* (6th ed., pp. 85–133). John Wiley & Sons.

Castonguay, L. G., Barkham, M., Youn, S. J., & Page, A. C. (2021). Practice-based evidence: Findings from routine clinical settings. In M. Barkham, W. Lutz, & L. G. Castonguay (Eds.). *Bergin and Garfield's handbook of psychotherapy and behavior change* (7th ed., pp. 191–222). John Wiley & Sons.

Lutz, W., de Jong, K., Rubel, J. A., & Delgadillo, J. (2021). Measuring, predicting and tracking change in psychotherapy. In M. Barkham, W. Lutz, & L. G. Castonguay (Eds.), *Bergin and Garfield's handbook of psychotherapy and behavior change* (7th ed., pp. 89–133). John Wiley & Sons.

SECTION I

PRACTICE-BASED EVIDENCE: APPROACHES AND APPLICATIONS

2

Practice-Based Evidence as a Cornerstone for Learning Health Systems

Michael Barkham, David Saxon, Nick Firth, and Jaime Delgadillo

In this chapter, we set out the arguments and vision for a paradigm of research in the psychological therapies that brings together the rigor of randomized controlled trials (RCTs) with the relevance of data drawn from routine clinical practice. We do so by documenting a program of research conducted in England that has spanned the past 40 years, starting with the development of outcome measures adopted in routine practice and enabling the activity of practice-based research that, over the years, cumulated in a body of knowledge we refer to as practice-based evidence. We document the yield of our practice-based research program, focusing on various ways of identifying and investigating natural variability, before outlining an approach to integrating the activities of practice-based research with trials-based methodology. We conclude by illustrating how practice-based evidence can become a natural cornerstone in transforming routine psychological health clinics into learning health systems where routinely collected patient health data becomes leverage for improving both local and national clinical practice. But first, we provide a preview of the main concepts and arguments set out in this chapter that will lay the groundwork for subsequent sections.

Research Paradigms: The Blueprint

A Tale of Two Paradigms

Research in the field of psychological therapies has been dominated by a tradition of controlled studies, primarily RCTs, yielding evidence for the efficacy of specific interventions, which has itself spawned a higher-level

Michael Barkham et al., *Practice-Based Evidence as a Cornerstone for Learning Health Systems*. In: *Practice-Based Evidence in the Psychological Therapies*. Edited by: Louis G. Castonguay et al., Oxford University Press.
 DOI: 10.1093/9780197748336.003.0002

pooling of evidence in the form of meta-analytic studies. Largely as a function of prioritizing internal validity via controlling extraneous variables and randomizing patients, the resulting studies have become the foundation underpinning the paradigm of *evidence-based practice* and have been hugely influential in informing national policies for the conduct and delivery of psychological therapies by practitioners in routine practice. It can therefore be considered a *top-down* model of informing best practice as shown in the left-hand box in Figure 2.1 and has been considered the pinnacle in the hierarchy of evidence that produces clinical guidelines to inform practitioners and clinical organizations on treatment to patients.

In contrast to the paradigm of evidence-based practice, there has been, since the turn of the century, an increasing recognition of a complementary paradigm that starts by collecting data from routine clinical practice as delivered by practitioners with few, if any, restrictions in terms of patient selection or allocation. This activity has been referred to as practice-based or practice-oriented research, and the product of such research yields the paradigm of *practice-based evidence*. This alternative paradigm takes a diametrically opposite approach to building an evidence base and can be summarized as a *bottom-up* model as shown in the right-hand box in Figure 2.1. Crucially,

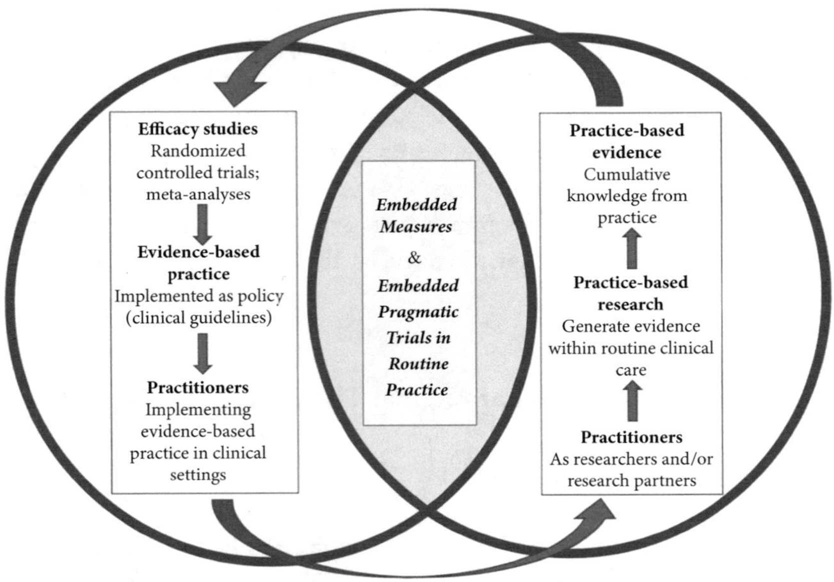

Figure 2.1 Complementary Paradigms of Evidence-Based Practice (Left) and Practice-Based Evidence (Right) Highlighting the Role of Embeddedness

however, these two paradigms complement each other in that evidence from RCTs needs to be tested in the real world, and findings from routine practice need to be tested under more controlled conditions (see Barkham & Mellor-Clark, 2003). The complementary nature of these two paradigms provides a framework for research via the intersectionality between these two paradigms, as indicated by the overlapping section in the center of Figure 2.1 comprising routine measurement *embedded* in practice and RCTs *embedded* within routine practice.

Embeddedness

The concept of embeddedness enables us to move beyond viewing each as a separate, albeit complementary, paradigm focused on its own model of research and toward providing an infrastructure whereby the two paradigms become interdependent. This development attempts to address concerns about generalizing trial results to routine practice and build on an understanding of mutual dependency. It is often the case that, although traditional effectiveness trials are indeed designed and implemented in routine practice, they introduce elements of the research design that are not actually part of routine practice. For example, they may introduce a specific outcome measure to address a question of generalizability from a prior efficacy trial but one that is not otherwise used in routine settings. In effect, these trials can be construed as *parachute* trials—that is, they are designed and dropped into practice settings to address a scientific question and once completed, the components of the effectiveness trial are wrapped up and withdrawn because they are not an intrinsic part of routine practice.

By contrast, suppose that trials are not only *pragmatic*—that is, capturing actual routine practice rather than imposing research components on it purely for the purposes of a trial—but are actually *embedded* in routine practice; in other words, where the trial uses the same outcome measure(s) that has already been adopted, accepted, and used within the wider clinical setting as intrinsic to routine practice. In this way, the findings of the trial component within a clinical organization can be assessed against the wider routine setting in which the trial is being conducted. Being able to ground trials in everyday routine practice would enable us to gain a richer and more realistic evaluation of the results and generalizability of findings from trials (i.e., evidence-based practice). Indeed, the notion of embeddedness is not novel, as it has close similarities to ideas initially presented by Relton et al. (2010) and labeled a cohort multiple RCT design that located an RCT within a patient cohort. Such designs have become known as Trials Within Cohorts (TwiCs; see also Nickolls et al., 2024) with the aim of maximizing the yield from both trial and observational data. However, while one of the main drivers for the TWiCs design is to support multiple trials within an existing organizational infrastructure and gain access to a broad range of patients, the focus in this chapter is more on providing the conditions for building an interdependent relationship between trial designs and routine practice that supports local and national agendas.

Variability and Learning Health Systems

In the context of utilizing both the complementary hallmarks of practice-based evidence and the stepped advance in the concept of trials embedded within routine practice, in this chapter we frame our research as addressing two specific aims. Our first aim is to present findings from practice-based research that are crucial in providing evidence that is invariably absent from RCTs by investigating the inherent *variability* at multiple levels over time that is characteristic of real-world clinical settings. Our second aim also makes an advance by framing practice-based research and its associated components as a key process in laying the cornerstone for clinics and clinical (i.e., health) organizations in the real world to develop as *learning health systems.* Crucially, they embed ongoing outcome monitoring as standard practice and are then able to develop and learn from their own practice-based research.

Figure 2.2 is a modification of the content of Figure 2.1 and shows a simplified representation of the relationship between practice-based evidence and learning health systems, how it is based on practitioners adopting routine outcome monitoring (ROM) and generating their own local knowledge that builds an evidence base locally and then, cumulatively, at a state, regional, and ultimately, national level. Both local and national levels are also informed by external evidence from trials, and, crucially, this combined evidence is fed back to practitioners, and owned by them, thereby lessening the need for such a direct top-down model (Figure 2.1, faded portion bottom-left).

Within this blueprint, our aim in this chapter is to set out an argument to academics, researchers, practitioners, and policy makers that evidence generated from everyday routine practice should not only have an equivalent

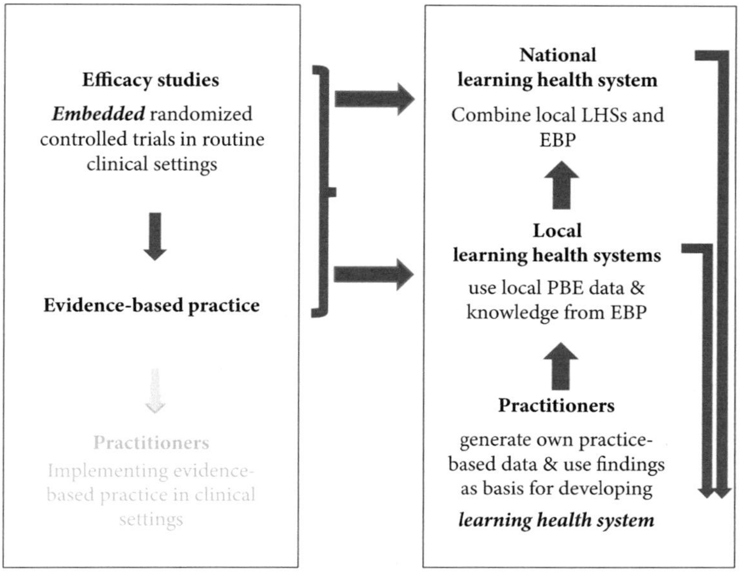

Figure 2.2 Reframing Practice-Based Evidence as the Development of Local and National Learning Health Systems: A Simplified Representation
Note: EBP = evidence-based practice; LHS = learning health system; PBE = practice-based evidence.

role and status to that bestowed on findings from RCTs but also be viewed as essential to the delivery of a sustainable integration of research and practice. We do so from the perspective that no single research paradigm alone can deliver a robust, reliable, and relevant knowledge base for the psychological therapies.

Developing Practice-Based Evidence: Building the Foundations

The scope and content of this chapter reflect the personal and professional impetus behind a 40-year quest to bridge the gap between research and practice by developing a program of research that builds a rigorous and relevant evidence base, complementary to that obtained from RCTs. Inspiration came from early evidence that findings from trials carried out in highly rarefied settings may not generalize or, worse, may be misleading. Specifically, a small-scale routine UK National Health Service (NHS) replication (Barkham, Rees, et al., 1996) of a comparative, psychological therapies trial originally conducted in a research clinic at the University of Sheffield (Shapiro et al., 1994) found that while the immediate effects of treatments were similar in both studies, at 3-month follow-up the patients in the replication study carried out in routine settings had lost most of the gains they had made during therapy. Crucially, this result challenged the credibility of randomized trials carried out in research clinics as providing reliable evidence upon which to base policy decisions in routine clinical services. But the alternative evidence from routine practice, at that time, was unsystematic, comprising uncoordinated research reports from practice settings that had no overarching framework or common method of measurement. What was needed was a credible research paradigm and program to act as an alternative—or rather as a complement—to trial-based methodologies.

Responding to this observation, a small group with varied research and practitioner experiences—Michael Barkham, Chris Evans, Frank Margison, and John Mellor-Clark—saw the need to develop a free-to-use patient self-report outcome measure that could easily be adopted in routine services and become the heart of a system for securing evidence derived from routine practice and thereby building a paradigm of practice-based evidence in the United Kingdom (Barkham et al., 1998). The result was a patient-reported outcome measure informed by feedback from practitioners that could be freely adopted by clinics—the Clinical Outcomes in Routine Evaluation–Outcome Measure (CORE-OM; Evans et al., 2002). The CORE-OM assessed the domains of subjective wellbeing, symptoms, functioning (general, social, and relationships), and risk (to self and to others). The measurement of outcomes was set within the broader CORE System that captured contextual information at the start and end of treatment, such as patient demographics, the form of intervention delivered, and the duration of treatment (Mellor-Clark et al., 1999).

The CORE-OM and System were implemented in multiple clinical organizations and, by benchmarking the outcomes, recorded the variability of patient outcomes across these clinical organizations (Barkham et al., 2001). Subsequently, a family of related CORE outcome measures was developed for specific requirements and populations (for a summary, see Barkham et al., 2006, 2010, 2015) as well as over 30 translations carried out according to documented procedures under the guidance of Chris Evans (e.g., Elfström et al., 2013). In addition, outputs summarizing the conceptual relationship between the paradigms of practice-based evidence and evidence-based practice (i.e., trials) were published (e.g., Barkham & Margison, 2007; Barkham & Mellor-Clark, 2003; Margison et al., 2000).

The cumulative effect of this work established a clear vision for a paradigm of practice-based evidence that has, since the turn of the century, yielded multiple outputs using the various CORE measures (see Barkham et al., 2015). More latterly, the program expanded into utilizing data from local and national psychological clinics in the English NHS Talking Therapies program (previously known as the Improving Access to Psychological Therapies [IAPT] program; Clark, 2018) in which the primary outcome measures are the Patient Health Questionnaire (PHQ-9), Generalized Anxiety Disorder Assessment (GAD-7), and the Work and Social Adjustment Scale (WSAS).

While the nascent program was developed in the research clinic at the University of Sheffield, the program moved in 1995 and became established at the University of Leeds (Psychological Therapies Research Centre). It subsequently relocated back to the University of Sheffield in 2007, initially in the form of the Centre for Psychological Services Research (Barkham et al., 2011) and then within the Psychotherapy Evaluation and Research Lab at Sheffield (PEARLS) comprising the current authors and other researchers committed to investigating a range of topics focused on psychological therapies (see https://pearlsresearchlab.sites.sheffield.ac.uk/).

Components of Practice-Based Evidence

Features and Approaches

The development of the family of CORE outcome measures and its adoption in routine clinical practice highlighted key *features* of the paradigm of practiced-based evidence, which have remained central to subsequent work. They comprise a focus on *routine* treatment as delivered in practice that has the potential to generate very *large* data sets resulting in greatly enhanced *statistical power* and better inclusion of *diversity* across a range of domains (e.g., cultural, clinical, biological) that are features of national populations. At its center lies a free-to-use *common outcome measure(s)* that has clinical utility and is adopted by multiple practices with, ideally, data-sharing agreements. This information derives from the practice of administering the outcome measure routinely—hence the term *routine outcome monitoring*—and integrating this practice naturally into the process of therapy, ideally on a session-by-session basis and using feedback to adjust the course of therapy as indicated by a mismatch between current and archival data where previous successful outcomes were achieved with similar patients. Crucially, there is a recognition of the *nested nature of data* that reflects the architecture (i.e., the hierarchy) of everyday routine practice. That is, sessions are nested within patients, who are nested within therapists, who are nested within clinics, and so on. In this way, both the structure and process of therapy become naturally *data informed*, enabling the prediction and *modeling of treatment responses* that focus on what is best for *this* specific patient, and hence giving due credence to *statistical* as well as clinical data.

These features can be found in three related *approaches* to practice-based evidence—practice-based research, patient-focused research, and practice research networks—each of which is summarized in Castonguay et al. (2013). The term *practice-oriented research* is variously used but, in our view, all research should be oriented toward practice. Rather, what is distinctive for this research paradigm is that it is *based in* practice, hence our preference for the term *practice-based research*. But the overall agenda is the same.

Figure 2.3 provides a schematic diagram of these three approaches with the vertical line within the circle representing a focus on the *hierarchical*

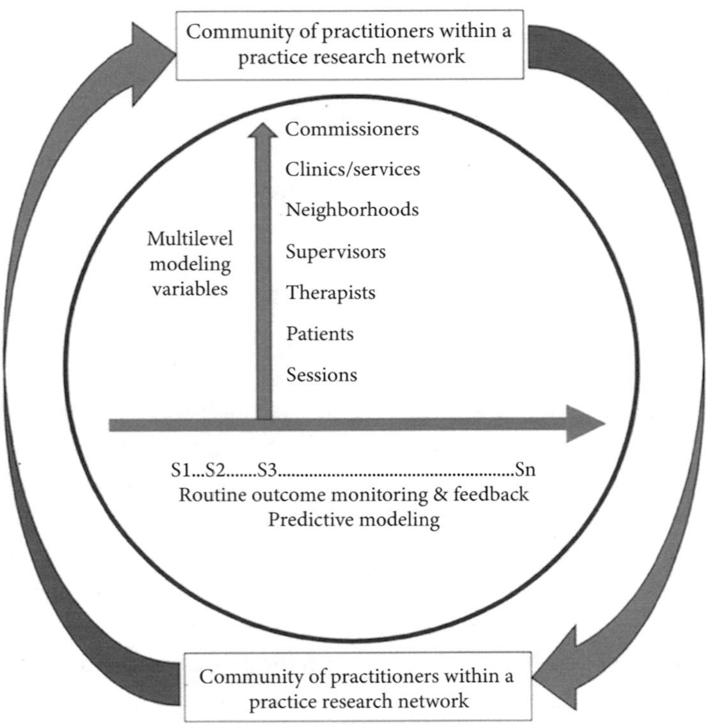

Figure 2.3 Schematic Diagram Comprising Three Approaches to Acquiring Practice-Based Evidence

nature of nested data (i.e., sessions nested within patients, nested within therapists, etc.) and the horizontal line representing a focus on the *temporal* nature of data in therapy (i.e., the use of session-by-session data). The third approach, practice research networks, captures a structural or organizational relationship in which communities of practitioners coalesce around a research center that supports their pursuit of local research agendas (see Castonguay et al., 2013).

The Yield: Identifying and Investigating Natural Variability

A key feature of routine practice data, in contrast to trials-based data, is its suitability to identify and investigate sources of variability in treatment outcomes. This is a crucial difference between the paradigms given Osler's (1904) axiom "Variability is the law of life." While trial designs aim to *reduce* variability in their implementation, practice-based evidence examines naturally occurring variability. The data reported in this chapter derived from patients receiving psychological therapies in routine clinical settings, and the studies in this section have been organized along the two key dimensions identified in the previous section: (1) *hierarchical levels*, initially using single-level analyses of patient outcomes and benchmarking and subsequently adopting multilevel analyses in recognition of the nested nature of data; and (2) *temporal sequencing*, using temporal categorization of data and determining the relationship with treatment response (i.e., predictive ability). Each of these two groups of studies addresses differing questions arising in the real-world delivery of patient care. But they also reflect a developing sophistication in the analytic approaches adopted by researchers in moving from profiling what was happening in practice toward efforts at predicting treatment outcomes and attempting to better match patients to treatments and therapists.

Hierarchical Levels

Initial attention focused on implementing the CORE-OM in routine practices and developing methods and technologies for data collection across collaborating clinics within a psychological therapies practice research network (Audin et al., 2001).

Single Level Analyses: Determining the Effectiveness of Routine Therapy Practice

Early in our program, the focus was on evaluating the outcomes of therapies as delivered in real-world clinical settings. These efforts analyzed routine data and then benchmarked them against each other, given the use of a common outcome measure, thereby evidencing the variability in outcomes across many secondary care clinics[1] (Barkham et al., 2001) and primary care counseling clinics (Evans et al., 2003). Benchmarking represented an early strategy for providing an account of the collective efforts of multiple clinics using the CORE-OM (see Mullin et al., 2006) and is still a favored approach using NHS Talking Therapies data, both conceptually (Delgadillo, McMillan, Leach, et al., 2014) and empirically (Gaskell et al., 2023). However, most clinics early in the program that adopted the CORE-OM implemented it only at pre- and post therapy, as this was the dominant design for evaluating UK psychological therapies at the turn of the millennium. Although the CORE-OM was designed within this form of practice, two shorter versions were also constructed at the same time—CORE Short Form A and B (Evans et al., 2002)—for repeated use, and a few clinics saw the potential for using shorter versions to obtain session-by-session data. But, on the whole, the challenge was getting clinics to adopt simple pre-post assessments and make their data available for research purposes.

Accumulating increasingly larger data sets using the CORE-OM provided the opportunity to address questions that RCTs had focused on for many years, namely, whether one therapy yielded consistently better outcomes than another, but to do so using data from routine practices. We published findings from an initial study, as well as a subsequent larger replication, comparing cognitive-behavioral therapy (CBT), person-centered therapy, and psychodynamic therapy in which no significant differences in patient outcomes were obtained (Stiles et al., 2006, 2008, respectively). While these (replicated) results gave much needed support for non-CBT modalities, one methodological issue was that the data relied on patients completing the post-therapy CORE-OM form and many patients left therapy without completing their post-treatment assessment. Hence, the view developed that post-therapy data can be potentially biased, as patients

[1] In the United Kingdom, the term *services* denotes a higher organizational level that might comprise multiple clinics serving a wide catchment area. We have used the term *clinics* as being more easily understood but also referred to the organizational level when referring to multiple clinics in a specific geographical area.

remaining in therapy to the end of their treatment are more likely to be those who benefit most, leading to the outcomes being artificially inflated. Such concerns played a part in national moves in England via the implementation of the Improving Access to Psychological Therapies (IAPT) program (later renamed NHS Talking Therapies; see Clark, 2018) toward adopting routinely administered outcome measures—the PHQ-9, GAD-7, and WSAS—at each therapy session and thereby ensuring that an assessment was available at the last attended therapy session regardless of whether treatment termination was negotiated or not.

Several systematic reviews of routine practice data have been conducted using the CORE-OM (Cahill et al., 2010) and the NHS Talking Therapies measures (Gaskell et al., 2023; Wakefield et al., 2021). Overall, and perhaps most reassuringly, these reviews have all shown routine practice to yield positive outcomes. But the question remains as to how the outcomes of routine practice compare with those from RCTs, raising the issue about the relationship between evidence arising from each of these paradigms. In trials, it is assumed that treatments are delivered under optimal conditions and patients are randomly assigned to treatments, thereby reducing the impact of confounding variables. In a study using crosswalk tables that enabled direct comparisons to be made between published routine practice data using the CORE-OM and five published efficacy trials using the Beck Depression Inventory, results showed the former to be disadvantaged by ≈12% compared with patient outcomes in trials (Barkham et al., 2008). The suggestion would be that treatment outcomes are more favorable in clinical trials as compared with routine practice, likely due to a myriad of factors that may lead to an overall better experience of therapy in a trial setting as compared with routine practice.

Multilevel Analyses: Therapist Effects and Their Relation to Key Clinic Variables

A significant step change in the sophistication of our research program occurred with the adoption of multilevel modeling (MLM), recognizing that data is naturally hierarchically structured. The underpinning science for this approach derived from the field of education, where pupils are nested within classes/teachers, who are themselves nested within schools, and so on. (Goldstein & Spiegelhalter, 1996). Such an approach yields considerably greater sensitivity to effects at differing levels within hierarchical data than provided by group means based solely on patient aggregated data analyzed at a single level, which does not acknowledge the non-independence of data (e.g., for a single therapist and all the patients seen by them). By contrast, MLM can address the issue of therapist effects and investigate both within- and between-therapist variability and inform the view that some therapists are generally more effective than others (Baldwin & Imel, 2013). A focus on therapist effects attracted particular attention because investigating this phenomenon is not the raison d'être for trials. Trials are constructed with a range of specific inclusion and exclusion criteria that makes patient samples more homogeneous and attempts to minimize variability in all variables other than the treatments being investigated, all of which work to attenuate therapist effects. Moreover, given the propensity for RCTs to be underpowered at the patient level, this is only more apparent in terms of the number of therapists. Hence, trials are not a reliable source for determining the extent of therapist effects. For example, in a recent review of this topic, we found therapist effects to account for ≈5%–7% of variability in treatment outcomes in routine clinical care, whereas this tends to be around 3% in clinical trials (Johns et al., 2019).

One of the larger and more robust studies of therapist effects was conducted using CORE-OM data from 119 therapists and counselors, all of whom had seen at least 90 patients each (Saxon & Barkham, 2012). The key findings were that some therapists consistently obtained better patient outcomes than others, while another group consistently yielded worse-than-average outcomes. The outcomes for these two groups did not overlap; that is, they were significantly different from each other to the extent of the better-than-average therapists achieving at least twice as good patient outcomes as the less effective therapists. Moreover, the therapist effect increased as a function of patient initial severity: the more severe a patient's condition at intake, the more it mattered which therapist treated them. This illustrates another advantage of MLM—it allows both higher-level variables (e.g., therapists, clinics) as well as lower-level variables (e.g., within-session micro-level processes and outcomes) to be included—to better understand and explain patient outcomes. Including a therapist's "risk caseload" was such an example and showed that the greater the number of cases with risk issues (e.g., risk of harm) in a therapist's caseload, the poorer the patient outcomes were.

Multilevel modeling became a key analytic approach underpinning our research program and was applied in studies of psychological wellbeing practitioners (PWPs), who provide the initial step (i.e., assessment and low-intensity treatment) within the NHS Talking Therapies program. Given that low-intensity treatments involve brief (e.g., ≤8 sessions) guided self-help interventions, it might be expected that variability between PWPs would be more constrained in this context. However, results were very similar to those of high-intensity therapists sampled by Saxon and Barkham (2012) with PWPs yielding effects of 6%–7%, such that more effective PWPs achieved almost twice the clinical change in a session as less effective PWPs (Firth et al., 2015). We further investigated factors that distinguished between more and less effective practitioners, with the former displaying greater resilience and having better organizational skills (Green et al., 2014). Findings from a subsequent study suggested that the patients of PWPs who were more agreeable achieved poorer outcomes, a finding that did not apply to CBT therapists (Delgadillo, Branson, et al., 2020). It may be that in more time-limited practice requiring a readiness to implement coping strategies, excessively agreeable PWPs may be less able to engage in difficult conversations with patients who may be reluctant to adhere to the treatment approach.

These studies highlight the importance of identifying differential effects and characteristics *between* therapists/practitioners. A subsequent review of therapists' personality traits found they were associated with therapeutic orientation and interpersonal skills, but evidence was less clear as to their impact on patient outcomes (Fletcher & Delgadillo, 2022). In another study, therapists who had higher self-reported indices of occupational burnout (specifically the facet of *disengagement*) and lower job satisfaction tended to achieve significantly poorer treatment outcomes compared with therapists with better indices of burnout and job satisfaction (Delgadillo, Saxon, et al., 2018).

Finally, it is a salutary lesson regarding the prominence placed—or perhaps, misplaced—by policymakers on treatment modality and duration that we have found these factors to have minimal differential impact on patient outcomes compared with differences *between* therapists and whether or not a patient completes a course of treatment (Saxon et al., 2017).

Beyond Therapist Effects: Clinics and Neighborhoods

Looking beyond therapists, there are additional layers within the wider community that might impact on therapy outcomes, with two such factors being the clinics within which therapists work and the various neighborhoods within which people (i.e., patients) live that are served by any specific clinic (recall Figure 2.3). Given the nature of this structure, we can build statistical models that show the relative impact these variables assert on patient outcomes.

Extending beyond two-level (sessions–patients or patients–therapists) analyses of therapist effects, we conducted a three-level—patients, therapists, and clinics—analysis of CORE-OM data from 26,888 patients comprising 462 therapists across 30 clinics (Firth et al., 2019). Analyses showed a clinic effect of ≈8%, which decreased to ≈2% once sociodemographic and clinical factors were included in the model. By contrast, the therapist effect at just under 4% remained relatively stable. Hence, the case-mix of patients and treatment delivery context (primarily patient-level symptomatology, employment status, the percentage of White patients within the clinic, and the healthcare sector) accounted for a much larger proportion of the variance in the outcomes of clinics compared with therapists. A subsequent study established the differential size of therapist effects across the different health sectors: therapist effects in primary care settings (≈8%) were twice that of secondary clinics (≈4%), which, in turn, were twice that of university and voluntary settings (≈2%), which were twice that of workplace settings (≈1%) (Firth et al., 2020). It is clear that the phenomenon of therapist variability differs at an organizational and systemic care delivery level, underpinning the argument that evidence relating to psychological therapies needs to be derived from *local* clinics in order to take account of such levels of variability.

Nevertheless, risks of confounding and misinterpretation remain. For example, apparent variability in effectiveness between clinics or therapists may actually represent differences in need or barriers to effectiveness in the neighborhoods and communities they offer treatment in. As such, clustering effects may be evident between patient neighborhoods (i.e., where a patient lives) independent of therapist and clinic effects. Firth et al. (2023) carried out a study using a large data set generated from the NHS Talking Therapies program comprising a retrospective, observational cohort design with both low-intensity (N = 773,675) and high-intensity psychological intervention samples (N = 617,375). Samples included 55 clinics, 9,000–10,000 therapists/practitioners, and over 18,000 neighborhoods in England. Results showed a significant neighborhood and clinic effect, such that people responded differently to treatments as a function of the neighborhood where they lived and the clinic they attended. The neighborhood effect (but not clinic effect) was significantly accounted for by patient severity and socioeconomic deprivation factors.

It should be noted that the non-significant effect at the clinic level may be related to confidence intervals and therefore power at this level ($N = 55$ clinics), mirroring the challenge we raised earlier in relation to underpowered RCTs. In contrast, neighborhood and therapist effects were estimated with high precision. Thus, it could be argued that despite great leaps toward robust samples at the patient, therapist, and neighborhood level, we continue to experience challenges at these higher levels of clustering. Arguably, these may only be suitably addressed with even greater standardization and collaboration in routine data collection and sharing.

Temporal Sequencing

In the same way that multilevel modeling generated a step change in analytic sophistication and better reflected the natural structure of data, so the adoption of session-by-session data collection enabled research to better reflect the process of change along the course of therapy. It enabled researchers to investigate what happens *between* pre- and post-therapy assessment, thereby providing the potential for evidence on the process of patient outcomes. Much earlier work, predating our current program, using the Personal Questionnaire method (Mulhall, 1977) collected data multiple times a week and showed distinct shapes of change across time (Barkham et al., 1993). One of the four patterns captured the phenomenon of *variability*, showing 17 times the extent of variability *within* a course of treatment compared with *between* treatments, a phenomenon that could not be captured using pre-post data.

Trajectories of Change

One focus of interest to researchers and practitioners has always been the amount of therapy to provide, with the traditional model being determined by the number of sessions delivered: the more sessions, the better, but with a pattern of diminishing returns yielding a negatively accelerating curve (see Barkham & Lambert, 2021). However, an alternative model has emerged from our research program in which it has been proposed that rather than the number of sessions, it is the specific rate of change of each individual patient that determines how long a patient remains in therapy. Thus, patients only leave therapy when they have reached a good enough level of improvement, thereby leading to the name good enough level (GEL) model (Barkham, Connell, et al., 2006; see also Bone, Delgadillo, et al., 2021). In many ways, the GEL model is a clinically appealing model because it does not set predetermined limits on the number of sessions, as its key hallmark is recognizing that each individual patient has differing rates of change. Notwithstanding the different models and the well-documented fact that different patients require different numbers of sessions to improve, a comprehensive review of the dose–effect literature suggested that most patients who attain clinically reliable improvements through therapy do so usually within 24 sessions (Robinson et al., 2020).

Sudden Gains and Early Response

In contrast to investigating the overall response to therapy, there has been interest in discrete patterns within the course of therapy, particularly in terms of *sudden gains* and *early response* to therapy. The phenomenon of sudden gains was initially reported in trials of cognitive therapy for depression (Tang & DeRubeis, 1999), and our focus has been on investigating the phenomenon in non-trial patients. An initial study examined sudden gains in routine practice settings using one of the CORE-Short Forms and found that while sudden gains occurred approximately half as frequently as in trials (17% vs. 39%, respectively), they were present across a broad range of presenting conditions and in response to a range of therapeutic approaches (Stiles et al., 2003). Another study included a sample of NHS patients but within a university-based clinic and found the phenomenon to occur in 41% of patients and with sudden gainers having significantly lower end therapy distress scores compared with non-sudden gainers (Hardy et al., 2005). Similarly, a subsequent practice-based study found that 42% of patients receiving CBT for panic disorder had a sudden gain, which predicted better post-treatment outcomes compared with those who did not show sudden gains (Lee et al., 2024). Hence, the occurrence of sudden gains appears to provide a good prognosis of a patient's final outcome. But it also shows that meaningful change can occur in a dramatic way. Conceptually, it is likely that sudden gains are an extreme form of the variability that is inherent in the course of therapy: recall the earlier finding regarding variability within a course of therapy (Barkham et al., 1993).

A related but different expression of change has been the phenomenon of *early response* and its prognostic value in relation to eventual outcome status. This phenomenon has been observed in practice-based data from

CBT-based interventions (Delgadillo, McMillan, Lucock, et al., 2014) and in person-centered experiential therapy (PCET; Duffy et al., 2022). In the latter study, in a sample of 3,321 patients within a single NHS Talking Therapies organization comprising multiple clinics, almost 30% of patients who made an early response to therapy by Session 4 achieved reliable and clinically significant improvement (RCSI) by the end of therapy. By contrast, a quarter of patients showed a mirrored pattern by making an eventual rather than early response to therapy and achieving RCSI by the end of therapy. Early responders were 6 times more likely to make RCSI by the end of therapy. Indeed, these patients made three-quarters (74.4%) of their overall gains during the initial four sessions compared with 15.6% of gains by Session 4 and 84.4% afterward for eventual responders. Compared with early responders, eventual responders were more likely to be taking medication, present with lower severity of depression, but have higher impaired functioning. To date, there is ample evidence that early response is a reliable prognostic indicator across a variety of psychological therapies and settings (see review by Beard & Delgadillo, 2019).

The phenomenon of early response features in another way when comparing different treatment modalities. In a national audit of the NHS Talking Therapies program, we found that when comparing the two most widely available therapy modalities—CBT and PCET—there was an advantage to PCET over CBT in the initial therapy sessions but this was later reversed at around Sessions 7–8 (Pybis et al., 2017). This effect has been replicated in a larger sample of >11,000 patients within the NHS Talking Therapies program (Saxon et al., 2024). However, this later study found that the reversal effect only occurred for moderately severe or severe patients; that is, the initial advantage to PCET did not occur for less severe patients. Hence, results from studies of practice-based data suggest that while overall overcomes may be broadly similar between contrasting therapy modalities, in this case CBT and PCET, such results may be masking more nuanced patterns in which the outcome depends on the individual rate of change or how much therapy has been delivered, precisely what the GEL model would predict. Such findings challenge the reliance on defining treatment differences based on a single time point.

Therapist (and Patient) Feedback

The area of feedback derived from ROM has become a major focus for research and is supported by a broad evidence base (Barkham et al., 2023).

Implementing ROM yields, overall, ≈8% advantage in patient outcomes. In the NHS Talking Therapies program, the feasibility and yield of using feedback technology was initially evaluated in a quasi-experimental study that adopted a before-and-after design (Delgadillo, Overend, et al., 2017). Early findings from this study indicated that the method was acceptable to patients and therapists, although the design and relatively small sample precluded drawing firm conclusions about its efficacy. In subsequent studies, the clinical- (Delgadillo et al., 2018) and cost-effectiveness (Delgadillo et al., 2021) of feedback-informed treatment was established in a pragmatic multisite RCT (N = 2233) conducted across eight healthcare organizations in England. In light of the status of ROM and feedback in routine practice and in trials, we have coauthored a text specifically for practitioners that sets out a practice-based guide to implementing and maximizing the yield from ROM and feedback (de Jong et al., 2023). This effort has been further enhanced by the production of a series of 10 videos covering the main components of ROM and feedback freely available on YouTube: https://www.youtube.com/playlist?list=PLwS02kBxHd2HwzeRkANo5O212U0BM30yG.

Prediction of Treatment Response and Matching

In the same way that feedback has focused on reducing instances of patients failing to achieve their expected gains while in therapy, efforts have also focused on ensuring better assignment of patients to the most appropriate therapy and/or therapist. The simple premise is that clinical judgment is fallible and that the use of actuarial data is more reliable but underutilized (Lutz et al., 2022; Meehl, 1954). Such a view has underpinned a major strand of research through the application of machine learning, which refers to "algorithms that are capable of discovering patterns in data and of recognizing them in new samples" (Delgadillo, 2021, p. 1). Such an approach increases the ability to make predictions about the course of a patient's response to treatment. This work builds on earlier work using CORE-SF data and adopting the strategy of predicting a patient's progress based on their nearest neighbors (i.e., the pattern of response to the treatment of patients best approximating the presenting conditions of the target patient; Lutz et al., 2005). The field has now progressed such that dynamic prediction models have been shown to be superior to standard approaches that use expected treatment responses (Bone, Simmonds-Buckley, et al., 2021). These models leverage information from the early response phenomenon discussed previously, thereby maximizing the value of data derived from early sessions to make accurate predictions about each patient's expected treatment outcome.

In a study comprising >1,500 patients within the NHS Talking Therapies program, patients classified as having complex needs (using a machine learning algorithm) were found to have poor outcomes if they received low-intensity treatments as part of a stepped care pathway (Delgadillo, Huey, et al., 2017). These findings, albeit from an observational study, suggested that applying a stratification method guided by a machine learning algorithm could potentially improve clinical outcomes, by initially matching complex cases to high-intensity treatments, and other cases to low-intensity treatments.

In a subsequent experimental test of this hypothesis, N = 951 patients within the NHS Talking Therapies program participated in a pragmatic RCT where some followed an algorithm-driven stratified care treatment pathway, while others followed a usual stepped care pathway (Delgadillo, Ali, et al., 2022). Importantly, the treatments as delivered comprised the standard treatment options available (i.e., either high- or low-intensity). What was randomized was whether the treatment *decision* was made by the clinician (as per usual stepped care) or recommended by an algorithm (stratified care). Results showed that patients in receipt of stratified care were significantly more likely to attain remission of depression symptoms (52.3%) compared with usual stepped care (45.1%). These findings suggest that the adoption of machine learning enables better assignment of patients according to their unique characteristics (clinical, demographic and personality features) and expected (i.e., predicted) prognosis.

This approach has also been applied to the investigation of assignments to different types of high-intensity treatments. Hence, rather than being a question of whether a patient would be better assigned a high- or low-intensity intervention, the question moves to asking which of the available interventions within each step of care is better suited to a given patient. Using the standard research strategy of initially developing a training model that is then applied to a hold-out test sample (i.e., which is independent of the training sample), we found that, among depressed patients who received either CBT or PCET in a single NHS Talking Therapies organization, patients who received their algorithm-indicated assignment had a 20% better improvement rate compared with receiving the other treatment (62.5% vs. 41.7%, respectively) (Delgadillo & Gonzalez Salas Duhne, 2020). Similarly, in a test of the generalizability of an algorithm determining the optimal matched treatment for patients receiving either CBT or PCET in a sample drawn from NHS Talking Therapies, we found patients receiving the optimal treatment showed ≈12% advantage compared with those patients receiving a non-optimal matched treatment (Moggia et al., 2024). And finally, in a study using practice-based data from over 80,000 patients, Gonzalez Salas Duhne et al. (2022) developed a machine learning algorithm to select the optimal treatment modality (e.g., computerized vs. in person) for patients eligible for low-intensity guided self-help.

In considering the findings from this section focusing on the identification and investigation of natural variability in psychological therapies, evidence has shown the role that therapists and contextual features (i.e., clinics and neighborhoods) have on the effectiveness of psychological therapies. In addition, research focusing on trajectories and models of patient change, indicators of positive outcomes (e.g., sudden gains and early response), as well as ROM have provided insights into patterns of patients' responses to treatments. And the adoption of machine learning methods to identify features that enable patients to be matched with their optimal treatment has provided a novel method for enhancing the effectiveness of psychological therapies.

Chiasmus: Evidence-Based Practice and Practice-Based Evidence

At the outset of this chapter, we flagged our view of the need for both trial-based and practice-based paradigms and our commitment to both paradigms (Barkham & Lambert, 2021; Castonguay et al., 2013, 2021; Lutz et al., 2021). Indeed, these complementary paradigms produce the chiasmus of *practice-based evidence and evidence-based practice*[2] (Barkham & Mellor-Clark, 2003). Beyond espousing the paradigm of practice-based evidence, our research program shows how the yield from trials methodologies and practice-based research can confirm, combine, or challenge the existing evidence base on the premise that these two paradigms are complementary. However, we now take a step forward from presenting these two paradigms as separate, albeit complementary, and toward a paradigm in which there is a defined space where both evidence-based practice and practice-based evidence are integrated and contribute equally (recall Figure 2.1).

[2] A common example of a chiasmus is the idiom "When the going gets tough, the tough get going."

Trials and Tribulations

While the strength of an RCT lies in its valuing internal validity, many commentators have railed against trials methodology, some of them, in our view, unreasonably. Methodologists have long tried to make the purified RCT more relevant, including designing adaptive trials that are more responsive to the realities of day-to-day clinical decision-making. However, such designs are still rare in the field of psychological therapies, and a more standard modified design is that of the pragmatic RCT that is carried out in real-world settings and focuses on effectiveness rather than determining explanatory factors (Schwartz & Lellouch, 1967). However, in a somewhat humorous quip, it has been commented that "RCTs are the worst outcome designs except for all other designs that have been tried" (Lilienfeld et al. 2018, p. 537).

That said, our view is that two general issues remain crucial. The first relates to the failure to represent the wider population of users in trials, resulting in a *lack of generalizability*. Over the past 50 years, our societies have become increasingly multicultural and diverse, but the selection processes into research trials do not favor the inclusion of such diversity in terms of culture or socioeconomic status, which undermines the generalizability and potential transportability of research efforts. However, in recent years, there has been a developing focus on the promise of *real-world evidence*, drawing on real-world data obtained beyond traditional trials, including pragmatic trials as they are carried out under real-world conditions (DeAngelis, 2021; National Institute for Health and Care Excellence [NICE], 2022). The real promise is securing data in everyday settings that does not set up barriers to inclusion and will thereby utilize data that is representative of a given population.

The second issue concerns the design of trials, such that a constant shortcoming in the psychological therapies has been delivering *underpowered trials*. A trial with a standard design comparing two active psychological therapies needs to be able to detect a small effect (i.e., $d = .20$), and it has been calculated that trial samples need to be more than 500 (Cuijpers, 2016) in order to detect a minimally important difference where $d = .24$. Underpowered trials make results vulnerable to Type II errors (i.e., not sufficiently powerful to detect a difference should one be present), yielding findings of no or small effects between therapy modalities and that are largely interpreted as being of little or no consequence at the study level. But, when such small effects are considered at a *population* level, they can convert into potentially differential benefits for hundreds or thousands of patients (Barkham, 2023).

As the field of psychological therapies increasingly adopts precision methods (see Delgadillo & Lutz, 2020), it becomes imperative that our science be built on methods and sample sizes that allow such precision as well as being adequately powered to determine interactions and moderators. The cost and investment for trials to adopt such a strategy would be vast and likely impractical in addressing the range and variety of questions that, as a collection of diverse societies, we need to address in order to deliver quality care for the greatest number of patients. By contrast, thousands of people are attending for psychological treatments every single day of every year across multiple clinical settings. It might be thought that there is both a huge waste of relevant information (i.e., data) and an apparent lack of a creative research and collaborative effort focused on harnessing such data. Kazdin (2008) captured exactly this sentiment when commenting on routine practice with the statement: "we are letting data slip through the holes of a colander" However, if trials were embedded in routine clinical practice, both the issue of diversity and statistical power could be addressed.

Building a More Comprehensive Evidence Base

Embedding trials in routine practice in England within the NHS Talking Therapies program provides unrivaled access to large cohorts of patients who are willing to participate in research. Three examples within our research program are (1) the PRaCTICED trial, which recruited 510 patients in receipt of high-intensity therapies (Barkham et al., 2021); (2) the Strat-Care trial, which recruited 951 patients (Delgadillo, Ali, et al., 2022); and (3) the IAPT-FIT Trial, which recruited 2,233 patients (Delgadillo et al., 2018). Importantly, these are *pragmatic* trials, and the interventions delivered by practitioners are the same as delivered to patients not enrolled in the trials. In effect, they comprise two layers of data: first, the routine data—namely, the PHQ-9, GAD-7, and WSAS—collected at every attended session as is standard within the NHS Talking Therapies program, and second, the "independent" trial data that is collected at specific time points and provides richer and more comprehensive data but is collected less frequently.

The relationship between the two layers of data is important, as they yield both practice-based and trial-based results in parallel within the same study.

As an example, the primary outcome of the PRaCTICED trial found that at 6 months post randomization, PCET was non-inferior to CBT but not so at 12 months post randomization. Further, analysis of the routinely collected data within the trial contrasting first- and last-session data (mirroring the standard analysis in the Talking Therapies national program) found no difference between treatments. This latter finding is important, not only because it confirms the findings from routine practice-based data analyzed outside of a trial that there is little, if any difference, between therapy modalities, but it does so for patients who were *randomized* to treatments. As such, it challenges the views of commentators that practice-based data is unreliable, as it is subject to confounding effects. In short, in this instance, practiced-based (randomized) routinely collected data embedded within a trial confirmed findings from routinely collected non-trial data. But, on the other hand, the trial data at 12 months post randomization significantly favored CBT, of which comparable practice-based data was not available (i.e., not collected as part of routine practice).

This example shows how relying on results from only one of these research paradigms fails to provide a full picture of the effects of psychological therapies. Of course, each of the evaluation points occurred at a different time: for the trial data at 6 months and 12 months post randomization, and for the routine data at end of treatment (last session). Hence, findings regarding psychological therapies depend not only on the paradigm used, but also, as noted earlier, on when and under what conditions questions are asked, and data is collected.

While such data can relate trial-based data with routine clinical data from trial participants, because we also collected all the routine outcome data from patients in the service as a whole who were *not* in the trial, we could go a step further and compare data from the trial—both routine and trial-specific—with routine data derived from patients in the wider clinical organization. In such a comparison of the PRaCTICED data set with non-trial data from the wider service, we found that as the data sets became increasingly representative of routine clinical practice, therapist effects increased (i.e., accelerated). By contrast, while controlling for therapist effects, treatment effects remained relatively constant (i.e., generalized but did not accelerate) and favored CBT but not significantly (Barkham et al., 2025). Evidence indicates that tighter controls in RCTs reduce differences between treatments and between therapists that emerge in routine practice. Hence, unless routine data also contributes to the evidence, the application of trial results to real-world practice will always be tenuous.

With such rich sources of data, it becomes a natural progression to build policies for practitioners based on both local routine data as well as evidence cited in the wider scientific literature, which leads us to the concluding heading of this chapter, namely, the concept of learning health systems as initially presented in the outline of this chapter (see Blueprint) and represented earlier in Figure 2.2.

Learning Health Systems: Generating Local and National Policies for Practitioners

Practice-based evidence has been presented as a "bottom-up" approach, which at an organizational level places the lens of change on local settings. Hence, each local health system should be able to learn from its own data as well as being informed by nationally based data and evidence from the wider research literature. These are the central components of a *learning health system*, as first outlined by the Institute of Medicine (2001) in which generating evidence (i.e., data) is a "by-product of care delivery." In effect, "evidence is both generated and applied as a natural product of the care process" (Ramsberg & Platt, 2017). A learning health system has been defined as "a health system in which internal data and experience are systematically integrated with external evidence, and that knowledge is put into practice" (Agency for Healthcare Research and Quality, 2019, p.1).

Figure 2.4 sets out the main components, which comprise an organizational leadership committed to pursuing the integration of internal evidence (i.e., derived from embedded or routinely collected patient data from within the organization) with external, research evidence, used to feed back to the healthcare team to improve the quality and effectiveness of the healthcare system through continuous and iterative learning. Given that embedded and routinely collected data are hallmarks of the Talking Therapies program, it is a natural progression for practice-based evidence arising from these data to become a cornerstone for transforming standard clinical organizations into learning health systems.

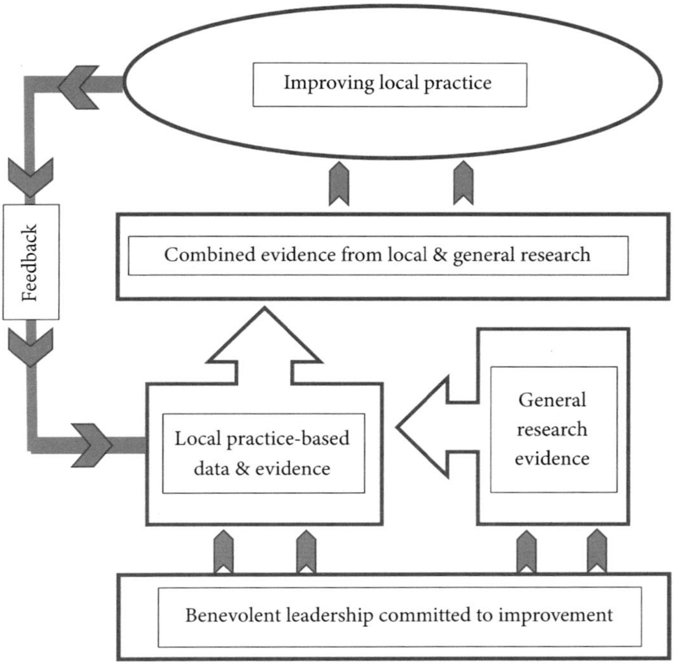

Figure 2.4 Schematic Representation of the Continuous Cycle of a Learning Health System

Practice-Based Research Underpinning a Learning Health System: A Case Study

As an example of how practice-based data can underpin the naturally occurring process of a learning health system, James et al. (2024) report a study in which an NHS Talking Therapies psychological therapy organization in England, which was deemed by a national body to be underperforming, embarked on a recovery program utilizing components of an informal learning health system utilizing three key elements. First, there was already preexisting outcome data embedded in the organization and administered at every attended therapy session, thereby enabling the clinics in the organization to use their own generated data to monitor and feed back on the process of recovery. Second, a leadership culture was in place that was committed to remedying the situation by allocating resources to the program that included a dedicated clinical manager who analyzed the local data and also sourced relevant research from the wider scientific community. Third, practitioners engaged in new learning activities aimed at creating a positive learning environment in which clinical feedback was a key component and developing a compassionate climate of support to all staff.

The recovery program comprised the analysis of the preexisting data followed by a management-led focus on improving patient outcomes over 18 months, which was then followed by a further 18-month program comprising a clinician-led focus on clinical feedback as well as a modified form of deliberate practice and compassionate support to staff. These combined interventions yielded not only improved patient outcomes (effectiveness) but also a marked reduction in therapist variability (equity). The latter impact is consistent with analyses of trial data in which the use of feedback reduced the gap between therapists' outcomes and yielded greater therapist equity (Delgadillo, Deisenhofer, et al., 2022).

The use of embedded and routinely collected data within a clinical organization (in this case, the PHQ-9) was facilitated by the application of sophisticated data analytics (i.e., multilevel modeling) and represented by impactful graphics (i.e., caterpillar plots; see Saxon & Barkham, 2012). And the delivery was located within a climate of self-reflection that enabled the organization to be both a provider and user of its own data for the betterment of both patients and practitioners, the defining hallmark of a learning health system.

Conclusions

The program of practice-based research we have documented in this chapter illustrates how academics can work with healthcare providers to yield routinely collected data that complements trial-based data and underpins a cycle of learning that delivers innovations and informs future clinical care. Such a model is consistent with the concept of a learning health system, which can be located within the wider context of data-driven healthcare that includes registries, databases, clinical audits, and other forms of collection, storage, and analysis of patient data that are consistent with real-world data and real-world evidence.

The approach set out in this chapter will hopefully yield a greater interdependence between practice-based and trial-based methodologies that will support psychological health clinics and clinical organizations adopting more data-informed practice (Lutz et al., 2022). The result will yield a science of psychological therapies grounded in routine practice and guided by greater precision.

References

Agency for Healthcare Research and Quality (AHRQ). (2019). *National healthcare quality and disparities report*. https://www.ahrq.gov/research/findings/nhqrdr/nhqdr19/index.html

Audin, K., Mellor-Clark, J., Barkham, M., Margison, F., McGrath, G., Lewis, S., Cann, L., Duffy, J., & Parry, G. (2001). Practice research networks for effective psychological therapies. *Journal of Mental Health, 10*(3), 241–251. https://doi.org/10.1080/09638230125294

Baldwin, S., A., & Imel, Z. E. (2013). Therapist effects: Findings and methods. In M. J. Lambert (Ed.), *Bergin and Garfield's handbook of psychotherapy and behavior change* (6th ed., pp. 258–297*)*. John Wiley & Sons.

Barkham M. (2023). Smaller effects matter in the psychological therapies: 25 years on from Wampold et al. (1997). *Psychotherapy Research, 33*(4), 530–532. https://doi.org/10.1080/10503307.2022.2141589

Barkham, M., Connell, J., Stiles, W. B., Miles, J. N. V., Margison, F., Evans, C., & Mellor-Clark, J. (2006). Dose-effect relations and responsive regulation of treatment duration: The good enough level. *Journal of Consulting and Clinical Psychology, 74*(1), 160–167. https://doi.org/10.1037/0022-006X.74.1.160

Barkham, M., de Jong, K., Delgadillo, J., & Lutz, W. (2023). Routine outcome monitoring (ROM) and feedback: Research review and recommendations. *Psychotherapy Research, 33*(7), 841–855. https://doi.org/10.1080/10503307.2023.2181114

Barkham, M., Evans, C., Margison, F., McGrath, G., Mellor-Clark, J., Milne, D., & Connell, J. (1998). The rationale for developing and implementing core outcome batteries for routine use in service settings and psychotherapy outcome research. *Journal of Mental Health, 7*(1), 35–47. https://doi.org/10.1080/09638239818328

Barkham, M., Hardy, G. E., & Mellor-Clark, J. (Eds.). (2010). *Developing and delivering practice-based evidence: A guide for the psychological therapies*. John Wiley & Sons.

Barkham, M., Hardy, G. E., & Shapiro, D. A. (2011). The Sheffield-Leeds psychotherapy research program. In J. C. Norcross, G. R. VandenBos, & D. K. Freedheim (Eds.), *History of psychotherapy: Continuity and change* (2nd ed., pp. 382–388). American Psychological Association.

Barkham, M., & Lambert, M. J. (2021). The efficacy and effectiveness of psychological therapies. In M. Barkham, W. Lutz, & L. G. Castonguay (Eds.), *Bergin and Garfield's handbook of psychotherapy and behavior change* (7th ed., pp. 135–189). John Wiley & Sons.

Barkham, M., & Margison, F. (2007). Practice-based evidence as a complement to evidence-based practice: From dichotomy to chiasmus. In C. Freeman & M. Power (Eds.), *Handbook of evidence-based psychotherapies: A guide for research and practice* (pp. 443–476). John Wiley & Son.

Barkham, M., Margison, F., Leach, C., Lucock, M., Mellor-Clark, J., Evans, C., Benson, L., Connell, J., Audin, K., & McGrath, G. (2001). Service profiling and outcomes benchmarking using the CORE-OM: Toward practice-based evidence in the psychological therapies. *Journal of Consulting and Clinical Psychology, 69*(2), 184–196. https://doi.org/10.1037/0022-006x.69.2.184

Barkham, M., & Mellor-Clark, J. (2003). Bridging evidence-based practice and practice-based evidence: Developing a rigorous and relevant knowledge for the psychological therapies. *Clinical Psychology & Psychotherapy, 10*(6), 319–327. https://doi.org/10.1002/cpp.379

Barkham, M., Mellor-Clark, J., Connell, J., & Cahill, J. (2006). A core approach to practice-based evidence: A brief history of the origins and applications of the CORE-OM and CORE System. *Counselling and Psychotherapy Research, 6*(1), 3–15. https://doi.org/10.1080/14733140600581218

Barkham, M., Mellor-Clark, J., & Stiles, W. B. (2015). A core approach to progress monitoring and feedback: Enhancing evidence and improving practice. *Psychotherapy, 52*(4), 402–411. https://doi.org/10.1037/pst0000030

Barkham, M., Rees, A., Shapiro, D. A., Stiles, W. B., Agnew, R. M., Halstead, J., Culverwell, A., & Harrington, V. M. G. (1996). Outcomes of time-limited psychotherapy in applied settings: Replicating the Second Sheffield Psychotherapy Project. *Journal of Consulting and Clinical Psychology, 64*(5), 1079–1085. https://doi.org/10.1037/0022-006X.64.5.1079

Barkham, M., Saxon, D., Hardy, G. E., Bradburn, M., Galloway, D., Wickramasekera, N., Keetharuth, A. D., Bower, P., King, M., Elliott, R., Gabriel, L., Kellett, S., Shaw, S., Wilkinson, T., Connell, J., Harrison, P., Ardern, K., Bishop-Edwards, L., Ashley, K., . . . Brazier, J. E. (2021). Person-centred experiential therapy versus cognitive behavioural therapy delivered in the English Improving Access to Psychological Therapies service for the treatment of moderate or severe depression (PRaCTICED): A pragmatic, randomised, non-inferiority trial. *The Lancet Psychiatry, 8*(6), 487–499. https://doi.org/10.1016/S2215-0366(21)00083-3

Barkham, M., Saxon, D., Hardy, G. E., Delgadillo, J., & Lutz, W. (2025). Mapping the relation between trials methodology and practice-based evidence in the real world of smaller effects: Generalizability and research recommendations. *Psychotherapy Research*, https://doi.org/10.1080/10503307.2025.2541710

Barkham, M., Stiles, W. B., Connell, J., Twigg, E., Leach, C., Lucock, M., Mellor-Clark, J., Bower, P., King, M., Shapiro, D. A., Hardy, G. E., Greenberg, L., & Angus, L. (2008). Effects of psychological therapies in randomized trials and practice-based studies. *British Journal of Clinical Psychology, 47*(4), 397–415. https://doi.org/10.1348/014466508X311713

Barkham, M., Stiles, W. B., & Shapiro, D. A. (1993). The shape of change in psychotherapy: Longitudinal assessment of personal problems. *Journal of Consulting and Clinical Psychology, 61*(4), 667–677. https://doi.org/10.1037/0022-006x.61.4.667

Beard, J. I. L., & Delgadillo, J. (2019). Early response to psychological therapy as a predictor of depression and anxiety treatment outcomes: A systematic review and meta-analysis. *Depression and Anxiety, 36*(9), 866–878. https://doi.org/10.1002/da.22931

Bone, C., Delgadillo, J., & Barkham, M. (2021). A systematic review and meta-analysis of the good-enough level (GEL) literature. *Journal of Counseling Psychology, 68*(2), 219–231. https://doi.org/10.1037/cou0000521

Bone, C., Simmonds-Buckley, M., Thwaites, R., Sandford, D., Merzhvynska, M., Rubel, J., Deisenhofer, A. K., Lutz, W., & Delgadillo, J. (2021). Dynamic prediction of psychological treatment outcomes: Development and validation of a prediction model using routinely collected symptom data. *The Lancet Digital Health, 3*(4), e231–e240. https://doi.org/10.1016/S2589-7500(21)00018-2

Cahill, J., Barkham, M., & Stiles, W. B. (2010). Systematic review of practice-based research on psychological therapies in routine clinic settings. *The British Journal of Clinical Psychology, 49*(4), 421–453. https://doi.org/10.1348/014466509X470789

Castonguay, L. G., Barkham, M., Lutz, W., & McAleavey, A. A. (2013). Practice-oriented research: Approaches and applications. In M. J. Lambert (Ed.), *Bergin and Garfield's handbook of psychotherapy and behavior change* (6th ed., pp. 85–133). John Wiley & Sons.

Castonguay, L. G., Barkham, M., Youn, S. J., & Page, A. C. (2021). Practice-based evidence: Findings from routine clinical settings. In M. Barkham, W. Lutz, & L. G. Castonguay (Eds.), *Bergin and Garfield's handbook of psychotherapy and behavior change* (7th ed., pp. 191–222). John Wiley & Sons.

Clark, D. M. (2018). Realizing the mass public benefit of evidence-based psychological therapies: The IAPT Program. *Annual Review of Clinical Psychology, 14*(1), 159–183. https://doi.org/10.1146/annurev-clinpsy-050817-084833

Cuijpers, P. (2016). Are all psychotherapies equally effective in the treatment of adult depression? The lack of statistical power of comparative outcome studies. *Evidence-Based Mental Health, 19*(2), 39–42. https://doi.org/10.1136/eb-2016-102341

DeAngelis, T. (2021, September 1). Can real-world data lead to better interventions? *Monitor on Psychology, 52*(6). https://www.apa.org/monitor/2021/09/news-real-world-data

de Jong, K., Delgadillo, J., & Barkham, M. (2023). *Routine outcome monitoring and feedback in psychological therapies*. Open University Press.

Delgadillo J. (2021). Machine learning: A primer for psychotherapy researchers. *Psychotherapy Research, 31*(1), 1–4. https://doi.org/10.1080/10503307.2020.1859638

Delgadillo, J., Ali, S., Fleck, K., Agnew, C., Southgate, A., Parkhouse, L., Cohen, Z. D., DeRubeis, R. J., & Barkham, M. (2022). Stratified care vs stepped care for depression: A cluster randomized clinical trial. *JAMA Psychiatry, 79*(2), 101–108. https://doi.org/10.1001/jamapsychiatry.2021.3539

Delgadillo, J., Asaria, M., Ali, S., & Gilbody, S. (2016). On poverty, politics and psychology: The socioeconomic gradient of mental healthcare utilisation and outcomes. *The British Journal of Psychiatry, 209*(5), 429–430. https://doi.org/10.1192/bjp.bp.115.171017

Delgadillo, J., Branson, A., Kellett, S., Myles-Hooton, P., Hardy, G. E., & Shafran, R. (2020). Therapist personality traits as predictors of psychological treatment outcomes. *Psychotherapy Research, 30*(7), 857–870. https://doi.org/10.1080/10503307.2020.1731927

Delgadillo, J., Deisenhofer, A. K., Probst, T., Shimokawa, K., Lambert, M. J., & Kleinstäuber, M. (2022). Progress feedback narrows the gap between more and less effective therapists: A therapist effects meta-analysis of clinical trials. *Journal of Consulting and Clinical Psychology, 90*(7), 559–567. https://doi.org/10.1037/ccp0000747

Delgadillo, J., de Jong, K., Lucock, M., Lutz, W., Rubel, J., Gilbody, S., Ali, S., Aguirre, E., Appleton, M., Nevin, J., O' Hayon, H., Patel, U., Sainty, A., Spencer, P., & McMillan, D. (2018). Feedback-informed treatment versus usual psychological treatment for depression and anxiety: A multisite, open-label, cluster randomised controlled trial. *The Lancet Psychiatry, 5*(7), 564–572. https://doi.org/10.1016/S2215-0366(18)30162-7

Delgadillo, J., Farnfield, A., & North, A. (2018). Social inequalities in the demand, supply and utilisation of psychological treatment. *Counselling and Psychotherapy Research, 18*(2), 114–121. https://doi.org/10.1002/capr.12169

Delgadillo, J., & Gonzalez Salas Duhne, P. (2020). Targeted prescription of cognitive-behavioral therapy versus person-centered counseling for depression using a machine learning approach. *Journal of Consulting and Clinical Psychology, 88*(1), 14–24. https://doi.org/10.1037/ccp0000476

Delgadillo, J., Huey, D., Bennett, H., & McMillan, D. (2017). Case complexity as a guide for psychological treatment selection. *Journal of Consulting and Clinical Psychology, 85*(9), 835–853. https://doi.org/10.1037/ccp0000231

Delgadillo, J., & Lutz, W. (2020). A development pathway towards precision mental health care. *JAMA Psychiatry, 77*(9), 889–890. https://doi.org/10.1001/jamapsychiatry.2020.1048

Delgadillo, J., McMillan, D., Gilbody, S., de Jong, K., Lucock, M., Lutz, W., Rubel, J., Aguirre, E., & Ali, S. (2021). Cost-effectiveness of feedback-informed psychological treatment: Evidence from the IAPT-FIT trial. *Behaviour Research and Therapy, 142*, Article 103873. https://doi.org/10.1016/j.brat.2021.103873

Delgadillo, J., McMillan, D., Leach, C., Lucock, M., Gilbody, S., & Wood, N. (2014). Benchmarking routine psychological services: A discussion of challenges and methods. *Behavioural and Cognitive Psychotherapy, 42*(1), 16–30. https://doi.org/10.1017/S135246581200080X

Delgadillo, J., McMillan, D., Lucock, M., Leach, C., Ali, S., & Gilbody, S. (2014). Early changes, attrition, and dose–response in low intensity psychological interventions. *British Journal of Clinical Psychology, 53*(1), 114–130. https://doi.org/10.1111/bjc.12031

Delgadillo, J., Overend, K., Lucock, M., Groom, M., Kirby, N., McMillan, D., Gilbody, S., Lutz, W., Rubel, J. A., & de Jong, K. (2017). Improving the efficiency of psychological treatment using outcome feedback technology. *Behaviour Research and Therapy, 99*, 89–97. https://doi.org/10.1016/j.brat.2017.09.011

Delgadillo, J., Saxon, D., & Barkham, M. (2018). Associations between therapists' occupational burnout and their patients' depression and anxiety treatment outcomes. *Depression and Anxiety*, *35*(9), 844–850. https://doi.org/10.1002/da.22766

Duffy, K. E. M., Simmonds-Buckley, M., Saxon, D., Delgadillo, J., & Barkham, M. (2022). Early response as a prognostic indicator in person-centered experiential therapy for depression. *Journal of Counseling Psychology*, *69*(6), 803–811. https://doi.org/10.1037/cou0000633

Elfström, M. L., Evans, C., Lundgren, J., Johansson, B., Hakeberg, M., & Carlsson, S. G. (2013). Validation of the Swedish version of the Clinical Outcomes in Routine Evaluation Outcome Measure (CORE-OM). *Clinical Psychology & Psychotherapy*, *20*(5), 447–455. https://doi.org/10.1002/cpp.1788

Evans, C., Connell, J., Barkham, M., Margison, F., McGrath, G., Mellor-Clark, J., & Audin, K. (2002). Towards a standardised brief outcome measure: Psychometric properties and utility of the CORE-OM. *The British Journal of Psychiatry*, *180*(1), 51–60. https://doi.org/10.1192/bjp.180.1.51

Evans, C., Connell, J., Barkham, M., Marshall, C., & Mellor-Clark, J. (2003). Practice-based evidence: Benchmarking NHS primary care counselling services at national and local levels. *Clinical Psychology & Psychotherapy*, *10*(6), 374–388. https://doi.org/10.1002/cpp.384

Finegan, M., Firth, N., Wojnarowski, C., & Delgadillo, J. (2018). Associations between socioeconomic status and psychological therapy outcomes: A systematic review and meta-analysis. *Depression and Anxiety*, *35*(6), 560–573. https://doi.org/10.1002/da.22765

Firth, N., Barkham, M., Delgadillo, J., Allery, K., Woodward, J., & O'Cathain, A. (2022). Socioeconomic deprivation and dropout from contemporary psychological intervention for common mental disorders: A systematic review. *Administration and Policy in Mental Health and Mental Health Services Research*, *49*(3), 490–505. https://doi.org/10.1007/s10488-021-01178-8

Firth, N., Barkham, M., Delgadillo, J., Bell, A., & O'Cathain, A. (2023). The role of socioeconomic deprivation in explaining neighborhood and clinic effects in the effectiveness of psychological interventions. *Journal of Consulting and Clinical Psychology*, *91*(2), 82–94. https://doi.org/10.1037/ccp0000784

Firth, N., Barkham, M., Kellett, S., & Saxon, D. (2015). Therapist effects and moderators of effectiveness and efficiency in psychological wellbeing practitioners: A multilevel modelling analysis. *Behaviour Research and Therapy*, *69*, 54–62. https://doi.org/10.1016/j.brat.2015.04.001

Firth, N., Saxon, D., Stiles, W. B., & Barkham, M. (2019). Therapist and clinic effects in psychotherapy: A three-level model of outcome variability. *Journal of Consulting and Clinical Psychology*, *87*(4), 345–356. https://doi.org/10.1037/ccp0000388

Firth, N., Saxon, D., Stiles, W. B., & Barkham, M. (2020). Therapist effects vary significantly across psychological treatment care sectors. *Clinical Psychology & Psychotherapy*, *27*(5), 770–778. https://doi.org/10.1002/cpp.2461

Fletcher, A. C., & Delgadillo, J. (2022). Psychotherapists' personality traits and their influence on treatment processes and outcomes: A scoping review. *Journal of Clinical Psychology*, *78*(7), 1267–1287. https://doi.org/10.1002/jclp.23310

Gaskell, C., Simmonds-Buckley, M., Kellett, S., Stockton, C., Somerville, E., Rogerson, E., & Delgadillo, J. (2023). The effectiveness of psychological interventions delivered in routine practice: Systematic review and meta-analysis. *Administration and Policy in Mental Health and Mental Health Services Research*, *50*(1), 43–57. https://doi.org/10.1007/s10488-022-01225-y

Goldstein, H., & Spiegelhalter, D. J. (1996). League tables and their limitations: Statistical issues in comparisons of institutional performance. *Journal of the Royal Statistical Society. Series A (Statistics in Society)*, *159*(3), 385–443. https://doi.org/10.2307/2983325

Gonzalez Salas Duhne, P., Delgadillo, J., & Lutz, W. (2022). Predicting early dropout in online versus face-to-face guided self-help: A machine learning approach. *Behaviour Research and Therapy, 159*, Article 104200. https://doi.org/10.1016/j.brat.2022.104200

Green, H., Barkham, M., Kellett, S., & Saxon, D. (2014). Therapist effects and IAPT Psychological Wellbeing Practitioners (PWPs): A multilevel modelling and mixed methods analysis. *Behaviour Research and Therapy, 63*, 43–54. https://doi.org/10.1016/j.brat.2014.08.009

Hardy, G. E., Cahill, J., Stiles, W. B., Ispan, C., Macaskill, N., & Barkham, M. (2005). Sudden gains in cognitive therapy for depression: A replication and extension. *Journal of Consulting and Clinical Psychology, 73*(1), 59–67. https://doi.org/10.1037/0022-006X.73.1.59

Institute of Medicine (US) Committee on Quality of Health Care in America. (2001). *Crossing the quality chasm: A new health system for the 21st century*. National Academies Press (US). https://doi.org/10.17226/10027

James, K., Saxon, D., & Barkham, M. (2024). Transforming the effectiveness and equity of a psychological therapy service: A case study in the English NHS Talking Therapies program. *Administration and Policy in Mental Health and Mental Health Services Research, 51*, 970–987. https://doi.org/10.1007/s10488-024-01403-0

Johns, R. G., Barkham, M., Kellett, S., & Saxon, D. (2019). A systematic review of therapist effects: A critical narrative update and refinement to Baldwin and Imel's (2013) review. *Clinical Psychology Review, 67*, 78–93. https://doi.org/10.1016/j.cpr.2018.08.004

Kazdin, A. E. (2008). Evidence-based treatment and practice: New opportunities to bridge clinical research and practice, enhance the knowledge base, and improve patient care. *American Psychologist, 63*(3), 146–159. https://doi.org/10.1037/0003-066X.63.3.146

Lee, R., McMillan, D., Delgadillo, J., Alexander, R., & Lucock, M. (2024). Cognitive change before sudden gains in cognitive behavioural therapy for panic disorder. *Behavioural and Cognitive Psychotherapy, 52*(2), 107–118. https://doi.org/10.1017/S1352465823000449

Lilienfeld, S. O., McKay, D., & Hollon, S. D. (2018). Why randomised controlled trials of psychological treatments are still essential. *The Lancet Psychiatry, 5*(7), 536–538. https://doi.org/10.1016/S2215-0366(18)30045-2

Lutz, W., de Jong, K., Rubel, J. A., & Delgadillo, J. (2021). Measuring, predicting and tracking change in psychotherapy. In M. Barkham, W. Lutz, & L. G. Castonguay (Eds.), *Bergin and Garfield's handbook of psychotherapy and behavior change* (7th ed., pp. 89–133). John Wiley & Sons.

Lutz, W., Leach, C., Barkham, M., Lucock, M., Stiles, W. B., Evans, C., Noble, R., & Iveson, S. (2005). Predicting change for individual psychotherapy clients on the basis of their nearest neighbors. *Journal of Consulting and Clinical Psychology, 73*(5), 904–913. https://doi.org/10.1037/0022-006X.73.5.904

Lutz, W., Schwartz, B., & Delgadillo, J. (2022). Measurement-based and data-informed psychological therapy. *Annual Review of Clinical Psychology, 18*, 71–98. https://doi.org/10.1146/annurev-clinpsy-071720-014821

Margison, F. R., Barkham, M., Evans, C., McGrath, G., Clark, J. M., Audin, K., & Connell, J. (2000). Measurement and psychotherapy: Evidence-based practice and practice-based evidence. *The British Journal of Psychiatry, 177*, 123–130. https://doi.org/10.1192/bjp.177.2.123

Meehl, P. E. (1954). *Clinical versus statistical prediction: A theoretical analysis and a review of the evidence*. University of Minnesota Press. https://doi.org/10.1037/11281-000

Mellor-Clark, J., Barkham, M., Connell, J., & Evans, C. (1999). Practice-based evidence and standardized evaluation: Informing the design of the CORE system. *European Journal of Psychotherapy & Counselling, 2*(3), 357–374. https://doi.org/10.1080/13642539908400818

Moggia, D., Saxon, D., Lutz, W., Hardy, G. E., & Barkham, M. (2024). Applying precision methods to treatment selection for moderate/severe depression in person-centered experiential therapy or cognitive behavioral therapy. *Psychotherapy Research, 34*(8), 1035–1050. https://doi.org/10.1080/10503307.2023.2269297

Mulhall, D. J. (1977). Systematic self-assessment by P.Q.R.S.T. (Personal Questionnaire Rapid Scaling Technique). *Psychological Medicine, 6*(4), 591–597. https://doi.org/10.1017/S0033291700018225

Mullin, T., Barkham, M., Mothersole, G., Bewick, B. M., & Kinder, A. (2006). Recovery and improvement benchmarks in routine primary care mental health settings. *Counselling and Psychotherapy Research, 6*(1), 68–80. https://doi.org/10.1080/14733140600581515

National Institute for Health and Care Excellence. (2022). *NICE real-world evidence framework*. www.nice.org.uk/corporate/ecd9

Nickolls, B. J., Relton, C., Hemkens, L., Zwarenstein, M., Eldridge, S., McCall, S. J., Griffin, X. L., Sohanpal, R., Verkooijen, H. M., Maguire, J. L., & McCord, K. A. (2024). Randomised trials conducted using cohorts: A scoping review. *BMJ Open, 14*(3), Article e075601. https://doi.org/10.1136/bmjopen-2023-075601

Osler, W. (1904). *Aequanimitas: With other addresses to medical students, nurses and practitioners of medicine*. P. Blakiston's Son & Co. https://doi.org/10.5962/bhl.title.2395

Pybis, J., Saxon, D., Hill, A., & Barkham, M. (2017). The comparative effectiveness and efficiency of cognitive behaviour therapy and generic counselling in the treatment of depression: Evidence from the 2nd UK National Audit of psychological therapies. *BMC Psychiatry, 17*, Article 215. https://doi.org/10.1186/s12888-017-1370-7

Ramsberg, J., & Platt, R. (2017). Opportunities and barriers for pragmatic embedded trials: Triumphs and tribulations. *Learning Health Systems, 2*(1), Article e10044. https://doi.org/10.1002/lrh2.10044

Relton, C., Torgerson, D., O'Cathain, A., & Nicholl, J. (2010). Rethinking pragmatic randomised controlled trials: Introducing the "cohort multiple randomised controlled trial" design. *BMJ* (Clinical Research Edition), 340, Article c1066. https://doi.org/10.1136/bmj.c1066

Robinson, L., Delgadillo, J., & Kellett, S. (2020). The dose-response effect in routinely delivered psychological therapies: A systematic review. *Psychotherapy Research, 30*(1), 79–96. https://doi.org/10.1080/10503307.2019.1566676

Saxon, D., & Barkham, M. (2012). Patterns of therapist variability: Therapist effects and the contribution of patient severity and risk. *Journal of Consulting and Clinical Psychology, 80*(4), 535–546. https://doi.org/10.1037/a0028898

Saxon, D., Broglia, E., Duncan, C., & Barkham, M. (2024). Variability in treatment effects in an English national dataset of psychological therapies: The relationships between severity, treatment duration, and therapy type. *Journal of Affective Disorders, 362*, 244–255. https://doi.org/10.1016/j.jad.2024.06.115

Saxon, D., Firth, N., & Barkham, M. (2017). The relationship between therapist effects and therapy delivery factors: Therapy modality, dosage, and non-completion. *Administration and Policy in Mental Health and Mental Health Services Research, 44*(5), 705–715. https://doi.org/10.1007/s10488-016-0750-5

Schwartz, D., & Lellouch, J. (1967). Explanatory and pragmatic attitudes in therapeutical trials. *Journal of Chronic Diseases, 20*(8), 637–648. https://doi.org/10.1016/0021-9681(67)90041-0

Shapiro, D. A., Barkham, M., Rees, A., Hardy, G. E., Reynolds, S., & Startup, M. (1994). Effects of treatment duration and severity of depression on the effectiveness of cognitive-behavioral and psychodynamic-interpersonal psychotherapy. *Journal of Consulting and Clinical Psychology, 62*(3), 522–534. https://doi.org/10.1037/0022-006x.62.3.522

Stiles, W. B., Barkham, M., Mellor-Clark, J., & Connell, J. (2008). Effectiveness of cognitive-behavioural, person-centred, and psychodynamic therapies in UK primary-care routine practice: Replication in a larger sample. *Psychological Medicine, 38*(5), 677–688. https://doi.org/10.1017/S0033291707001511

Stiles, W. B., Barkham, M., Twigg, E., Mellor-Clark, J., & Cooper, M. (2006). Effectiveness of cognitive-behavioural, person-centred and psychodynamic therapies as practised in UK

National Health Service settings. *Psychological Medicine*, *36*(4), 555–566. https://doi.org/10.1017/S0033291706007136
Stiles, W. B., Leach, C., Barkham, M., Lucock, M., Iveson, S., Shapiro, D. A., Iveson, M., & Hardy, G. E. (2003). Early sudden gains in psychotherapy under routine clinic conditions: Practice-based evidence. *Journal of Consulting and Clinical Psychology*, *71*(1), 14–21. https://doi.org/10.1037/0022-006X.71.1.14
Tang, T. Z., & DeRubeis, R. J. (1999). Sudden gains and critical sessions in cognitive-behavioral therapy for depression. *Journal of Consulting and Clinical Psychology*, *67*(6), 894–904. https://doi.org/10.1037/0022-006x.67.6.894
Wakefield, S., Kellett, S., Simmonds-Buckley, M., Stockton, D., Bradbury, A., & Delgadillo, J. (2021). Improving Access to Psychological Therapies (IAPT) in the United Kingdom: A systematic review and meta-analysis of 10-years of practice-based evidence. *British Journal of Clinical Psychology*, *60*(1), 1–37. https://doi.org/10.1111/bjc.12259

3

Practice-Based Evidence and Data-Informed Psychological Therapy

Wolfgang Lutz, Miriam I. Hehlmann, Anne-Katharina Deisenhofer, Danilo Moggia, Jana Schaffrath, Antonia Vehlen, Steffen T. Eberhardt, and Brian Schwartz

The aim of this chapter is to help readers understand the need for a research paradigm that focuses on data collection in routine care and the use of information generated directly in practice to study and improve the practice of psychological therapies as they unfold. In this introduction and throughout the text, I (W. L.) will also give a few personal notes about how I came to conduct this kind of research and make it my research team's focus at the Trier University. Since the beginning of my career, my research has focused on measurement, outcome prediction, and providing therapists and patients with feedback on change processes. I have also focused on patient-focused research and the classification of change trajectories, and I have illustrated how empirically derived clinical recommendations can be applied to improve outcomes in routine mental health care.

Capturing psychological change using the latest methods available in the field of psychology has fascinated me since I was a student at the Department of Psychology at the University of Heidelberg. I have always tried to test new methods developing in psychology, including the latest statistical or data collection technologies, to enrich my own research, improve the knowledge base about change in psychological therapies, and test their applicability in clinical practice. These methods include improving measurement accuracy, investigating patterns of change and therapist effects, and providing valuable feedback to therapists in clinical practice about their individual patients' progress in therapy.

Pursuing these research interests would not have been possible without the input and nurturing environment provided by colleagues at the

Wolfgang Lutz et al., *Practice-Based Evidence and Data-Informed Psychological Therapy*. In: *Practice-Based Evidence in the Psychological Therapies*. Edited by: Louis G. Castonguay et al., Oxford University Press.
 DOI: 10.1093/9780197748336.003.0003

Society for Psychotherapy Research (SPR). I did my BSc, MSc (Diploma), and doctoral thesis at the University of Heidelberg (Peter Fiedler, Christoph Mundt) and the Center for Psychotherapy Research in Stuttgart, Germany (Hans Kordy, Horst Kächele) with my thesis already focusing on patient-focused feedback and outcome research. I then completed a postdoctoral fellowship at Northwestern University, USA, working with Kenneth I. Howard, one of the founders of SPR and a central pioneer of patient-focused feedback and outcome research, followed by a position as a research associate with the Psychotherapy Research Group at the University of Bern (Klaus Grawe) in Switzerland. After these experiences as well as my visits to the research groups at the University of Sheffield (Michael Barkham) and Brigham Young University (Michael J. Lambert), all of which are closely associated with the SPR and provided an excellent research and learning environment in practice-oriented research, it became clear to me that I wanted to stay in this field of investigation at the center of the scientist–practitioner divide.[1]

I subsequently secured a full professor position at the Trier University, Germany, in 2007. For over 15 years now, my students and I have built a research program that simultaneously integrates research with clinical practice, reflecting the core concept of patient-focused research. The goal of this program is to generate practice-based evidence by studying treatment progress, therapist differences, the implementation of change measurement for clinical and research purposes, as well as the development and utilization of tools to guide clinical interventions. This research on empirically derived clinical recommendations and personalized mental health care is also the foundation of our clinical training program, and more recently it has focused on bridging the gap between research and private practices and clinics on a broader scale.

As a whole, this chapter discusses key issues around implementing practice-based evidence into clinical practice and training. We discuss new ways to develop empirically derived clinical recommendations and to implement them into clinical training as well as community clinics and private practices using modern technology and software solutions. The goal is to establish a data-informed approach to psychological therapy that not only allows clinical practice to be informed by ongoing research but also allows

[1] I (W. L.) do want to use this opportunity here to thank Ken Howard, who strongly supported me embarking on an academic career. I am also particularly grateful to my long-term mentors and friends, Michael Barkham and Mike Lambert. I also want to thank Klaus Grawe and Hans Kordy for supporting me in my research endeavors over many years.

ongoing research to generate practice-based evidence in research, practice, and clinical training settings. Furthermore, we describe the implementation of these concepts in a research and training clinic and provide recommendations to readers who are interested in setting up their own clinic or private practice or conducting research using a similar practice-based evidence framework. We present examples from the University of Trier's outpatient clinic to illustrate the concepts and research that led to its development.

Research Informs Practice and Practice Informs Research

We begin by discussing conclusions from psychotherapy outcome, therapist, process, and patient-focused feedback research that can form the basis of a pragmatic clinical framework for treatment planning, monitoring, and intervention systems.

Usually, in psychotherapy (now often referred to as *psychological therapy* to include the various newer theoretical concepts) there is a long road from research to practice. First, a new treatment must be developed over several years and then tested via case studies and later randomized controlled trials (RCTs). Finally, new clinicians must be trained to apply it, and at the end of this long developmental pathway, the new psychological treatment is eventually implemented into clinical practice (Lutz, Castonguay, et al., 2021). It is therefore no wonder that over the years a research–practice gap has developed within the profession. Further, new clinical developments often have difficulty demonstrating that they can significantly improve outcomes compared with treatments that are already well established (e.g., Barkham & Lambert, 2021).

As a result, over the years several streams of research have taken a more practice-oriented approach to implement research findings directly into clinical practice and improve clinical care. Several terms besides "practice-based evidence" have been used to describe these approaches in the literature: that is, patient-focused research, practice-oriented research, feedback-informed treatment, measurement-based care, routine outcome monitoring (ROM), and data-informed clinical practice (e.g., Barkham et al., 2010, 2023; Castonguay et al., 2013, 2021; Lutz, de Jong, et al., 2021; Lutz, Schwartz, & Delgadillo, 2022; see also Chapter 1). While they differ regarding the use of research results and/or empirically based algorithms to plan and monitor treatment, these streams of research all use data from clinical practice to learn about and improve clinical practice. In addition, these approaches rely on data not only collected before and after, but also during, treatment. In the following section, we begin by discussing patient-focused research, as this approach was our research group's leading research paradigm for many years, extended by additional precision mental health concepts as of about 2015.

Patient-Focused Research

In 1996, patient-focused research was introduced to psychotherapy research by Ken Howard as a practice-based research paradigm (Howard et al., 1996). In 2001, it was more broadly discussed for the first time in a special issue of the *Journal of Consulting and Clinical Psychology* (JCCP) organized by Mike Lambert (Lambert, 2001). From the beginning, this approach was concerned with improving treatments implemented in practice, rather than the efficacy of treatment manuals in clinical trials (Lutz, 2002). To this end, research is conducted on individual change trajectories in patients undergoing routine treatment, which can reveal differences in such trajectories and subgroups of patients with similar ones. Patient-focused research aims to monitor individual treatment progress and feed this information back to therapists (e.g., Howard et al., 1996; Lambert, 2001).

Patient-focused research and ROM (the terms are often used synonymously) aim to support clinical decisions via routine assessments and feedback throughout treatment. Evaluating treatment progress repeatedly during treatment enhances information quality, providing the information necessary for empirically based decision support. Extensive research examining various problem areas and services, including several meta-analyses, has consistently demonstrated the positive impact of patient-focused research and ROM on treatment progress and outcomes, particularly benefiting patients at risk for treatment failure (Barkham et al., 2023; de Jong et al., 2021). Furthermore, applications that enrich patient-focused research and ROM with clinical support tools available to therapists to support treatment adjustments when patients are at risk of negative treatment outcomes seem to be very effective additions to evidence-based psychological treatments. These clinical support tools advise therapists on how to approach and address specific critical clinical areas associated with a patient not progressing as expected (e.g., Lutz, de Jong, et al., 2021).

Expected Treatment Response

One of patient-focused research's early goals was to go beyond average change patterns to address the question of expected treatment response (ETR; Howard et al., 1996). Instead of making assumptions about each patient gradually improving based on an average patient's progress, researchers began calculating individual change trajectories. To do this, patient characteristics such as problem chronicity, previous treatments, treatment expectations, and global assessment of functioning served as predictors to establish ETR curves in growth curve models (Lutz et al., 1999). These predictions and the corresponding measures of variance (e.g., confidence intervals) were then used to identify patients at risk for deterioration (e.g., Finch et al., 2001; Lutz et al., 1999). With the increasing availability of machine learning algorithms, methods such as nearest neighbors (NNs) were applied to improve predictions (Lutz et al., 2005, 2006). From a clinical perspective, this early ETR research laid the groundwork for identifying patients at risk for adverse outcomes and has been widely implemented in ROM systems.

Patterns of Change and Early Response

Early response is a concept describing symptom improvement that occurs at the very beginning of psychotherapy. Initially classified by basic measures such as clinically significant change, more complex statistical methods such as growth mixture modeling (GMM) have emerged, with findings supporting the complementary function of both methods (Rubel et al., 2015). The importance of this pattern of change for treatment outcome has been confirmed for a variety of disorders (e.g., Lutz et al., 2009, 2014; Moggia et al., 2020; Stulz et al., 2007). A meta-analysis observed a large pooled effect size of early response on treatment outcome ($g = 0.87$) and an even larger effect for anxiety measures ($g = 1.37$; Beard & Delgadillo, 2019). Findings further suggest that patient intake characteristics, such as symptom severity, global functioning, chronicity, prior psychotherapy, treatment expectation, and daily affect dynamics, modulate early positive or negative responses to treatment, which in turn are predictive of outcome at the end of treatment (e.g., Husen et al., 2016; Stulz et al., 2007). For example, in a study by Lutz et al. (2014), four latent early-change subgroups were identified, showing clusters of change trajectories over the first five sessions of psychological treatment for patients with panic disorder. One of the subgroups consisted of patients whose symptoms decreased rapidly and who also had the best outcomes at the end of treatment. This early change information improved treatment prediction by 16.1% over patient intake characteristics alone. The early change patterns also significantly predicted patients' early treatment discontinuation. Patient intake characteristics that significantly predicted class membership included functional impairment and anxiety symptoms.

Sudden Gains and Losses

A particular change pattern that often appears over the course of psychological therapy is the so-called sudden gain. Sudden gains, as defined by Tang and DeRubeis (1999), describe nonlinear changes in symptom severity that occur rapidly from one session to the next. In addition to requirements for the magnitude of positive (gain) and/or negative (loss) changes, these changes must show a certain level of stability (e.g., persist for at least three sessions). Sudden gains have been found to occur more frequently early in treatment (Lutz et al., 2013) and depend on the therapist's ability to initiate them (Deisenhofer et al., 2022). Moreover, they are associated with enhanced therapeutic alliance and treatment outcomes (Wucherpfennig et al., 2017; Zilcha-Mano et al., 2019). The latter has been investigated in a meta-analysis of 50 studies, which found a link between sudden gains and improved post-treatment and follow-up outcome assessments (Shalom & Aderka, 2020). The literature on sudden losses, on the other hand, is more limited. However, differences between sudden losses and sudden gains have been identified in terms of timing (more evenly distributed across treatment) and frequency (less frequent) (e.g., Krüger et al., 2014; Lutz et al., 2013). It is also important to note that sudden losses or negative responses during treatment can indicate patients at risk for a negative treatment outcome. This information, in combination with the ETR research mentioned earlier, can provide useful feedback to therapists during treatment.

Tailoring Psychological Treatments

Treatment responses vary widely among individual patients, and, consequently, a patient starting an evidence-based treatment, even with an initially average level of effectiveness, might not necessarily attain a successful outcome. Although therapists have always tailored treatments to individual patients in their everyday work, this decision-making process can vary significantly, as it can be based on intuitive judgments, theoretical models, evidence from clinical guidelines, or a combination of these sources, among others. Clinical guidelines are often based on RCTs, which frequently neglect the heterogeneity of treatment effects (e.g., Kaiser et al., 2022) and thus often overlook individual characteristics (beyond the diagnostic category) that might be associated with treatment effects. Consequently, over the past decade, new models have emerged using new digital and statistical tools, such as machine learning algorithms on large databases, to provide a more precise, data-driven strategy for tailoring psychological therapy, often referred to as treatment personalization and precision mental health (Lutz et al., 2022). These approaches rely on predictive algorithms and feedback, encompassing a broad range of patient characteristics, and employing large data sets as well as advanced statistical models, such as machine learning (e.g., Delgadillo & Lutz, 2020).

Similar to the ETR, several additional indices have been applied to support treatment selection in recent years, including the Prognostic Index (PI; e.g., Cohen et al. 2023; Lorenzo-Luaces et al., 2017), the Leeds Risk Index (LRI; e.g., Delgadillo et al., 2016, 2022), and the Personalized Advantage Index (PAI; e.g., DeRubeis et al., 2014). Several of these studies were conducted by or in cooperation with our research group and were able to show a benefit in outcome or dropout rates for patients who were treated with their recommended treatment approach (package/protocol; e.g., Deisenhofer et al., 2018), strategy (modules/processes; e.g., Gómez Penedo et al., 2022; Rubel et al., 2020), setting (online vs. face-to-face; e.g., Gonzalez Salas Duhne et al., 2022), or who were matched to a suitable therapist (e.g., Constantino et al., 2021; Delgadillo et al., 2020; Lutz et al., 2007).

In the following example, we will take a closer look at a measurement-based and data-informed model for strategy selection at the beginning of treatment as well as a tool for monitoring and adjusting treatment during the therapeutic process. This example demonstrates the potential of integrating the practice-based evidence and patient-focused research described earlier with precision mental health methods to tailor interventions, especially for patients at risk for negative treatment outcomes.

Practice-Based Evidence and Data-Informed Psychological Therapy in Practice and Training: An Example

In the first chapter of Bergin and Garfield's *Handbook of Psychotherapy and Behavior Change*, Urban and Ford (1971) highlighted the discontinuous nature of the evolution of psychotherapy. After originating in the late 19th century, the advancement of the field did not adhere to a linear progression toward increasingly sophisticated and effective psychological techniques, strategies, or principles of change. Rather, the proliferation of diverse psychotherapeutic treatments and orientations led to progress along various lateral paths, and the field has seen the emergence of numerous therapeutic approaches and schools, each with its own concepts of psychopathology and change.

This has led to a highly diverse landscape of approaches and regulations for clinical training and practice, both within and between countries (e.g., Lutz et al., 2023). Furthermore, the significant heterogeneity within treatment schools makes it difficult to establish a unified set of concepts or mechanisms applicable across all variants. Moreover, none of the therapeutic orientations have yet established a scientifically grounded and clearly defined causal connection between their proposed mechanisms of change and treatment outcomes (e.g., Crits-Christoph et al., 2021; Kazantzis et al., 2018; Wester et al., 2024).

Data-Informed Clinical Practice and Training

We attempt to address these challenges with a clinical and training framework that remains receptive to ongoing research, serving as a road map for process- and feedback-oriented transtheoretical and transdiagnostic interventions (Lutz et al., 2023). This model incorporates findings from practice-based evidence and patient-focused research on psychotherapy outcomes, processes, and feedback, creating a clinical and training framework that allows for potential adaptations depending on the respective treatment concepts. More specifically, this framework is based on recent psychotherapy research results, especially outcome and patient-focused feedback research and research on therapist effects, predictors, moderators, and mediators of change. Central to this framework is a data-informed decision system (Trier Treatment Navigator, TTN) that was specifically developed to support therapists in making evidence-based clinical decisions during the ongoing treatment process.

Trier Treatment Navigator (TTN)

The TTN (e.g., Lutz et al., 2019) exemplifies a comprehensive decision and navigation system employing modern technology to simultaneously facilitate data-informed, measurement-based care and general practice-based evidence. It was developed, investigated, and has now been applied for several years at our clinic at the Trier University, which has served as a "living lab" for system and procedure development. With the aim of adapting the TTN for broader application in routine practices, we have recently collaborated with clinicians to develop an adapted Web-based version, the Treatment Navigator Pro (TN-Pro). The idea is to make the capabilities of the system, which has been applied and tested in our clinic and training program, available to private practitioners interested in generating and learning from practice-based evidence.

Therapists participate in data collection and the generation of a research database, while the navigation system provides them with algorithm-based treatment recommendations, both at the beginning of and during ongoing therapy. Therapists at the University of Trier's outpatient center receive training in the use of the evidence-based decision support system, which integrates sociodemographic data and process/outcome measures to tailor predictions to the individual patient. The TTN's session-by-session measures monitor treatment progress, offering personalized support for treatment selection, outcome monitoring, and adaptations to the treatment strategy.

At the onset of treatment, therapists receive an overview of patients' potential issues, including suicidality risk, substance abuse, treatment expectations, symptomatology, and interpersonal challenges. The TTN calculates the individual dropout risk based on predictors like initial impairment, personality traits, and treatment expectations, comparing it with clinic averages. The TTN then offers personalized treatment recommendations for the initial 10 sessions[2] based on an archival data set, aiding

[2] On average, patients receive 30.85 treatment sessions (*SD* = 20.24) (see Lutz et al., 2019).

therapists in deciding between motivation-oriented, problem-oriented, or mixed strategies. A graph displays the likely outcome for each approach (see Figure 3.1).

Throughout treatment, the TTN assesses patient symptoms at each session. The system calculates an expected change curve based on similar patients, issuing a risk value after four sessions. If a patient's symptom severity exceeds the risk value, a warning symbol is displayed and therapists receive access to relevant clinical problem-solving tools (CPST). These CPSTs include deliberate practice videos that simulate challenging situations to train therapists' skills. The TTN thus supports the personalized, evidence-based adaptation of ongoing therapy (e.g., Schaffrath et al., 2022).

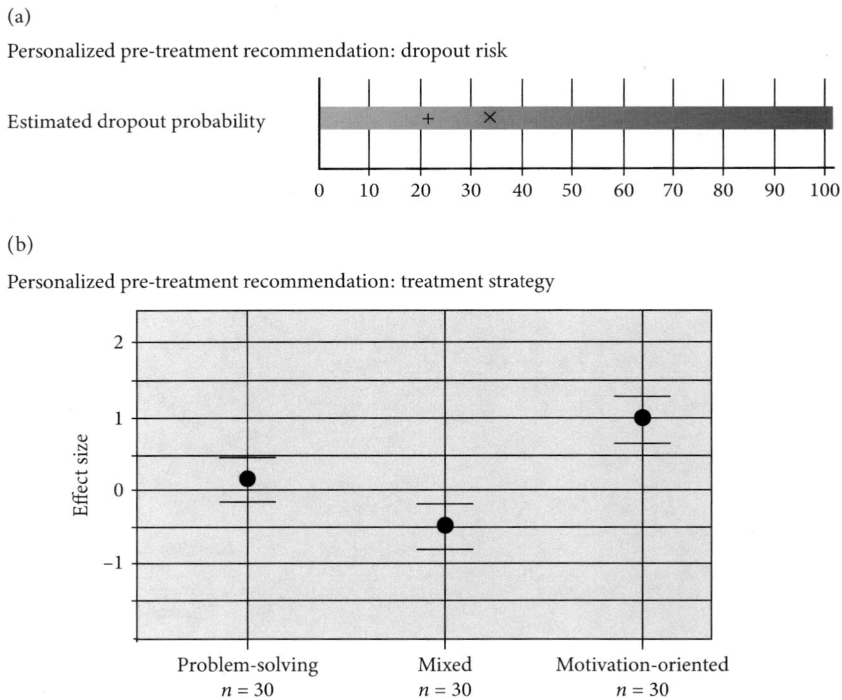

Figure 3.1 The Trier Treatment Navigator (TTN) Interface With Examples of Pretreatment Recommendations

Note: (a) Patient's dropout risk (+ is the average dropout rate; X is the patient's dropout risk). (b) Treatment strategy recommendation for the first 10 sessions based on similar treated cases. Effect sizes are shown in Cohen's d of the particular treatment strategy. n indicates how many similar patients were used to calculate effect sizes for each treatment strategy.

For example, the results displayed in Figure 3.1 are based on data from a middle-aged, female patient treated at our outpatient clinic. She reported suffering from a depressed mood, low energy, poor appetite, disturbed sleep, low self-confidence, and latent suicidal thoughts. After the Structured Clinical Interview for DSM-5 Disorders (SCID-5), she was diagnosed with moderate recurrent depression. The TTN's pre-treatment recommendations revealed that she had a slightly elevated dropout risk (Figure 3.1a), while the system recommended starting treatment with a motivation-oriented strategy (Figure 3.1b) before problem and disorder-specific interventions should be applied. Following this recommendation, the therapist was able to initiate a promising therapeutic process.

In Session 7, she reported that she had lost her job. She was very upset and angry with her boss and colleagues, who had never understood how much work and energy she had put into the job. She also expressed doubts about therapy, as she had not noticed any progress so far and was unsure whether this was the right path for her. In the TTN, a deterioration of her symptomatic progress was observed, and the therapist was prompted with a signal that she was "off-track" and at risk for treatment failure (see Figure 3.2). Crossing the risk threshold also activated CPSTs targeting areas of unexpected stagnation or even deterioration. CPSTs provide therapists

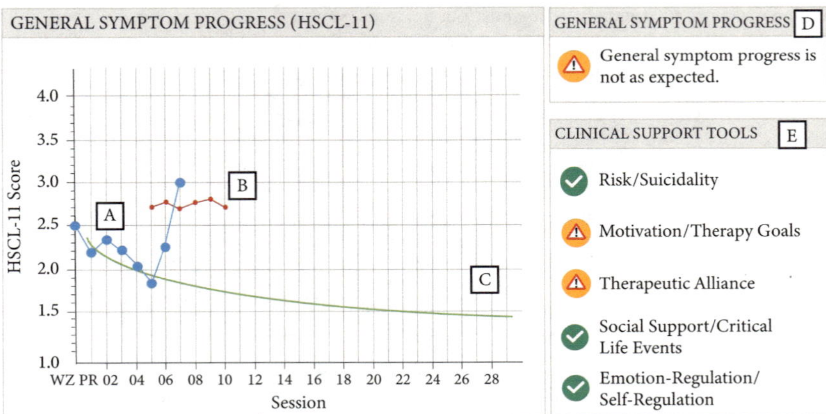

Figure 3.2 The Trier Treatment Navigator (TTN) Interface With Examples of Treatment Monitoring, and Treatment Adaptations

Note: Screenshot of the Trier Treatment Navigator (TTN) interface when the threshold for increased risk of a negative development is exceeded. The blue line (A) indicates the actual symptom severity, the green line (B) represents the expected course of symptom severity, and the red line (C) represents the individual risk value. On the right-hand side, the warning sign (D) and the domains relevant to the current problem are displayed (E). For this case, the domains "Motivation / Therapy Goals" and "Therapeutic Alliance" especially seem to be affected. HSCL, Hopkins Symptom Checklist; PR, pretreatment; WZ, waitlist.

with suggestions on how to get a clearer understanding of the therapeutic problem and give recommendations for potential interventions, including worksheets or instructions. The clinical support tools cover five areas, including (1) risk estimation (suicidal ideation, substance abuse), (2) motivation and treatment goals, (3) therapeutic relationship, (4) social support and life events, and (5) emotion regulation. In our example, the therapist had access to CPSTs for motivation and treatment goals, as well as the therapeutic alliance (see Figure 3.2). To target these problems, the therapist asked the patient about her opinion of their previous collaboration and where she would like to have more support. They also revisited the therapy goals to check whether they were still suitable.

The system has been prospectively evaluated on 538 patient–therapist dyads in our clinic, which were randomized to either the therapist having access to the TTN (intervention group; n = 335) or not (treatment as usual; n = 203; Lutz, Deisenhofer, et al., 2022). The analyses regarding the personalized pre-treatment strategy recommendation showed that patients whose therapists used the predicted optimal strategy had greater early improvements (d = 0.3). The analyses regarding adaptive feedback during treatment showed that specific therapist variables significantly predicted or moderated the effects of the system. For example, therapists' symptom awareness, their attitudes toward feedback, and their confidence in using psychometric feedback affected treatment outcomes. Overall, the results showed that using feedback significantly helps therapists (both trainee and licensed therapists in our clinic) to foster their skills and improve their practice. However, implementation quality and therapist acceptance are crucial and will be a central future aim alongside the continuous improvement of the system.

Improving Precision, Implementation, and Dissemination

Further advancing the field of practice-based evidence and data-informed psychological therapy requires improving data assessment accuracy and analysis as well as addressing implementation and dissemination issues. Therefore, although the TTN system has been established and used successfully in our clinic and training program for several years, we have recently pursued several additional research goals and potential improvements, examined implementation issues, and expanded practitioner support for therapists who wish to use the TTN in their private practices.

Precision: Improving Measurements and Predictions

As described earlier, prognostic models can help to assign patients to their optimal treatment approach or strategy. These models have a long-standing tradition but have recently benefited from the rise of machine learning (ML) algorithms that can handle increasingly complex data from advanced assessments, modeling methods, and research designs (Delgadillo & Lutz, 2020, 2023). Due to the rapid development of ML algorithms and model architectures, the suitability of a specific algorithm can vary greatly depending on the task. Researchers typically experiment with multiple algorithms to identify the one that yields the best results for a particular application. Further, what works best today might be outperformed by new advancements in the near future. However, initial methodological studies have begun to systematically examine different parameter settings (e.g., resampling methods, sample sizes, variable selection methods) for specific prediction problems (e.g., Bennemann et al., 2022; Giesemann et al., 2023; Moggia et al., 2023). Some early prospective studies have already demonstrated the practical use of such prediction models as described earlier for the TTN (Lutz, Deisenhofer, et al., 2022). However, further validation and prospective studies are needed (e.g., Deisenhofer et al., 2024; Delgadillo & Lutz, 2023).

To date, many studies have primarily relied on cross-sectional data or a restricted set of patient variables (e.g., diagnosis, symptom severity, interpersonal problems) to predict treatment outcome, select the most suitable treatment for an individual, or model treatment progress. However, recent advancements in innovative technologies are introducing novel digital data collection methods that create diverse data sets, such as Ecological Momentary Assessment (EMA) and video analyses. EMA, for example, employs various methods, including signal- or event-contingent self-reports and passive sensing. Passive sensing, also known as digital phenotyping, involves gathering data from personal digital devices such as smart phones or fitness trackers. Various types of data can be captured, for example, GPS, accelerometry, heart rate, stress levels, and sleep. To improve predictive accuracy and treatment recommendations, we have recently also begun to employ intensive longitudinal assessments and procedures to translate individual network models into personalized predictions and treatment recommendations (e.g., Hehlmann et al., 2024; Husen et al., 2016; Lutz et al., 2018; Rubel et al., 2018). One example is providing feedback to clinicians about patients' sleep duration, activity, and stress levels throughout the week and testing whether this information is helpful to therapists when interacting with patients about their problems.

Another potential way to improve precision when measuring clinical processes and interventions is the video analysis of therapy sessions (e.g., Atzil-Slonim et al., 2024). The automated analysis of the patient's and therapist's nonverbal synchrony is a well-established field of research based on the quantification of movement as a time- and cost-saving alternative to manual human coding (e.g., Lutz et al., 2020; Paulick et al., 2018; Schwartz et al., 2022). However, technological advances in the availability and accuracy of ML algorithms may further improve the assessment of social and emotional dynamics in the patient–therapist dyad. One of our team's recent studies has demonstrated the validity of these novel measures by comparing them to traditional self-report measures (Terhürne et al., 2022). The study used the Non-Verbal Behavior Analyzer (NOVA, Baur et al., 2020) to apply video-based emotion recognition, automatically capturing arousal and valence during therapy sessions. Using self-trained models based on facial expressions, the study found significant correlations between therapist-rated emotions, such as sadness and anxiety, and emotion recognition scores. Notably, automatically detected negative valence was linked to anxiety levels, highlighting its potential as a predictive tool for anxiety severity assessment.

Another recent study using natural language processing (NLP) explored the validity of a pre-trained sentiment analysis model on psychotherapy transcripts, offering a complementary approach to nonverbal measures (Eberhardt et al., 2024). By analyzing sentiment within session transcripts, the study found significant correlations between automatically rated sentiment and therapist and patient reports of emotion in the same session. The finding that increasing positive sentiment throughout therapy predicted better outcomes underscores the value of NLP in assessing emotional changes over time. Both studies suggest that automated video, audio, and transcript analysis could serve as an additional metric for tracking treatment progress. Future research could focus on combining these modalities to create a more comprehensive assessment of therapeutic processes and outcomes. With these promising findings and ongoing advancements in computerized session transcription, analyzing key therapeutic processes and outcomes automatically could become increasingly accessible. For example, in feedback-informed psychotherapy, automated multimodal assessments could provide an in-depth analysis of off-track sessions. They provide information that may help therapists understand why a patient is not improving as expected. This additional insight could help guide the patient back on track (Lutz et al., 2024).

Implementation and Acceptance: Improving Commitment and Overcoming Procedural Barriers

The successful implementation of practice-based evidence and data-informed psychological therapy into clinical practice depends on the acceptance and commitment of everyone involved, including therapists, patients, and administrators. While patient acceptance is vital, as the quality of data depends on their honest and thoughtful input, fortunately, about 90% of patients appear to embrace this aspect of care (Lutz, de Jong, et al., 2021). In contrast, it seems significantly more challenging to gain therapists' support. Several studies have shown that effects depend on therapists' attitudes, application, and commitment (e.g., Barkham et al., 2023; de Jong et al., 2021). For example, in our studies, therapists' perceived usefulness of feedback and therapists' positive attitudes toward feedback were significantly associated with improved effects (Lutz, Deisenhofer, et al., 2022).

Therefore, to ensure the success of practice-based evidence, the primary focus needs to lie on the implementation process, which is widely recognized as the main barrier due to human, organizational, and systemic factors (e.g., Douglas et al., 2023). The recently published Implementing Precision Methods (IPM) Framework provides a practical overview and guidelines (Deisenhofer et al., 2024). According to this framework, clinical and practical aspects must be considered, technical and statistical challenges must be overcome, and contextual factors need to be taken into account. Considering these multiple barriers to implementation, there is a broad consensus that no single strategy is likely to succeed. Instead, successful implementation requires multifaceted strategies tailored to address locally relevant barriers and all participating groups (Lutz et al., 2021).[3] This collaborative design approach guarantees that the systems are both useful and efficient for individuals facing significant

[3] https://www.zotero.org/google-docs/?GoY9Ef

time constraints in real-world situations. Organizations should facilitate this process by providing resources such as computerized systems, staff support, and dedicated time in daily practice. To increase acceptance, it seems important to motivate therapists and scientist-practitioners to participate in developing computerized systems as key stakeholders. The process involves potentially making cultural adjustments within the clinical setting to prevent discrimination and identifying potential obstacles early to ensure the engagement of those involved. Furthermore, considering technical aspects, such as implementing user-friendly systems that are easy to interpret (e.g., visual feedback) and applying short, robust, and relevant measures, is crucial to garner organizational support (Lutz, de Jong, et al., 2021).

Finally, training is an important factor in the implementation process, increasing positive attitudes toward practice-based evidence and data-informed psychological therapy. It is necessary for therapists to learn a reflective professional approach to such models, integrating clinical judgment and statistical predictions into their treatment concept (e.g., Deisenhofer et al., 2024).

Reaching Out: Practice-Based Evidence Goes Local and Global

The utilization of practice-based evidence has often been confined to individual academic research settings and some associated clinics and private practices. This has resulted in a very heterogeneous landscape of assessment routines and measures, both within and across countries. To improve the situation, data collection should be made more comparable between institutes, and algorithms such as those implemented in the TTN should be made more broadly available. For example, the European Psychotherapy Consortium (EPoC), an association of European research outpatient clinics, has taken up this cause across Europe (a Latin American consortium has also been recently established). Although agreement on the single item and its translations (now in 14 languages) was not easy, and widespread implementation will take some time, this internationally coordinated effort within psychotherapy research has the potential to collect data from tens of thousands of patients per year and to integrate practice-based evidence concepts (i.e., TTN or similar systems) into clinical practice on a larger scale (Gonçalves et al., 2024).

In a recent project, our research group at the Trier University is acting as a communication hub to help local private practices implement the TTN into their services. Instead of immediate implementation, we are collaborating with clinicians to develop an adapted Web-based version, the TN-Pro. Development is guided by the IPM Framework (Deisenhofer et al., 2024), ensuring that the TN-Pro reflects both patient needs and clinician requirements. For instance, we balanced comprehensive data collection to improve therapy prognoses with maintaining practical feasibility in daily clinical practice. Clinician concerns about usability and time efficiency were integrated by using a co-design approach, allowing for active feedback on realistic time commitments and desired features. Feedback on integrating the TN-Pro into routine procedures proved particularly valuable. For example, the automatic activation of interim measurements at the beginning of each quarter was implemented. Additionally, regular, short questionnaires that patients complete on their smart phones before each session have also proven less time consuming and more sustainable than longer questionnaires administered every few sessions, due to the efficiency of habitual use.

In the initial phase, we invited potential scientist-practitioners to participate in the project—a majority of whom accepted. These clinicians were involved in the developmental feedback loops. Subsequently, additional colleagues will be included. The idea is that successful, enthusiastic use of the TN-Pro by initial participants will inspire others, fostering a growing network of scientist-practitioners. So far, feedback from the initial users has been positive, as the TN-Pro provides support for diagnostics, case formulations, difficult therapeutic processes, as well as helping to reflect on one's clinical impressions.

Discussion

One of the main goals of my research career (W. L.) has been to make use of psychotherapy research to help students and colleagues develop patient-focused and practice-based research programs and implement them in their clinics. Sharing the lessons that my students and I have derived from our work has led me to believe in the importance of international learning experiences to improve psychotherapy research. We try to implement and enable this approach in our research and training program and hope we have communicated it in this chapter. During clinical training at the Trier University, therapists actively engage with practice-based evidence, and a data-informed psychological therapy training concept, developing their ability to adeptly manage feedback and seamlessly integrate it into their clinical practice. The curriculum encompasses theoretical courses that play a pivotal role in developing an understanding of practice-based evidence and data-informed treatment.

A further aspect of training involves hands-on experience in the outpatient center under supervision, facilitating direct application in individual cases. In addition, therapists receive support, especially when they are confronted with challenges. For example, if a patient deviates from the expected course of treatment according to the TTN feedback system, that is, develops into a potential risk case, a therapist meeting is held to discuss this development and possible ways of dealing with it. It is important to remember that these systems have limitations. They can provide empirically based guidelines and work as navigation systems, but they are not automated in the sense that they could provide treatment autonomously. Such systems can only be applied with the critical reflective ability of a clinically and scientifically well-trained therapist.

Overall, we believe it is a worthwhile endeavor to establish practice-based evidence in various forms, either as research clinics, practice-research networks, or as private clinics or practices, and to collect information from clinical practice to learn about it and use it to improve practice. We think that these types of investigations have the potential to improve the knowledge base of psychotherapy research and help bridge the gap between research and practice. While RCTs have been the cornerstone of evidence-based practice, these studies alone seem insufficient to expand our knowledge base about the complexities of clinically meaningful change for patients in real-world clinical settings. Their focus on average change neglects patients at risk for negative outcomes or patient groups for whom psychological therapy hasn't yet found optimal treatment solutions. Therefore, psychotherapy research should be accompanied by high-quality, high-intensity investigations in research clinics serving as "living laboratories" for the development and evaluation of systems and procedures. The key, of course, is to then apply and adopt them in routine practice to improve care at the individual patient level. Such systems, methods, and procedures have the potential to transform routine practice and clinical training precisely through the process of coproduction and collaboration with practitioners (Lutz, et al., 2024).

We hope that the future will see many such practice-based evidence endeavors and initiatives in different countries around the world. Such developments will help to advance psychotherapy research and ground psychological therapy in better science that could result in improved practice- *and* evidence-based therapy and training.

Acknowledgments

This work was supported by the German Research Foundation (DFG) under project nos. 493169211 and 504507043.The authors are most thankful for the tremendously helpful proofreading by Kaitlyn Poster (Trier University).

References

Atzil-Slonim, D., Penedo, J. M. G., & Lutz, W. (2024). Leveraging novel technologies and artificial intelligence to advance practice-oriented research. *Administration and Policy in Mental Health and Mental Health Services Research, 51*, 306–317. https://doi.org/10.1007/s10488-023-01309-3

Barkham, M., de Jong, K., Delgadillo, J., & Lutz, W. (2023). Routine Outcome Monitoring (ROM) and feedback: Research review and recommendations. *Psychotherapy Research, 33*(7), 841–855. https://doi.org/10.1080/10503307.2023.2181114

Barkham, M., Hardy, G. E., & Mellor-Clark, J. (Eds.). (2010). *Developing and delivering practice-based evidence: A guide for the psychological therapies* (1st ed.). Wiley. https://doi.org/10.1002/9780470687994

Barkham, M., & Lambert, M. J. (2021). The efficacy and effectiveness of psychological therapies. In M. Barkham, W. Lutz, & L. G. Castonguay (Eds.), *Bergin and Garfield's handbook of psychotherapy and behavior change* (7th ed., pp. 135–190). Wiley.

Baur, T., Clausen, S., Heimerl, A., Lingenfelser, F., Lutz, W., & André, E. (2020). NOVA: A tool for explanatory multimodal behavior analysis and its application to psychotherapy. *MultiMedia Modeling: 26th International Conference, MMM 2020, Daejeon, South Korea, January 5–8, 2020, Proceedings, Part II, 26*, 577–588. https://doi.org/10.1007/978-3-030-37734-2_47

Beard, J. I. L., & Delgadillo, J. (2019). Early response to psychological therapy as a predictor of depression and anxiety treatment outcomes: A systematic review and meta-analysis. *Depression and Anxiety, 36*(9), 866–878. https://doi.org/10.1002/da.22931

Bennemann, B., Schwartz, B., Giesemann, J., & Lutz, W. (2022). Predicting patients who will drop out of out-patient psychotherapy using machine learning algorithms. *The British Journal of Psychiatry, 220*(4), 192–201. https://doi.org/10.1192/bjp.2022.17

Castonguay, L. G., Barkham, M., Lutz, W., & McAleavey, A. (2013). Practice-oriented research: Approaches and applications. In M. J. Lambert (Ed.), *Bergin and Garfield's handbook of psychotherapy and behavior change* (6th ed., pp. 85–133). Wiley.

Castonguay, L. G., Barkham, M., Youn, S. J., & Page, A. C. (2021). Practice-based evidence—Findings from routine clinical settings. In M. Barkham, W. Lutz, & L. G. Castonguay (Eds.), *Bergin and Garfield's handbook of psychotherapy and behavior change* (7th ed., pp. 191–222). Wiley.

Cohen, Z. D., DeRubeis, R. J., Hayes, R., Watkins, E. R., Lewis, G., Byng, R., Byford, S., Crane, C., Kuyken, W., Dalgleish, T., & Schweizer, S. (2023). The development and internal evaluation of a predictive model to identify for whom mindfulness-based cognitive therapy offers superior relapse prevention for recurrent depression versus maintenance antidepressant medication. *Clinical Psychological Science*, *11*(1), 59–76. https://doi.org/10.1177/21677026221076832

Constantino, M. J., Boswell, J. F., Coyne, A. E., Swales, T. P., & Kraus, D. R. (2021). Effect of matching therapists to patients vs assignment as usual on adult psychotherapy outcomes: A randomized clinical trial. *JAMA Psychiatry*, *78*(9), 960–969. https://doi.org/10.1001/jamapsychiatry.2021.1221

Crits-Christoph, P., Connolly Gibbons, M. B., & Mukherjee, D. (2021). Psychotherapy process-outcome research. In M. Barkham, W. Lutz, & L. G. Castonguay (Eds.), *Bergin and Garfield's handbook of psychotherapy and behavior change* (7th ed., pp. 263–296). Wiley.

de Jong, K., Conijn, J. M., Gallagher, R. A. V., Reshetnikova, A. S., Heij, M., & Lutz, M. C. (2021). Using progress feedback to improve outcomes and reduce drop-out, treatment duration, and deterioration: A multilevel meta-analysis. *Clinical Psychology Review*, *85*, Article 102002. https://doi.org/10.1016/j.cpr.2021.102002

Deisenhofer, A.-K., Barkham, M., Beierl, E. T., Schwartz, B., Aafjes-van Doorn, K., Beevers, C. G., Berwian, I. M., Blackwell, S. E., Bockting, C. L., Brakemeier, E.-L., Brown, G., Buckman, J. E. J., Castonguay, L. G., Cusack, C. E., Dalgleish, T., de Jong, K., Delgadillo, J., DeRubeis, R. J., Driessen, E., . . . Cohen, Z. D. (2024). Implementing precision methods in personalizing psychological therapies: Barriers and possible ways forward. *Behaviour Research and Therapy*, *172*, 1–16. https://doi.org/10.1016/j.brat.2023.104443

Deisenhofer, A., Delgadillo, J., Rubel, J. A., Böhnke, J. R., Zimmermann, D., Schwartz, B., & Lutz, W. (2018). Individual treatment selection for patients with posttraumatic stress disorder. *Depression and Anxiety*, *35*(6), 541–550. https://doi.org/ggxdg3

Deisenhofer, A.-K., Rubel, J. A., Bennemann, B., Aderka, I. M., & Lutz, W. (2022). Are some therapists better at facilitating and consolidating sudden gains than others? *Psychotherapy Research*, *32*(3), 343–357. https://doi.org/mc26

Delgadillo, J., Ali, S., Fleck, K., Agnew, C., Southgate, A., Parkhouse, L., Cohen, Z. D., DeRubeis, R. J., & Barkham, M. (2022). Stratified care vs stepped care for depression: A cluster randomized clinical trial. *JAMA Psychiatry*, *79*(2), 101–108. https://doi.org/10.1001/jamapsychiatry.2021.3539

Delgadillo, J., & Lutz, W. (2020). A development pathway towards precision mental health care. *JAMA Psychiatry*, *77*(9), 889–890. https://doi.org/gjw3z3

Delgadillo, J., & Lutz, W. (2023). Precision mental health care for depression. In J. Pettit (Ed.), *APA handbook of depression*. American Psychological Association.

Delgadillo, J., Moreea, O., & Lutz, W. (2016). Different people respond differently to therapy: A demonstration using patient profiling and risk stratification. *Behaviour Research and Therapy*, *79*, 15–22. https://doi.org/10.1016/j.brat.2016.02.003

Delgadillo, J., Rubel, J., & Barkham, M. (2020). Towards personalized allocation of patients to therapists. *Journal of Consulting and Clinical Psychology*, *88*(9), 799–808. https://doi.org/10.1037/ccp0000507

DeRubeis, R. J., Cohen, Z. D., Forand, N. R., Fournier, J. C., Gelfand, L. A., & Lorenzo-Luaces, L. (2014). The Personalized Advantage Index: Translating research on prediction into individualized treatment recommendations. A demonstration. *PLOS One*, *9*(1), Article 83875. https://doi.org/10.1371/journal.pone.0083875

Douglas, S., Bovendeerd, B., Van Sonsbeek, M., Manns, M., Milling, X. P., Tyler, K., Bala, N., Satterthwaite, T., Hovland, R. T., Amble, I., Atzil-Slonim, D., Barkham, M., de Jong, K., Kendrick, T., Nordberg, S. S., Lutz, W., Rubel, J. A., Skjulsvik, T., & Moltu, C. (2023). A clinical leadership lens on implementing progress feedback in three countries: Development of a multidimensional qualitative coding scheme. *Administration and Policy in Mental Health and Mental Health Services Research*. https://doi.org/10.1007/s10488-023-01314-6

Eberhardt, S. T., Schaffrath, J., Moggia, D., Schwartz, B., Jaehde, M., Rubel, J. A., Baur, T., André, E., & Lutz, W. (2024). Decoding emotions: Exploring the validity of sentiment analysis in psychotherapy. *Psychotherapy Research*. https://doi.org/10.1080/10503307.2024.2322522

Finch, A. E., Lambert, M. J., & Schaalje, B. G. (2001). Psychotherapy quality control: The statistical generation of expected recovery curves for integration into an early warning system. *Clinical Psychology & Psychotherapy*, *8*(4), 231–242. https://doi.org/bqmqp3

Giesemann, J., Delgadillo, J., Schwartz, B., Bennemann, B., & Lutz, W. (2023). Predicting dropout from psychological treatment using different machine learning algorithms, resampling methods, and sample sizes. *Psychotherapy Research*, *33*(6), 683–695. https://doi.org/10.1080/10503307.2022.2161432

Gómez Penedo, J. M., Schwartz, B., Giesemann, J., Rubel, J. A., Deisenhofer, A.-K., & Lutz, W. (2022). For whom should psychotherapy focus on problem coping? A machine learning algorithm for treatment personalization. *Psychotherapy Research*, *32*(2), 151–164. https://doi.org/10.1080/10503307.2021.1930242

Gonçalves, M., Lutz, W., Schwartz, B., Oliveira, J. T., Saarni, S. E., Tishby, O., Rubel, J. A., Boehnke, J., Montesano, A., Paiva, D., Ceridono, D., Zech, E., Willemsen, J., Saarni, S. I., Kompan Erzar, K., Janeiro, L., Gelo, O. C. G., Errazuriz, P., Holas, P., & Barkham, M. (2024). *Developing a European Psychotherapy Consortium (EPoC): Scientific objectives and logistical challenges* [Manuscript submitted for publication]. School of Psychology, University of Minho.

Gonzalez Salas Duhne, P., Delgadillo, J., & Lutz, W. (2022). Predicting early dropout in online versus face-to-face guided self-help: A machine learning approach. *Behaviour Research and Therapy*, *159*, Article 104200. https://doi.org/10.1016/j.brat.2022.104200

Hehlmann, M. I., Moggia, D., Schwartz, B., Driver, C. C., Eberhardt, S. T., & Lutz, W. (2024). Outcome prediction in psychological therapy with continuous time dynamic modeling of affective states and emotion regulation. *Journal of Consulting and Clinical Psychology*. https://doi.org/10.1037/ccp0000862

Howard, K. I., Moras, K., Brill, P. L., Martinovich, Z., & Lutz, W. (1996). Evaluation of psychotherapy: Efficacy, effectiveness, and patient progress. *American Psychologist*, *51*(10), 1059–1064. https://doi.org/10.1037/0003-066X.51.10.1059

Husen, K., Rafaeli, E., Rubel, J. A., Bar-Kalifa, E., & Lutz, W. (2016). Daily affect dynamics predict early response in CBT: Feasibility and predictive validity of EMA for outpatient psychotherapy. *Journal of Affective Disorders*, *206*, 305–314. https://doi.org/10.1016/j.jad.2016.08.025

Kaiser, T., Volkmann, C., Volkmann, A., Karyotaki, E., Cuijpers, P., & Brakemeier, E.-L. (2022). Heterogeneity of treatment effects in trials on psychotherapy of depression. *Clinical Psychology: Science and Practice*, *29*(3), 294–303. https://doi.org/mc27

Kazantzis, N., Luong, H. K., Usatoff, A. S., Impala, T., Yew, R. Y., & Hofmann, S. G. (2018). The processes of cognitive behavioral therapy: A review of meta-analyses. *Cognitive Therapy and Research*, *42*(4), 349–357. https://doi.org/gdp2bp

Krüger, A., Ehring, T., Priebe, K., Dyer, A. S., Steil, R., & Bohus, M. (2014). Sudden losses and sudden gains during a DBT-PTSD treatment for posttraumatic stress disorder following childhood sexual abuse. *European Journal of Psychotraumatology*, *5*(1), Article 24470. https://doi.org/10.3402/ejpt.v5.24470

Lambert, M. J. (2001). Psychotherapy outcome and quality improvement: Introduction to the special section on patient-focused research. *Journal of Consulting and Clinical Psychology*, *69*(2), 147–149. https://doi.org/10.1037/0022-006X.69.2.147

Lorenzo-Luaces, L., DeRubeis, R. J., van Straten, A., & Tiemens, B. (2017). A prognostic index (PI) as a moderator of outcomes in the treatment of depression: A proof of concept combining multiple variables to inform risk-stratified stepped care models. *Journal of Affective Disorders*, *213*, 78–85. https://doi.org/10.1016/j.jad.2017.02.010

Lutz, W. (2002). Patient-focused psychotherapy research and individual treatment progress as scientific groundwork for an empirically based clinical practice. *Psychotherapy Research, 12*(3), 251–272. https://doi.org/10.1080/713664389

Lutz, W., Castonguay, L. G., Lambert, M. J., & Barkham, M. (2021). Traditions and new beginnings: Historical and current perspectives on research in psychotherapy and behavior change. In M. Barkham, W. Lutz, & L. G. Castonguay (Eds.), *Bergin and Garfield's handbook of psychotherapy and behavior change* (7th ed., pp. 3–18). Wiley.

Lutz, W., Deisenhofer, A.-K., Rubel, J., Bennemann, B., Giesemann, J., Poster, K., & Schwartz, B. (2022). Prospective evaluation of a clinical decision support system in psychological therapy. *Journal of Consulting and Clinical Psychology, 90*(1), 90–106. https://doi.org/10.1037/ccp0000642

Lutz, W., Deisenhofer, A.-K., Weinmann-Lutz, B., & Barkham, M. (2023). Data-informed clinical training and practice. In L. G. Castonguay & C. E. Hill (Eds.), *Becoming better psychotherapists: Advancing training and supervision.* (pp. 191–213). American Psychological Association. https://doi.org/10.1037/0000364-010

Lutz, W., de Jong, K., Rubel, J. A., & Delgadillo, J. (2021). Measuring, predicting and tracking change in psychotherapy. In M. Barkham, W. Lutz, & L. G. Castonguay (Eds.), *Bergin and Garfield's handbook of psychotherapy and behavior change* (7th ed., pp. 89–133). Wiley.

Lutz, W., Ehrlich, T., Rubel, J., Hallwachs, N., Röttger, M.-A., Jorasz, C., Mocanu, S., Vocks, S., Schulte, D., & Tschitsaz-Stucki, A. (2013). The ups and downs of psychotherapy: Sudden gains and sudden losses identified with session reports. *Psychotherapy Research, 23*(1), 14–24. https://doi.org/gd3vjv

Lutz, W., Hofmann, S. G., Rubel, J., Boswell, J. F., Shear, M. K., Gorman, J. M., Woods, S. W., & Barlow, D. H. (2014). Patterns of early change and their relationship to outcome and early treatment termination in patients with panic disorder. *Journal of Consulting and Clinical Psychology, 82*(2), 287–297. https://doi.org/10.1037/a0035535

Lutz, W., Leach, C., Barkham, M., Lucock, M., Stiles, W. B., Evans, C., Noble, R., & Iveson, S. (2005). Predicting change for individual psychotherapy clients on the basis of their nearest neighbors. *Journal of Consulting and Clinical Psychology, 73*(5), 904–913. https://doi.org/10.1037/0022-006X.73.5.904

Lutz, W., Leon, S. C., Martinovich, Z., Lyons, J. S., & Stiles, W. B. (2007). Therapist effects in outpatient psychotherapy: A three-level growth curve approach. *Journal of Counseling Psychology, 54*(1), 32–39. https://doi.org/10.1037/0022-0167.54.1.32

Lutz, W., Martinovich, Z., & Howard, K. I. (1999). Patient profiling: An application of random coefficient regression models to depicting the response of a patient to outpatient psychotherapy. *Journal of Consulting and Clinical Psychology, 67*(4), 571–577. https://doi.org/10.1037/0022-006X.67.4.571

Lutz, W., Prinz, J. N., Schwartz, B., Paulick, J., Schoenherr, D., Deisenhofer, A.-K., Terhürne, P., Boyle, K., Altmann, U., Strauß, B., Rafaeli, E., Atzil-Slonim, D., Bar-Kalifa, E., & Rubel, J. (2020). Patterns of early change in interpersonal problems and their relationship to nonverbal synchrony and multidimensional outcome. *Journal of Counseling Psychology, 67*(4), 449–461. https://doi.org/10.1037/cou0000376

Lutz, W., Rubel, J. A., Schwartz, B., Schilling, V., & Deisenhofer, A.-K. (2019). Towards integrating personalized feedback research into clinical practice: Development of the Trier Treatment Navigator (TTN). *Behaviour Research and Therapy, 120,* https://doi.org/10.1016/j.brat.2019.103438

Lutz, W., Saunders, S. M., Leon, S. C., Martinovich, Z., Kosfelder, J., Schulte, D., Grawe, K., & Tholen, S. (2006). Empirically and clinically useful decision making in psychotherapy: Differential predictions with treatment response models. *Psychological Assessment, 18*(2), 133–141. https://doi.org/ddgpk5

Lutz, W., Schwartz, B., & Delgadillo, J. (2022). Measurement-based and data-informed psychological therapy. *Annual Review of Clinical Psychology, 18*(1), 71–98. https://doi.org/10.1146/annurev-clinpsy-071720-014821

Lutz, W., Schwartz, B., Hofmann, S. G., Fisher, A. J., Husen, K., & Rubel, J. A. (2018). Using network analysis for the prediction of treatment dropout in patients with mood and anxiety disorders: A methodological proof-of-concept study. *Scientific Reports, 8*(1), 7819. https://doi.org/10.1038/s41598-018-25953-0

Lutz, W., Stulz, N., & Köck, K. (2009). Patterns of early change and their relationship to outcome and follow-up among patients with major depressive disorders. *Journal of Affective Disorders, 118*(1), 60–68. https://doi.org/10.1016/j.jad.2009.01.019

Lutz, W., Vehlen, A., & Schwartz, B. (2024). Data-informed psychological therapy, measurement-based care, and precision mental health. *Journal of Consulting and Clinical Psychology, 92*(10), 671–673. https://doi.org/10.1037/ccp0000904

Moggia, D., Lutz, W., Arndt, A., & Feixas, G. (2020). Patterns of change and their relationship to outcome and follow-up in group and individual psychotherapy for depression. *Journal of Consulting and Clinical Psychology, 88*(8), 757–773. https://doi.org/10.1037/ccp0000562

Moggia, D., Saxon, D., Lutz, W., Hardy, G. E., & Barkham, M. (2023). Applying precision methods to treatment selection for moderate/severe depression in person-centered experiential therapy or cognitive behavioral therapy. *Psychotherapy Research*, 1–16. https://doi.org/10.1080/10503307.2023.2269297

Paulick, J., Rubel, J. A., Deisenhofer, A.-K., Schwartz, B., Thielemann, D., Altmann, U., Boyle, K., Strauß, B., & Lutz, W. (2018). Diagnostic features of nonverbal synchrony in psychotherapy: Comparing depression and anxiety. *Cognitive Therapy and Research, 42*(5), 539–551. https://doi.org/10.1007/s10608-018-9914-9

Rubel, J. A., Fisher, A. J., Husen, K., & Lutz, W. (2018). Translating person-specific network models into personalized treatments: Development and demonstration of the Dynamic Assessment Treatment Algorithm for Individual Networks (DATA-IN). *Psychotherapy and Psychosomatics, 87*(4), 249–251. https://doi.org/gf7kbh

Rubel, J. A., Zilcha-Mano, S., Giesemann, J., Prinz, J., & Lutz, W. (2020). Predicting personalized process-outcome associations in psychotherapy using machine learning approaches—A demonstration. *Psychotherapy Research, 30*(3), 300–309. https://doi.org/10.1080/10503307.2019.1597994

Rubel, J., Lutz, W., Kopta, S. M., Köck, K., Minami, T., Zimmermann, D., & Saunders, S. M. (2015). Defining early positive response to psychotherapy: An empirical comparison between clinically significant change criteria and growth mixture modeling. *Psychological Assessment, 27*(2), 478–488. https://doi.org/f7fztt

Schaffrath, J., Weinmann-Lutz, B., & Lutz, W. (2022). The Trier Treatment Navigator (TTN) in action: Clinical case study on data-informed psychological therapy. *Journal of Clinical Psychology, 78*(10), 2016–2028. https://doi.org/10.1002/jclp.23362

Schwartz, B., Cohen, Z. D., Rubel, J. A., Zimmermann, D., Wittmann, W. W., & Lutz, W. (2021). Personalized treatment selection in routine care: Integrating machine learning and statistical algorithms to recommend cognitive behavioral or psychodynamic therapy. *Psychotherapy Research, 31*(1), 33–51. https://doi.org/ghbwb2

Schwartz, B., Rubel, J. A., Deisenhofer, A.-K., & Lutz, W. (2022). Movement-based patient-therapist attunement in psychological therapy and its association with early change. *Digital Health, 8*. https://doi.org/10.1177/20552076221129098

Shalom, J. G., & Aderka, I. M. (2020). A meta-analysis of sudden gains in psychotherapy: Outcome and moderators. *Clinical Psychology Review, 76*, Article 101827. https://doi.org/10.1016/j.cpr.2020.101827

Stulz, N., Lutz, W., Leach, C., Lucock, M., & Barkham, M. (2007). Shapes of early change in psychotherapy under routine outpatient conditions. *Journal of Consulting and Clinical Psychology, 75*(6), 864–874. https://doi.org/10.1037/0022-006X.75.6.864

Tang, T. Z., & DeRubeis, R. J. (1999). Sudden gains and critical sessions in cognitive-behavioral therapy for depression. *Journal of Consulting and Clinical Psychology, 67*(6), 894–904. https://doi.org/10.1037/0022-006X.67.6.894

Terhürne, P., Schwartz, B., Baur, T., Schiller, D., Eberhardt, S. T., André, E., & Lutz, W. (2022). Validation and application of the Non-Verbal Behavior Analyzer: An automated tool to assess non-verbal emotional expressions in psychotherapy. *Frontiers in Psychiatry, 13*. https://doi.org/10.3389/fpsyt.2022.1026015

Urban, H. B., & Ford, D. H. (1971). Some historical and conceptual perspectives on psychotherapy and behavior change. In A. E. Bergin & S. L. Garfield (Eds.), Handbook of psychotherapy and behavior change. (pp. 3–35). Wiley.

Wester, R. A., Schwartz, B., Lutz, W., Hall, M., Hoos, T., & Rubel, J. (2024). Treatment credibility as a mechanism of change in cognitive behavioral therapy: Effects on depression and anxiety. *Journal of Consulting and Clinical Psychology*. Advance online publication. https://doi.org/10.1037/ccp0000866

Wucherpfennig, F., Rubel, J. A., Hofmann, S. G., & Lutz, W. (2017). Processes of change after a sudden gain and relation to treatment outcome—Evidence for an upward spiral. *Journal of Consulting and Clinical Psychology, 85*(12), 1199–1210. https://doi.org/10.1037/ccp0000263

Zilcha-Mano, S., Eubanks, C. F., & Muran, J. C. (2019). Sudden gains in the alliance in cognitive behavioral therapy versus brief relational therapy. *Journal of Consulting and Clinical Psychology, 87*(6), 501–509. https://doi.org/10.1037/ccp0000397

4

Practice-Research Networks

Collaborative Partnerships for the Integration of Science, Clinical Work, and Training

Louis G. Castonguay

As it pertains to psychotherapy, practice-oriented research is aimed at understanding and improving psychosocial treatments as they are conducted in clinical routine (Castonguay et al., 2021). By investigating the accessibility, implementation, process, and impact of day-to-day mental health services, practice-oriented research contributes to the accumulation of practice-based evidence. Practice-research networks (PRNs) represent one type of practice-oriented research, and thus one source of practice-based evidence. PRNs are defined as groups of practitioners or, more typically, groups of practitioners and other stakeholders of mental health practice who work together to conduct empirical research (Castonguay et al., 2013). In contrast with other approaches of practice-oriented research, PRNs do not focus on specific topics of investigation—such as clients' patterns of change and therapists' responses to feedback that are emphasized in patient-focused research (see Lutz et al., this volume). Rather, PRNs' distinctive feature is the collaborative engagement of individuals with various responsibilities, tasks, needs, resources, and knowledge in the collection of data that they jointly viewed as clinically meaningful. By fostering the combination of different types of expertise and experiences, PRNs can be viewed as an optimal pathway for the integration of science and practice. In this chapter, I will present two PRNs initiatives, briefly highlighting their respective goals, organizational structure, and a few studies that emerged from them. I will also describe how such PRNs exemplify the hallmarks of practice-oriented research and thus the unique value of practice-based evidence for the scientific foundations of psychotherapy. First, however, I will provide the context that led to my engagement in PRNs.

Louis G. Castonguay, *Practice-Research Networks*. In: *Practice-Based Evidence in the Psychological Therapies*.
Edited by: Louis G. Castonguay et al., Oxford University Press.
DOI: 10.1093/9780197748336.003.0004

Context: Pathways of Integration

I have been guided by an integrative perspective for a long time. A significant part of my undergraduate studies at l'université de Sherbrooke in Quebec was devoted to reading several major psychodynamic, behavioral, and humanistic authors, which eventually led me to an almost paralyzing state of confusion—how can Freud, Skinner, and Rogers be so convincing and yet, at least on the surface, so different? To help me move beyond this uncomfortable state of mind, my first academic mentor, Yves St-Arnaud, introduced me to a book that offered a new model of therapeutic change based on convergences and complementarities between various approaches: *Systems of Psychotherapy: A Transtheoretical Analysis* (Prochaska, 1979). He also guided me in applying to a master's degree program that was based on the integration of different theoretical orientations—something unheard of in the late '70s and early '80s. The review of literature on common factors that I conducted for my master's thesis, under the supervision of Conrad Lecomte, led me to discover the work of Marv Goldfried, in particular his seminal publications on principles of change that cut across different forms of psychotherapy. Starting with my PhD at Stony Brook University under Goldfried's mentorship, my empirical and scholarly work has been primarily focused on understanding therapeutic change from an integrative lens, examining numerous types of factors that are common and unique to different types of therapy.

This integrative perspective is still guiding my work, but when I started my career as a faculty member at Penn State University in 1994, I delved into another type of integration—this time between science and practice. What was particularly attractive to me in this type of integration was the possibility of moving the scientific-practitioner model beyond its conceptual framework and of "bringing it to life" through an active and in "real-time" partnership between practitioners and researchers. PRNs quickly appeared to me as an ideal pathway for the type of partnership that I thought could advance the field of mental health via a concrete and seamless merging of practical and scientific knowledge. This is because PRNs are based on an active collaboration in various aspects of a study (from the selection of a topic to examine, the design and the implementation of a research protocol, through to the presentation of the results), thus relying on a diversity of expertise and experiences to conduct and disseminate empirically rigorous, as well as clinically feasible and helpful, investigations. Rather than being primarily guided by the interest and knowledge of academicians (many of them seeing few, if any clients), PRN studies allow practitioners to voice what they need to know to improve their clinical work and how a study might be conducted in day-to-day clinical routine with minimum burden imposed on them, their clients, and the center/system where they provide mental health care.

In retrospect, I realize that my wish and excitement to work with practitioners in designing, implementing, and presenting studies can be traced back to my undergraduate years. The program that I attended had been created by clinicians for the sake of offering academic training that focused more on professional development in the fields of human relationships than on research development. While science in general and experimental psychology in particular were recognized as crucial sources of knowledge, the emphasis was given to theory (thus my extensive reading of Freud, Rogers, and Skinner) and clinical expertise. The respect for practitioners' expertise that I acquired in this early formative period has never left me.

This new professional and scientific adventure began under the mentorship of Tom Borkovec, who was a close friend of Ken Howard, whose work led him to implement an outcome measure (the now defunct Compass Assessment System [COMPASS], Howard et al. 1993) in the training clinic associated with the adult clinical program at Penn State University. Borkovec's ultimate goal was to create a national PRN of training clinics using the same outcome measure in order to generate large data sets—thereby allowing students to investigate, in reliable and valid ways, complex issues that were relevant to their own training and practice of psychotherapy. As a first step, however, the feasibility and validity of the data collection in our own clinic needed to be improved. This is when I collaborated with Aaron Pincus to gradually transform our training clinic into a PRN.

When I arrived at Penn State, Borkovec, a full-time academician, had also paired up with Steve Ragusea, a full-time clinician, to create another PRN, this one involving practitioners in private practice across the state of Pennsylvania. The two of them had been engaged for years in private and public debates about the relevance of science to practice. Ragusea argued that research published in peer-review journals was so removed from day-to-day practice that most practitioners saw little, if any at all, clinical value to it. Borkovec defended the view that unless it is informed with solid empirical evidence it may be precarious to assume that the impact of psychotherapy, as practiced in the real world, is strong, extensive, and robust. As an attempt to resolve their disputes, they decided to join forces and test whether or not it would be possible to design and conduct clinically valid and informative research. Using the COMPASS, they led a study assessing the effectiveness of psychotherapy as delivered in private practice (Borkovec et al., 2001).

When the study was completed, I took the lead of this PRN and oversaw its next studies. The following sections will describe my quest, in collaboration with many colleagues and students, for the integration of science and practice in these two clinical settings (a third PRN where I have been pursuing the same collaborative endeavor is presented in another chapter: Hayes and Castonguay, this volume).

Pennsylvania State University Training Clinic PRN

From my perspective, the schism between science and practice is experienced by many scholars (at least in North America) in the initial stage of their careers. Graduate students must learn clinical and research skills, and, traditionally, they do so under the supervision of different mentors/supervisors and in different settings. It is typical to hear former graduate students say that their master's thesis and dissertation projects had limited clinical implications, let alone direct relevance to what they were learning when seeing clients during training. As an effort to address this disjointed state of affairs, the training clinic associated with the adult clinical graduate program was transformed into the Penn State University Training Clinic Practice Research Network (PSU-TCPRN), with the goal of creating optimal conditions for students to conduct studies (including their master's and dissertation projects) examining clinical questions within the setting where they are trained—thus, fostering a seamless integration of empirical, clinical, and training purposes.

Several factors facilitated this transformation. First, all tenure track faculty members in the program are involved in research on assessment and/or psychotherapy, and the core of the required supervision (clinical teams in cognitive behavioral and psychodynamic treatment) is conducted "in house" by tenure-track faculty members. Thus, students are trained by and work with some of the same people across their graduate courses, clinical responsibilities, and research endeavors. Second, the training clinic allows for relatively large naturalistic samples for archival and prospective studies: typically, between 200 and 250 clients per given year with diverse clinical problems, and approximately 25 therapists at any given time—most of them are doctoral trainees but some are licensed mental health providers—at any given time.

PSU-TCPRN Structure

The transformation of the training clinic into a PRN involved the gradual implementation of key structural components. A crucial piece has been the standardization of our routine assessment with the aim of assimilating research and practice into the same activities. This means that the core instruments that we have used and the procedures that we have implemented in collecting some of our primary research data correspond to what we want to assess, as well as how and when we want to measure it for clinical purposes. At a basic level, *the research protocol is the clinical protocol.* This not only increases the external validity of our studies (because we are investigating practice as it is conducted routinely) but also avoids a potential ethical problem of coercion that researchers can have on clients when asked to provide data and/or the conflicts of interest that a trainee may experience between the needs of a client and the need to collect data for their professional development.

In terms of instruments, our core battery assesses dimensions of psychopathology that are both clinically important and relevant to the research interests of many of our students, faculty members, and clinical staff. Central to this battery are two symptomatic measures, one self-report (Treatment Outcome Package [TOP, Kraus et al., 2005]) and one observer-rated (a slightly modified version of the Anxiety and Related Disorders Interview Schedule for DSM-5 (ADIS-5 [Brown & Barlow, 2014])), as well as two measures assessing interpersonal difficulties, also from self-report and interview-based perspectives: the Inventory of Interpersonal Problems-Short Circumplex (IIP-SC; Hopwood et al., 2008) and the International Personality Disorders Examination (Loranger, 1995). Other measures assessing suicide risk and trauma have been recently added to the core battery, for the same dual clinical and research purposes.

The assessment procedure has also been guided by an effort to seamlessly integrate research and practice. For example, while the TOP was originally assigned to a restricted number of sessions during treatment, a students' initiative led to its implementation before every session (as well as from a paper to a digital administration). Because the data are immediately processed and available, therapists are now being informed before the beginning of each session of their client's current scores on the subscales of the TOP and their scores at the previous administrations. In line with one of the major goals of practice-oriented research (see Castonguay et al., 2021), the data collected by and for the therapists are immediately (and continually) actionable. From a research perspective, a more frequent measurement of outcome was motivated by the possibility of investigating fine-grained patterns of change.

Another key component of our PRN infrastructure is a clinic research committee (CRC) which is responsible for the evaluation of research proposals. These proposals are short and are aimed at assessing the utility and feasibility of the proposed study. Applicants are asked to describe the clinical relevance of the investigation, as well as the burden it will impose on the clinical routine (e.g., time and tasks required by clients, therapists, administrators). They must also describe how their project is consistent with the goal of conducting research in our training clinic and how this clinic provides optimal conditions to conduct such a project. In order to benefit from the expertise of various stakeholders of our PRN and of full-time practitioners in evaluating the proposals, the CRC comprises faculty members, staff members, a graduate student, and a private practice clinician.

The structure of this PRN is also based on an agreement with the Office of Research Protections (ORP) regarding the approval of studies by the institutional review board (IRB) of our university. This arrangement recognizes that two types of studies can be conducted at the training clinic. Level I studies are investigations conducted within Penn State and only involve the use of completely de-identified data collected as part of clinic's routine standard of clinical care. As such, the IRB has deemed these studies as de-identified chart reviews that do not require formal IRB approval and instead are reviewed and approved by our CRC. The arrangement also stipulates that studies involving any collection of data outside of our standardized assessment, in terms of instruments and/or procedures, or include any form of protected health information (PHI), or are to be shared with external collaborators (i.e., Level II studies) require both IRB and CRC approval. This collaborative partnership with the IRB saved considerable time and effort for the trainees interested in better understanding care provided in their training environment.

Studies Conducted Within the PSU-TCPRN

Over the last 20 years, many studies have been generated within the PSU-TCPRN. Only a few are briefly presented here, and, to be consistent with the specific pathway of integration described in this chapter, I focus only on studies that students in my lab and I have been involved in. For his master's thesis, Samuel Nordberg conducted a Level 1 type of study examining patterns of change as measured by the TOP (Nordberg et al., 2014). As an example of patient-focused research (see Lutz et al., this volume), the study involved 147 clients treated by 45 therapists and replicated findings obtained in a different clinical setting with a different outcome measure (Stulz et al., 2007). Specifically, clients beginning therapy with high levels of depression showed different outcome profiles, with one group showing rapid response during treatment and the other remaining highly depressed. As an extension of Stulz and colleagues' findings, clinical factors that predicted clients whose symptom level did not change were identified: high levels of suicidality and social conflicts. These findings are not only clinically relevant but also potentially actionable, as they are generated from the setting where our students are acquiring therapeutic skills. The results can indeed inform them about clients who are at risk of not benefiting from treatment, as well as potential targets of assessment and treatment that may help them to be more responsive to clients who may not otherwise benefit from the care provided at the clinic.

To pursue his clinical, training, and research interests in the process of change, James Boswell needed to collect data that were not part of the clinic assessment routine. As an example of a Level 2 study (Boswell et al., 2010), his master's thesis required therapists (n = 19) to report their use of empirically supported interventions (via the Multitheoretical List of Therapeutic Interventions, MULTI; McCarthy & Barber, 2009) at the end of every session. It also required clients (n = 42) to rate each session in terms of its level of helpfulness using the Session Progress Scale (SPS; Kolden, 1991). Interestingly, interventions reported by therapists during therapy did not correlate with their own theoretical orientation nor with the theoretical orientation of the training provided by their supervisors. Some of the techniques, however, predicted clients' perceived level of session helpfulness: clients whose therapist typically used high levels of common factor techniques with them perceived sessions to be less helpful when their therapist used high levels of cognitive behavioral therapy (CBT) interventions.

Notably, this effect was particularly strong when CBT techniques were used by therapists who generally used high levels of common techniques with their clients. At a general level, the results suggest that shifts of interventions across conceptually different theoretical approaches may at times interfere with the process of therapy. At a more specific level, the findings suggest that knowing how and when to use CBT techniques (as you would also expect for interventions associated with all theoretical approaches) requires therapists to be attuned and responsive to the client's needs. From a training perspective, these findings point to advanced skills that therapists should learn in the early phases of their clinical careers.

Another Level 2 study suggested a possible context within which trainees can learn to successfully use CBT interventions. As part of his master's research and with a sample of 11 therapists and 26 clients, Andrew McAleavey also measured the use of interventions and the level of session helpfulness after every session (McAleavey et al., 2014). The results showed that therapists' reports of cognitive techniques related to clients' perceived helpfulness, but only when these techniques were used by trainees who identified primarily as cognitive therapists *and* when these trainees were supervised by a cognitive therapy supervisor. The results also indicated that process-experiential interventions were negatively related to the session helpfulness when used by therapists who identified themselves strongly with the humanistic tradition. Furthermore, psychodynamic interventions related negatively to the client's perception of the session helpfulness when used by therapists who were supervised by psychodynamic supervisors. Taken together, the results suggest that while some combinations of theoretical preference (on the part of the therapist) and expertise (on the part of the supervisor) may foster the effective implementation of particular techniques, others may not—perhaps because they engender rigidity, which in turn may have a hindering impact on the process of change.

As part of his master's research, but with a larger sample (16 therapists and 31 clients), McAleavey also investigated the link between therapists' use of interventions and client level of insight at the end of every session (McAleavey & Castonguay, 2014). The findings indicated insight-oriented techniques did not predict a high level of insight. Surprisingly, behavioral-change-oriented techniques were associated with client insight level—but only in the context of sessions with a high level of common factors. In addition to highlighting the interaction between technical and relational factors, these findings showed that some factors assumed to be unique to a particular type of therapy can explain part of the positive impact of other approaches.

Current studies conducted by students in my lab are further advancing previous work and opening new areas in research, practice, and training. For example, Katherine Davis and Hongjun Michael Tan are investigating the complexity of the process of change by assessing the link between techniques and different facets of the therapeutic relationship, including the client's perception of the therapist's interpersonal style, as well as alliance ruptures and their repair. Using mixed qualitative and quantitative methods, another study being conducted by Natalie Pottschmidt is exploring the feasibility and helpfulness of a repeated idiographic assessment of clients' distress and concerns, therapeutic change, as well as satisfaction with services during and after treatment. One goal of this study is to examine whether such idiographic assessment could add information to the nomothetic instruments routinely used at the clinic—information that could potentially help trainees, staff therapists, supervisors, and administrators to provide care that is most responsive to the needs of a particular client. At a broader level, this study is the first step in a program aimed at engaging primary stakeholders of our PRN, the clients, in evaluating and improving the clinic functioning and the services it provides to the community.

Pennsylvania Psychological Association PRN

Whereas the overarching goal of the training clinic PRN is to foster a seamless integration of science and practice at the early phase of a mental health professional's training, one of the raisons d'être of the Pennsylvanian Psychological Association PRN (PPA-PRN) is to provide experienced clinicians opportunities to do something that many of them (in particular those who applied to a PhD program) have wanted to do even before applying to graduate school: conduct research and, in doing so, advance scientific knowledge. What has motivated my own involvement in both PRNs is, in some respect, very different. While the building and maintaining of the PSU-TCPRN has been geared toward the empirical and professional actualization of trainees, my commitment to the PPA-PRN is much more personal: How can I continue to learn about how to conduct therapy despite the fact that my academic position does not give me time to see many clients? This being said, in both cases I am driven by the possibility of contributing to a specific path of the scientific-practitioner model, one that rests on investigating what some clinicians want to know and to do so in ways that are actionable. And in both cases, I am driven, no doubt more strongly, by the reward of working with others who share my interest in understanding and improving psychotherapy, but who are coming at it from a different angle.

Although there are converging sources of purposes and motivations, the two PRNs are very distinct structurally. The structure of the PSU-TCPRN is formal, and while changes have been made to be responsive to the needs and responsibilities of various stakeholders, its operation has remained anchored within the same basic components described earlier. In contrast, the PPA-PRN is not dependent on a highly complex and stable administrative structure. It is sponsored by a statewide professional organization, which has provided some financial support despite having limited resources itself, and administrative members of this organization have contributed to the development and implementation of some of the studies. However, the "structure" of the PRN is defined by each of the studies that are conducted, one at the time. Reflecting these idiosyncratic structures, more space will be given to the design and implementation of each study that I describe in the next section, as compared with the previous one.

Studies Conducted Within the PPA-PRN

As mentioned earlier in this chapter, the first study conducted within the PPA-PRN was primarily aimed at examining the impact of psychotherapy in day-to-day practice. Using a simple pre and post research design, it involved 50 therapists across the state of Pennsylvania who agreed to use a standardized outcome monitoring measure as part of the clinical routine of their private practice. Process-wise, the study demonstrated that it was feasible for clinicians and researchers to collaborate in the selection of research questions to be investigated, as well as in the development and implementation of a study protocol that would not interfere with clinical work. Outcome-wise, the findings revealed significant pre–post symptomatic change, as well as various predictors of treatment outcome (Borkovec et al., 2001; Ruiz et al., 2004). Yet, for core members of the PRN, the study left much to be desired: Clinically, it did not investigate issues or questions that clinicians are directly faced with when working with clients, and it did not provide immediately actionable findings. Empirically, it did not address what could be argued as the ultimate goal of science, namely, establishing a cause-and-effect relationship (Borkovec & Castonguay, 1998).

Helpful and Hindering Events in Psychotherapy

From these limitations, core members of this PRN concluded that investigating immediately useful questions in a rigorous manner requires a more complex protocol, and that such a protocol would be best designed and implemented through frequent and regular meetings between all practitioners and researchers involved. It was thus decided that the context for the second study would shift from the entire state of Pennsylvania to the much smaller community surrounding Penn State University.

A group of therapists and researchers then met regularly for 12 months to decide what to study and how to study it. The primary question that we decided to investigate was voiced in our first meeting by one of the clinicians: "What I would really like to know is what my clients found helpful during a session we just conducted." Raised by a researcher, a second question that we agreed to pursue was whether knowing from the clients what they find helpful and/or unhelpful can improve treatment effectiveness. The discussions that took place over the following months focused on all aspects of the study, for example: What instruments are relevant to our investigation? What parts of these instruments should we use? How and when should we use them so that they will not interfere with or impose too much burden on clinical work? The collaborative process that fed and sustained these discussions allowed for the distinct and complementary expertise of the practitioners and researchers to shape every component of the research protocol that we built together. This collaborative process also led to a new and unexpected experience for me. Whereas I had previously faced ambivalence on the part of clinicians when I had asked them to fill out questionnaires as part of a research trial designed by researchers ("Oh, Louis, these are a lot of questions that you are asking me and my clients to answer!"), such "resistance" disappeared when we designed our study within the context a full partnership. In fact, I was the one who many times showed ambivalence about the use of questionnaires: "Oh, yes, this would lead to fascinating data, but are you sure that you want to fill this out after every session? I think that this would be a lot of work, don't you think?" I should also mention that during the many months of meetings devoted to design and implementation of the study, clinicians and researchers learned from each other about broader issues, for example: "So what is the current status of the research on this?" "How do you handle this type of crisis in your practice?" These discussions are as nourishing as they are rare when professional contacts are limited to our own community of mental health stakeholders.

When building our research protocol, we decided that for the duration of the study, clinicians would integrate within their clinical routine the TOP to measure at pre and post treatment several dimensions of symptoms and functioning. Furthermore, we agreed that unless counter-indicated clinically, all new clients (children, adolescents, adults) in their private practice would be asked if they would be willing to participate in a study where participants are randomly assigned to two conditions. In the experimental condition, the clients and therapists were asked, after each session, to describe any helpful and/or hindering events that may have happened during the session and to rate such events in terms of how helpful or hindering they were. Therapists were instructed to read the client's answers (after having recorded their own) before the next session and consider how these might help them to be most attuned to the client's needs. However, the research protocol did not prescribe (or proscribe) any other tasks. It was up to the therapists if they wanted to do something, and what they wanted to do, with the information provided by their clients. In the control condition, only the therapists answered the questions about helpful and hindering events. This was to address a possible confounding variable in our attempt to assess whether receiving feedback from clients has a causal effect on treatment outcome (i.e., the potential beneficial impact of having the therapists identifying and addressing meaningful events). While randomization of clients is associated with studies conducted in controlled settings, the use of such methodology in this study, as well as other practice-oriented research (e.g., Lambert et al., 2001; Whipple et al., 2003) did not dictate a major change to clinicians' work (e.g., adhering to treatment manuals, receiving specialized training, or implementing specific tasks to particular helpful or hindering events). As they reflected the treatment delivered in usual care, albeit slightly modified, the findings can be viewed, arguably, as practice-based evidence.

The study was implemented by 13 practitioners up to a period of 18 months. A total of 146 clients were recruited, and more than 1,600 helpful or hindering events were recorded by them and their therapists. These events were then coded by graduate students with respect to the *types* of events reported and their *content* (i.e., what these events were about). For the combined groups of adolescent and adult clients, events identified as an increase in awareness (such as the exploration of painful events and the experience of negative feelings) were viewed as particularly helpful events by both clients and therapists (Castonguay, Boswell, et al., 2010). Therapists also viewed as particularly helpful the events reflecting the strengthening of the therapeutic relationship. In addition, issues related to the therapeutic relationship were among the most frequent content referred to in the helpful events (such as the formation of a close bond), as well as in the hindering events (such as the client feeling under attack and needing to withdraw)—for both clients and therapists. This suggests that in day-to-day practice, the therapeutic relationship is perceived as a key component that can either facilitate or interfere with the process of change. However, an insufficient number of clients completed the TOP at the end of treatment to allow us to examine whether the experimental and control group differed in terms of therapeutic outcome.

Following the completion of the study, 11 of the 13 participating therapists were interviewed about their engagement in designing and implementing the investigation. Their answers, which were submitted to a qualitative analysis (Castonguay, Nelson, et al., 2010) provided extensive information about what they found most interesting and/or beneficial (e.g., getting feedback from clients and using it to adjust their interventions; developing a sense of community based on a shared goal); what they found most difficult and/frustrating (e.g., remembering components of the research protocol; extra time and work added to practice); what did they saw as beneficial (e.g., writing down thoughts about what took place during the session) or detrimental (e.g., filling out instruments being perceived by some as inconvenient) to their clients; what they did to overcome obstacles that they were confronted to (e.g., consulting with each other and researchers; developing strategies to remember research procedures); and what they would recommend for future PRNs studies (e.g., having research tasks being clinically useful, providing incentives to increase motivation). Needless to say, we derived lessons from these interviews to guide our next studies.

Techniques and Impact of Therapy

The third study from our PRN (Castonguay et al., 2024), also conducted in communities surrounding Penn State University, was guided by two primary goals. One was to examine the relationship between techniques and session impact and thus deliver a replication of the Boswell et al. (2010) findings in a different clinical setting. A second one was to assess whether collecting data about techniques and impact on a session-to-session basis could improve treatment effectiveness. A total of 11 private practice therapists (one of them also a full-time academician) met for several months to design and implement the study, while engaging in the same collaborative process that characterized the helpfulness and hindering study. Adopting the TOP as part of their respective clinical routine, clinicians invited for up to 2 years new individual therapy clients (18 years old or older) to be randomly assigned to either an experimental or a control group. However, to reduce the burden that practitioners experienced during the helpful and hindering events study, each therapist could only recruit up to four clients at any given time during the study.

In the experimental group, client and therapist filled out at the end of each session the MULTI, two questions to identify techniques that they viewed as particularly helpful or hindering, as well the same brief questionnaire on the impact of the session used in Boswell et al. (2010). Similar to what was done in the helpful and hindering events study, therapists were asked to read the information provided by their clients (after they filled out their own questionnaires but prior to the next session), but no instruction was given about if, when, or how to react to the collected information.

With regard to the first goal of this study, the findings indicated that although clients who received a higher use of common factors (relative to their own therapist's caseload average) tended to report better session outcomes, such outcomes were poorer in sessions with higher use of behavioral change techniques (relative to the client's own average). In contrast, clients who received the lowest use of common factors tended to perceive as the most helpful sessions those that involved higher levels of behavioral change techniques. These results appear to share a general pattern with Boswell et al.'s (2010) results, one that suggests that with respect to the client experience of the impact of a session, consistency in therapist technique use matters.

It is worth noting that in designing this study, we attempted to learn from our previous experience not only by making the study protocol more manageable (by limiting the recruitment of clients for each clinician) but by improving our data collection—including the provision of financial incentives to clients for filling out the TOP at post-treatment. Yet, we still failed to collect sufficient outcome data to meet the second goal of the study, namely, assessing whether monitoring and receiving information about techniques and session impact may have a causal effect on client improvement.

Peer Supervision

The next and current phase of our PRN represents a double shift from the last two studies, first by returning to Pennsylvania-wide investigations and, second, by moving from a focus on therapy to one on supervision. The first step of this new phase was a preliminary study on the feasibility and helpfulness of peer consultation for early career practitioners (Kilcullen et al., 2023). The study was designed and implemented by a senior researcher, an experienced clinician, an early career researcher, two administrative staff members of the PPA, and a graduate student. Recruited from different parts of Pennsylvania, eight psychologists with less than 10 years of post-licensure experience were assigned to one of two peer consultation groups (one dropped out early on in the study).

Before the peer consultation began, participants filled out a measure (with both Likert-scale and open-ended questions) to assess what they anticipated, in terms of feasibility and helpfulness, from their participation. The experience of their actual participation was assessed after the completion of the peer consultation, which took place via Zoom videoconferencing over 7 months. The research protocol was designed with the goal of making the peer consultation as actionable and as close as possible to what takes place in clinical practice: Participants in each of their respective groups decided how frequently they were going to meet (e.g., once every 2 weeks), as well as the length (e.g., 2 hours), process (e.g., formal case presentations), and the focus (e.g., personal experience of the therapists) of the meetings. Quantitative and qualitative analyses revealed that participants generally had positive expectations toward the consultation meetings. They also experienced them positively in terms of feasibility and implementation (e.g., easy to participate, engaging, cohesive). Numerous benefits were reported with respect to their clinical development (e.g., improving case formulation and interventions skills), professional development (e.g., expanding their network of connections), and emotional support (e.g., reducing a sense of isolation, experiencing feelings of empowerment and validation). In addition, a number of factors that interfere with peer supervision were identified, including lack of structure and unhelpful interpersonal dynamics.

Combined with the lessons from our previous studies, what we learned in terms of fostering the actionability and impact of peer supervision is currently being used in the design of a large process and outcome study.

Concluding Remarks: Implications, Limitations, and Recommendations for PRNs

This chapter was aimed at presenting PRNs as one approach to collect practice-based evidence. While emerging from different clinical settings, the studies briefly described here (as well as in Hayes and Castonguay, this volume) exemplify defining features of practice-oriented research, as they were conducted in naturalistic milieux, reflected the clinical routine of such milieux, and sought to minimize research-driven restrictions or prescriptions to the utilization or implementation of day-to-day practice in these milieux. Most salient to PRNs, these practice-oriented research studies have been designed and implemented as part of an active collaboration of clinicians and other stakeholders invested in better understanding and improving mental health care.

Having practitioners involved in deciding what to study can open windows of investigation into unanswered questions and unresolved issues that they face as part of clinical routine. Having them involved in creating and implementing a research protocol and/or an infrastructure can provide invaluable insights about the hurdles to avoid and feasible ways to cope with them in collecting meaningful data within day-to-day clinical work. This is one way for the field to correct what Alan Kazdin (2008) colorfully described as a major faux pas in the field of psychotherapy: letting clinicians' experience-based knowledge drip through the holes of a colander. Rather than paying limited attention to clinicians' observations, questions, and experience, PRN initiatives can give them a voice in setting the research agenda (Zarin et al., 1997), as well as in creating feasible and actionable studies—thereby setting up a potentially fruitful pathway for the actualization of the scientific-practitioner model.

Implications

Not surprisingly, studies planned in part by and for clinicians (as trainees, early professionals, or senior therapists) can lead to helpful lessons, as suggested by some of the clinical implications briefly mentioned earlier. Among them is the recommendation of maintaining a general stance of consistency in implementing different types of interventions. Yet, findings described in this chapter suggest that one should remain vigilant about the potential negative impact of high levels of and/or rigid adherence to particular techniques.

More general clinical *and* empirical implications can be derived from the previously described studies, which in turn highlight some of the contributions of practice-based evidence toward the scientific foundations of psychotherapy. In contrast with most randomized clinical trials (RCTs) conducted in controlled settings, a substantial number of therapists have been involved in both of the PRNs outlined in this chapter, enhancing the generalizability of their findings, at least in the respective setting in which they have been obtained. The external validity of the results obtained is likely to be especially high within the unique and specific environment where an investigation has been conducted. For example, therapists at the Penn State University training clinic do not have to wonder whether the finding that a substantial (and identifiable) number of clients who started therapy with a high level of symptoms will remain so during treatment is or is not relevant to their caseload. As long as the structure of this PRN does not change, this finding is not only relevant to their caseload—it *is* about their caseload and those of their colleagues.

In addition to being directly applicable, findings in some of the studies summarized earlier are immediately actionable. Engaging in a seamless integration of science and practice, therapists in the second PPA-PRN study were not only collecting empirical data about what is helpful or hindering in therapy but also simultaneously gathering clinical information that could potentially help them, right as they were implementing the research protocol they designed, to be more responsive to their clients' individual needs. Similarly, when therapists in the PPA-PRN peer supervision study were meeting (whenever they wanted and for how long they wanted) to discuss what they wanted to discuss and how they wanted to discuss it, they were not only providing evidence that this form of postgraduate training is feasible and helpful—they were, in the here and now, acquiring skills to work with their current clients, as well as ways to cope with current professional and personal challenges (including the emergence of the COVID epidemic). Were these therapists advancing science when they consulted with each other, or were they learning clinically—not only for the future but for what was going on in their current practice and their life? At these exact and key moments of the study procedures they were doing both. In the same vein, the aspiration of seamlessly integrating science and practice was guiding the establishment of the PSU training PRN when stakeholders were endeavoring for the basic research protocol to be the clinical protocol.

Limitations

Several limitations are inherent in the PRNs studies described in this chapter. By far, the most frustrating one was the inability to collect sufficient post-treatment outcome data to answer questions about the possibility that the addition of specific interventions within clinicians' own practices could cause client improvement. Difficulties in collecting post-treatment data have also been experienced in the early phase of another practice-based initiative but was corrected by more frequent monitoring of outcome (see Barkham et al., this volume). We are anticipating using this strategy in planning our next PPA-PRN study. As emphasized by one of the clinicians involved in this PRN, learning how to do better practice-oriented research has been a main benefit of past and current collaborative efforts (Hemmelstein, 2012).

Although larger than in most RCTs conducted in controlled settings, conducting studies with a greater sample of therapists (and thus clients) would improve generalizability of findings and provide adequate power for the use of sophisticated analyses aimed at addressing, precisely and rigorously, complex clinical questions. Working with a limited number of therapists and clients has been a price to pay for conducting studies within "local" communities—in contrast to investigations that I have conducted with graduate students and other stakeholders within a PRN infrastructure involving more than 800 university counseling centers (see Hayes & Castonguay, this volume). Addressing this current limitation is the main reason for our intention to return to a statewide recruitment of clinicians in planning the next PPA-PRN study. We have also not forgotten Tom Borkovec's dream of creating a network of training clinics using the same outcome measures. Actualizing this dream would allow trainees access to large samples of clients and therapists. In both cases, these future developments would reflect one of the recommendations for future practice-oriented research, namely, working locally and collaborating globally (Castonguay et al., 2021).

Recommendations

In addition to addressing limitations to our previous studies, I would suggest that future PRN research should focus on a number of broad issues. Among them is the creation and completion of synergetic loops involving, firstly, the collection of data in a natural setting to better understand its clinical routine; secondly, the generation of strategies to improve delivery of care based on the findings of the initial data collection; and thirdly, the investigation of the feasibility and helpfulness of these strategies within the same setting. Collaboratively designed by various stakeholders (e.g., graduate students, supervisors, academicians, administrative/clinical staff members), an RCT could be involved in the third phase of these loops where, for example, diverse actionable strategies (none of them imposing drastic changes to clinical routine) might be compared in their ability to help clinicians in the PSU training clinic to be more responsive to clients who begin with and maintain high levels of distress. This type of trial could provide particularly strong evidence for the convergence and complementarity between PRNs and RCT studies conducted in controlled settings.

A second broad issue that deserves attention in future PRN efforts is sustainability. Designing and implementing a non-burdensome and potentially helpful intervention is a challenging task, but having clinicians sustain it as part of their routine is a more daunting one. For example, one of the participants in the peer supervision study reported that the group was going to continue meeting after the completion of the study. Has it and, if so, for how long? PRN researchers are likely to benefit from implementation science in assessing and enhancing the retainability of their findings (Youn et al., 2024).

An even broader, and certainly bolder, issue would be to promote the dissemination of PRNs. A substantial number of PRN infrastructures have already been developed, with several of them linked to professional organizations, specific clinical disorders, or common healthcare settings (Castonguay et al., 2013). Yet, more PRNs should be built as they represent an optimal strategy for addressing two major limitations of traditional RCT studies. First, like all methods aimed at collecting practice-based evidence, PRNs can attenuate concerns of external validity intrinsic to findings that emerge from studies that are not conducted in naturalistic settings or are not reflecting the clinical routine of such settings. Second, traditional studies are typically conceived by academicians and primarily aimed at improving care via a top-down approach of dissemination. PRNs can be a transformative alternative to such an approach by moving the field beyond the metaphor of the bridge between science and practice, where representatives of different perspectives stand on opposite sides of a river and where the exchange of knowledge is, for the most part, unidirectional—with the clinicians being informed or trained about what researchers tell them is evidence-based practice. In contrast, PRNs provide opportunities for the creation of new landscapes of knowledge and action that are based on and grow from diverse needs, convergent interests, and complementary expertise. As such, fostering the dissemination of PRNs can not only broaden the scientific foundations of psychotherapy but also reduce the schism between researchers and clinicians that prevails in the field of mental health—a schism that has been maintained in part by the predominant weight that has been given to traditional RCTs in clinical, training, and policy guidelines.

Acknowledgments

I am grateful for the feedback provided by James Boswell, Neil Hemmelstein, Sam Knapp, Andrew McAleavey, Sandra Testa Michelson, and Soo Jeong Youn on a previous version of this chapter.

References

Borkovec, T. D., & Castonguay, L. G. (1998). What is the scientific meaning of empirically supported therapy? *Journal of Consulting and Clinical Psychology*, *66*(1), 136–142. https://doi.org/10.1037/0022-006X.66.1.136

Borkovec, T. D., Echemendia, R. J., Ragusea, S. A., & Ruiz, M. (2001). The Pennsylvania practice research network and future possibilities for clinically meaningful and scientifically rigorous psychotherapy research. *Clinical Psychology: Science and Practice*, *8*, 155–167. https://doi.org/10.1093/clipsy.8.2.155

Boswell, J. F., Castonguay, L. G., & Wasserman, R. H. (2010). Effects of psychotherapy training and intervention use on session outcome. *Journal of Consulting and Clinical Psychology*, *78*, 717–723. https://doi.org/10.1037/a0020088

Brown, T. A., & Barlow, D. H. (2014). *Anxiety and related disorders interview schedule for DSM-5 (ADIS-5) - adult and lifetime version: Clinician manual.* New York: Oxford University Press.

Castonguay, L. G., Barkham, M., Lutz, W., & McAleavy, A. (2013). Practice oriented research: Approaches and applications. In M. J. Lambert (Ed.), *Bergin and Garfield's handbook of psychotherapy and behavior change* (6th ed., pp. 85–133). New York: Wiley.

Castonguay, L. G., Barkham, M., Youn, S. J., & Page, A. C. (2021). Practice-based evidence—Findings from routine clinical settings. In M. Barkham, W. Lutz, & L. G. Castonguay (Eds.), *Bergin and Garfield's handbook of psychotherapy and behavior change* (7th ed., pp. 191–222). New York: Wiley.

Castonguay, L. G., Boswell, J. F., Zack, S. E., Baker, S., Boutselis, M. A., Chiswick, N. R., Damer, D. D., Hemmelstein, N. A., Jackson, J. S., Morford, M., Ragusea, S. A., Roper, J. G., Spayd, C., Weiszer, T., Borkovec, T. D., & Grosse Holtforth, M. (2010). Helpful and hindering events in psychotherapy: A practice research network study. *Psychotherapy, 47*(3), 327–344. https://doi.org/10.1037/a0021164

Castonguay, L. G., Nelson, D. L., Boutselis, M. A., Chiswick, N. R., Damer, D. D., Hemmelstein, N. A., Jackson, J. S., Morford, M., Ragusea, S. A., Roper, J. G., Spayd, C., Weiszer, T., & Borkovec, T. D. (2010). Psychotherapists, researchers, or both? A qualitative analysis of psychotherapists' experiences in a practice research network. *Psychotherapy, 47*(3), 345–354. https://doi.org/10.1037/a0021165

Castonguay, L. G., Youn, S. J., Boswell, J. F., Kilcullen, J. R., Xiao, H., McAleavey, A. A., Boutselis, M. A., Braver, M., Chiswick, N. R., Hemmelstein, N. A., Jackson, J. S., Lytle, R. A., Morford, M. E., Scott, H. S., Spayd, C. S., & O'Leary Wiley, M. (2024). Therapeutic techniques and session impact: A practice-research network study in private practice. *Psychotherapy Research, 34*(7), 845–857. https://doi.org/10.1080/10503307.2023.2262099

Hemmelstein, N. A. (2012, January). Scientist-practitioner networks from the practitioner's point of view. *International Federation for Psychotherapy Newsletter*, 6–7.

Hopwood, C. J., Pincus, A. L., DeMoor, R. M., & Koonce, E. A. (2008). Psychometric characteristics of the Inventory of Interpersonal Problems—Short Circumplex (IIP-SC) with college students. *Journal of Personality Assessment, 90*(6), 615–618. https://doi.org/10.1080/00223890802388665

Howard, K. L, Brill, P. L., Lueger, R. J., O'Mahoney, M. T., & Grissom, G. R. (1993). *Integra outpatient tracking assessment.* Compass Information Systems.

Kazdin, A. E. (2008). Evidence-based treatment and practice: New opportunities to bridge clinical research and practice, enhance the knowledge base, and improve patient care. *American Psychologist, 63*(3), 146–159. https://doi.org/10.1037/0003-066X.63.3.146

Kilcullen, J. R., Castonguay, L., Carney, D. M., Davis, K. A., Pottschmidt, N. R., Knapp, S. J., Jackson, C. L., Hemmelstein, N. A., & Frakes, A. M. (2023). Peer consultation for early career psychotherapists: A preliminary study. In L. G. Castonguay & C. E. Hill (Eds.), *Becoming better psychotherapists: Advancing training and supervision* (pp. 267–287). American Psychological Association. https://doi.org/10.1037/0000364-013

Kolden, G. G. (1991). The generic model of psychotherapy: An empirical investigation of patterns of process and outcome relationships. *Psychotherapy Research, 1*, 62–73.

Kraus, D. R., Seligman, D. A., & Jordan, J. R. (2005). Validation of a behavioral health treatment outcome and assessment tool designed for naturalistic settings: The Treatment Outcome Package. *Journal of Clinical Psychology, 61*(3), 285–314. https://doi.org/10.1002/jclp.20084

Lambert, M. J., Whipple, J. L., Smart, D. W., Vermeersch, D. A., Nielsen, S. L., & Hawkins, E. J. (2001). The effects of providing therapists with feedback on patient progress during psychotherapy: Are outcomes enhanced? *Psychotherapy Research, 11*(1), 49–68. https://doi.org/10.1080/713663852

Loranger, A. W. (1995). *International Personality Disorders Examination (IPDE).* World Health Organization.

McAleavey, A. A., & Castonguay, L. G. (2014). Insight as a common and specific impact of psychotherapy: Therapist-reported exploratory, directive, and common factor interventions. *Psychotherapy, 51*(2) 283–294. https://doi.org/10.1037/a0032410

Mcaleavey, A. A., Castonguay, L. G., & Xiao, H. (2014). Therapist orientation, supervisor match, and therapeutic interventions: Implications for session quality in a psychotherapy training PRN. *Counselling and Psychotherapy Research, 14*(3), 192–200. https://doi.org/10.1080/14733145.2014.929418

McCarthy, K. S., & Barber, J. P. (2009). The Multitheoretical List of Therapeutic Interventions (MULTI): Initial report. *Psychotherapy Research, 19*, 96–113. DOI: 10.1080/10503300802524343

Nordberg, S. S., Castonguay, L. G., Fisher, A. J., Boswell, J. F., & Kraus, D. (2014). Validating the rapid responder construct within a practice research network. *Journal of Clinical Psychology*, *70*, 886–903. https://doi.org/10.1002/jclp.22077

Prochaska, J. O. (1979). *Systems of psychotherapy: A transtheoretical analysis*. Dorsey Press.

Ruiz, M. A., Pincus, A. L., Borkovec, T. B., Echemendia, R., Castonguay, L. G., & Ragusea, S., (2004). Validity of the Inventory of Interpersonal Problems (IIP-C) for predicting treatment outcome: An investigation with the Pennsylvania Practice Research Network. *Journal of Personality Assessment*, *83*(3), 213–222. https://doi.org/10.1207/s15327752jpa8303_05

Stulz, N., Lutz, W., Leach, C., Lucock, M., & Barkham, M. (2007). Shapes of early change in psychotherapy under routine outpatient conditions. *Journal of Consulting and Clinical Psychology*, *75*(6), 864–874. https://doi.org/10.1037/0022-006X.75.6.864

Whipple, J. L., Lambert, M. J., Vermeersch, D. A., Smart, D. W., Nielsen, S. L., & Hawkins, E. J. (2003). Improving the effects of psychotherapy: The use of early identification of treatment failure and problem-solving strategies in routine practice. *Journal of Counseling Psychology*, *50*(1), 59–68. https://doi.org/10.1037/0022-0167.50.1.59

Youn, S. J., Boswell, J. F., Douglas, S., Harris, B. A., Aajmain, S., Arnold, K. T., Creed, T. A., Gutner, C. A., Orengo-Aguayo, R., Oswald, J. M., & Stirman, S. W. (2024). Implementation science and practice-oriented research: Convergence and complementarity. *Administration and Policy in Mental Health*, *51*(3), 336–347. https://doi.org/10.1007/s10488-023-01296-5

Zarin, D. A., Pincus, H. A., West, J. C., & McIntyre, J. S. (1997). Practice-based research in psychiatry. *The American Journal of Psychiatry*, *154*(9), 1199–1208. https://doi.org/10.1176/ajp.154.9.1199

SECTION II

PARTICIPANTS AND STAKEHOLDERS: THERAPISTS AND PATIENTS

5

How the Therapist Matters

Practice-Based Evidence for Improving Therapist Effectiveness

Helene A. Nissen-Lie

Every client knows this well: The person of the therapist is crucial. Indeed, clients often refer to the therapist's personal qualities when describing whether the therapist managed to help them—or not, with statements like "The moment she picked me up in the waiting room, I knew she was different from my former therapist, by her way of smiling at me and her tone of voice," "She was far too distant for me," "He managed to put me at ease by his sense of humor," and "I felt that he was too judgmental and so I could not open up."

Despite the common wisdom that the effectiveness of psychotherapy depends in large part on the person of the therapist, and some notable empirical programs describing *who* the therapist is (e.g., Henry et al., 1971), until recently there were few empirical investigations into therapist effects and the nature of those effects. In fact, fewer than 0.25% of clinical trials published between 1965 and 2013 examined the effect of the therapist, a fact that made Wampold and Owen (2021) conclude that "studying differences among therapists is not a priority in psychotherapy research" (pp. 8–9). Things have gradually changed, and today researchers have started to include the systematic study of individual therapist differences in psychotherapy research studies, both in controlled studies and, more notably, in practice-oriented research studies (see Castonguay & Hill, 2017; Nissen-Lie et al., 2024).

One needs to apply suitable methods (such as advanced statistical models) to find answers to *if* (how much of variability in outcomes are due to individual characteristics of the therapist) and *how* (i.e., what characterizes more and less effective psychotherapists and under which circumstances these factors have more or less impact) the individual therapist makes a difference to

Helene A. Nissen-Lie, *How the Therapist Matters*. In: *Practice-Based Evidence in the Psychological Therapies*.
Edited by: Louis G. Castonguay et al., Oxford University Press.
DOI: 10.1093/9780197748336.003.0005

client progress in psychotherapy. Fortunately, prior research has produced some answers to these important questions, and I will briefly review some of the main findings in the field before turning to a line of research that I have taken part in during the last decade. Using different therapist samples, but all under the umbrella of practice-oriented research (i.e., conducted within and reflecting clinical routine practice), this research has sought to delineate some of the therapist's contribution to psychotherapeutic change. As noted by Barkham et al. (2010), one of the contributions of practice-oriented research / practice-based evidence is precisely the legitimization of the therapist as a key focus of empirical investigation. As compared with the randomized controlled trial (RCT) design, naturalistic designs used in practice-oriented research make it optimal to explore naturally occurring differences in therapist effectiveness and how different therapist behaviors relate to differential client outcomes. Finally, I will make the claim that this knowledge has important implications for the training of therapists, as well as for therapist self-care.

Several meta-analytic studies indicate that therapists differ in their general effectiveness (i.e., Johns et al., 2019). In studies using multilevel models, the proportion of total outcome variability that is attributable to therapists is typically presented as an *intraclass correlation coefficient (ICC)* denoting the ratio of the variance due to therapists divided by the sum of between-therapist variance and within-therapist (i.e., between-patient) variance. These studies indicate that the therapist explains about *half the variation in outcomes* that is related to having been in therapy versus not having received therapy (i.e., 14% of outcome variation can be attributed to having been treated in psychotherapy; see Barkham & Lambert, 2021; Wampold & Imel, 2015). In a recent review of therapist effects (Johns et al., 2019), the authors conclude that the aggregate effect size across therapists, weighted by the number of patients per therapist in RCTs, was .08 (=8%), while the aggregate ICC for naturalistic studies was .07. An ICC of .07 is equivalent to a standardized effect size or standardized mean difference (SMD) of 0.55,[1] which is a moderate effect size. Reflecting a SMD of 0.55–0.60, therapist effects are in fact considerably larger than the effects related to specific therapeutic methods (that is, e.g., cognitive behavior therapy vs. psychodynamic therapy),

[1] If one considers an ICC of .07 as the proportion of variance accounted for by therapists, it is comparable to a *squared correlation coefficient*. A correlation coefficient of about 0.26 ($=\sqrt[2]{.07}$) is equivalent to an SMD = 0.55 (see Wampold & Imel 2015).

and several other components of psychotherapy, but are close to the effect explained by the working alliance (Nissen-Lie et al., 2024).

During the last decade I have been exploring some of the characteristics that may explain these therapist effects. My earlier work at the University of Oslo focused on both the *context* and *content* of therapist effects in a practice-oriented research study, that is, the *Norwegian Multisite Study for the Process and Outcome of Psychotherapy* (NMSPOP; see Nordmo et al., 2020) and its collaboration with the international Collaborative Research Network (CRN) of the Society of Psychotherapy Research (SPR). The researchers of the CRN had developed the comprehensive survey battery *Development of Psychotherapists Common Core Questionnaire* (DPCCQ) (Orlinsky & Rønnestad, 2005), which was designed to measure a large variety of therapists' professional and personal characteristics and experiences. I had contributed to the data collection in Norway of the DPCCQ, and now was the time to explore whether these self-reported measures of psychotherapists could predict therapy processes and outcomes in a practice-oriented research setting where patients received treatment by clinicians from seven different sites who were willing to take part in the study. In collaboration with my mentors, Helge Rønnestad, Jon Monsen, Per Høglend, and others, we investigated whether therapists' own reports of their interpersonal styles and skills, difficulties in practice and coping strategies, among other variables, were associated with alliance ratings and patient outcomes in three different domains (i.e., symptomatic distress, interpersonal problems, and psychosocial functioning).

Both researchers and clinicians were eager to learn what characterized more effective therapists back in 2010, but few studies had gathered data on the therapists beyond simple demographics and had sufficient numbers of patients per therapist enrolled in the study. Moreover, many studies did not include patients that one actually meets in routine clinical care, with a high degree of comorbidity and different levels of motivation for therapy. Hence, in this Norwegian practice-oriented research program, we made an effort to gather data that would reflect ordinary, routine practice. Further, we wanted to study therapist effects (i.e., how the therapists contributed to differential patient outcomes) in an environment where therapist traits, characteristics, self-perceptions, feelings, and coping would naturally unfold and where there were few constraints as to diagnoses and type of therapy conducted, including frequency of sessions and length of treatment. Simply put, we wanted to study *how the therapist matters* in a naturalistic context so as to increase ecological validity and generalizability of our findings to ordinary clinical practice.

I will organize the description of the findings that came out of these studies into three sections, as they can be seen to reflect the following broader themes: (1) the power of professional humility;(2) the relational matrix of psychotherapy—the role of the therapists' interpersonal functioning; and (3) the merging of the professional and the personal. Finally, I will discuss potential implications of the findings of these studies that I have been a part of.

The Power of Professional Humility[2]

One of the findings from this line of studies that has received the most attention was the, at first surprising, *positive* association between a construct called professional self-doubt (PSD) and early patient-rated working alliance, as well as change in patient-rated interpersonal problems measured via the Inventory of Interpersonal Problems (IIP-64) (Horowitz et al., 2000). PSD is a factor that emerged through factor analysis of the 21-item scale, Difficulties in Practice, of the DPCCQ (Orlinsky & Rønnestad, 2005). This questionnaire was developed after an elaborate qualitative process gathering experiences in therapy practice that clinicians found challenging or difficult, which were later developed into a 21-item questionnaire.

The items were subjected to factor analysis, and along with the PSD factor, two additional factors also appeared in the international data of about 4,000 therapists that had been collected at the time (see Orlinsky & Rønnestad, 2005). These were termed *Frustrating Treatment Case* (e.g., frustrations related to aspects of a client's life over which one had little control such as health-related and financial issues), and *Negative Personal Reaction* (NPR) (i.e., negative emotional reactions toward a patient, such as having trouble finding something to like or respect in a client or difficulty withstanding a patient's emotional neediness). Only the PSD and NPR came out in our Norwegian data, and using these two factors as predictors of outcome,[3] expecting both to be negatively related to alliance and outcome, we found

[2] This subtitle is borrowed from the podcast series *Making Therapy Better* by Professor Bruce E. Wampold for CarePath, in which I was a guest.

[3] We also found an effect of the NPR factor, to be discussed further.

that therapists' higher scores on PSD instead were beneficial for clients in our studies (Nissen-Lie et al., 2010; Nissen-Lie, Monsen, Ulleberg et al. 2013).

Although it may be argued that psychotherapists should possess professional *self-confidence*, not professional *self-doubt*, our own findings, and those of other researchers, converge toward suggesting that, in the words of Hook et al. (2015), "An expert therapist is first and foremost a humble therapist" (p. 13). In fact, even though this finding was surprising at first glance, we now believe that PSD may have tapped into the broader and more positively connoted virtue of *professional humility*, which was put on the map in the helping professions as early as the mid-19th century, by the Danish philosopher and existentialist, Sören Kierkegaard. Kierkegaard famously said this about the matter: "But all true help begins with a humbling. (. . .) for to help is not to dominate, but to serve" (Kierkegaard, 1859). One hundred and sixty years later this declaration seems to receive increasing empirical support in modern psychotherapy.

One example is a study in Germany that compared therapists' assessments of their clients' progress with clients' measurements of their actual improvement, where the authors found that more modest or conservative therapist estimations (relative to their clients' actual improvement) predicted *greater* reductions of clients' symptoms and greater improvements in quality of life as assessed by the patients themselves (Ziem & Hoyer, 2020). Similarly, in a recent American study, Constantino et al. (2023) found that therapists who consistently overestimated their effectiveness (in different problem domains) had patients who reported worse global outcomes than patients whose therapist more accurately estimated their effectiveness. Moreover, therapists who assessed their effectiveness to be lower than it was had patients who reported better outcomes compared with therapists who accurately estimated their effectiveness or overestimated their effectiveness (Constantino et al., 2023). These findings indicate that a more modest attitude, or as the authors framed it, *professional humility*, seemed to have paved the way for therapists' performances that helped the clients reduce their symptoms or improve functioning.

When trying to grasp what these performances or behaviors might be, we are reminded of studies by Lutz et al. (2015) and de Jong et al. (2012), who found that positive therapist attitudes toward client feedback predicted better outcomes. Recently, in a study in the United Kingdom, in which I took part (Delgadillo et al., 2025), we found that utilization of feedback (i.e., routine outcome monitoring; ROM) reduced the variability in outcomes between therapists and was particularly effective for therapists with higher caseloads as well as for those with a so-called high external feedback propensity (EFP; see Herold & Fedor, 2003). EFP refers to a preference for evaluating task performance based on other peoples' perspective and opinions; hence, therapists with a strong EFP benefited most from using progress feedback, probably since this feedback provided them with a clear and structured way to support patients who were not on track.

We may draw the conclusion that a therapist who is motivated to collect feedback from their patients, and especially when one relies more on external feedback, who is willing to accept that they are not optimally knowledgeable or effective, is open to learn and to improve their skills and adapt their relational behaviors to suit the needs of the client (Nissen-Lie et al., 2023). It also seems reasonable to believe that some level of self-doubt makes therapists more alert to signals indicating that they need to change the course of therapy in collaboration with the client and as such may stand a better chance of detecting ruptures and taking responsibility for repairing them (Eubanks et al., 2018).

Interestingly, in recent research a potentially negative effect of therapist overconfidence has been found to be particularly prominent when working with patients with *more severe pretreatment impairment* (Constantino et al., 2023; see also Saxon & Barkham, 2012). This aligns with our own findings in Norway that professional self-doubt in the therapist was more beneficial for clients with higher levels of interpersonal problems (and likely more personality pathology) before the start of treatment (Nissen-Lie, Monsen, Ulleberg et al., 2013). As we know, treating patients with more relational problems can be challenging—and maybe "therapists who espouse a humbler and more vigilant stance (are) more alert and responsive to such challenges" (Constantino et al., 2023, p. 482). It might well be that patients with more severe problems find therapist overconfidence particularly negative, especially if they have suffered from mental health issues over lengthy periods of time and as such know more about what might be helpful for them than do their therapists.

In fact, treating clients with more symptomatic or relational distress seems to expose greater differences between therapists as seen in several recent studies (see Johns et al., 2019), and this is precisely when openness to feedback, and a flexible attitude toward modifying once's stance, makes a greater difference. However, one may ask, is professional humility always a positive resource, or might there be situations in which the therapist's authority and self-confidence are (relatively) more important? Does the cultural context in which the therapy takes place, including the cultural background of the patient and therapist—whether different or similar—affect whether humility is more of an asset to the therapist? And how does a therapist who endorses a sound level of PSD behave in the actual therapy room?

Some of our additional data bring nuance into the picture. After finding that PSD is positively associated with alliance and patient improvement, we addressed the interplay between self-doubt and patient outcome by also including therapists' ratings of a self-affiliative introject, based on the Structural Analysis of Social Behaviors (SASB) methodology (Benjamin, 1996). The SASB self-affiliative introject indexes the extent to which therapists treat themselves in a more or less affiliative manner (i.e., self-love versus self-attack; Nissen-Lie et al., 2017). We anticipated that therapists' level of personal self-affiliation might moderate the effect that PSD has on change. Indeed, this hypothesis was supported: Therapists who reported more self-doubt in their work facilitated change in patient distress to a greater extent if they also reported to have an affiliative introject (or way of treating themselves), while those who combined low scores on professional self-doubt with higher scores of self-affiliation contributed to the least change. The findings imply that a healthy self-critical stance is an ingredient of successful professional performance or expertise, while treating oneself as a person with care and nurturance, but lacking capacity to critically evaluate (i.e., doubt) one's therapeutic work, is a less fruitful pathway (Nissen-Lie & Rønnestad, 2016).

Psychotherapy as a Relational Matrix: Therapists' Relational Skills and Their Impact on Alliance and Outcome

Psychotherapy is fundamentally a relational matrix in which both patient and therapist are mutually shaped and transformed over time, even if they have different responsibilities and roles in the therapeutic setting (Atzil-Slonim & Tschacher, 2020, Bernhardt et al., 2019). Many studies suggest that the interpersonal functioning of the therapist, either in the form of their empathic communication, attachment style, interpersonal skills, or interpersonal problems, is central to therapeutic effectiveness (e.g., Anderson et al., 2016; Dinger et al., 2007). Typically, though, it has been hard to find a link between self-rated interpersonal (or social) skills (see Anderson et al., 2009;

Wampold & Owen, 2021) and patient outcomes. Notwithstanding this, in the Norwegian studies using the DPCCQ, we did find a quite robust relationship between seeing oneself as espousing a warm interpersonal style and patient-rated as well as therapist-rated alliances (Nissen-Lie et al., 2010, 2013b). This has been found previously; that is, an affiliative style in therapists characterized by acceptance, tolerance, and nurturance has been found to be among the most robust positive predictors of therapeutic alliances (Bohart et al., 2002; Norcross, 2002). The contribution from this line of inquiry (see Nissen-Lie et al., 2010) is the revelation that such a positive association remained even when therapists' warmth was self-assessed. In fact, we may infer that therapists assessed their own interpersonal style with a certain level of "accuracy" and that they had a good sense of their actual level of warmth toward patients, given that we found a strong connection between self-rated therapist warmth and patient-rated working alliance. Interestingly, therapists' self-assessed warmth also predicted their own alliance ratings, that is, how they perceived the quality of the working alliance during therapy with their patients. This indicates that there is a *mutually reinforcing dynamic* between patients and therapists—in the sense that the more therapists were expressing affirmation and nurturance, the more their patients perceived the alliance to be good and the more the therapists themselves espoused a positive view of the alliance.

Regarding therapists' relational skills, on the other hand, among the more perplexing findings in these studies was the association between a therapist factor called "advanced relational skills" (ARS) and patient-rated alliance and observer-rated global assessment of functioning (GAF) scores (Nissen-Lie, et al., 2013b, 2017). ARS reflects one's self-assessed skills in using the patients' emotional reactions toward oneself as a therapist (or skills in using the immediate or transference feelings arising) as well as one's own emotional reactions to the patient (i.e., one's countertransference feelings) in the therapeutic work. The term *advanced* was chosen because this factor contains items denoting skills that are assumed to be more sophisticated or advanced and because higher scores were more often reported by senior therapists in the large-scale sample of therapists from around the world (Orlinsky & Rønnestad, 2005). Despite this positive connotation, ARS was found to relate *negatively* to early patient-rated alliance, alliance over time, and observer-rated outcome (increase in GAF scores). We were puzzled by this finding—that something embedded in these self-evaluations was not as beneficial as one might expect. Some nuances in our findings may give us a clue to explain the complex role of therapists' use of their emotions and the patients' emotions toward them in therapeutic work. Some research points to the unhealthy tendency whereby strains in the therapeutic relationship are met by a higher proportion of interpretations, which in turn may lead to resistance in patients (see, e.g., Schut et al., 2005). The tendency to use more interpretations with patients may in some way reflect the therapists' own (stable) psychological makeup, which was suggested in the work of Hersoug (2004), who found that the use of interpretations was inversely correlated with the therapists' representation of a caring mother up to their adolescence. This may indicate that "advanced relational skills" may involve a somewhat critical propensity in the therapists, which may in part explain the negative relationship between these self-assessed skills and alliance and outcome in our data.

A central characteristic of ARS is therapists' use of their own emotional reactions in therapy. This requires an adequate management of their feelings so as to avoid a spill-over of *negative* emotions (or countertransference reactions) into interpersonal communications that leave the patient feeling criticized or blamed. Moreover, too much focus on one's own reactions as therapists may take the shape of an overly self-centered stance. Evidence that therapists who are hostile toward themselves are more prone to engage in countertransference enactments has been presented (Castonguay et al., 2006), which may tie in with the finding that the negative effect of ARS on early patient-rated alliance was attenuated by the therapists' "negative personal reaction" (Nissen-Lie et al., 2010). The specific direction of this effect revealed that in the case of *lower* levels of NPR, ARS represented a more constructive focus, whereas in the face of high NPR, ARS was related to poorer alliance ratings perhaps because this combination led to a risk of communicating negative (countertransference) reactions resembling criticism or blame toward patients.

We also found that therapists' level of ARS did not differentiate the response to treatment for patients with *lower* levels of global interpersonal distress before therapy (see Nissen-Lie, Monsen, Ulleberg et al., 2013). It appeared that less disturbed patients benefited equally from treatment regardless of their therapists' self-estimated advanced relational skills. Relatedly, Schauenburg et al. (2010) also found that only with more disturbed patients did therapists' secure attachment representation differentiate between the therapists. When the patients had more moderate amounts of relational disturbance, the attachment style of the therapist did not make a difference.

An alternative mechanism when interpreting the negative effect of ARS could be related to the aforementioned finding of a positive effect of PSD in the same data. The ARS scale measured the extent to which the therapists perceived themselves as *skillful* in the constructive use of the emotional reactions pertaining to themselves or the patients, not their actual behavior or interventions. This may be of vital importance, since higher scores on these skills may be reflective of an exaggerated self-confidence or lack of humility in therapists when judging their skills, rather than the use of these interventions or their actual skill level.

It seems that when patients report more impairment and more suffering, the emotional makeup of the psychotherapist becomes particularly important. This notion aligns with the findings that therapist effects increase with longer treatments (Goldberg et al., 2018), and as mentioned, with more clinical distress (Saxon & Barkham, 2012).

It seems vital when observing therapists' interpersonal functioning that the stimulus material (i.e., the client behaviors) needs to reflect some degree of clinical *challenge*, rather than just any therapy situation, to differentiate between more- from less-effective therapists. This has been convincingly demonstrated in the FIS (facilitative interpersonal skills) studies of Timothy Anderson and colleagues (2009, 2016).

We may conclude this part of the chapter, with the results from these practice-based studies, that *who* the therapist is more important when the patient suffers more and has traumatic relationships in their history and therefore is in greater need of a responsive, non-defensive, and flexible therapist who can listen carefully and modify their therapeutic stance to match the changing needs of the patient through the process.

The Merging of the Professional and the Personal

Both quantitative and qualitative research demonstrate that there is a close link between the therapists' personal functioning and their professional performance (Nissen-Lie et al., 2021, 2024). This third part of the chapter will be devoted to the intersection of the personal and the professional in the lives of psychotherapists. At the end of this chapter, I will derive implications to help practitioners improve their own effectiveness, hopefully without losing sight of our need to take care of ourselves along the way.

Whichever therapeutic model therapists use to guide their work, they must have sufficient *emotional* resources to be receptive and responsive to the emotional state and needs of the client in order to build a strong alliance and productively pursue therapeutic goals (Nissen-Lie et al, 2021). Inevitably though, sometimes the emotional reserves of the therapist are depleted as a result of personal or occupational burdens. This depletion can have negative consequences, as has been found in prior studies. For example, in the large-scale Improving Access to Psychological Therapies (IAPT)—now rebranded as the Talking Therapies for Anxiety and Depression—program in the United Kingdom, Delgadillo et al. (2018) investigated the associations between therapist burnout and reduction of symptoms for patients presenting with anxiety and depression. The authors found that higher scores on the part of burnout that deals with emotionally distancing yourself from the work (i.e., disengagement) and lower scores on job satisfaction were associated with poorer treatment outcomes.

In one of our own practice-oriented research studies (Nissen-Lie, Monsen, Høglend et al., 2013), we studied emotional burdens and satisfactions in one's personal lives as predictors of working alliance scores, provided by both patients ($N = 227$) and therapists ($N = 70$). Therapists' burdens were operationalized with items denoting stress in one's personal life, feeling burdens of responsibility, worry or concern, or feeling significant conflict with family members or loss of a loved one. Personal satisfactions denoted therapists' reports of a satisfying private life, with elements of unreserved joy, satisfying intimacy, and emotional support. These scales were assessed once every year for 5 years and turned out to be stable across this period of time. The relative constancy of those personal burdens might reflect an enduring vulnerability, a maladaptive coping style, or a prolonged unsatisfactory life situation in psychotherapists that could represent a potential threat to their therapeutic effectiveness (Nissen-Lie et al., 2021).

Our findings revealed that both these scales were strong predictors of alliance as rated by both patients and therapists, but an interesting discrepancy was revealed: Therapists' reports of their burdens were inversely related to the alliance when it was rated by the patients but was unrelated to therapist-rated alliance (Nissen-Lie, Monsen, Høglend et al., 2013). Conversely, therapists' reports of their satisfactions were positively associated with therapist-rated alliance but were unrelated to the patients' ratings of the alliance. The puzzling finding suggested to us that patients are particularly sensitive to their therapists' private life experience of distress, which at some level must be communicated through the therapists' in-session behaviors, making the therapist more absentminded, or defensive, or less able to scrutinize their own contribution to impasses, and less warm, caring and empathetic. On the other hand, when the therapists judged the alliance, it seems that feeling satisfied in one's personal life constituted a bias when evaluating the alliance with patients.

In a later study, as part of the CRN study mentioned earlier, David Orlinsky, Helge Rønnestad, and I aimed to identify past and current personal and situational factors that are linked to increased levels of emotional burdens in therapists' personal lives (with 12,036 participating therapists), since this was a factor that came out as a strong predictor of how patients experienced the therapeutic process. In a subsample of therapists (N = 1243) who had also responded to a standard measure of attachment in close relationships, we investigated the importance of attachment avoidance and attachment anxiety in explaining current personal burdens. We found that both personality-related and past and current life circumstances contributed considerably to therapists' experience of burdens.

In terms of their personality dimensions, the therapists reporting being guarded and reserved or dominant and demanding in close relationships had higher risk of experiencing personal burdens. Conversely, therapists who reported being warmer and more accepting in close relationships had fewer emotional burdens. This accords with other findings suggesting that satisfying personal relationships work as a buffer against burnout and secondary traumatic distress when working as therapists (Lakioti et al., 2020), and that therapists' level of social support is inversely related to burnout (Rzeszutek & Schier, 2014). Further, we also found that therapists' attachment anxiety was positively linked to personal burdens. The same finding has emerged in other therapist samples (e.g., Lingiardi et al., 2018; Simionato & Simpson, 2018), and these results align with findings that individuals with less secure attachment, especially a pattern of anxious attachment, typically report lower well-being (Karreman & Vingerhoets, 2012). Other studies find that insecure attachment in the form of attachment anxiety can be detrimental to client progress (Leitemo et al., 2019), especially if treating more interpersonally troubled individuals (Schauenburg et al., 2010). Interestingly, an avoidant attachment style was not predictive of therapists' personal burdens. Maybe more avoidantly attached therapists are less prone to experiencing and reporting on strong emotional burdens in their personal lives (cf. Mikulincer & Shaver, 2016), but this style may still be unfavorable in terms of the therapist's emotional capacity to meet the client's needs and thus is a barrier in their work.

As can be deduced from these studies, there is a close interplay between therapists' professional and personal well-being. It is fair to say that it is vital for therapists to cultivate personal relationships aside from their work, and work on emotional issues that stem from early traumatic events and current emotional conflicts and difficulties in private relationships in order to improve their own well-being and quality of life.

All the studies mentioned earlier on how the psychotherapist as a person matters to patient change used quantitative methods to explore the interrelationships of potentially relevant therapist variables and detecting some pattern of covariation between these and alliance and/or outcome scores. Of course, even if interesting and sometimes surprising, these studies provide little "flesh on the bone" or phenomenological description of *how* the personal affects the professional, and vice versa (see Bernhardt et al., 2021). Hence, we are left with many questions when attempting to translate these findings into clinical guidelines and recommendations for practicing therapists or trainers. In order to remedy this and fill out the picture, we have conducted a series of in-depth qualitative studies of interviews or in-session video recordings, and I will now briefly summarize some of the findings that shed light on the contribution of the psychotherapist and supplement the studies outlined earlier.

One of our recently published, in-depth, single-case studies (Raddum, Nissen-Lie, et al., 2024) was inspired by the FIS studies (Anderson et al., 2009, 2016), where therapists are presented with interpersonally challenging cases to which they are asked to respond in the most constructive way. The original results of the FIS and many later replications demonstrated that therapists' composite scores on eight different FIS dimensions, tapping into verbal fluency and focusing on the client, warmth, and so on, as rated by trained expert evaluators, strongly correlate with the change achieved by these therapists in their actual clinical work. As such, the FIS studies are the ones to provide the most potent link between therapists' qualities and patient outcome that we have to date. However, since the FIS studies rely on correlations between responses to a non-interactive stimulus and patient outcome, they do not clarify how the therapist's interpersonal skills come into play in an actual clinical setting.

In order to understand more of this, we need case studies that explore the dynamic and changing interplay between patients and therapists in challenging therapy cases as they unfold over time. Recently, we conducted such an in-depth case study (Raddum et al., 2024) following an entire psychodynamic psychotherapy process of 39 sessions, where a female therapist saw a male client with relational problems and traumatic experiences in his upbringing. The client in the case achieved a particularly good outcome, expressing that "the therapy had changed his life in terms of creating a positive spiral of beneficial relational experiences and made it possible to engage in less destructive relationships" (Raddum et al., 2024, p. 3). He made active use of the therapy but often in a way that put the interpersonal skills and empathy of the therapist to the test. By means of qualitative analysis conducted among four authors of all video-recorded sessions, focusing on instances that were judged to be especially challenging, we saw how the therapist consistently "detoxified" the client's aggressive, critical, and self-destructive communications. By using this term from psychoanalytic theory (i.e., "detoxification," Bion, 1962), one could grasp the special quality of responding to the patient's skepticism and criticism by focusing on the patient's underlying feeling and resisting an enactment of the kind of scenario that the patient invited her to. We found many examples of this non-defensive and constructive response to direct criticism and aggression played out in the therapeutic relationship. Without getting defensive or overly pleasing, she accompanied the client with a warm appearance, smile, and eye contact and validated his difficult feelings. The therapist also met the client's excessive self-destructive behaviors in a non-judgmental way, making sense of how his reinforcing of his shame might have been a way for him to punish himself and paradoxically take control. Finally, she tentatively interpreted his rejection of her as a therapist as a form of separation anxiety related to the termination of the therapy, which made sense to him, as he had experienced the loss of many important figures in his early life. More than anything, it was the *manner* in which she did all this that seemed to have made the difference.

The use of the term *detoxification* to denote the mechanism by which the patient's more destructive material is transformed into understandable and tolerable experiences with the help of the therapist is taken from the model of the container-contained by Wilfred Bion (1962, 1970). Using this model, we could say that an interpersonally skilled therapist may function as a container for the patient's anxieties, fears, and painful inner states. We conclude that being able to tolerate these feelings and respond to them in an empathic way, rather than with invalidation, subtle retaliation, or pleasing behaviors, is of crucial importance to facilitate a favorable therapeutic outcome, especially, we may add, with patients who have endured relational trauma and/or have more interpersonal distress.

How do therapists handle this undoubtedly challenging task? What do they draw from to be able to respond in a genuinely empathic way when their emotional capacities and interpersonal skills are put to the test? We know that psychotherapists' personal histories and personal characteristics influence their therapeutic work (Heinonen & Nissen-Lie, 2020; Rønnestad & Skovholt, 2013), possibly even more than their training and professional experience, but how do psychotherapists draw from their personal lives in the work with patients? In another line of research (i.e., the Art & Science of Psychotherapy, Råbu et al., 2013), in which therapists ($N = 16$) who obtained good outcomes with clients and were regarded as especially resourceful and skilled by their managers, we tried to get closer to this by exploring the junction between the personal and the professional of the therapist using qualitative interviews of both therapists and patients and in-depth investigation of therapy sessions. All the therapists in the sample described in one way or another how their personal qualities represented both "a strength and a drawback" in the therapeutic setting (Bernhardt et al., 2019). There was an undeniable tension that they constantly needed to be mindful of, to understand what was going on inside them—while at the same time focusing on the emotional needs of the client (for more details, see Bernhardt et al., 2019, 2021). As we know, this can be particularly challenging when faced with aggression and rejection from clients, such as that which was described previously (Raddum et al., 2024). They also expressed how challenging it could be to regulate closeness and distance in the therapeutic relationship, and how their preference (for more or less closeness) was rooted in their own attachment history but also in that of the patient. If both parties are willing to risk something and change, a negotiation between these two can be quite productive.

What was striking in this highly selected and resourceful sample of psychotherapists was their willingness to open up about their limitations and shortcomings with the interviewers. Describing actual therapeutic work with patients, they were able to admit how they were struggling with issues that were likely caused by their own shortcomings or vulnerabilities, which, in meeting the vulnerabilities of the patient, could bring about challenging instances in their therapeutic work. They provided detailed accounts of how they worked with these issues in their everyday work and in particular therapy cases (see Bernhardt et al., 2019). They would also stress that their shortcomings are not resolved once and for all; rather, they require constant attention. Maybe this non-defensive willingness to scrutinize their own contribution in alliance ruptures or stagnant therapeutic work was the single most important ingredient in their successful therapeutic work. There is reason to believe that in these studies we observed the unfolding of what an attitude of benign professional self-doubt in therapists actually looks like, to tie in with the first section of this chapter.

Summary and Implications

Considerable empirical evidence, especially from practice-oriented research settings where therapists, patients, and clinics are varied and reflective of routine practice, has confirmed what most patients, trainers, and supervisors have experienced: Some therapists are more effective than others (Nissen-Lie et al., 2024; Castonguay & Hill, 2017). This knowledge has important implications for the training of therapists, as well as for therapist self-care. In this chapter, I have described findings from several practice-oriented research programs I have taken part in, which yield a complex picture of how professional humility and the therapist's interpersonal functioning come into play, describing some factors related to the well-being of the therapists in their personal lives.

If we take the research described in this chapter seriously, that differences among therapists accumulate to have large real-life effects over time, and that this differential effectiveness can be traced to certain qualities and attitudes in practicing therapists, we should seek to maximize the development of these qualities in our training programs. The findings reviewed highlight, more than anything, the therapist's capacity for *self-awareness* or *self-observation* as an invaluable asset in their work. Several findings indicate the need for therapists to be willing to critically evaluate their contribution in therapy processes, but also to strive toward an accepting and tolerant attitude of themselves, to be of help to the client.

Our research on the personal burdens of psychotherapists has relevance for therapist self-care in clinical practice, training, and supervision. An implication of these findings is that the focus on therapists' well-being should be an important part of clinical training and supervision (Wise & Barnett, 2016). Mindfulness practices and other forms of reflective practice that increase self-awareness are empirically supported methods for improving self-care and are thus recommended (see Bennett-Levy, 2019).

Ultimately, I claim that the findings of practice-oriented studies on psychotherapists support an intersubjective and humanistic view of psychotherapy over a more medical model where therapists are instruments of specific techniques that work irrespective of whoever delivers them (see also Wampold, 2007). We need to foster in ourselves a responsiveness to the unique human being in front of us and develop both our personal and professional capacities. Much research supports the claim that effective therapists do not avoid conflict or challenging moments; rather, they work with them, and this work is therapeutic in and of itself (Eubanks et al., 2018). They are open to feedback, seek support from colleagues, and are aware of the demanding nature of psychotherapy. A therapist who is willing to change and grow herself will likely facilitate that in the other.

References

Anderson, T., Crowley, M. E., Himawan, L., Holmberg, J. K., & Uhlin, B. D. (2016). Therapist facilitative interpersonal skills and training status: A randomized clinical trial on alliance and outcome. *Psychotherapy Research*, *26*(5), 511–529. https://doi.org/10.1080/10503307.2015.1049671

Anderson, T., Ogles, B. M., Patterson, C. L., Lambert, M. J., & Vermeersch, D. A. (2009). Therapist effects: Facilitative interpersonal skills as a predictor of treatment outcome. *Journal of Clinical Psychology*, *65*(7), 755–768. https://doi.org/10.1037/ccp0000060

Atzil-Slonim, D., & Tschacher, W. (2020). Dynamic dyadic processes in psychotherapy: Introduction to a special section. Psychotherapy Research, 30(5), 555–557.

Barkham, M., Hardy, G. E., & Mellor-Clark, J. (Eds.). (2010). *Developing and delivering practice-based evidence. A guide for the psychological therapies*. Wiley-Blackwell.

Barkham, M., & Lambert, M. J. (2021). The efficacy and effectiveness of psychological therapies. In M. Barkham, W. Lutz, & L. G. Castonguay (Eds.), *Bergin and Garfield's handbook of psychotherapy and behavior change: 50th anniversary edition* (7th ed., pp. 135–189). John Wiley & Sons, Inc.

Benjamin, L. S. (1996). A clinician-friendly version of the interpersonal circumplex: Structural analysis of social behavior (SASB). Journal of Personality Assessment, *66*, 248–266.

Bennett-Levy, J. (2019). Why therapists should walk the talk: The theoretical and empirical case for personal practice in therapist training and professional development. *Journal of Behavior Therapy and Experimental Psychiatry*, *62*, 133–145. https://doi.org/10.1016/j.jbtep.2018.08.004

Bernhardt, I. S., Nissen-Lie, H., Moltu, C., McLeod, J., & Råbu, M. (2019). "It's both a strength and a drawback": How therapists' personal qualities are experienced in their professional work. *Psychotherapy Research*, *29*(7), 959–970. https://doi.org/10.1080/10503307.2018.1490972.

Bernhardt, I. S., Nissen-Lie, H. A., & Råbu, M. (2021). The embodied listener: A dyadic case study of how therapist and patient reflect on the significance of therapist's personal presence for the therapeutic change process. *Psychotherapy Research*, *31*(5), 682–694. https://doi.org/10.1080/10503307.2020.1808728

Bion, W. R. (1962). *Learning from experience*. Heinemann.

Bion, W. R. (1970). *Attention and interpretation*. Karnac.

Bohart, A. C., Elliott, R., Greenberg, L. S., & Watson, J. C. (2002). Empathy. In J. C. Norcross (Ed.), *Psychotherapy relationships that work. Therapist contributions and responsiveness to clients* (pp. 89–108). Oxford University Press.

Castonguay, L. G., Constantino, M. J., & Grosse Holtforth, M. (2006). The working alliance: Where are we and where should we go? *Psychotherapy: Theory, Research, Practice, and Training, 43*, 271–279. https://doi.org/10.1037/0033-3204.43.3.271

Castonguay, L. G., & Hill, C. E. (Eds.). (2017). *How and why are some therapists better than others?: Understanding therapist effects.* American Psychological Association. https://doi.org/10.1037/0000034-000.

Constantino, M. J., Boswell, J. F., Coyne, A. E., Muir, H. J., Gaines, A. N., & Kraus, D. R. (2023). Therapist perceptions of their own measurement-based, problem-specific effectiveness. *Journal of Consulting and Clinical Psychology, 91*(8), 474–484. https://doi.org/10.1037/ccp0000813

Delgadillo, J., Saxon, D., & Barkham, M. (2018). Associations between therapists' occupational burnout and their patients' depression and anxiety treatment outcomes. *Depression and Anxiety, 35*(9), 844–850. https://doi.org/10.1002/da.22766

Delgadillo, J., Nissen-Lie, H. A., De Jong, K., Schröder, T. A., & Barkham, M. (2025). An examination of therapists' professional characteristics as moderators of the effect of feedback on psychological treatment outcomes. *Psychotherapy Research, 35*(3), 501–511, DOI: 10.1080/10503307.2024.2310635

de Jong, K., van Sluis, P., Nugter, M. A., Heiser, W. J., & Spinhoven, P. (2012). Understanding the differential impact of outcome monitoring: Therapist variables that moderate feedback effects in a randomized clinical trial. *Psychotherapy Research, 22*(4), 464–474. https://doi.org/10.1080/10503307.2012.673023

Dinger, U., Strack, M., Leichsenring, F., & Schauenburg, H. (2007). Influences of patients' and therapists' interpersonal problems and therapeutic alliance on outcome in psychotherapy. *Psychotherapy Research, 17*(2), 148–159. https://doi.org/10.1080/10503300600865393

Eubanks, C. F., Muran, J. C., & Safran, J. D. (2018). Alliance rupture repair: A meta- analysis. *Psychotherapy, 55*(4), 508–519. https://doi.org/10.1037/pst0000185

Henry, W. E., Sims, J. H., & Spray, S. I. (1971). *The fifth profession.* Jossey-Bass.

Herold, D. M., & Fedor, D. B. (2003). Individual differences in feedback propensities and training performance. *Human Resource Management Review, 13*(4), 675–689. https://doi.org/10.1016/j.hrmr.2003.11.008

Hersoug, A. G. (2004). Assessment of therapists' and patients' personality: Relationship to therapeutic technique and outcome in brief dynamic psychotherapy. *Journal of Personality Assessment, 83*(3), 191–200. https://doi.org/10.1207/s15327752jpa8303_03

Goldberg, S. B., Hoyt, W. T., Nissen-Lie, H. A., Nielsen, S. L., & Wampold, B. E. (2018). Unpacking the therapist effect: Impact of treatment length differs for high- and low-performing therapists. *Psychotherapy Research, 28*(4), 532–544. https://doi.org/10.1080/10503307.2016.1216625

Heinonen, E., & Nissen-Lie, H. A (2020). What are the characteristics of effective psychotherapists? A systematic literature review. *Psychotherapy Research, 30*(4), 417–432. https://doi.org/10.1080/10503307.2019.1620366

Hook, J. N., Watkins, Jr., C. E., Davis, D. E., & Owen, J. (2015). Humility: The paradoxical foundation for psychotherapy expertise. *Psychotherapy Bulletin, 50*(2), 11–13.

Horowitz, L. M., Alden, L. E., Wiggins, J. S., & Pincus, A. L. (2000). *Inventory of Interpersonal Problems manual.* The Psychological Corporation.

Johns, R. G., Barkham, M., Kellett, S., & Saxon, D. (2019). A systematic review of therapist effects: A critical narrative update and refinement to review. *Clinical Psychology Review, 67*, 78–93. https://doi.org/10.1016/j.cpr.2018.08.004

Karreman, A., & Vingerhoets, A. J. J. M. (2012). Attachment and well-being: The mediating role of emotion regulation and resilience. *Personality and Individual Differences, 53*(7), 821–826. https://doi.org/10.1016/j.paid.2012.06.014

Kierkegaard, S. (1859). *Fra synspunkter fra min forfattervirksomhet: En ligefrem meddelelse. Rapport til historien* [*Viewpoints from my authorship: An honest disclosure. Report to history*]. A. E. Reitzel Publishing.

Lakioti, A., Stalikas, A., & Pezirkianidis, C. (2020). The role of personal, professional, and psychological factors in therapists' resilience. *Professional Psychology: Research and Practice, 51*(6), 560–570. https://doi.org/10.1037/pro0000306

Leitemo, K., Vestbø, H., Bakali, J. V., & Nissen-Lie, H. A. (2019). The role of attachment anxiety and avoidance for reduced interpersonal problems in training group analytic therapy. *Group Dynamics*. Advance online publication. https://doi.org/10.1037/gdn0000112

Lingiardi, V., Muzi, L., Tanzilli, A., & Carone, N. (2018). Do therapists' subjective variables impact on psychodynamic psychotherapy outcomes? A systematic literature review. *Clinical Psychology & Psychotherapy, 25*(1), 85–101. https://doi.org/10.1002/cpp.2131

Lutz, W., De Jong, K., & Rubel, J. (2015). Patient-focused and feedback research in psychotherapy: Where are we and where do we want to go? Psychotherapy Research, 25(6), 625–632. https://doi.org/10.1080/10503307.2015.1079661

Mikulincer, M., & Shaver, P. R. (2016). An attachment perspective on psychopathology. *World Psychiatry, 11*(1), 11–15. https://doi.org/10.1016/j.wpsyc.2012.01.003

Nissen-Lie, H. A. (2023). The power of professional humility. Episode 7. In Wampold, B. E., Making Therapy Better. Podcast.

Nissen-Lie, H. A., Heinonen, E., & Delgadillo, J. (2023). Therapist factors. In S. D. Miller, D. Chow, S. Malins, & M. A. Hubble (Eds.), *The field guide to better results: Evidence-based exercises to improve therapeutic effectiveness* (pp. 79–106). American Psychological Association. https://doi.org/10.1037/0000358-005

Nissen-Lie, H. A., Monsen, J. T., Høglend, P. A., Havik, O. E., & Rønnestad, M. H. (2013). The contribution of therapists' personal life quality to the development of the working alliance. *Journal of Counseling Psychology, 60*(4), 483–495. https://doi.org/10.1037/a0033643

Nissen-Lie, H. A., Monsen, J. T., & Rønnestad, M. H. (2010). Therapist predictors of early patient-rated working alliance: A multilevel approach. *Psychotherapy Research, 20*(6), 627–646. https://doi.org/10.1080/10503307.2010.497633

Nissen-Lie, H. A., Monsen, J. T., Ulleberg, P., & Rønnestad, M. H. (2013). Psychotherapists' self-reports of their interpersonal functioning and difficulties in practice as predictors of patient outcome. *Psychotherapy Research, 23(1)*, 86–104. https://doi.org/10.1080/10503307.2012.735775

Nissen-Lie, H. A., Oddli, H. W., & Heinonen, E. (2024). Do therapists differ in their general effectiveness? Therapist effects and their determinants. In F. T. L. Leong, J. L. Callahan, J. Zimmerman, M. J. Constantino, & C. F. Eubanks (Eds.), *APA handbook of psychotherapy: Evidence-based practice, practice-based evidence, and contextual participant-driven practice* (pp. 213–226). American Psychological Association. https://doi.org/10.1037/0000354-014

Nissen-Lie, H. A., Orlinsky, D. E., & Rønnestad, M. H. (2021). The emotionally burdened psychotherapist: Personal and situational risk factors. *Professional Psychology: Research Practice, 52*(5), 429–438. https://doi.org/10.1037/pro0000387

Nissen-Lie, H. A., & Rønnestad, M. H. (2016). The empirical evidence for psychotherapist humility as a foundation for psychotherapist expertise. Psychotherapy Bulletin, 51, 7–9.

Nissen-Lie, H. A., Rønnestad, M. H., Høglend, P. A., Havik, O. E., Stiles, T. C., Solbakken, O. A., & Monsen, J. T. (2017). Love yourself as a person, doubt yourself as a therapist? *Clinical Psychology & Psychotherapy, 24*(1), 48–60. https://doi.org/10.1002/cpp.1977

Norcross, J. C. (2002). Empirically Supported Therapy Relationships. In J. C. Norcross (Ed.), *Psychotherapy Relationships that Work. Therapist contributions and responsiveness to clients* (pp. 3–17). Oxford University Press.

Nordmo, M., Sønderland, N. M., Havik, O. E., Eilertsen, D. E., Monsen, J. T., & Solbakken, O. A. (2020). Effectiveness of open-ended psychotherapy under clinically representative conditions. *Frontiers in Psychiatry, 11*, Article 384. https://doi.org/10.3389/fpsyt.2020.00384

Orlinsky, D. E., & Rønnestad, M. H. (2005). *How psychotherapists develop: A study of therapeutic work and professional growth.* American Psychological Association.

Raddum, H. S., Nissen-Lie, H. A., Hillestad-Hoff, C., & Strømme, S. (2024): "Detoxification" of destructive clinical material in psychodynamic psychotherapy: A case study of how the therapists' interpersonal skills are used in a challenging treatment case with a successful outcome. *Counselling Psychology Quarterly, 7*(4), 651–672. https://doi.org/10.1080/09515070.2023.2291199

Råbu, M., Moltu, C., & McLeod, J. (2013). *The art and science of conducting psychotherapy: How collaborative action between client and therapist generates and sustains productive life change.* University of Oslo. Department of Psychology.

Rønnestad, M. H., Orlinsky, D. E., & Wiseman, H. (2016). Professional development and personal therapy. In J. C. Norcross, G. R. VandenBos, D. K. Freedheim, & L. F. Campbell (Eds.), *APA handbook of clinical psychology: Education and profession* (pp. 223–235). American Psychological Association. https://doi.org/10.1037/14774-015

Rønnestad, M. H., & Skovholt, T. M. (2013). *The developing practitioner: Growth and stagnation of therapists and counselors.* Routledge.

Rzeszutek, M., & Schier, K. (2014). Temperament traits, social support, and burnout symptoms in a sample of therapists. *Psychotherapy, 51*(4), 574–579. https://doi.org/10.1037/a0036020

Saxon, D., & Barkham, M. (2012). Patterns of therapist variability: Therapist effects and the contribution of patient severity and risk. *Journal of Consulting and Clinical Psychology, 80*(4), 535–546. https://doi.org/10.1037/a0028898

Schauenburg, H., Buchheim, A., Beckh, K., Nolte, T., Brenk-Franz, K., Leichsenring, F., Strack, M., & Dinger, U. (2010). The influence of psychodynamically oriented therapists' attachment representations on outcome and alliance in inpatient psychotherapy. *Psychotherapy Research, 20*(2), 193–202. https://doi.org/10.1080/10503300903204043

Schut, A. J., Castonguay, L. G., Bedics, J. D., Smith, T. L., Barber, J. P., Flanagan, K. M., & Yamasaki, A. S. (2005). Therapist interpretation, patient-therapist interpersonal process, and outcome in psychodynamic psychotherapy for avoidant personality disorder. *Psychotherapy: Theory, Research, Practice, Training, 42*(4), 494–511. https://doi.org/10.1037/0033-3204.42.4.494

Simionato, G. K., & Simpson, S. (2018). Personal risk factors associated with burnout among psychotherapists: A systematic review of the literature. *Journal of Clinical Psychology, 74*(9), 1431–1456. https://doi.org/10.1002/jclp.22615

Wampold, B. E., & Imel, Z. E. (2015). *The great psychotherapy debate: The evidence for what makes psychotherapy work* (2nd ed.). Routledge.

Wampold, B. E. (2007). Psychotherapy: The humanistic (and effective) treatment. *American Psychologist, 62*(8), 857–873. https://doi.org/10.1037/0003-066X.62.8.857

Wampold, B. E., & Owen, J. (2021). Therapist effects: History, methods, magnitude, and characteristics of effective therapists. In L. G. Castonguay, M. Barkham, & W. Lutz (Eds.), *Bergin and Garfield's handbook of psychotherapy and behavior change* (7th ed., pp. 301–330). Wiley.

Wise, E. H., & Barnett, J. E. (2016). Self-care for psychologists. In J. C. Norcross, G. R. VandenBos, D. K. Freedheim, & L. F. Campbell (Eds.), *APA handbook of clinical psychology: Education and profession* (pp. 209–222). American Psychological Association.

Ziem, M., & Hoyer, J. (2020). Modest, yet progressive: Effective therapists tend to rate therapeutic change less positively than their patients. *Psychotherapy Research, 30*(4), 433–446. https://doi.org/10.1080/10503307.2019.1631502

6

Improving Mental Health Care by Leveraging Therapists' Own Practice-Based Evidence

Michael J. Constantino, James F. Boswell, Alice E. Coyne, Anuj H. P. Mehta, and Ashleigh E. Smith

Practice-oriented research focuses on the knowledge gained (i.e., practice-based evidence) from customarily administered psychotherapy that is largely (if not fully) unconstrained by traditional stipulations of controlled research (see Castonguay et al., 2021; Leong et al., 2024). As a counterbalance to more unidirectional, researcher-imposed practice recommendations that risk being (or at least seeming) out of step with certain clinical realities, practice-oriented research honors "the inherent complexities and individualized nature of psychotherapy as practiced in real-world versus tightly controlled research settings" (Constantino & Eubanks, 2024, p. 173). Partly owing to advances in routine measurement (e.g., repeated, systematic collection of patient-reported outcomes data) and data analytic methods (e.g., machine learning), practice-oriented research creates a bidirectional laboratory that privileges the investigation of questions that are important and ecologically germane to frontline clinicians, their patients, and psychotherapy researchers alike. To us, such partnership among multiple psychotherapy stakeholders, whether implicit or explicit, represents an energizing and inclusive way to help guide evidence-informed clinical practice.

Although the practice-oriented research landscape is necessarily broad and multi-shaped, one relevant area reflects the influence of the mental health care therapist, irrespective of the type(s) of treatment they deliver, on their patients' outcomes. This maturing empirical focus addresses an important historical gap: namely, whereas variability in patient outcomes has long been attributed to differences between patient characteristics

Michael J. Constantino et al., *Improving Mental Health Care by Leveraging Therapists' Own Practice-Based Evidence*. In: *Practice-Based Evidence in the Psychological Therapies*. Edited by: Louis G. Castonguay et al., Oxford University Press. © Oxford University Press (2026). DOI: 10.1093/9780197748336.003.0006 (see Constantino et al., 2021) or treatment approaches (see Barkham & Lambert, 2021), relatively little attention has been paid to the treating therapist beyond the methods they use (see Constantino et al., 2017; Wampold & Owen, 2021). Indeed, the provider was historically viewed as a controllable factor, especially in clinical trials where their skills and influence were assumed to be standardized via pointed training, close supervision, and adherence to a specific treatment manual. This notion always struck our team members as problematic, and, as it turns out, even with such standardization attempts, compelling practice-based evidence points to the inescapable fact that the therapist's contribution to patient change (whether positive or negative) cannot be fully concealed (Wampold & Imel, 2015).

Accordingly, our team followed these data and joined researchers who began to increasingly analyze "big data" from patient-reported routine outcome measures, which are a hallmark of the practice-based evidence paradigm, at the *therapist* level. Such analysis has revealed, most basically, the robust existence of general *between*-therapist effectiveness differences across diverse treatment settings (e.g., clinical trials, naturalistic care) and after controlling for various patient case-mix variables (Johns et al., 2019; Nissen-Lie et al., 2024). This classic version of a "therapist effect" explains a clinically meaningful average of about 5% of patient outcome variance, with outcome typically assessed as general symptomatic and functional improvement. Thus, research accentuates that mental health care can be meaningfully improved not just by promoting the use of evidence-based *interventions*, but also by trying to harness in some way therapist effectiveness data (Constantino & Muir, 2024).

Inspired by this notion, as opposed to viewing the therapist effect as a methodological nuisance to be controlled, our team has developed over the past decade or so a collaborative, multimethod, and community-engaged practice-oriented research program that aims to uncover additional complexities of therapist effectiveness differences and harness them prospectively (in routine practice settings) for therapeutic benefit. Specifically, we are interested in *within*-therapist effects, or caseload-level effectiveness strengths and weaknesses when treating different types of patients in the context of routinely delivered psychotherapy (Coyne, 2024). In this chapter, we summarize the main facets of this evolving practice-oriented research and the practice-based evidence it has generated.

We begin by reviewing our foundational research showing that many therapists possess unique and stable strengths and weaknesses in treating patients with different types of presenting problems, and that therapists have potential biases when *self*-assessing their effectiveness. We also summarize our stakeholder-engaged research that explicitly asked patients how much they would value using therapist effectiveness data when making treatment decisions. Next, we summarize the results of our clinical trial that tested the benefit of prospectively harnessing within-therapist effectiveness data by matching patients to therapists' problem-specific, measurement-based strengths (a type of responsive, personalized mental health care), as well as our in-progress work on broadly implementing our match system. Finally, we provide potential practice, training, and policy recommendations based on existing research on the multidimensional within-therapist effect, and we outline possible future directions to advance research on the compound question—*who works best for whom, and why?*

Uncovering Within-Therapist Effectiveness Differences

Building on the classic between-therapist effect on patients' globally measured treatment outcomes, *multidimensional* outcome measures (i.e., those that granularly assess varied specific symptom and functioning domains) can also assess within-therapist differences in treating those different mental health problems. For example, Therapist A's average patient with primary depression or social conflict may achieve exceptional outcomes (two clear domain-specific strengths). For this same therapist, their average patient with quality-of-life concerns may fail to improve or even reliably deteriorate (a clear domain-specific weakness). Finally, and simultaneously, Therapist A's average patient with primary sleep problems may change to a minimally expected degree, as determined with a predictive analytic (neither a remarkable strength nor weakness).

To create such an effectiveness profile, our team analyzes patient data from a routinely administered and psychometrically sound outcome measure—the Treatment Outcome Package (TOP; Kraus et al., 2005)—which has been administered for years in numerous mental health care systems across the United States. As the foundation of our research program, the TOP includes 58 items that dimensionally assess 12 clinical scales: work functioning, sexual functioning, social conflict, depression, panic/somatic anxiety, psychosis, suicidal ideation, violence, mania, sleep, substance misuse, and quality of life. To classify therapist effectiveness, we have applied a multistep method (Kraus et al., 2011, 2016). First, in a large sample of approximately 28,000 adult patients with pre- to post-treatment TOP data from their naturalistically administered treatment, we used machine learning to determine the most potent patient-level predictors (e.g., problem severity, prior hospitalizations, medical comorbidities) of TOP-based, domain-specific change. The resulting best-fitting models produced normative change rates for each TOP domain based on patients' TOP responses and case-mix profiles. Second, for any new patient, the machine learning algorithms compare their personally predicted/expected change rate to their actual change on each of the TOP domains. Finally, we then examine these data at the therapist level; that is, for any therapist who has treated at least 10—15 cases with TOP data, we calculate a confidence interval for each of their patient's mean difference (positive, negative, or none) from their case-mix-adjusted expected outcomes for each of the 12 TOP domains.

Resulting from this analysis, we have created three classifications that are applied to each TOP domain. An "effective" classification represents a therapist whose average patient in a given domain reliably *exceeds* their personally predicted/expected rate of improvement. A "neutral" classification represents a therapist whose average patient in a given domain changes right about to the *expected* degree (not exceptional, but still a positive outcome history). Finally, an "ineffective" classification represents a therapist whose average patient in a given domain *falls short* of their personally expected rate of improvement. Using this classification system, we have examined therapists' multidimensional effectiveness patterns in community-based naturalistic care settings.

In one study for which we classified approximately 700 therapists based on a subsample of 10 patients each, we found that virtually all clinicians possessed some areas of relative strength and some areas of relative weakness (Kraus et al., 2011). The majority of therapists were classified as effective in treating three to seven domains, whereas none were effective in all domains, and 4% were ineffective or harmful across all domains. Notably, therapists who were reliably effective in treating their average patient within a given problem area had large and *positive* pre- to post-treatment improvement effect sizes, whereas therapists who were reliably ineffective in a given domain had large and *negative* pre- to post-treatment improvement effects. Next, in a separate study of 59 therapists, we extended our work to show that clinicians' strengths and weaknesses, as determined with one wave of 30 cases, were largely stable across a second wave of 30 patients (Kraus et al., 2016). For example, among the 40% of therapists who were particularly effective in reducing substance misuse in the first wave, 91% remained effective with the subsequent wave. Further, therapist past performance significantly predicted future performance for 11 of the 12 TOP domains (with the exception being mania).

Based on these results, it seemed highly plausible to us that therapist-level outcomes data could be useful for making case assignments within a mental health care system, perhaps especially if therapists were unable to make accurate *self*-assessments of their differential measurement-based abilities. We examined this latter question in a study of 50 community therapists who treated an average of 27 historical patients who had completed the TOP at pre- and post-treatment (Constantino, Boswell, Coyne, et al., 2023). As part of a broader survey, therapists (who were unaware of their measurement-based outcomes) rated their perceived effectiveness (using our three-level classification system) on each of the same 12 outcomes the TOP assesses. For seven of these domains, the majority of therapists *overestimated* their own effectiveness classification. Arguably, these domains represented the most common presenting problems, such as depression, anxiety, and quality-of-life issues. Thus, if therapists encounter a problem often, they may be more likely to believe they are good at treating it—a possible overconfidence bias. Moreover, there were no TOP domains for which the majority of therapists *underestimated* their measurement-based effectiveness. Finally, for all but the one outcome domain of psychosis, therapists were *no better than chance* at predicting their measurement-based effectiveness classification.

Hence, our research to this point underscored the limitations of status quo therapist case assignment and referral practices in mental health systems, as well as the potential need to use therapists' measurement-derived effectiveness profiles to help pair patients with personally well-suited providers. That said, despite us researchers thinking this was an exciting idea, it remained unclear if patients themselves would value using therapist effectiveness information when making treatment decisions. Therefore, we set out to answer this question in another thread of our practice-oriented research program.

Patient Valuing of Therapist Effectiveness Data

Based on a survey of adult patients who were receiving community-based outpatient therapy, the answer is "yes"—patients would value having therapist effectiveness data inform their referrals and case assignment (Boswell et al., 2021). Namely, over 90% of the 403 respondents indicated that (a) they would use therapist track record data to make treatment decisions if it were made available to them; (b) patients should have access to therapist track records when making decisions; (c) it is important to be assigned to therapists based on their track records, especially when having previously failed to benefit from treatment; and (d) having access to and matching on therapist effectiveness information would increase the likelihood of being helped by treatment. As a multimethod study, these sentiments were generally corroborated through qualitative analysis of 15 patients' semistructured interview data (note that these transcripts were randomly selected from 37 participants who volunteered for the follow-up interview through convenience sampling; see Boswell et al., 2021). For example, in light of common experiences having difficulty finding a mental health care provider, patients indicated they would welcome accessing (or having their referring physician access) a measurement-derived list of well-matched providers and that they would be willing to wait longer to see one of the clinicians on this personal shortlist. However, patient valuing of therapist effectiveness data did not occur in a vacuum; they still expressed valuing, to some degree, other non-measurement-based therapist factors, such as therapy style and cultural sensitivity.

Additionally, drawing on a discounting task, we found that patients would be willing to sacrifice the greatest amount of general therapist effectiveness to ensure working with a provider who had known success in treating their *most specific need area*; notably, this general effectiveness discount was far more than what patients were willing to "give up" in order to experience other things like a match on a social identity variable or the therapist being more experienced (Boswell et al., 2018). Overall, our findings across the studies reviewed to this point suggested there is a patient-centered opportunity to facilitate personalized mental health care through provider specialization to their unique measurement-informed skills and away from their measurement-informed shortcomings. Accordingly, we next tested this patient-valued and practice-oriented idea.

Prospectively Harnessing Therapists' Strengths

Informed by our foundational research, we conducted a double-masked randomized controlled trial that tested the effectiveness of measurement-based matching (at the time of intake) of patient problems to therapists' strengths prior to naturalistic outpatient therapy with adults in a mental health care network in the Midwestern United States (Constantino et al., 2021). As a first step, prior to the trial, we applied our aforementioned TOP-based classification protocol to the 48 participating therapists. After establishing these multidimensional effectiveness profiles, the second step included the recruitment of 218 new trial patients who completed the TOP at intake, which revealed their personally most elevated mental health concerns. For the third step, these patients were then randomly assigned to therapists empirically (the match condition) or pragmatically as usual (the control condition). For the match arm, patients were assigned to a clinician with a historical track record of effectiveness in treating their most personally salient problem(s). For the control arm, patients were assigned based on typical provider parameters, such as roster openings, office location, and self-described expertise, with an empirical match being left purely to chance. Finally, after case assignment, therapists simply treated patients as they normally would, and we followed patients through their actual termination or a maximum of 16 weeks. Notably, therapists treated patients in *both* the match and control conditions, which allowed us to examine our hypothesized within-therapist effect of matching; that is, within a given therapist's study-based caseload, did patients who were matched have better outcomes than those who were not intentionally matched?

For the primary outcome of general symptomatic and functional impairment, results indicated that the match versus control patients showed significantly more improvement, with a large effect size of $d = .75$ (Constantino et al., 2021). This effect was also clinically meaningful—the average match, but not control, patient demonstrated a post-treatment impairment level (i.e., estimated through 16 weeks of therapy) that was indistinguishable from a community norm of nondistressed, non-treatment-seeking individuals. In a follow-up analysis, we also found that the positive effect of matching was even stronger for patients who presented with more severe primary concerns (Boswell et al., 2022). Notably, this severity moderator also emerged in another secondary study, but this time at the therapist level: namely, for clinicians who tended to treat patients with higher versus lower average severity levels, the positive match effect was especially potent (Coyne, Constantino, Boswell, Gaines, & Kraus, 2024). Further informing precision care, the match effect was also stronger for patients who identified with an underrepresented race/ethnicity, which suggested that leveraging therapist effectiveness differences may hold promise for increasing mental health care equity (Boswell et al., 2022).

In terms of current implications, measurement-based matching to therapists' effectiveness strengths (and away from their weaknesses) represents a practice-oriented research innovation that can complement other evidence-based efforts to improve mental health care. It is also worth reiterating that as a form of precision care, which occurs at the time of case assignment, matching had a substantive positive impact even though nothing else about treatment changed and neither participant knew about the dyad's match status. Thus, if applied in this way, matching is likely non-burdensome to any mental health care network; as long as a multidimensional outcome tool is being used at baseline and follow-up, a reality that's becoming more common (Barkham et al., 2023), then therapist effectiveness data can prime a match system in a way that does not have to threaten clinicians' *treatment* autonomy. Accordingly, matching to therapists' problem-specific effectiveness strengths is a readily scalable innovation for which mental health care systems are rather easily positioned for widespread adoption. To this end, and fully consistent with the practice-oriented research paradigm, we recently launched a large-scale, multiphase implementation project.

Implementing Matching to Therapists' Strengths

For our in-progress implementation work (Constantino, Kraus, et al., 2023), we aim in Phase 1 to demonstrate that routine TOP assessment, development of therapist effectiveness profiles, and prospective matching can be successfully integrated into the current operations within a large regional mental health care network in the Eastern United States. Based on an initial quantitative assessment, we have learned that project-engaged therapists have generally favorable attitudes toward using evidence-based practices in general, monitoring patients' progress with the TOP, and data-driven matching (Aajmain et al., 2023). Moreover, based on the qualitative analysis of interview data, therapists have expressed being intrigued to learn about their problem-specific effectiveness profiles, provided the information is delivered in a growth-oriented versus punitive manner; they have also largely endorsed a belief that data-driven matching to therapists' strengths would promote better patient outcomes and might result in higher therapist satisfaction with their work (Harris et al., 2023). Such therapist-focused data are another outgrowth of practice-oriented research, and they demonstrate how multiple stakeholders can be meaningfully engaged to help shape the implementation of evidence-informed practices about which they care. And consistent with therapists' favorable attitudes, we have now successfully launched Phase 1 TOP administration, established therapist effectiveness profiles, and enabled the TOP-based match system for case assignments. Assessments of fidelity, reach, and effectiveness are forthcoming.

In Phase 2, we will rely on the survey and interview data we collect and analyze, materials we develop, and lessons we learn in Phase 1 to replicate our implementation efforts more widely across a large national network of mental health care centers in the United States. Our strategy follows the Framework for Dissemination (Mendel et al., 2008), which approaches implementation with the expectation that some degree of adaptation to the evidence-based intervention (i.e., data-driven matching) will be necessary for long-term sustainment. Thus, broader activities in the partner mental health care networks will include working to integrate the TOP-Match system into their existing electronic health record, establishing training protocols for future adoptions, assessing and refining the match system to meet the network's needs, and demonstrating fidelity and beneficial patient treatment outcomes that meet or exceed those observed in the original trial—again, without requiring that clinicians change *how* they directly administer psychotherapy (Constantino et al., 2021). In its adoption of a Hybrid Type I design (Youn et al., 2024), our implementation project underscores the intersection of practice-oriented research and implementation science. Specifically, the project aims to examine the health impact of outcomes-based matching in additional naturalistic settings, while prospectively collecting information on implementation processes to inform future implementation activities (Curran et al., 2012).

Practice and Policy Recommendations Related to Within-Therapist Effects

In this section, we highlight several possible (though certainly preliminary) practice, training, and policy recommendations based on existing research on the multidimensional within-therapist effect. Following from our foundational research that uncovered such effectiveness differences (Kraus et al., 2011, 2016) and showed that therapists are inaccurate assessors of their own problem-specific strengths and weaknesses (Constantino, Boswell, Coyne, et al., 2023), it seems important that independent clinicians and group practices of all guises adopt the use of a multidimensional routine outcome measure to help determine more accurately which therapists work best for whom—at least in terms of patients with certain elevated presenting problems. Such data can then be more transparently reported to relevant mental health care decision makers, which would address a seemingly major concern that patients often choose a therapist based on the therapist's self-assessed (and therefore potentially overestimated) areas of expertise. As Constantino, Boswell, Coyne, et al. (2023) noted, "With more widespread replication of such inaccuracies, mental health care stakeholders would be right to question the veracity of therapists' self-marketing of effectiveness in the absence of data" (p. 481). Instead, these stakeholders, and the various systems in which they are embedded, could focus on explicit and measurement-driven personalization efforts that center more so on the provider than, say, the type or format of treatment (Constantino & Muir, 2024). Our prospective match intervention (Constantino et al., 2021), which was tested with the rigor of a randomized trial within a practice-oriented research paradigm, represents one such promising and rather minimalist avenue to precision care.

It may also be important to incentivize such efforts to increase therapist accuracy in "knowing thyself" in terms of their effectiveness strengths and weaknesses. For example, such incentives could come in the form of insurance companies offering higher reimbursement rates for therapists who quantify and advertise their areas of expertise based on patient-reported outcomes data (see Rousmaniere et al., 2020). Although not uniquely based on patient-reported outcomes data, such effectiveness-based incentives have already been implemented at scale for psychologists who work with Centers for Medicare and Medicaid Services patients in the United States (Boswell et al., 2023). Additionally, administrators in multi-provider practices can incentivize, such as through referral volume, therapists being willing to specialize to their strengths (i.e., see only empirically well-matched patients). Alternatively, these practices can provide training resources to help clinicians (especially those who wish to remain more of a generalist) address their areas of shortcoming—a type of personalized continuing education and training (Constantino et al., 2021).

Finally, efforts to reduce the systemic health disparities faced by patients with underrepresented identities (Alegría et al., 2008; Lê Cook et al., 2014) may wish to include matching to therapists' measurement-based, problem-specific strengths. Although replication is needed, including with more diverse samples, our work demonstrated that the beneficial effect of such matching was roughly double for people of color (POC) versus white patients (Boswell et al., 2022). Given that POC themselves have expressed a valuing of using provider effectiveness information in this manner (Constantino, Gaines, et al., 2023; Gaines et al., 2023), matching could be an efficient patient-centered and practice-oriented way to increase mental health care equity. As a complement to building awareness of, and ultimately improving, therapists' problem-specific strengths and growth areas, training methods and resources can be developed to enhance therapists' self-awareness of their patient identity-based strengths and improve their effectiveness in areas where they may be less effective. That said, this should be just one prong in a comprehensive and urgently needed effort to redress the mental health care disparities that POC have historically faced, typically as a function of structural barriers, attitudinal barriers, and discrimination within mental health care systems (e.g., American Psychological Association, 2021).

Future Directions for Research on Within-Therapist Effects

In this section, we outline several future directions that can help advance research on *who works best for whom, and why?* Inspired by our aforementioned trial's moderator result that POC benefited even more strongly from matching to therapists' problem-specific strengths (Boswell et al., 2022), we have recently begun repeating our program of research, but now with a focus on within-therapist effectiveness differences in treating patients with different racial/ethnic identities—another multidimensional factor for which clinicians may demonstrate strengths and weaknesses. For the first step (uncovering differences), and by adapting our previously reviewed classification system, we have built on prior research (e.g., Hayes et al., 2015, 2016; Kivlighan et al., 2019) to demonstrate that therapists do indeed possess measurement-based and identity-specific effectiveness differences. Namely, in a study of 40 providers in a naturalistic care context, we found that 10% of therapists were more effective when working with POC than white patients, whereas 18% were more effective working with white patients than POC (Coyne, Constantino, Boswell, Lukowitsky, & Kraus, 2023). Moreover, similar to our foundational problem-specific matching, we also showed retrospectively that patients who had been assigned (purely by chance) to a provider with a historical identity-specific strength had better outcomes than naturalistically unmatched patients.

For the second step in our program sequence (patient valuing), we have also demonstrated that POC, in particular, would generally value using therapist effectiveness information in their treatment decision-making (Gaines et al., 2023). Moreover, based on a discounting task, they would also sacrifice other preferences (such as the type of treatment they receive or identifying in the same way as their provider) to work with a therapist known to possess their personally relevant identity-specific strength (Constantino et al., 2024). The next steps of testing identity-based matching in a prospective randomized trial and implementing it widely, should the results warrant it, are coming soon.

Another future direction can focus on determining whether the size of the current evidence-based effect of matching patients to therapists' strengths changes when the case assignment system is unmasked and both participants are aware of their match status (in contrast to our aforementioned double-masked trial). Future research can also focus on mechanisms of patient–therapist match effects. For example, for the unmasked scenario, the match effect might operate through an increase in patients' expectation for being helped (given their knowledge of a therapist's historical and personally relevant effectiveness strength). As a transtheoretical and transdiagnostic variable, such outcome expectation has been shown to correlate with greater improvement (see Constantino et al., 2018). Of course, this is just one possible mechanism, and others should be tested as well. For example, at the therapist level, it may be that the in-session mechanisms that transmit the match effect are specific to different outcome domains. That is, what therapists do to drive their exceptional track record when working with patients with primary depressive symptoms (e.g., ability to maximize social support) may be distinct from what exceptionally effective therapists do when treating anxiety (e.g., competently using exposure strategies; Coyne, 2024).

Moreover, future research can focus on determining additional moderators of patient–therapist match effects. In this vein, and in addition to the distinct severity and race/ethnicity moderators revealed in our previously discussed problem-specific match trial, we also found (at a non-significant trend level) that the match effect was stronger for patients with higher baseline existential isolation (Constantino, Gaines, Coyne, et al., 2023). This finding will, of course, require replication. Additional moderators should also be explored, including in relation to unmasked matching of patients to therapists' problem-specific strengths and future tests of matching to therapists' identity-specific strengths.

Also, knowing that therapists possess different types of domain-specific effectiveness strengths and weaknesses necessitates research that can identify determinants of such differences (Coyne, 2024). For example, knowing immutable therapist factors that determine whether they will be well- or ill-suited to treat certain types of mental health problems or patients can help inform the *selection* of therapists into the field or the types of specializations they may choose once in the profession. Additionally, unearthing mutable therapist factors that determine whether they will be well- or ill-suited to treat certain types of mental health problems or patients can help inform the contents and processes of future clinician *trainings*. For example, understanding factors that predict which therapists work especially well with POC would be a boon to future trainings on culturally effective practices. In general, therapist effects research conducted within a practice-oriented research framework can inform adaptation to our training models, perhaps especially for established therapists who wish to improve in their areas of shortcoming versus only specializing to their historical measurement-based strengths.

Finally, therapist-focused research can also expand match notions beyond initial assignment of patient to provider. For example, our team has pioneered work on uncovering in-session therapy processes that clinicians use to good, no, or poor effect (Coyne et al., 2022). In this study of naturalistically delivered therapy, we found that for some therapists, the alliance–improvement association was positive and strong (a typical, intuitive effect). For other therapists, though, the alliance–improvement association was null or negative (counterintuitive effects). To be sure, the latter result indicated that higher patient-rated alliance for *some* therapists associates with *poorer* patient outcomes. Such variability in process–outcome correlations spotlights another opportunity for precision care in the form of matching the provider to the processes they are most likely to use well. With replication and extension in this area, future work can help inform during-treatment, therapist-level feedback systems, as well as personalized training agendas (Constantino, 2024).

Concluding Thoughts

As noted, the practice-oriented research program discussed herein is evolving. Drawing on therapist-level practice-based evidence, we feel we have come a long way in uncovering types of within-therapist effectiveness differences and prospectively leveraging this knowledge for patients' benefit. Importantly, we see such work as a compelling complement to (vs. rival of) other major practice-oriented research innovations, such as measurement-based, feedback-informed psychotherapy at the individual patient level (e.g., Lutz et al, 2021). Of course, as we outlined in the previous section, there is also a long way to go in both replicating the work discussed herein and further understanding the full and complex ways in which providers influence patients' mental health outcomes. Notably, though, we have drawn on various methodologies to accomplish our existing aims, including sophisticated analysis of large practice-generated data sets and both quantitative and qualitative methods to ascertain stakeholder valuing of provider effectiveness information. As such assessment of patients' and therapists' perspectives, needs, and values is largely nonexistent in *traditional* controlled research "in the lab," this community-engaged thread of work underlines a unique contribution of practice-oriented research to psychotherapy science.

Moreover, we conducted a rigorous randomized trial to determine the causal effectiveness of measurement-based, problem-specific matching of patients to providers. For this latter method, we hope to have helped debunk a false dichotomy that prevails in the field: namely, that randomized clinical trials are restricted to controlled research settings that may bear limited resemblance to everyday practice settings (see Borkovec & Castonguay, 1998). Indeed, this method is simply a rigorous and versatile tool for understanding various forms of evidence-based practices, and it can be applied squarely within the practice-oriented research paradigm. In general, we hope that all of the various methods we have employed to date can serve as useful heuristics for future research. We also hope (and expect) to be inspired by new and ever-emerging methodologies that can help us understand the influence of the mental health care therapist—arguably a long-neglected factor in our field's definition of research-informed clinical work.

References

Aajmain, S., Gaines, A. G., Constantino, M. J., Boswell, J. F., & Kraus, D. R. (2023, October 12–14). *Mental healthcare stakeholder attitudes toward measurement-based care and perspectives on the implementation of evidence-based practices* [Paper presentation]. North American Society for Psychotherapy Research Meeting, Amherst, MA, United States.

Alegría, M., Chatterji, P., Wells, K., Cao, Z., Chen, C., Takeuchi, D., Jackson, J., & Meng, X. L. (2008). Disparity in depression treatment among racial and ethnic minority populations in the United States. *Psychiatric Services, 59*(11), 1264–1272. https://doi.org/10.1176/ps.2008.59.11.1264

American Psychological Association. (2021). *Apology to people of color for APA's role in promoting, perpetuating, and failing to challenge racism, racial discrimination, and human hierarchy in U.S.* https://www.apa.org/about/policy/racism-apology

Barkham, M., De Jong, K., Delgadillo, J., & Lutz, W. (2023). Routine outcome monitoring (ROM) and feedback: Research review and recommendations. *Psychotherapy Research, 33*(7), 841–855. https://doi.org/10.1080/10503307.2023.2181114

Barkham, M., & Lambert, M. J. (2021). The efficacy and effectiveness of psychological therapies. In M. Barkham, W. Lutz, & L. G. Castonguay (Eds.), *Bergin and Garfield's handbook of psychotherapy and behavior change: 50th anniversary edition* (7th ed., pp. 135–189). John Wiley & Sons.

Borkovec, T. D., & Castonguay, L. G. (1998). What is the scientific meaning of empirically supported therapy? *Journal of Consulting and Clinical Psychology, 66*(1), 136–142. https://doi.org/10.1037/0022-006X.66.1.136

Boswell, J. F., Constantino, M. J., Coyne, A. E., & Kraus, D. R. (2022). For whom does a match matter most? Patient-level moderators of evidence-based patient–therapist matching. *Journal of Consulting and Clinical Psychology, 90*(1), 61–74. https://doi.org/10.1037/ccp0000644

Boswell, J. F., Constantino, M. J., Oswald, J. M., Bugatti, M., Coyne, A. E., Goodwin, B., & Morrison, N. (2021). A multimethod study of mental health care patients' attitudes toward clinician-level performance information. *Psychiatric Services, 72*(4), 452–456. https://doi.org/10.1176/appi.ps.202000366

Boswell, J. F., Constantino, M. J., Oswald, J. M., Bugatti, M., Goodwin, B., & Yucel, R. (2018). Mental health care consumers' relative valuing of clinician performance information. *Journal of Consulting and Clinical Psychology, 86*(4), 301–308. https://doi.org/10.1037/ccp0000264

Boswell, J. F., Hepner, K. A., Lysell, K., Rothrock, N. E., Bott, N., Childs, A. W., Douglas, S., Owings-Fonner, N., Wright, C. V., Stephens, K. A., Bard, D. E., Aajmain, S., & Bobbitt, B. L. (2023). The need for a measurement-based care professional practice guideline. *Psychotherapy, 60*(1), 1–16. https://doi.org/10.1037/pst0000439

Castonguay, L. G., Barkham, M., Youn, S. J., & Page, A. C. (2021). Practice-based evidence—Findings from routine clinical settings. In M. Barkham, W. Lutz, & L. G. Castonguay (Eds.),

Bergin and Garfield's handbook of psychotherapy and behavior change (7th ed, pp. 191–222). John Wiley & Sons.

Constantino, M. J. (2024). Measurement-based matching of patients to psychotherapists' strengths. *Journal of Consulting and Clinical Psychology, 92*(6), 327–329. https://doi.org/10.1037/ccp0000897

Constantino, M. J., Boswell, J. F., & Coyne, A. E. (2021). Patient, therapist, and relational factors. In M. Barkham, W. Lutz, & L. G. Castonguay (Eds.), *Bergin and Garfield's handbook of psychotherapy and behavior change* (7th ed, pp. 225–262). John Wiley & Sons.

Constantino, M. J., Boswell, J. F., Coyne, A. E., Kraus, D. R., & Castonguay, L. G. (2017). Who works for whom and why? Integrating therapist effects analysis into psychotherapy outcome and process research. In L. G. Castonguay & C. E. Hill (Eds.), *How and why are some therapists better than others? Understanding therapist effects* (pp. 55–68). American Psychological Association. https://doi.org/10.1037/0000034-004

Constantino, M. J., Boswell, J. F., Coyne, A. E., Muir, H. J., Gaines, A. N., & Kraus, D. R. (2023). Therapist perceptions of their own measurement-based, problem-specific effectiveness. *Journal of Consulting and Clinical Psychology, 91*(8), 474–484. https://doi.org/10.1037/ccp0000813

Constantino, M. J., Boswell, J. F., Coyne, A. E., Swales, T. P., & Kraus, D. R. (2021). Effect of matching therapists to patients vs assignment as usual on adult psychotherapy outcomes: A randomized clinical trial. *JAMA Psychiatry, 78*(9), 960–969. https://doi.org/10.1001/jamapsychiatry.2021.1221

Constantino, M. J., & Eubanks, C. F. (2024). Introduction to Volume 2, Parts II and III. In F. T. L. Leong, J. L. Callahan, J. Zimmerman, M. J. Constantino, & C. F. Eubanks (Eds.), *APA handbook of psychotherapy: Evidence-based practice, practice-based evidence, and contextual participant-driven practice, Vol. 2* (pp. 173–176). American Psychological Association. https://doi.org/10.1037/0000354-011

Constantino, M. J., Gaines, A. N., Coyne, A. E., Boswell, J. F., & Kraus, D. R. (2023). Existential isolation as a correlate of mental health problems, predictor of treatment outcome, and moderator of a patient-therapist match effect. *Journal of Social and Clinical Psychology, 42*(1), 1–28. https://doi.org/10.1521/jscp.2023.42.1.1

Constantino, M. J., Gaines, A. N., Hart, N., & Boswell, J. F. (2024). *People of Color's relative valuing of having therapist performance data inform the referral/assignment process. Cogent Mental Health, 3*(1), 1–21. https://doi.org/10.1080/28324765.2024.2305405

Constantino, M. J., Kraus, D. K., & Boswell, J. F. (December 10–13, 2023). *Implementing matching of patients to mental healthcare therapists' strengths* [Paper presentation]. 16th Annual Conference on the Science of Dissemination and Implementation in Health, Washington, DC, United States.

Constantino, M. J., & Muir, H. J. (2024). Can we harness therapist effects for therapeutic benefit? In F. T. L. Leong, J. L. Callahan, J. Zimmerman, M. J. Constantino, & C. F. Eubanks (Eds.), *APA handbook of psychotherapy: Evidence-based practice, practice-based evidence, and contextual participant-driven practice, Vol. 2* (pp. 243–254). American Psychological Association. https://doi.org/10.1037/0000354-016

Constantino, M. J., Vîslă, A., Coyne, A. E., & Boswell, J. F. (2018). A meta-analysis of the association between patients' early treatment outcome expectation and their posttreatment outcomes. *Psychotherapy, 55*(4), 473–485. https://doi.org/10.1037/pst0000169

Coyne, A. E. (2024). Therapist performance report cards: Do clinicians differ in their specific effectiveness? In F. T. L. Leong, J. L. Callahan, J. Zimmerman, M. J. Constantino, & C. F. Eubanks (Eds.), *APA handbook of psychotherapy: Evidence-based practice, practice-based evidence, and contextual participant-driven practice, Vol. 2* (pp. 227–242). American Psychological Association. https://doi.org/10.1037/0000354-015

Coyne, A. E., Constantino, M. J., Boswell, J. F., Gaines, A. G., & Kraus, D. R. (2024). Therapist-level moderators of patient-therapist match effectiveness in community psychotherapy.

Administration and Policy in Mental Health and Mental Health Services Research, 51, 738–752. https://doi.org/10.1007/s10488-024-01360-8

Coyne, A. E., Constantino, M. J., Boswell, J. F., & Kraus, D. R. (2022). Therapist-level moderation of within- and between-therapist process-outcome association. *Journal of Consulting and Clinical Psychology, 90*(1), 75–89. https://doi.org/10.1037/ccp0000676

Coyne, A. E., Constantino, M. J., Boswell, J. F., Lukowitsky, M. R., & Kraus, D. R. (2023, August 3–5). *Harnessing therapists' strengths in treating patients with specific racial/ethnic identities* [Paper presentation]. American Psychological Association 131st Annual Meeting, Washington, DC, United States.

Curran, G. M., Bauer, M., Mittman, B., Pyne, J. M., & Stetler, C. (2012). Effectiveness-implementation hybrid designs: Combining elements of clinical effectiveness and implementation research to enhance public health impact. *Medical Care, 50*(3), 217–226. https://doi.org/10.1097/MLR.0b013e3182408812

Gaines, A. N., Constantino, M. J., Kmetz, H., & Boswell, J. F. (2023). Patients' race/ethnicity in relation to their experiences of and attitudes toward therapist referral/assignment. *Cogent Mental Health, 2*(1). Advance online publication. https://doi.org/10.1080/28324765.2023.2277920

Harris, B., Boswell, J. F., Schwartzman, C. M., Constantino, M. J., Scharff, A., Muir, H. J., Gaines, A. N., King, B. R., & Kraus, D. R. (2023, October 12–14). *A qualitative analysis of stakeholder attitudes regarding personalized provider selection and patient-therapist matching* [Paper presentation]. North American Society for Psychotherapy Research Meeting, Amherst, MA, United States.

Hayes, J. A., McAleavey, A. A., Castonguay, L. G., & Locke, B. D. (2016). Psychotherapists' outcomes with White and racial/ethnic minority clients: First, the good news. *Journal of Counseling Psychology, 63*(3), 261–268. https://doi.org/10.1037/cou0000098

Hayes, J. A., Owen, J., & Bieschke, K. J. (2015). Therapist differences in symptom change with racial/ethnic minority clients. *Psychotherapy, 52*(3), 308–314. https://doi.org/10.1037/a0037957

Johns, R. G., Barkham, M., Kellett, S., & Saxon, D. (2019). A systematic review of therapist effects: A critical narrative update and refinement to Baldwin and Imel's (2013) review. *Clinical Psychology Review, 67*, 78–93. https://doi.org/10.1016/j.cpr.2018.08.004

Kivlighan, D. M., III, Hooley, I. W., Bruno, M. G., Ethington, L. L., Keeton, P. M., & Schreier, B. A. (2019). Examining therapist effects in relation to clients' race-ethnicity and gender: An intersectionality approach. *Journal of Counseling Psychology, 66*(1), 122–129. https://doi.org/10.1037/cou0000316

Kraus, D. R., Bentley, J. H., Alexander, P. C., Boswell, J. F., Constantino, M. J., Baxter, E. E., & Castonguay, L. G. (2016). Predicting therapist effectiveness from their own practice-based evidence. *Journal of Consulting and Clinical Psychology, 84*(6), 473–483. https://doi.org/10.1037/ccp0000083

Kraus, D. R., Castonguay, L., Boswell, J. F., Nordberg, S. S., & Hayes, J. A. (2011). Therapist effectiveness: Implications for accountability and patient care. *Psychotherapy Research, 21*(3), 267–276. https://doi.org/10.1080/10503307.2011.563249

Kraus, D. R., Seligman, D. A., & Jordan, J. R. (2005). Validation of a behavioral health treatment outcome and assessment tool designed for naturalistic settings: The Treatment Outcome Package. *Journal of Clinical Psychology, 61*(3), 285–314. https://doi.org/10.1002/jclp.20084

Lê Cook, B., Zuvekas, S. H., Carson, N., Wayne, G. F., Vesper, A., & McGuire, T. G. (2014). Assessing racial/ethnic disparities in treatment across episodes of mental health care. *Health Services Research, 49*(1), 206–229. https://doi.org/10.1111/1475-6773.12095

Leong, F. T. L., Callahan, J. L., Zimmerman, J., Constantino, M. J., & Eubanks, C. F. (Eds.). (2024). *APA handbook of psychotherapy: Evidence-based practice, practice-based evidence, and contextual participant-driven practice, Vol 2*. American Psychological Association. https://doi.org/10.1037/0000354-000

Lutz, W., de Jong, K., Rubel, J. A., & Delgadillo, J. (2021). Measuring, predicting, and tracking change in psychotherapy. In M. Barkham, W. Lutz, & L. G. Castonguay (Eds.), *Bergin and Garfield's handbook of psychotherapy and behavior change* (7th ed., pp. 89–133). John Wiley & Sons.

Mendel, P., Meredith, L. S., Schoenbaum, M., Sherbourne, C. D., & Wells, K. B. (2008). Interventions in organizational and community context: A framework for building evidence on dissemination and implementation in health services research. *Administration Policy in Mental Health and Mental Health Services Research, 35*, 21–37. https://doi.org/10.1007/s10488-007-0144-9

Nissen-Lie, H. A., Oddli, H. W., & Heinonen, E. (2024). Do therapists differ in their general effectiveness? Therapist effects and their determinants. In F. T. L. Leong, J. L. Callahan, J. Zimmerman, M. J. Constantino, & C. F. Eubanks (Eds.), *APA handbook of psychotherapy: Evidence-based practice, practice-based evidence, and contextual participant-driven practice, Vol. 2* (pp. 213–226). American Psychological Association. https://doi.org/10.1037/0000354-014

Rousmaniere, T., Wright, C. V., Boswell, J. F., Constantino, M. J., Castonguay, L. G., McLeod, J., Pedulla, D., & Nordal, K. (2020). Keeping psychologists in the driver's seat: Four perspectives on quality improvement and clinical data registries. *Psychotherapy, 57*(4), 562–573. https://doi.org/10.1037/pst0000227

Wampold, B. E., & Imel, Z. E. (2015). *The great psychotherapy debate: The evidence for what makes psychotherapy work, 2nd ed.* Routledge/Taylor & Francis Group.

Wampold, B. E., & Owen, J. (2021). Therapist effects: History, methods, magnitude, and characteristics of effective therapists. In M. Barkham, W. Lutz, & L. G. Castonguay (Eds.), *Bergin and Garfield's handbook of psychotherapy and behavior change* (7th ed., pp. 297–326). John Wiley & Sons.

Youn, S. J., Boswell, J. F., Douglas, S., Harris, B. A., Aajmain, S., Arnold, K. T., Creed, T. A., Gutner, C. A., Orengo-Aguayo, R., Oswald, J. M., & Stirman, S. W. (2024). Implementation science and practice-oriented research: Convergence and complementarity. *Administration and Policy in Mental Health, 51*, 336–347. https://doi.org/10.1007/s10488-023-01296-5

7

Collaborating With Patients and Therapists in Practice-Research Networks

The Norse Feedback Action Research Program

Christian Moltu, Heidi Brattland, Samuel S. Nordberg, and Andrew A. McAleavey

Back in 2007, working as a full-time outpatient psychologist and therapist, I (C. M.) had an important experience. In the weekly intake meeting at the specialist mental health outpatient clinic, all the referrals from primary care physicians sat as a pile of papers before the clinic leader, representing people seeking help for mental health problems. This pile was the subject of a meeting of about 15 healthcare workers, psychologists, psychiatrists, nurses and social workers with different competencies, and therapeutic focuses. Importantly, all 15 already had significant caseloads. My colleagues were, as a group, highly competent: All had completed lengthy postgraduate training in cognitive behavioral therapies, intensive short-term dynamic therapies, trauma-focused therapies, or mentalization-based therapies. In the meeting, the clinic leader presented each referral from the pile one by one, in the hope that one of the team members would have an open space. When no one had an open slot for a new patient, the leader assigned the case to whoever put forward less opposition to adding another patient to their caseload.

In this rather common situation, I found one experience particularly striking. When discussing whether they could take on a given patient, it became clear that many of my colleagues knew many of the patients from earlier treatments. In fact, many of the referrals, maybe even a majority, were for a second, third, or even fourth treatment course. The referrals described problems that would be considered treatable given the experience and therapeutic tools that the group possessed. In this situation, first-time referrals

Christian Moltu et al., *Collaborating With Patients and Therapists in Practice-Research Networks*. In: *Practice-Based Evidence in the Psychological Therapies*. Edited by: Louis G. Castonguay et al., Oxford University Press. © Oxford University Press (2026). DOI: 10.1093/9780197748336.003.0007 were far more popular and easier to assign, whereas people who had been in unsuccessful treatment processes before were significantly harder to find a willing therapist for. Interestingly, at that point in time, patients' outcomes, or even how many times they had been referred previously, were not recorded systematically at all.

These three challenges, achieving precision in patient assignment, tailoring treatments to individuals to reduce dropouts, and recording outcomes while learning from treatment responses in the clinic, formed the foundation for the research journey we initiated. In this chapter we will present and discuss the strategies and methods for participatory research, development, implementation, and refinement that have guided the process leading up to the Norse Feedback (NF) program, currently in use in Norway (Nordberg et al., 2021) and the United States (Nordberg et al., 2024; Youn et al., 2024). But before going into those details, some important questions should be clarified. Why did we need to establish this research program and outcome monitoring system at all, as opposed to adopting another existing system? Which problems were we trying to solve, and who did they impact the most? What do the most important stakeholders—the patients and therapists using NF—need it to do for them? And how do the approaches that we have chosen differ from other methods?

What Did We Aim to Achieve by Establishing a Practice-Based Research Program?

In the early 2000s, the core messages from psychotherapy research that made it all the way to the lay clinicians in our context seemed to be that psychotherapy is generally effective and that 80% of treated people are better off than the average non-treated person. Furthermore, the lay understanding was that the prioritized research strategy was to discover whether a given therapeutic modality would outperform another by achieving higher improvement rates on the population level. However, these methods did not seem to directly address the fundamental needs in our clinic. First, we had all the evidence-based therapeutic modality competence and formal training within the team, but, apparently, we were not reproducing the results from the randomized control trials (RCTs). Second, the theoretical 20%, or, as I later learned from practice-based evidence, the much larger portion who didn't benefit from treatment, seemed a much more salient area for improvement (Clark et al., 2009, 2018; McAleavey, 2022). This was especially true because their re-referrals constituted a major strain on the system, and because, more basically, they continued to suffer and without sufficient help. Third, it seemed that the clinicians and patients in the clinic knew something else, something important, about suffering and recovery, unhealthy social situations, treatment processes, impasses, and outcomes. The everyday clinical knowledge seemed to suggest that patients' and therapists' situation and context seemed to impact treatment outcomes more than techniques in themselves.

To address these everyday clinical questions with a research program, we formed a collaborative team. When we embarked on developing our research infrastructure, the following three points formed basic premises and values that we aimed to integrate into our plans and research:

- Ordinary clinical practice is different from RCT research in ways we do not fully understand.
- It may be more impactful to improve services for patients who have negative treatment outcomes, rather than slightly improving the effect for those patients who already benefit.
- Stakeholders in ordinary practice, predominantly clinicians and patients, have untapped knowledge that should be possible to translate into research designs.

What Is Norse Feedback?

To have a context for understanding the background for the project, we need to briefly describe the outcome of it. NF, the key result of the research, development, and implementation processes that will be described in this chapter, is a patient-centered system used for routine outcome monitoring (ROM) and clinical feedback (CF) in mental health treatment processes. Patients are typically asked to respond to NF prior to each session in outpatient treatment, or once every week during inpatient care. The system is continuously evolving based on collaborative research and is currently in its third generation. It is widely implemented in primary, secondary, and private mental health care settings, with over 10,000 administrations per month in Norway at the time of writing.

Figure 7.1 Norse Feedback Adult Clinical Report

NF measures a range of constructs that are relevant to treatment, including different symptom expressions, problem-maintaining processes, impacts on functioning, therapeutic alliance, and patient preferences, across 20 potential scales and 96 potential items. To be feasible for sessional use, NF is fully digital and employs a dynamic empirical personalization algorithm (McAleavey et al., 2021; Moltu et al., 2018), so that only items that are relevant for any individual patient are administered. This feature has led the system to be acceptable to clinicians and patients (Hovland et al., 2023), and implementable in routine care (Nordberg et al., 2021). The patient-centered measurement strategy is befitting newer explainable machine learning approaches to developing clinical tools (Westbye et al., 2024). For the sake of illustration, Figure 7.1 presents a clinical report from NF content.

Collaboration and Participatory Approaches to Research

Our team's research journey started from the context of psychiatry, rather than from within psychotherapy research specifically. Within psychiatry, a service user movement had developed over several decades. Psychiatry patients had formed activist and survivor movements, due to earlier and continued oppression and coercion of patients in these settings. These countermovements resulted in significant contributions to the methods and values of psychiatry research: Ideologically, they manifested in the form of rights-based, democratic, and citizenship approaches to participation (Davidson et al., 2010), under the slogan "nothing about us, without us" (Nelson et al., 1998). Methodologically, they manifested in the form of research methods frameworks for co-creation, co-research, user-led research, and similar manifestations of first-person perspectives empowerment in research design and implementation (Moltu et al., 2012). Clinically, these movements manifested in the form of recovery perspectives and theories, such as, for example, CHIME (Connectedness, Hope, Identity, Meaning, and Empowerment) (Leamy et al., 2011), and dialogical and user-led practices (Davidson et al., 2010).

Reading the psychotherapy research literature from within this psychiatry research perspective, we found comparatively less focus on patient participation as co-researchers in developing and implementing research programs. Perhaps this is due to psychotherapy having been considered a friendlier practice, not fueling a countermovement to advocate for the user perspective within the discourse. It is, after all, only recently that adverse outcomes, deterioration, and harmful psychotherapy processes have become prominent foci of research. Yet, when we started we felt that the importance of collaboration had received insufficient attention in the field of psychotherapy research.

Within the context of the clinical, philosophical, social, and empirical factors described earlier, the NF research program emerged from a clinical setting in which focusing on patients with unsatisfactory benefits from treatment was a priority, and from an approach to science in which all stakeholders have a legitimate say. At the time that this program was initiated, ROM and CF were showing promise to improve outcomes, in particular for patients who were not on track to recovery (Shimokawa et al., 2010), and if implemented well in clinical practice (Krägeloh et al., 2015). However, implementation was notoriously hard (Boswell et al., 2015). We hypothesized that this resulted in part from (a) the stakeholders who were to use and benefit from ROM and CF not having a strong enough role in their development, and (b) the outcomes and concepts that researchers had been interested in not fully mirroring the needs experienced within clinical practice.

In response, the NF research program aimed to (1) develop a clinically sensible and useful ROM and CF system, while (2) focusing on implementation as widely as possible, and (3) using research methods to continually evaluate and develop it further. To do so, we decided that the project needed to be designed collaboratively with clinicians and patients in ordinary practices, and be implemented as a continuous participatory process within a responsive and responsible research and innovation framework (Stilgoe et al., 2013).

Collaboration in Practice

As the stakeholders of the NF program began collaborating on the development of a useful ROM system, the first question that emerged among them was: What is an outcome? This significant question can be reformulated in multiple ways, such as, for example: What is a good outcome? What is an adverse outcome? Who decides what a relevant outcome is? How close to the desired outcome is close enough? How should different relevant outcomes, such as, for example, increased agentic capacity and reduced depressive symptoms, be prioritized against each other, in reality and within measures? In our understanding, such questions were relevant to planning the ROM research but might also be key to understanding why many implementations might not fully succeed. Implicit understanding of what the most relevant outcome is, and consequently, an implicit understanding of what psychotherapy is, will always be built into a ROM system.

Important methodological learning points that emerged for us by collaborating closely with patient stakeholders, therapist stakeholders, and leader stakeholders across a range of specific projects, can be summarized:

1. A thorough analysis of who the different stakeholders are, and an appraisal of what their stake consists of, need to come first. In this process, stakeholders need to be given space to self-define their participatory role in the project (Moltu et al., 2012) rather than being invited to a limited role based on the researchers' perception of their interest.
2. A thorough process of researcher reflexivity, in which the collaboration with partners and stakeholders is used to become aware of implicit preconceptions that we as researchers (Veseth et al., 2017) brought to the table, is key to starting research projects on a common and solid foundation.
3. For someone to collaborate well, there needs to be a mutual recognition of the validity and value of each other's point of view. To bring about true collaboration, we as researchers have needed to cede some control, which was occasionally uncomfortable, inconvenient, and difficult—as we wanted to speed ahead.

In the NF research program, we experienced these three points exerting a significant influence on our process on multiple occasions. In participatory research approaches, one will oftentimes have to back up some steps to find the right place to start. In particular, we experienced this when talking with other people makes us aware of implicit preconceptions we have brought to the project that might not be helpful to science. One key example is from a project studying how patients used ROM and CF during hospital admissions for mental health problems (e.g., Eldal et al., 2019). In this project, the collaborative approach resulted in the service user co-researchers halting the process and asking the researchers: Do we really know what a mental health hospital admission is and what the basic patient needs are during inpatient care? In response, we needed to roll the project back and spend 3 years of research just to establish what we initially had thought was the point of departure. It is a key experience in our program that to implement participatory research methods, the researchers must be responsive and willing to truly recognize the input brought to the table by the partners (Moltu et al., 2012). From a positive viewpoint, this shows how collaborative approaches can support researcher reflexivity and conceptual clarity. On the other hand, taking collaboration seriously has made us lose some speed from time to time.

Collaborative Organization: An Expanding Practice Research Network

As a foundation, the NF research program has incorporated the structures and principles involved in practice research networks (PRNs). PRNs are collaborative organizations that include clinical researchers and clinical practitioners in active interactions to direct not just the conduct of research, but also the focus of research and development of research projects at each stage (Castonguay et al., 2013, 2021). Forming a PRN requires that researchers actively seek participation from providers who have historically been excluded from decision-making processes in the conduct of research and that they conduct research that addresses their concerns and that occurs in their regular practice. Successful PRNs maximize the clinical relevance and immediate applicability to clinical practice of their research. Importantly, our program has extended a particular emphasis of PRN by adding service user voices to the basic model.

In the beginning, the NF research program was primarily located in one health organization: Førde Hospital Trust. This is itself a larger hospital system that encompasses several regional clinics. The NF PRN has later developed into a larger group of mental health clinics and substance abuse centers, for adult and adolescent populations across several geographical areas (e.g., Grindheim, Moltu, et al., 2024; Nordberg et al., 2021). Thus, our program represents an alternative implementation to the more traditional PRNs, which are highly locally organized through physical colocation in a single treatment clinic and in-person interactions (Castonguay et al., 2010, 2015). It should be noted that this alternative is not unique, as several large infrastructures have created PRNs with various organizations (see Hayes & Castonguay, this volume).

The development of the NF PRN is described in greater detail elsewhere (Nordberg et al., 2021). Briefly, we started locally in Western Norway by establishing basic technological and ethical requirements for the collection of data. As the NF tool itself has become more widespread, we have fostered both explicit engagement with clinical providers at each treatment center and multiple research hubs with overlapping research agendas. One such group, primarily located in Trondheim and Central Norway, has been focused on the application of the NF in substance use treatments (e.g., Grindheim, McAleavey, et al., 2024). Simultaneously, the NF has been applied increasingly in the United States, including a research group focused on the use of the NF to guide initial assessment, triage, and assignment of digital clinical tools (Youn et al., 2024).

The central organization in Western Norway continues to develop the NF actively in collaboration with technical partners and has several formal methods for collecting clinical feedback and researchable questions from clinical partners. One such method is a weekly meeting for technological and research stakeholders to hear suggestions and feedback collected by clinical-implementation liaisons. This feedback from providers has been the driving force behind several development steps of the NF, including significant changes to items and scales (Moltu et al., 2021). Given the complexity of the NF solution, we have needed to include several stakeholders as often as possible, and the PRN infrastructure has helped ensure that clinicians' needs are met.

Norse Feedback Pre-Phase: Which Psychotherapy Outcomes Are Important to Which Stakeholders?

While symptom reduction is fundamental to any treatment, psychotherapy has always targeted additional processes, to varying degrees. Consequently, an ongoing debate has been about what the most relevant outcomes to measure were. This debate started when outcomes were measured purely for psychotherapy research projects. Now, when we move beyond discrete outcome studies and aim to measure outcomes session by session, it seems very important that the measurement constructs fit the outcomes that therapists and patients work collaboratively toward.

Early on, Connolly and Strupp (1996) developed outcome clusters with the input from 80 patients in the Vanderbilt Psychotherapy Research Project.

Of the clusters that they reported, the cluster *improved symptoms* corresponds with what has most typically been measured across later ROM approaches. However, the authors also reported the outcome clusters of improved *self-understanding, improved self-confidence,* and *greater self-definition,* which are less frequently addressed. Some 10 years later, Klein and Elliott (2006) revisited the questions from a humanistic perspective. In line with Connolly and Strupp (1996), they report *affective change,* a symptom-oriented concept, as important, underscoring again how symptoms of mental distress are key to both treatment focus and outcome. However, Klein and Elliott (2006) also report *self-improvement, experiential processing, life functioning,* and *interpersonal relationships* as core outcomes of psychotherapy. Other studies have emphasized, in addition to symptomatic distress, the themes of interpersonal relationships, self-understanding, and self-acceptance (Binder et al., 2010) as pivotal. In our own pre-phase qualitative exploration we reported *strengthened approach behavior, relational change, new understanding,* and *collaborative acceptance* as important outcome concepts (Moltu et al., 2017).

There is no question that monitoring relevant symptoms has a significant place in ROM approaches. It is likely that both patients and therapists would feel estranged if the ROM did not address symptoms, which are often among the core precipitants of treatment. Moreover, it seems that symptom reduction is associated with non-symptom outcomes, or perhaps a prerequisite for those to emerge (Skar-Fröding et al., 2022). Perhaps it is even possible to predict from relevant symptom outcomes what more function-oriented quality of life or specific process outcomes would be. However, in the specific context of ROM and CF, we have found that it is important not to limit the scope to the concepts that are most easily and traditionally measured.

Instead, we have started from the core idea that ROM is to be used clinically in the here and now of the encounter, to mirror and support the conversational processes that are already ongoing in therapy (Moltu et al., 2018). This approach is supported by findings from research into idiographic ROM approaches (Solstad et al., 2023). For example, Sales and colleagues (2018) suggested that between 71% and 95% of patients wanted to track outcomes that were not covered by a symptom-oriented measure. This seems particularly important when new technology and growing research evidence mandate continuously monitoring and interpreting patient outcomes as part of ordinary practice. Previously, the omission of patient-relevant outcomes in a measure might have meant that the corresponding research project, reliant on the collected data, might overlook some significant insights, albeit without any risk to the treatment process. In routine clinical feedback, however, in which outcomes are continuously fed back to the clinical process, failing to track relevant outcomes may foster patient disenfranchisement and misalign therapeutic interventions or conversations (Solstad et al., 2019, 2021). We consider it an ethical imperative to scrutinize the choice to only measure symptoms, especially in a highly restrictive form, during psychotherapy, except in highly specific treatment contexts. For example, the Patient Health Questionnaire-9 (PHQ-9; Kroenke et al., 2001), a widely used measure of depression is likely not sufficient for routine clinical feedback among patients with eating disorders, despite its clear strengths for many patients and its validity as a measure of depressive symptoms within that population specifically (Wisting et al., 2021).

Implementing this line of thinking into our own program, we started with establishing a baseline understanding of what relevant outcomes and clinical measure concepts were for different populations, by reviewing the literature and conducting our own basic research. Different subgroups seemed to need significantly different outcome concepts for the ROM system to meaningfully support clinical conversation and exploration. For example, adolescent mental health patients between 13 and 19 years of age underscored how (a) affect consciousness, (b) safer identities, (c) safer connections with others, (d) approach behavior, and (e) boundaries were the relevant outcomes for them (Lavik et al., 2018a). In contrast, adult mental health stakeholders underscored how social role safety and performance, therapeutic preferences, problem ownership, and agency were important measurement concepts for them, while substance abuse patients underscored impulsivity and coping as key points (Moltu et al., 2021). On the basis of a wide exploration of potentially relevant outcome concepts, we embarked on studies aimed at constructing, implementing, evaluating, and changing a ROM system.

The First Iteration of Norse Feedback Adult Version

We launched the program with the general adult outpatient population and adult substance abuse population (Moltu et al., 2018). Preparing for this cornerstone study of our program, we performed a stakeholder analysis. This process resulted in defining treatment providers as one group of key stakeholders, including psychologists, psychiatrists, psychiatric nurses, and clinical social workers. Another key group of stakeholders was mental health and substance abuse patients. Within this group we found it important to represent all age groups, both outpatients and inpatients, and patients in various diagnostic and treatment groups. The first study comprised a selective sample of 55 stakeholders across these categories (36 women, 19 men). We used individual interviews and focus groups to explore the foundational research question: *What do patients and clinicians want and need from a ROM and CF system?* (Moltu et al., 2018).

The key learning was that different stakeholder groups had simultaneously overlapping and idiosyncratic needs from the ROM system. This is a point that we have developed later in the Norse Feedback Action Research Program. Moreover, we have learned that our early focus on therapists and patients as stakeholders was insufficient, and that leaders, supervisors, and managers are important both in a development and implementation perspective (Douglas et al., 2023; Douglas et al., 2024; Hovland & Moltu, 2019). However, the overlapping area between therapists and patients was the dominant need for the ROM system to support their treatment collaboration directly. Put colloquially, both therapists and patients wanted a ROM system to be developed and designed to help them achieve open conversations, make it easier to develop trust, and make it easier to define and monitor shared treatment goals. Needs that were specific to the patient perspective were of particular interest for patients' functioning in everyday roles during treatment, as well as early warning signals for worsening status (Moltu et al., 2018). Therapists in particular defined needs for the ROM system to let them monitor the degree to which patients felt ownership and agency in the therapeutic process. They also wanted the ROM system to monitor some symptoms, and risk factors, such as suicidal ideation and intention.

The resulting NF adult system for ROM/CF, in its most current version at the time of writing, included a total bank of 96 items necessary for measuring the stakeholder needs with moderate to good precision (McAleavey et al., 2021), within a multidimensional strategy. But, except in very rare instances, no patient ever responds to all items. An algorithm continuously learns which items and constructs are most relevant for any individual and automatically selects those at each administration. Some items, such as those measuring social determinants of health, are administered at regular time intervals throughout a process. Due to the complexities of a real-time personalization algorithm, the NF system is predominantly delivered over a bespoke technological solution integrated with the electronic health record (EHR) system but is in some installations implemented directly within the EHR (Youn et al., 2024).

The First Iteration of the Norse Adolescent Version

For the adolescent patient population, we replicated the study design that we had employed in the adult arm of the program. The stakeholder analyses resulted in child and adolescent psychiatrists, clinical psychologists, clinical social workers, and clinical pedagogues being the treatment provider stakeholders, and adolescents between 13–18 years, all with mental health treatment experiences, some with child welfare and protection service experiences, as well as a group from an adolescent service user movement, being invited as participants and co-developers of the ROM system for adolescents (Lavik et al., 2023). This study included 56 selected stakeholders across these categories. We used individual interviews and focus groups to explore the major research question: *What do adolescent service users and their therapists need from a clinical feedback system?*

The key learning that resulted was that the needs of adolescents and their providers were very different from what we learned in the adult treatment context. For adolescents, relevant outcomes were more future oriented, directed toward personally relevant future goals and autonomy. This is consistent with our own studies for this population (e.g., Lavik et al., 2018a; Stige et al., 2021) and those of others (e.g., Jacob et al., 2023). Put colloquially, adolescents seem to want to be going places, and going there autonomously, rather than returning where they previously were. Moreover, the stakeholders in this study were also clear that ROM systems would need to support very delicate relational processes, in which the adolescent patients worked hard to trust the adult helper. The therapeutic relationship, and the way a ROM system can support it, seemed much closer to "the real relationship" (Gelso, 2009), with its focus on authenticity and genuineness, rather than the working alliance (Bordin, 1979), for the young persons. Moreover, while adolescent therapists and the adolescents themselves agreed on most ROM needs, the therapists wanted the ROM system to help them know when an adolescent patient was ready to end therapy.

The resulting Norse Feedback Adolescent scales and measurement strategies follow the stakeholder needs studies including therapists and young patients (Lavik et al., 2023). In developing and testing item-level formulations, we implemented collaborative workshops with young expert-by-experience partners to find the language that communicated well.

Interestingly, while the adult population was happy about the system having automated algorithms to establish which would be relevant items for them, adolescents thought very differently about this. Adolescents, in general, are in the process of developing autonomy in several areas of their lives that coincide with their needing help from mental health services (e.g., Lavik et al., 2018a, 2018b). This manifested in the adolescents' desire to have a very strong say regarding what the ROM system asks of them. In interviews they explained that they were all too used to adults asking them sensitive and personal questions without being invited to do so, and that they did not want a ROM system to continue that trend. Rather, they themselves wanted to be the one inviting questions within different themes. Consequently, we did not implement an automatic algorithm for this population but, rather, as an example, ask voluntary screening items about each scale. For example: *Do you want to be asked questions about your family relationships?* If they say yes, the system opens the item within that scale, whereas if they say no, they remain collapsed. Figure 7.2 shows the clinician report from Norse Adolescent.

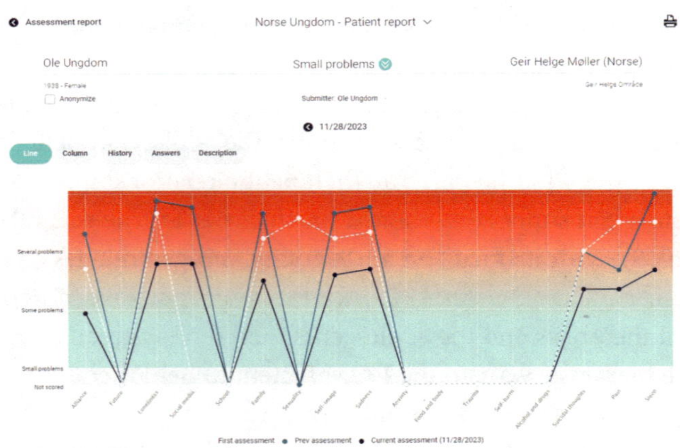

Figure 7.2 Norse Adolescent Clinician Report

Current Challenge: Maintaining the Norse Feedback Action Research Program Methods at Scale

Up until now, we have discussed our values and clinical background, and how the NF program established the principles for collaboration and conducted the first stages of development and implementation of ROM and CF for adults and adolescents. This constitutes the basis of the action research (AR) program. But AR is not finalized at initiation, but rather, it is a continuous process of revision, refinement, and further development based on collaboration and scientific methods (Veseth & Moltu, 2021). Given that NF is used more than 10,000 times each month, with new implementations doubling that number already scheduled, scaling issues emerge. The current NF iteration is the third cycle, and the program aims to develop generationally every 18–24 months (Nordberg et al., 2021). By which principles do we organize the collaboration within the AR program at this scale?

Importantly, not all clinics that use NF as a ROM and CF are active parts of the PRN. The key principle for the program is that all clinics using the system are invited to partake. For those who are members of the AR program, a guiding principle is that qualitative, clinical, quantitative, and psychometric knowledge are all important, potentially equally so. For example, in evaluating the clinical use and usefulness of an NF scale, our quantitative approach uses item response theory to establish which items have the most potentially clinically useful information for patients with various problem severity levels (McAleavey et al., 2021). Figure 7.3 illustrates such analyses from an early version of the NF Eating Problems scale. As we can observe from the figure, Items 47 and 86 do not provide meaningful information at any severity level. In practical terms, this means that a clinician cannot infer anything with certainty based on whether a patient's response is high or low to these items, at least in relationship to the other items on that scale: People with both high and low Eating Problems scores might endorse these items. These two items do not distinguish patients with severely disordered eating from those with healthier eating habits, in general. In the ongoing NF development process, this lack of information is grounds for evaluating if these items should be deleted, refined, or changed to something else. If psychometric analyses alone called the shots, these items would almost certainly be removed from the measure immediately.

However, in the NF AR program, this form of knowledge is balanced with clinical and qualitative knowledge. Clinicians in focus groups could,

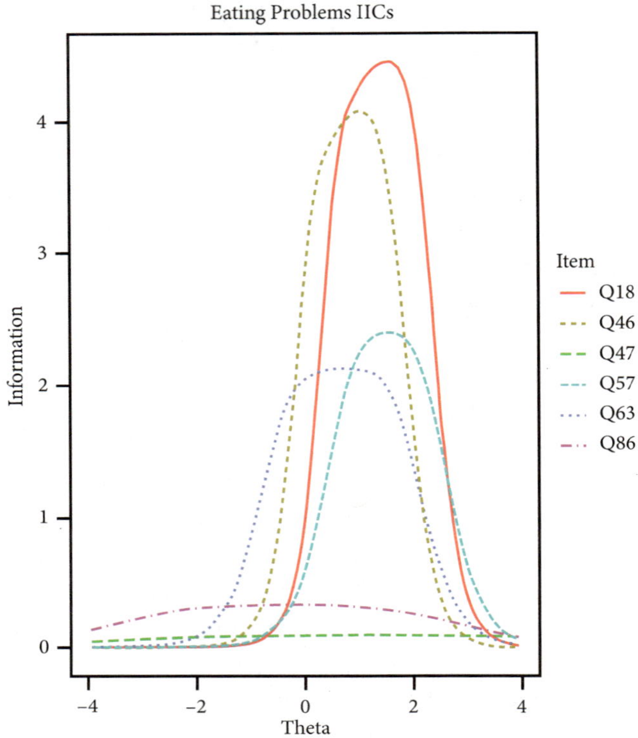

Figure 7.3 Item Information Curves Example for Eating Scale

for example, faced with the information that Item 47 did not contribute well psychometrically, underscore how the very same item helped them initiate important conversations about self-care with their patients, or that one patient–therapist dyad used these items as the main target for treatment, since they were uniquely appropriate to that case. Any such observations would alert us to important clinical content in the items and encourage revision and/or reorganization of these items into different scales. Focus group analyses are based on qualitative research methods (McAleavey & Moltu, 2021), which complement the quantitative psychometric development. From a psychometric perspective, these focus groups provide essential content-expert feedback, an essential method to ensure content validity (Skorupiński, 2015). Balancing clinical pragmatic usefulness with psychometric precision has been the guiding principle in the structure of evaluation for all versions of NF in collaboration with the PRNs.

Initially, while the use of NF was modest, the structure of the participatory stakeholder research processes was easy to understand and implement. At scale, a comprehensive organization is harder to achieve. A central technology to deliver, develop, and disseminate research developments has been important to our methods development. We believe that implementation science and technological development will become even more important in the future to support the established AR methodology. Key deliverables for these two strands of development within our program will be the anonymized and legitimate quantitative data pooled for real-time analyses, compliant with necessary regulatory and ethical standards, and solid infrastructures for qualitative and clinical perspectives to make their way to the core research team as efficiently and fully as possible.

Implementation Science Is a Pivotal Part

From the start of the program, we have conducted implementation studies to guide the use and development of the system. The first reason for this was the established knowledge, summarized by Boswell and colleagues (2015), that even the most well-documented ROM and CF systems were hard to implement in routine care. As part of our AR methodology, our practice-based collaborators have been mandated to have a strong voice in the systems development and implementation. Consequently, the eventual objections to using the systems were not to be seen as opposition, defensiveness, or barriers that needed to be overcome but, rather, as legitimate input that could potentially improve the process and product. Complementarily, our practice partners have been committed to playing constructive parts in development rather than rejecting ROM and CF at large. Based on this multiway commitment, our early implementation science projects resulted in establishing feasibility and systems development needs (Hovland & Moltu, 2020), accumulating implementation knowledge (Hovland & Moltu, 2019), and understanding the range of training needs underlying ROM and CF as a clinical skill (Hovland et al., 2023). Understanding the developers/implementers and the clinician/patients as equal partners in an implementation has been highly productive.

We have found that our views and experiences with implementation, clinical partnerships, and clinical training resonate with those of our international colleagues. Being part of international networks of researchers and developers, such as the International Network for Psychotherapy Innovations and Research into Effectiveness (INSPIRE) led by Dr. Kim de Jong (de Jong et al., 2024), has been pivotal to our learning and dissemination. As part of this collegial group we have studied implementation across different systems and countries (Douglas et al., 2023) in which we have tested concepts and methods from our own thinking alongside those of others (Douglas et al., 2024). In our experience, the INSPIRE group is pivotal in advocating the generous sharing of ideas, insights and collaboration between people working with different ROM systems toward the shared aim of improving services for our patients (Moltu et al., 2025).

Examples: Research and Quality Appraisal

As evident throughout this chapter, a range of data on different clinical constructs is collected through the routine clinical use of the NF system. Our objective is to measure constructs that are helpful to the clinical process for each individual dyad, while also supporting practiced-based research and clinical quality assurance processes with quality data. To exemplify how a research purpose and use case differs from an MBC quality assurance use case, we describe briefly two different projects and their characteristics. The Understanding and Improving Change processes in psychotherapy (U&I Change) is an example of a research application, and the Leadership dashboard projects is an example of a quality assurance application.

The *U&I Change* project has emerged as an adjunct to the NF AR program. It is driven primarily by questions derived from researcher stakeholders in the consortium. Focused primarily on the under-studied population of patients with substance use disorders (SUDs), the overarching research question is how people change through therapy—what changes when, under what circumstances, and why? The range of constructs measured routinely with NF supports research into these questions.

Based at the St. Olavs University Hospital and the Norwegian University of Science and Technology (NTNU) in Trondheim, Norway, the U&I Change project collaborates with four specialized substance use treatment clinics and one mental health center in Central Norway. In a first wave of data collection $N = 700$ patients consented to the inclusion of their NF responses as well as information on diagnoses, demographics, and session attendance in a longitudinal observational study.

A preliminary factor analysis of this data material explored what item response patterns on the NF might reflect early change or lack thereof in the early phase of SUD treatment (McAleavey et al., 2024). Results indicated that a negative affect or depression/anxiety scale, comprised of items that focus on internalizing symptoms across 12 NF scales and derived by factor analysis of the disaggregated within-patient deviation scores from each patient's average scores across time, is a structurally valid index to capture early change. This is especially useful for patients who, as is frequently the case in early SUD treatment, are currently abstinent from substance use. In a second preliminary analysis (Regueras et al., 2024), this depression/anxiety variable was found to predict next-session alliance scores, but not the other way around. This somewhat unexpected finding suggests that within-patient or statelike alliance might not drive therapeutic change in SUD treatment to the same degree as that which has been demonstrated in the treatment of mental health disorders (e.g., Zilcha-Mano & Fisher, 2022). Further analyses will seek to identify predictors of treatment outcome among the many treatment process indicators assessed with the NF.

Moving forward, the U&I Change project plans to utilize the existing research infrastructure to increase the sample size. Moreover, public registry information will be included such as usage of illness and welfare benefits, cost of care, and cause of death. This extension of the study will allow for the modeling of complex associations, in subgroups of patients, between NF-assessed treatment process indicators and "hard," definitive, observable outcomes.

The *clinical quality analytics approach* is based on a different set of questions by a different group of stakeholders. In a collaborative program, ROM and CF systems also need to address the needs of the clinical leadership (Douglas et al., 2023). These stakeholders have the distinct task of evaluating and comparing many patients' treatment outcomes at one time, which means they might have fundamentally different priorities with regard to what a ROM system should provide. Most administrators prioritize questions related to program evaluation and development: How well is the service performing? Which types of services within my center could use additional training or other resources? We have implemented a set of feedback tools designed to give clinic leaders an overview of their clinics' performance on key indicators and a relatively simple set of analyses that they can interpret. These reports have become increasingly automated, allowing for on-demand processing of reports when required in various treatment settings.

The *NF Leader Dashboard* distributes these data analyses. It is a live-updated website where administrators can observe basic interpretations of the aggregate NF data and receive relevant comparisons and analyses. In Figure 7.4 we show an example of a center that has several internal divisions that are compared, in this example, with a specialist mental health service norm population. In the example, the box-and-whisker plot shows the scale scores of patients in treatment processes across multiple sites, showing in broad strokes any differences. In this example, the Sad Affect scale is compared both visually and statistically across the current clinic divisions and the comparison sample. As indicated in the text, the smooth

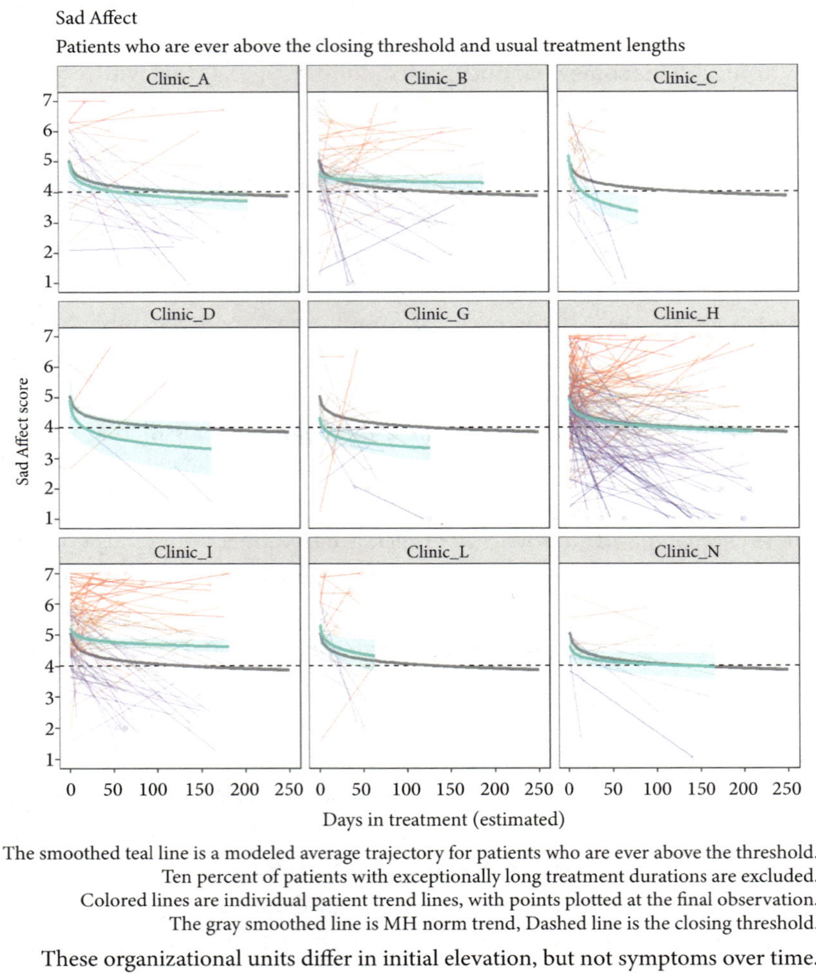

Figure 7.4 Quality Management via Patient Self-Report Data

lines are group-level averages, or the expected values for each group over time in treatments. The straight lines, which vary from red to blue, are individual-level trajectories, simplified in order to be more interpretable.

In this anonymized report, we can see that each subclinic has a different volume of data, different typical treatment lengths, and different average outcomes over time. The individual clinic leader may wish to evaluate several parts of this plot. Again, the text at the bottom is a summary of a statistical model that controls for several relevant features. Here, it suggests that the differences between these nine clinics are best understood as simply differences between initial severity: The clinics all have roughly equal change over time in Sad Affect, after controlling for relevant variables, in the underlying statistical model. This is addressing a question posed by many clinic leaders in our collaboration: How well do we do compared with benchmarks?

The advantage of using a computerized system for analysis and interpretation is that these reports can be run within a few minutes of receiving the request and can include quite complex analyses under the hood without overburdening the reader with technical details. The downsides are that it does not include very detailed clinical interpretation or expert advice, leaving these to the clinic administrator to determine on their own.

Conclusion and Future Development

In this chapter, we have presented the problem that made us initiate the NF AR program and discussed the values that made us think that developing a system bottom up by collaborating with clinicians and patients in a structured and committed way was necessary. From the qualitative and collaborative start, we have presented how we developed two main ROM and CFS—Norse Feedback adult and Norse Adolescent—and implemented them in practice. Presently, this local start has developed into an international program with multiple implementations, research projects, researchers, health organizations, and universities collaborating to change practice. Our current work is related to solidify the science in this collaborative organization at scale, and to develop our work further. When programs grow, they develop and change. What seemed the right choices early on might not be as constructive today. A growing program necessitates a strong and continuous assessment of ethical and regulatory aspects (Låver et al., 2024).

Recently, we won a major grant to develop and research the next step in the AR program, called Norse Impact. This grant gives us opportunity to make use of our significant data streams toward the goal of providing digital resources to equitably empower patients before and between treatment sessions. In implementing this next step of our program, collaboration within our PRNs and with our international colleagues will be the objective, the method, and the joy of working on it.

References

Binder, P. E., Holgersen, H., & Nielsen, G. H. (2010). What is a "good outcome" in psychotherapy? A qualitative exploration of former patients' point of view. *Psychotherapy Research, 20*(3), 285–294. https://doi.org/10.1080/10503300903376338

Bordin, E. S. (1979). The generalizability of the psychoanalytic concept of the working alliance. *Psychotherapy: Theory, Research & Practice, 16*(3), 252–260. https://doi.org/10.1037/h0085885

Boswell, J. F., Kraus, D. R., Miller, S. D., & Lambert, M. J. (2015). Implementing routine outcome monitoring in clinical practice: Benefits, challenges, and solutions. *Psychotherapy Research, 25*(1), 6–19. https://doi.org/10.1080/10503307.2013.817696

Castonguay, L. G., Barkham, M., Lutz, W., & McAleavey, A. A. (2013). Practice-oriented research. Approaches and applications. In M. J. Lambert (Ed.), *Bergin and Garfield's Handbook of Psychotherapy and Behavior Change. Sixth edition.* (pp. 85–133). John Wiley & Sons Ltd.

Castonguay, L. G., Barkham, M., Youn, S. J., & Page, A. C. (2021). Practice-based evidence—Findings from routine clinical settings. In M. Barkham, W. Lutz, & L. G. Castonguay (Eds.), *Bergin and Garfield's handbook of psychotherapy and behavior change: 50th anniversary edition* (7th ed., pp. 191–222). John Wiley & Sons, Inc.

Castonguay, L. G., Nelson, D. L., Boutselis, M. A., Chiswick, N. R., Damer, D. D., Hemmelstein, N. A., Jackson, J. S., Morford, M., Ragusea, S. A., Roper, J. G., Spayd, C., Weizer, T., & Borkovec, T. D. (2010). Psychotherapists, researchers, or both? A qualitative analysis of psychotherapists' experiences in a practice research network. *Psychotherapy: Theory, Research, Practice, Training, 47*(3), 345–354. https://doi.org/10.1037/a0021165

Castonguay, L. G., Pincus, A. L., & McAleavey, A. A. (2015). Practice research network in a psychology training clinic: Building an infrastructure to foster early attachment to the scientific-practitioner model. *Psychotherapy Research, 25*(1), 52–66. https://doi.org/10.1080/10503307.2013.856045

Clark, D. M., Canvin, L., Green, J., Layard, R., Pilling, S., & Janecka, M. (2018). Transparency about the outcomes of mental health services (IAPT approach): An analysis of public data. *The Lancet, 391*(10121), 679–686. https://doi.org/10.1016/S0140-6736(17)32133-5

Clark, D. M., Layard, R., Smithies, R., Richards, D. A., Suckling, R., & Wright, B. (2009). Improving access to psychological therapy: Initial evaluation of two UK demonstration sites. *Behaviour Research and Therapy, 47*(11), 910–920. https://doi.org/10.1016/j.brat.2009.07.010

Connolly, M. B., & Strupp, H. H. (1996). Cluster analysis of patient reported psychotherapy outcomes. *Psychotherapy Research, 6*(1), 30–42. https://doi.org/10.1080/10503309612331331558

Davidson, L., Shaw, J., Welborn, S., Mahon, B., Sirota, M., Gilbo, P., McDermid, M., Fazio, J., Gilbert, C., Breetz, S., & Pelletier, J.-F. (2010). "I don't know how to find my way in the world": Contributions of user-led research to transforming mental health practice. *Psychiatry*, *73*(2), 101–113. https://doi.org/10.1521/psyc.2010.73.2.101

de Jong, K., Douglas, S., Wolpert, M., Delgadillo, J., Aas, B., Bovendeerd, B., Carlier, I., Compare, A., Edbrooke-Childs, J., Janse, P., Lutz, W., Moltu, C., Nordberg, S., Poulsen, S., Rubel, J. A., Schiepek, G., Schilling, V. N. L. S., van Sonsbeek, M., & Barkham, M. (2024). Using progress feedback to enhance treatment outcomes: A narrative review. *Administration and Policy in Mental Health and Mental Health Services Research*. Advance online publication. https://doi.org/10.1007/s10488-024-01381-3.

Douglas, S., Bovendeerd, B., Van Sonsbeek, M., Manns, M., Milling, X. P., Tyler, K. S., Bala, N., Satterthwaite, T., Hovland, R. T., Amble, I., Atzil-Slonim, D., Barkham, M., de Jong, K., Kendrick, T., Nordberg, S. S., Lutz, W., Rubel, J. A., Skjulsvik, T., & Moltu, C. (2023). A clinical leadership lens on implementing progress feedback in three countries: Development of a multidimensional qualitative coding scheme. *Administration and Policy in Mental Health and Mental Health Services Research*. Advance online publication. https://doi.org/10.1007/s10488-023-01314-6

Douglas, S., Page, A. C., Moltu, C., Kyron, M., & Satterthwaite, T. (2024). The connections matter: Bi-directional learning in program evaluation and practice-oriented research. *Administration and Policy in Mental Health and Mental Health Services Research*, *51*(3), 318–335. https://doi.org/10.1007/s10488-023-01304-8

Eldal, K., Veseth, M., Natvik, E., Davidson, L., Skjølberg, Å., Gytri, D., & Moltu, C. (2019). Contradictory experiences of safety and shame in inpatient mental health practice—A qualitative study. *Scandinavian Journal of Caring Sciences*, *33*(4), 791–800. https://doi.org/10.1111/scs.12674

Gelso, C. J. (2009). The real relationship in a postmodern world: Theoretical and empirical explorations. *Psychotherapy Research*, *19*(3), 253–264. https://doi.org/10.1080/10503300802389242

Grindheim, Ø., McAleavey, A., Iversen, V., Moltu, C., Tømmervik, K., Govasmark, H., & Brattland, H. (2024). Response processes for patients providing quantitative self-report data: A qualitative study. *Quality of Life Research*, *33*(11), 2949–2961. https://doi.org/10.1007/s11136-024-03749-2.

Grindheim, Ø., Moltu, C., Iversen, V., McAleavey, A., Tømmervik, K., Govasmark, H., & Brattland, H. (2024). Points of departure: A qualitative study exploring relational facilitators and barriers in the first treatment session. *Psychotherapy Research*, *35*(1), 155–169. https://doi.org/10.1080/10503307.2023.2297996

Hovland, R. T., & Moltu, C. (2019). Making way for a clinical feedback system in the narrow space between sessions: Navigating competing demands in complex healthcare settings. *International Journal of Mental Health Systems*, *13*(1), Article 68. https://doi.org/10.1186/s13033-019-0324-5

Hovland, R. T., & Moltu, C. (2020). The challenges of making clinical feedback in psychotherapy benefit all users: A qualitative study. *Nordic Psychology*, *72*(3), 248–262. https://doi.org/10.1080/19012276.2019.1684348

Hovland, R. T., Ytrehus, S., Mellor-Clark, J., & Moltu, C. (2023). How patients and clinicians experience the utility of a personalized clinical feedback system in routine practice. *Journal of Clinical Psychology*, *79*(3), 711–728. https://doi.org/10.1002/jclp.22992

Jacob, J., Edbrooke-Childs, J., Costa da Silva, L., & Law, D. (2023). Notes from the youth mental health field: Using movement towards goals as a potential indicator of service change and quality improvement. *Journal of Clinical Psychology*, *79*(3), 697–710. https://doi.org/10.1002/jclp.23195

Klein, M. J., & Elliott, R. (2006). Client accounts of personal change in process–experiential psychotherapy: A methodologically pluralistic approach. *Psychotherapy Research*, *16*(1), 91–105. https://doi.org/10.1080/10503300500090993

Krägeloh, C. U., Czuba, K. J., Billington, D. R., Kersten, P., & Siegert, R. J. (2015). Using feedback from patient-reported outcome measures in mental health services: A scoping study and typology. *Psychiatric Services, 66*(3), 224–241. https://doi.org/10.1176/appi.ps.201400141

Kroenke, K., Spitzer, R. L., & Williams, J. B. (2001). The PHQ-9: Validity of a brief depression severity measure. *Journal of General Internal Medicine, 16*(9), 606–613. https://doi.org/10.1046/j.1525-1497.2001.016009606.x

Låver, J., McAleavey, A., Valaker, I., Castonguay, L. G., & Moltu, C. (2024). Therapists' and patients' experiences of using patients' self-reported data in ongoing psychotherapy processes - A systematic review and meta-analysis of qualitative studies. *Psychotherapy Research, 34*(3), 293–310. https://doi.org/10.1080/10503307.2023.2222896

Lavik, K. O., Veseth, M., Frøysa, H., Binder, P. E., & Moltu, C. (2018a). What are "good outcomes" for adolescents in public mental health settings? *International Journal of Mental Health Systems, 12*, Article 3. https://doi.org/10.1186/s13033-018-0183-5

Lavik, K. O., Veseth, M., Frøysa, H., Binder, P. E., & Moltu, C. (2018b). "Nobody else can lead your life": What adolescents need from psychotherapists in change processes. *Counselling and Psychotherapy Research, 18*(3), 262–273. https://doi.org/10.1002/capr.12166

Lavik, K. O., Veseth, M., Frøysa, H., Stefansen, J., Nøtnes, J. C., & Moltu, C. (2023). This is what I need a clinical feedback system to do for me: A qualitative inquiry into perspectives of adolescents and their therapists. *Journal of Clinical Psychology, 79*(3), 729–747. https://doi.org/10.1002/jclp.23100

Leamy, M., Bird, V., Le Boutillier, C., Williams, J., & Slade, M. (2011). Conceptual framework for personal recovery in mental health: Systematic review and narrative synthesis. *The British Journal of Psychiatry, 199*(6), 445–452. https://doi.org/10.1192/bjp.bp.110.083733

McAleavey, A. A. (2022). One in five, not one in 17, youth patients deteriorate during psychotherapy for depression. *European Child & Adolescent Psychiatry, 33*(1), 315–318. https://doi.org/10.1007/s00787-022-01943-6

McAleavey, A. A., & Moltu, C. (2021). Understanding routine outcome monitoring and clinical feedback in context: Introduction to the special section. *Psychotherapy Research, 31*(2), 142–144. https://doi.org/10.1080/10503307.2020.1866786

McAleavey, A. A., Nordberg, S. S., & Moltu, C. (2021). Initial quantitative development of the Norse Feedback system: A novel clinical feedback system for routine mental healthcare. *Quality of Life Research, 30*(11), 3097–3115. https://doi.org/10.1007/s11136-021-02825-1

McAleavey, A., Førde, H., Grindheim, Ø., Moltu, C., & Brattland, H. (2024, June 26–29). *A good outcome in early substance abuse treatment* [Panel presentation]. Society of Psychotherapy Research 55th Annual International Meeting, Ottawa, Canada.

Moltu, C., McAleavey, A. A., Helleseth, M. M., Møller, G. H., & Nordberg, S. S. (2021). How therapists and patients need to develop a clinical feedback system after 18 months of use in a practice-research network: A qualitative study. *International Journal of Mental Health Systems, 15*, Article 43. https://doi.org/10.1186/s13033-021-00465-z

Moltu, C., Stefansen, J., Nøtnes, J. C., Skjølberg, Å., & Veseth, M. (2017). What are "good outcomes" in public mental health settings? A qualitative exploration of clients' and therapists' experiences. *International Journal of Mental Health Systems, 11*, Article 12. https://doi.org/10.1186/s13033-017-0119-5

Moltu, C., Stefansen, J., Svisdahl, M., & Veseth, M. (2012). Negotiating the coresearcher mandate - service users' experiences of doing collaborative research on mental health. *Disability & Rehabilitation, 34*(19), 1608–1616. https://doi.org/10.3109/09638288.2012.656792

Moltu, C., van Sonsbeek, M., Bovendeerd, B., de Jong, K., Barkham, M., Sales, C., McAleavey, A., Mellor-Clark, J., Schwartz, B., Nordberg, S., Jacob, J., Lutz, W., Kaldo, V., Janse, P., Brattland, H., Compare, A., & Douglas, S. (2025). How can measurement based care improve psychotherapy processes and mental health service delivery? A synthesis of expert perspectives. *World Psychiatry, 24(2), 279*

Moltu, C., Veseth, M., Stefansen, J., Nøtnes, J. C., Skjølberg, Å., Binder, P. E., Castonguay, L. G., & Nordberg, S. S. (2018). This is what I need a clinical feedback system to do for me: A qualitative inquiry into therapists' and patients' perspectives. *Psychotherapy Research, 28*(2), 250–263. https://doi.org/10.1080/10503307.2016.1189619

Nelson, G., Ochocka, J., Griffin, K., & Lord, J. (1998). "Nothing about me, without me": Participatory action research with self-help/mutual aid organizations for psychiatric consumer/survivors. *American Journal of Community Psychology, 26*(6), 881–912. https://doi.org/10.1023/a:1022298129812

Nordberg, S. S., Jaso-Yim, B. A., Sah, P., Schuler, K., Eyllon, M., Pennine, M., Hoyler, G. H., Barnes, J. B., Murillo, L. H., O'Dea, H., Orth, L., Rogers, E., Welch, G., Peloquin, G., & Youn, S. J. (2024). Evaluating the implementation and clinical effectiveness of an innovative digital first care model for behavioral health using the RE-AIM framework: Quantitative evaluation. *Journal of Medical and Internet Research, 26*, Article e54528. https://doi.org/10.2196/54528

Nordberg, S. S., McAleavey, A. A., & Moltu, C. (2021). Continuous quality improvement in measure development: Lessons from building a novel clinical feedback system. *Quality of Life Research, 30*(11), 3085–3096. https://doi.org/10.1007/s11136-021-02768-7

Regueras, D. F., McAleavey, A., Grindheim, Ø., Moltu, C., & Brattland, H. (2024). *Longitudinal analysis of early change in therapy: link between treatment outcomes and therapeutic relationship in substance use disorders* [Panel presentation]. Society of Psychotherapy Research 55th Annual International Meeting, Ottawa, Canada.

Sales, C. M., Neves, I. T., Alves, P. G., & Ashworth, M. (2018). Capturing and missing the patient's story through outcome measures: A thematic comparison of patient-generated items in PSYCHLOPS with CORE-OM and PHQ-9. *Health Expectations, 21*(3), 615–619. https://doi.org/10.1111/hex.12652

Shimokawa, K., Lambert, M. J., & Smart, D. W. J. (2010). Enhancing treatment outcome of patients at risk of treatment failure: Meta-analytic and mega-analytic review of a psychotherapy quality assurance system. *Journal of Consulting and Clinical Psychology, 78*(3), 298–311. https://doi.org/10.1037/a0019247

Skar-Fröding, R., Clausen, H., Šaltytė Benth, J., Ruud, T., Slade, M., & Heiervang, K. S. (2022). Associations between personal recovery and service user-rated versus clinician-rated clinical recovery, a cross-sectional study. *BMC Psychiatry, 22*, Article 42. https://doi.org/10.1186/s12888-022-03691-y

Skorupiński, P. M. (2015). American Educational Research Association, American Psychological Association, National Council on Measurement in Education, Standards for educational and psychological testing. *Kwartalnik Pedagogiczny, 60*(4), 201–203.

Solstad, S. M., Castonguay, L. G., & Moltu, C. (2019). Patients' experiences with routine outcome monitoring and clinical feedback systems: A systematic review and synthesis of qualitative empirical literature. *Psychotherapy Research, 29*(2), 157–170. https://doi.org/10.1080/10503307.2017.1326645

Solstad, S. M., Cooper, M., Sundet, R., & Moltu, C. (2023). Effects and experiences of idiographic patient-reported outcome measures for feedback in psychotherapy: A systematic review and secondary analysis of the empirical literature. *Psychotherapy Research*, Advance online publication. https://doi.org/10.1080/10503307.2023.2283528

Solstad, S. M., Kleiven, G. S., Castonguay, L. G., & Moltu, C. (2021). Clinical dilemmas of routine outcome monitoring and clinical feedback: A qualitative study of patient experiences. *Psychotherapy Research, 31*(2), 200–210. https://doi.org/10.1080/10503307.2020.1788741

Stige, S. H., Barca, T., Lavik, K. O., & Moltu, C. (2021). Barriers and facilitators in adolescent psychotherapy initiated by adults—Experiences that differentiate adolescents' trajectories through mental health care. *Frontiers in Psychology, 12*, Article 633663. https://doi.org/10.3389/fpsyg.2021.633663

Stilgoe, J., Owen, R., & Macnaghten, P. (2013). Developing a framework for responsible innovation. *Research Policy*, *42*, 1568–1580. https://doi.org/10.1016/j.respol.2013.05.008

Veseth, M., Binder, P. E., Borg, M., & Davidson, L. (2017). Collaborating to stay open and aware: Service user involvement in mental health research as an aid in reflexivity. *Nordic Psychology*, *69*(4), 256–263. https://doi.org/10.1080/19012276.2017.1282324

Veseth, M., & Moltu, C. (2021). Å utvikle kunnskap i spenningen mellom ulike perspektiver - refleksjoner rundt brukermedvirkning i forskning. [Developing knowledge in the tension between different perspectives. Participatory approaches to research]. In D. von Heimburg & O. Ness (Eds.), *Aksjonsforskning. Samskapt kunnskap som endrer liv og samfunn*. [Action Research. Co-created knowledge that changes lives and societies]. Fagbokforlaget.

Westbye, H. J., Moltu, C., & McAleavey, A. A. (2024). eXplainable AI for routine outcome monitoring and clinical feedback. *Counselling and Psychotherapy Research*, Article e12764. https://doi.org/10.1002/capr.12764

Wisting, L., Johnson, S. U., Bulik, C. M., Andreassen, O. A., Rø, Ø., & Bang, L. (2021). Psychometric properties of the Norwegian version of the Patient Health Questionnaire-9 (PHQ-9) in a large female sample of adults with and without eating disorders. *BMC Psychiatry*, *21*(1), Article 6. https://doi.org/10.1186/s12888-020-03013-0.

Youn, S. J., Jaso, B., Eyllon, M., Sah, P., Hoyler, G., Barnes, J. B., Jarama, K., Murillo, L., O'Dea, H., Orth, L., Pennine, M., Rogers, E., Welch, G., & Nordberg, S. S. (2024). Leveraging implementation science to integrate digital mental health interventions as part of routine care in a practice research network. *Administration and Policy in Mental Health and Mental Health Services Research*, *51*, 348–357. https://doi.org/10.1007/s10488-023-01292-9

Zilcha-Mano, S., & Fisher, H. (2022). Distinct roles of state-like and trait-like patient–therapist alliance in psychotherapy. *Nature Reviews Psychology*, *1*(4), 194–210. https://doi.org/10.1038/s44159-022-00029-z

SECTION III

THERAPEUTIC CHANGE: PRECISION AND PROCESS

8

Leveraging Theoretical and Technological Innovations to Study the Mechanisms That Underlie Therapeutic Change

Dana Atzil-Slonim

The enduring question that has long intrigued clinicians and researchers—what works for whom in therapy, and when—remains as vital as ever. What has evolved, however, is our ability to investigate this question with greater precision and depth, leading to increasingly robust answers. Mental health is a complex, dynamic phenomenon, and the vast array of therapeutic options available to clinicians at any given moment makes addressing this question a formidable challenge. Practice-oriented research, which focuses on understanding and enhancing psychological treatments as they are delivered in real-world clinical settings, at times through close collaboration between clinicians and researchers, plays a pivotal role in driving this progress forward. By investigating treatments as they unfold in real-world clinical settings, practice-oriented research facilitates the accumulation of large and rich data sets of verbal and nonverbal information from psychotherapy sessions, which are essential for examining the complex dynamics that unfold in therapy. When based on strong partnerships between clinicians and researchers, practice-oriented research creates ecosystems where clinical practice and theory actively shape research, and research findings, in turn, continually refine and improve practice. These collaborations are especially crucial given recent breakthroughs in clinical science and technology, which offer great promise for deepening our understanding of the mechanisms underlying therapeutic change.

In this chapter, I will illustrate how adopting a practice-oriented research approach has enabled our interdisciplinary team of clinicians and researchers to work in close partnership, leveraging innovations in

Dana Atzil-Slonim, *Leveraging Theoretical and Technological Innovations to Study the Mechanisms That Underlie Therapeutic Change*. In: *Practice-Based Evidence in the Psychological Therapies*. Edited by: Louis G. Castonguay et al., Oxford University Press. DOI: 10.1093/9780197748336.003.0008 clinical science and cutting-edge technology to deepen our understanding of therapeutic change mechanisms. The chapter begins with a personal prologue that outlines the motivations behind our team's decision to establish a research clinic rooted in a practice-oriented research approach. The second section addresses critical challenges in the conceptualization, treatment, and research of mental health. Next, I describe significant theoretical shifts in clinical science that have opened new avenues for addressing these challenges, such as the transition from general treatment models to transtheoretical interventions and processes and the shift from one-person to two-person psychology. The fourth section details how our team has harnessed these theoretical innovations, alongside advancements in multimodal analysis and artificial intelligence (AI), to study intrapersonal (within clients) and interpersonal (between clients and therapists) dynamics associated with improved treatment outcomes. Finally, the chapter concludes by discussing the clinical and training implications derived from our studies.

Prologue

The first time I encountered the divide between practice and research in mental health care was when I found myself caught in a heated debate between clinicians at the university counseling center and researchers in the psychology department. The emotional intensity and deep conviction on both sides fascinated me. As an experienced clinician, I felt a strong connection to my colleagues in the counseling services. However, I was embarking on my PhD focused on psychotherapy research, and as I listened, I recognized significant merit in the arguments from both sides. On the one hand, I resonated with my fellow clinicians who argued that therapeutic interactions are incredibly complex, with each client–therapist encounter being unique and influenced by a range of factors such as momentary mindset and mood, transference, countertransference, culture, personal values, and life events. Such complexity makes studying what works for whom and when an immense challenge. The clinicians asserted that randomized controlled trials (RCTs) testing the efficacy of specific manualized treatments for specific diagnoses do not adequately address the needs of their real-world clients who often do not meet inclusion and exclusion criteria of typical RCT. They also felt that the pressure to adhere to manualized treatments, as suggested by such studies, hinder their ability to flexibly tailor interventions to their clients' immediate needs.

On the other hand, the researchers questioned how psychotherapy could remain unstudied, emphasizing our ethical obligation to determine what works (and what doesn't) to ensure our treatments are effective. While acknowledging the uniqueness and complexity of therapeutic encounters, they argued that achieving a certain level of evidence-based generalization is possible (for similar debates, see Safran, 2012).

The opportunity to bridge these polarized voices arose when following my PhD advisors, Orya Tishby and Gaby Shefler, and later my postdoctoral mentor, Hadas Wiseman, I became acquainted with the Society for Psychotherapy Research (SPR) community. It was through SPR that I discovered the paradigm of practice-oriented research. The idea of studying psychotherapy in naturalistic settings without imposing constraints on clinical routines, while fostering ongoing dialogue between clinicians and researchers (Castonguay, 2011), opened up the possibility of conducting systematic research that responds to clinicians' need to understand how they can improve their ability to help their clients achieve better therapeutic outcomes.

A few years later, as a new faculty member in the Department of Psychology at Bar-Ilan University (BIU), my colleagues—Eshkol Rafaeli, Eva Galboa-Schechtman, Tuvia Peri, Ilanit Hasson-Ohayon, and Rivka Tuval-Mashiach—and I led a transition in our departmental clinic inspired by the practice-oriented research approach. At the time, the clinic had a 50-year history of providing subsidized services to over 300 clients at any given time. Our team transformed this facility into a modern research clinic where all clinical activities are available for scientific inquiry. We designed a research protocol enabling session-by-session monitoring, within-session recording, and therapist feedback. This transition was greatly influenced by our close collaboration with Wolfgang Lutz from the University of Trier, whose generous sharing of research measures and procedures for continuous clinical monitoring was invaluable.

Transitioning a large mental health clinic into one with intensive research capabilities is challenging on many levels, including personal and ideological. The younger generation tended to embrace the project enthusiastically, but senior members expressed concerns. Wolfgang's extensive experience in establishing a similar center was instrumental in helping us navigate these challenges. Following his advice, we implemented a gradual transition process, offering the option to participate in research and fostering collaborative discussions where concerns could be raised and solutions brainstormed. This approach gradually reduced concerns and fostered engagement. Collaborative discussion groups of clinicians and researchers with expertise in psychotherapy and computer science shaped the research direction in our training clinic, determined the feedback provided to students and interns, and identified the research questions we wished to explore. It was particularly encouraging to see clinicians not previously involved in research actively participating in these discussions.

What started as building a bridge between research and practice has since grown, within our interdisciplinary team at BIU, into a vibrant ecosystem of co-creation. In this environment, complementary expertise of clinicians and researchers provides opportunities to develop studies that are both clinically meaningful and scientifically rigorous. Our work has been profoundly influenced by significant shifts in clinical science that emphasize the importance of identifying transtheoretical, intrapersonal, and interpersonal dynamics associated with improved treatment outcomes. Traditional research methods were insufficient for studying these complex dynamics, so we applied advances in AI and multimodal analyses. The large-scale, naturalistic data we gradually collected enabled us to use computational tools to address our research questions. In turn, research findings are fed back to clinicians and new questions are generated. This iterative process is a collective effort to address and overcome the key challenges that our field faces in practice and research.

Some Major Challenges for Mental Health Practice and Research

The prevalence of mental health issues is increasing, affecting millions of people worldwide (World Health Organization, 2019). At present, three major issues hinder the effectiveness of mental health services. First, the need for services greatly exceeds the availability of adequate providers (Kazdin, 2021). A major cause of this gap is the overreliance on the dominant treatment delivery model of one-on-one in-person sessions conducted by highly trained professionals.

Second, individuals who seek mental health services are often suboptimally diagnosed. Most clinicians and psychotherapy researchers administer semi-structured interviews following the *Diagnostic and Statistical Manual of Mental Disorders* (American Psychiatric Association, 2013) or the *International Classification of Diseases* (World Health Organization, 2019) for diagnostic purposes. However, these diagnostic systems have been increasingly criticized for focusing on categorical syndromes and failing to capture the high comorbidity, considerable interpersonal heterogeneity, and very pronounced intrapersonal variability of mental distress (Hofmann & Hayes, 2019).

Third, current mental health treatments are not sufficiently effective. Only 50% of clients receiving psychological, pharmacological, or combined interventions show adequate improvement in symptom severity following treatment. Moreover, among those who benefit from treatment, many experience a relapse within a year (Cuijpers et al., 2021).

The urgent need to identify mechanisms that facilitate therapeutic change and optimize healthcare practices has prompted researchers to study which therapy processes lead to positive treatment outcomes (e.g., Crits-Christoph & Gibbons, 2021). However, these efforts are constrained by four key factors. First, most previous studies rely on self-report measures. Although subjective measures are essential in psychotherapy research, they are limited by clients' self-awareness and motivation (Kazdin, 2008). Vast amounts of data from intake interviews and psychotherapy sessions, including both verbal and nonverbal behaviors of clients and therapists, remain largely untapped. Utilizing this data could significantly enhance diagnostic and treatment procedures, improve intervention selection, and deepen our understanding of the mechanisms driving therapeutic change.

Second, while researchers have developed numerous observer coding systems to tap what occurs within psychotherapy sessions (e.g., Pascual-Leone & Greenberg, 2005), observational coding is labor intensive and expensive. As such, these studies tend to focus on a small number of therapeutic components in relatively small samples of clients at limited time points (Crits-Christoph & Gibbons, 2021). Third, many of the efforts to explore how client characteristics are associated with treatment outcomes have produced mixed findings. While some characteristics have been robustly linked to outcomes, positively or negatively, others remain less clearly established, reflecting the complexity of mental health challenges and the need to move beyond pretreatment evaluations to consider the multifaceted and dynamic nature of mental distress (Constantino et al., 2021).

Fourth, attempts to identify effective interventions have produced promising findings for certain techniques but have not consistently yielded robust evidence across the broad range of techniques studied. The emphasis on single techniques and their direct links to treatment outcomes may oversimplify the inherently complex and dynamic therapeutic process (Hill & Norcross, 2023). This is because in actual clinical practice, clinicians attend to moment-by-moment verbal and nonverbal information to guide their clinical action. Expert therapists can quickly and flexibly tailor their interventions to meet a client's immediate needs and facilitate superior treatment outcomes. However, given the heterogeneous nature of mental distress and the vast array of potential interventions available to therapists at any given time, this presents a significant challenge that current research methods find hard to tackle. To truly understand what works for whom and when in psychotherapy, it is critical to consider the dynamic nature of the therapeutic interaction and the diverse contexts in which interventions are implemented (Hill & Norcross, 2023).

To tackle these challenges, our interdisciplinary team has combined a theory-based approach with a data-driven methodology to deepen our understanding of the intrapersonal and interpersonal dynamics underlying therapeutic change as it takes place in day-to-day clinical routine.

Leveraging Advances in Clinical Science to Study Intrapersonal and Interpersonal Dynamics in Psychotherapy

Recent theoretical shifts in clinical science have significantly influenced our work. The first major shift is the transition from manualized, disorder-focused treatments to a transtheoretical approach that emphasizes building a consensual knowledge base that integrates evidence-based interventions and processes that are central across diverse therapeutic models and tailoring interventions to meet clients' specific needs at specific times (Gaines & Goldfried, 2021; Hofmann & Hayes, 2019). Rather than perpetuating the long-standing competition among different schools of psychotherapy, contemporary research advocates for a unified language that synthesizes empirical evidence from across the spectrum of therapeutic approaches (Castonguay et al., 2021).

The second major shift is "the relational turn" (Aron & Harris, 2014). This shift marks the transition from a one-person psychology, focused solely on the client's mental experience, to a two-person psychology that acknowledges the therapist's significant involvement in the process of change (Eubank et al., 2018). The traditional view of a unidirectional therapeutic process (i.e., the therapist intervenes and the client is affected) has been replaced by the growing recognition that the therapist's role is dynamically intertwined with the client's experience (e.g., Atzil-Slonim & Tschacher, 2020). Relational psychotherapy theorists argue that the complexity of the therapeutic process can only be understood through the dynamic interplay between client and therapist, who are mutually but asymmetrically shaped and transformed over time (e.g., Aron & Harris, 2014).

Building on these theoretical advancements, as well as on clinical observations and collaborative discussions among clinicians in the community clinic, I developed the Multimodal Intrapersonal and Interpersonal Dynamics (MIND) framework, which shifts focus from categorical classification of traitlike psychopathology to modifiable intrapersonal dynamics, and from manualized disorder-focused treatments to interactive interpersonal dynamics tailored to clients' needs at specific moments (Atzil-Slonim, 2024). MIND begins by creating a transtheoretical coding scheme that breaks down clients' experiences and client–therapist interactions into core building blocks central to major therapeutic approaches, including cognitive behavioral therapy (CBT) and psychodynamic, interpersonal, relational, and experiential models. This framework highlights that human experience consists of multiple self-states that fluctuate and change over time (Beck et al., 2021; Bromberg, 1998; Stiles, 2001). Each self-state comprises identifiable elements characterized by specific combinations of Affect, Behaviour, Cognition, and Desire (ABCD; Revelle, 2007) that tend to be coactivated in a meaningful manner and directed either toward the self or others (Lazarus & Rafaeli, 2023). Self-states are a dynamic phenomenon—at any given moment, a particular self-state may dominate, with individuals varying in their ability to dynamically shift between self-states and/or reflect upon and foster dialogue among their self-states (Bromberg, 1998). Self-states often elicit complementary responses from others, creating cyclical self–other dynamics. Some of these dynamics are adaptive, fostering positive interactions; others are maladaptive, detrimental to the individual and their relationships. Along with the fundamental elements that shape an individual's experience, MIND integrates key therapist interventions central to a wide range of therapeutic theories—such as empathy, meaning-making, exploration, regulation, and guidance (Hill & Norcross, 2023), with common factors that define the therapeutic relationship, such as quality of the therapeutic alliance (Eubanks et al., 2018; Flückiger et al., 2020). Modern psychotherapy models increasingly emphasize the importance of enhancing a client's ability to transition from maladaptive to adaptive self-other dynamics (e.g., Fosha, 2001; McCullough et al., 2003). Focusing on self-states in theory, research, and practice can reveal within-person adaptive and maladaptive states, as well as between-person differences in typical self-states. Clients often seek therapy when they become stuck in a rigid self-state, where one dominant self-state overshadows the internal dialogue among diverse self-states. By attuning to clients' shifting self-states, therapists can help clients dampen maladaptive self-states and amplify adaptive ones.

The following clinical scenario demonstrates the coding scheme's application and illustrates a client's transition from a maladaptive to a more adaptive self-state (see Figure 8.1). Mika (a pseudonym), a woman from our sample in her late 30s, is diagnosed with major depressive disorder (MDD). She attributes this episode to a deep sense of hopelessness, doubting her ability to resume her career after years devoted to motherhood. She feels unsupported by her husband in rediscovering her path. In Session 9 she says,

> I just feel . . . stuck. I'm awful, like I have no direction. I was looking at this program I used to seriously consider before the kids and everything. But now? There's no way I'll get in. And even if I did, it's three years, and at my age, the chances of finding a job after that . . . they're so slim. It's just so frustrating. I mentioned the idea of enrolling to my husband yesterday, just casually, and he dismissed it right away. I knew he'd think it was unrealistic. I probably shouldn't have even brought it up.

Mika's dominant self-state seems to be self-critical and maladaptive. She expects rejection and anticipates criticism from her husband (D). She harshly judges herself, believing she's "awful," while perceiving her husband as critical (C). By avoiding a direct expression of her need for self-competence and casually mentioning it (B), she may have unintentionally signaled that it was unimportant, leading her husband to dismiss it, reinforcing her sense of defeat and hopelessness (A). The dialogue in Figure 8.1 illustrates how the therapist skillfully works with Mika, empathically reflecting her emotional experience, providing meaning to her experience, and helping her amplify the expression of her adaptive need for self-fulfillment and support in relationships.

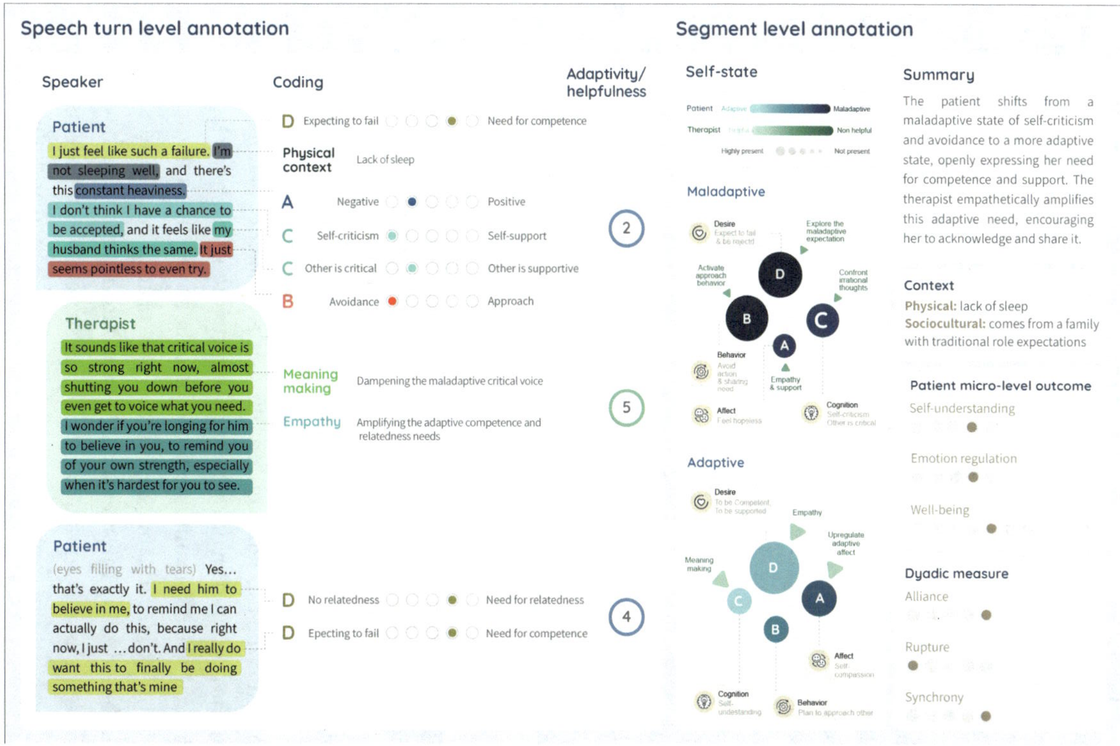

Figure 8.1 An Illustration of the MIND Coding Scheme in One Psychotherapy Session Drawn From Our Data Set

Note: Adaptivity (of the client), helpfulness (of the therapist), alliance, rupture, and synchrony (between the client and therapist) are all measured on a scale from 1 (low levels) to 5 (high levels). A = Affect; B = Behavior; C = Cognition; D = Desire.

Identifying moment-to-moment clients' self-states and therapists' interventions is a strong starting point for revealing intra- and interpersonal dynamics, predictive of positive (and negative) outcomes. Previous efforts to model clients' self-states and identify effective interventions relied on predefined theoretical frameworks (e.g., Arntz & Jacob, 2013) instead of data-driven analyses of how self-state elements cluster, contextual factors that correlate with self-states, and their temporal dynamics. The complexity of potential ABCD element combinations, the varying contexts in which they emerge, and the diverse interventions therapists might employ posed significant challenges for traditional research methodologies. However, recent advances in AI, natural language processing (NLP), signal processing, and machine learning offer tremendous potential to aid this process. Thus, the development of the MIND framework follows an iterative approach where core theoretical concepts provide a starting point, while advanced AI methods process large-scale psychotherapy data sets, including verbal but also nonverbal interaction, to reveal patterns in clients' states and therapist responses. This process aims to offer new insights into therapeutic dynamics, further refining the theoretical framework. By harnessing both theory-based and data-driven insights, this framework aims to illuminate what works, for whom, and when in psychotherapy.

Leveraging Advances in Multimodal Analysis and AI to Study Intrapersonal and Interpersonal Dynamics in Psychotherapy

Communication between clients and therapists occurs through verbal and nonverbal channels. While the content of the conversation offers valuable insights into internal thoughts and emotions, the subtleties of how things are said—the tone and rhythm of voice, facial expressions, and body language—provide crucial yet often underexplored facets of the therapeutic process. Recent technological advances in signal processing, NLP, and computer vision, combined with the rise of AI and machine learning, have shown great promise in assessing mental health constructs by employing quantitative methods that can capture and model key behavioral and physiological signals (Cohn et al., 2018). For instance, researchers have demonstrated the effectiveness of these technologies in automatically detecting the severity of individuals' depressive symptoms based on text, vocal tone, and facial expressions (e.g., Ringeval et al., 2019). These technologies have the potential to increase precision in diagnosis and deepen our understanding of the mechanisms of change in psychotherapy by enabling the coding of moment-by-moment verbal and nonverbal responses from clients and therapists (Aafjes-van Doorn et al., 2021). This granular focus on smaller units within therapy sessions allows researchers to process larger data sets, leading to more comprehensive insights into psychotherapy processes and outcomes.

AI-based models are particularly adept at handling the complexity of mental health data (Delgadillo & Atzil-Slonim, 2023). Among the AI techniques available, deep learning models—especially transformer-based language models—have emerged as the leading approach (Devlin et al., 2018). These models undergo pre-training on massive data sets of unlabeled text, using a process called unsupervised learning, where the model learns to predict randomly masked words, which enables it to identify patterns in language's underlying structure and context. After pre-training, the model can be fine-tuned for specific tasks, such as emotion recognition in psychotherapy texts, by adjusting parameters for optimal performance on the targeted task. The versatility and effectiveness of transformer-based language models have led to their widespread application across various research domains, including mental health (Delgadillo & Atzil-Slonim, 2023). Recent advancements in computing power and deep learning have propelled progress in generative AI and large language models (LLMs) (Bommasani et al., 2021). These models excel in understanding and generating human language, detecting intricate patterns, and capturing contextual nuances. By fine-tuning these models for specific tasks, researchers can significantly enhance their performance and accuracy (Stade et al., 2023). For example, after pre-training, the model can be fine-tuned for a specific task on a smaller labeled data set, such as emotion recognition in natural psychotherapy text by updating its parameters to optimize a task-specific objective.

In the next sections, I will describe how our research team has used these advanced techniques to analyze verbal and nonverbal data from recorded sessions to identify intrapersonal and interpersonal dynamics associated with improved psychotherapy outcomes. The data used for these analyses were collected as part of the day-to-day routine of our university-based community clinic, which serves both as a training facility and as a provider of subsidized services to the community. This routine clinical setting offers access to a large and diverse sample of clients and therapists, with natural variability in interventions that reflects real-world therapeutic conditions. Unlike data from RCTs, which often involve controlled and homogeneous samples, clinical routine data captures the richness and complexity of everyday practice, making it particularly well-suited for AI and machine learning analyses. This diversity allows advanced models to uncover patterns and dynamics that align closely with the nuanced realities of therapeutic interactions. Additionally, the comprehensive data set provides researchers with exceptional flexibility to tailor their analyses to various research questions. For instance, some studies focus on specific populations, such as clients diagnosed with depression, while others investigate broader phenomena using larger, heterogeneous samples. This flexibility ensures that the data serves as a robust foundation for addressing a wide range of research questions, enabling meaningful collaboration between researchers and clinicians and driving advancements in practice-oriented research that directly enhance therapeutic outcomes.

Using Multimodal Analysis and AI to Study Intrapersonal Dynamics in Day-to-Day Clinical Practice

Intrapersonal dynamics refer to the ways in which internal elements—such as emotions, behaviors, cognitions, desires, and physiological responses—fluctuate and interact within an individual over time (Bar-Kalifa & Atzil-Slonim, 2020). There are various intrapersonal dynamics such as variability (the range or amplitude of an internal element across time), instability (the magnitude of changes in an internal element from one moment to the next), and inertia (how well an internal element can be predicted from its previous state). Intrapersonal dynamics play a crucial role in psychological well-being and psychopathology and reflect an individual's ability to regulate their affect, behaviors, cognitions, and desires in response to environmental changes (Houben et al., 2015).

Our team has used advanced analytics to explore various intrapersonal dynamics and identify their links to treatment outcomes (e.g., Bar-Kalifa & Atzil-Slonim, 2020; Paz et al., 2021, 2024). A key dynamic consistently associated with positive outcomes across modalities is affective flexibility—the capacity to dynamically modulate emotional responses from one moment to the next (Houben et al., 2015). Greater affective flexibility implies increased sensitivity and adaptability to external (e.g., environmental changes) and internal (e.g., regulatory processes) factors fundamental to psychological well-being. Conversely, low levels of affective flexibility (rigidity) often underlie various psychopathologies.

In one study, we utilized network analysis to examine session-by-session intrapersonal emotional dynamics (Bar-Kalifa & Atzil-Slonim, 2020). The network approach conceptualizes emotions as interconnected constructs that influence one another over time. Our sample included clients from a university-based community clinic who provided at least 10 session reports (required for network analysis) and who scored below the clinical cutoff on the Outcome Rating Scale (ORS; Miller et al., 2003), indicating functioning below clinically defined levels. Clients reported their functioning at the start of each session and their emotional experiences at the end.

The dominant therapeutic approach in the clinic is short-term psychodynamic psychotherapy (Summers et al. 2024). However, a pan-theoretical training paradigm encourages therapists to be attuned to clinically meaningful scenarios and integrate evidence-based techniques from various approaches, including schema therapy (Arntz & Jacob, 2013) and cognitive behavioral therapy (Beck, 1993). Therapies lasted roughly 9 months to one year due to the academic calendar, and therapist assignment was based on availability and caseload. Our main goal was to identify differences in the temporal intrapersonal emotional network structures—specifically the density of emotional connections between treatment responders and non-responders. We found that clients who did not improve exhibited denser networks, suggesting less affective flexibility over time.

In this study, we relied on clients' self-reported emotions at the end of each session. While these reports provide valuable insights, they may not fully capture the range of emotions experienced throughout a session. Facial expressions offer an additional rich source of data on intrapersonal affective dynamics, as clinicians often use them to assess subtle emotional shifts. Computer vision methods, such as facial expression analysis, have been used to detect mood disorders (Girard et al., 2015). To examine the link between emotional flexibility and depression, we analyzed facial expression data from 283 video-recorded sessions of 58 clients diagnosed with MDD, as part of routine care at the clinic (Atzil-Slonim, Yehezkel, et al., 2024). Inclusion criteria required a primary MDD diagnosis based on the Mini-International Neuropsychiatric Interview (MINI; Sheehan et al., 1998) and a Beck Depression Inventory-II (BDI-II; Beck et al., 1996) score above 17 at intake. Although this subset was stringently defined, the clients were selected retrospectively from data originally collected in a naturalistic setting, thus preserving the routine-practice context. Emotional flexibility was measured using FaceReader (Höfling et al., 2020), an automated facial expression recognition system. Findings revealed a significant association between emotional flexibility and depressive symptoms at both the client and session levels. Clients with more severe depressive symptoms exhibited lower emotional flexibility overall, and sessions in which clients reported greater depressive symptoms were characterized by reduced emotional flexibility within that session. Importantly, this association remained significant beyond the overall valence of emotions. These results highlight emotional flexibility as a key factor in depression and demonstrate the utility of facial expression analysis in capturing moment-to-moment emotional fluctuations with greater time resolution.

While facial expressions convey emotional valence, vocal tone reflects affective arousal. In a recent study, we examined intrapersonal affective flexibility by analyzing both facial and vocal expression data from 279 therapy sessions involving 30 clients treated by 24 therapists (Paz et al., 2024). This data was retrospectively drawn from a larger data set of routine therapy sessions. Inclusion criteria required therapy to have dual-microphone recordings, last at least 15 sessions, and include adequate audio quality and pre-/post-session functioning measure (ORS) for at least every other session. Facial valence was measured using FaceReader, while vocal arousal was assessed through a computerized analysis of pitch, intensity, and energy features (Paz et al., 2021). Findings showed that clients with greater flexibility in both facial and vocal affective measures experienced more improvement in well-being, both within individual sessions and across treatment. Figure 8.2 illustrates this pattern, comparing two clients: one with higher affective flexibility, who showed treatment gains, and another with lower flexibility, who experienced declines in functioning.

The ongoing assessment of nonverbal measures, such as vocal tone and facial expressions, and the ability to track fluctuations in affect within sessions may offer valuable clinical insights for both clients and therapists. Our findings indicate that greater flexibility in vocal arousal and facial expressions is associated with better treatment outcomes. By integrating these observations into their practice, therapists can enhance their attunement to clients' evolving emotional states and tailor interventions that promote greater emotional and psychological flexibility, ultimately fostering more adaptive therapeutic change.

Whereas facial expression and vocal tone measures provide insights into nonverbal intrapersonal dynamics, text analysis offers a window into the verbal aspects of therapy. Many of our studies have utilized state-of-the-art NLP techniques to analyze text from transcribed psychotherapy sessions.

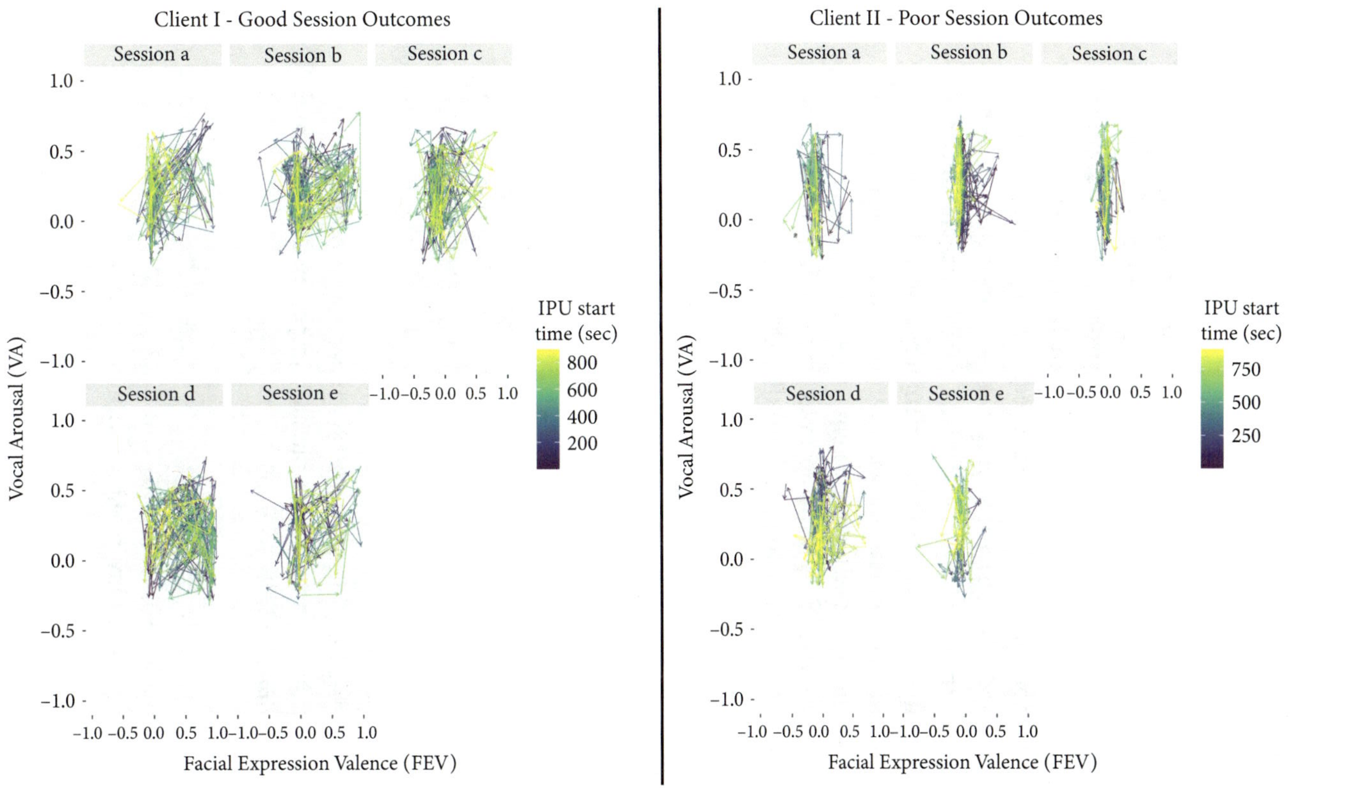

Figure 8.2 Intrapersonal Multimodal Flexibility Measures for Clients With Good and Poor Session Outcomes

Note: Each panel presents the affect dynamics of a single client over the course of five sessions. Each arrow represents the affective movement between consecutive interpausal units (IPUs). The x-axis represents the measured valence extracted from facial expressions; the y-axis represents the measured arousal extracted from the voice recordings of the clients. The color of the arrow represents the time course within the session: dark purple arrows represent measures from the beginning of the session. Yellow arrows represent measures from later parts of the session. Client I's flexibility was greater than Client II's flexibility. Correspondingly, Client I's average functioning improved during treatment, while Client II suffered a reduction in functioning across treatment. Importantly, for Client II, session d was marked by greater flexibility and greater improvement in well-being, but session e was marked by less flexibility and, accordingly, a reduction in functioning. Adapted from Paz et al., 2024.

For example, we employed transformer-based emotion recognition models to automatically label clients' emotions at the utterance level in a data set comprising 139,061 utterances from 872 sessions involving 68 clients and 52 therapists (Atzil-Slonim et al., 2024). The clients were selected from a sample of individuals who received treatment at the clinic as part of the routine monitoring. The selection criteria included: (a) a treatment duration of at least 15 sessions, and (b) complete data, including audio recordings for transcription and session-by-session questionnaires available for each client. We then used the labeled data to examine the coherence between verbally expressed emotions and self-reported emotions, employing multilevel modeling to assess the association between emotional coherence and improvement in functioning throughout treatment. The emotion recognition model demonstrated moderate performance, and we found a significant association between verbally expressed emotions and self-reported emotions. Coherence in clients' negative emotions was associated with improved functioning, underscoring the importance of emotional coherence to overall well-being.

These findings have important clinical implications, underscoring the need to help clients align their emotional experiences with the language they use to express them. Therapists can benefit from identifying clients or sessions where there is a pronounced dissociation between emotional experience and verbal expression, allowing them to tailor interventions that enhance emotional awareness and expression. Integrating computerized verbal and nonverbal assessments into existing feedback systems can provide therapists with valuable insights into within-session intrapersonal dynamics. By detecting moments when emotional flexibility or coherence fluctuate, therapists can adjust their interventions in real time to better support clients' emotional processing.

These studies focused on intrapersonal dynamics and processes; however, many intrapersonal dynamics occur in an interpersonal context, and psychotherapy is quintessentially such a context.

Using Multimodal Analysis and AI to Study Interpersonal Dynamics in Day-to-Day Clinical Practice

Interpersonal dynamics refer to the processes by which the affect, cognition, behavior, and desire of interacting individuals are interconnected and mutually influenced (Butler, 2015). When people interact, they naturally coordinate their emotions, perceptions, behavior, and physiology, leading to an interweaving of their self-states that enhance connection and communication (Feldman, 2012). For example, when people engage in a naturally flowing conversation, their vocal tones tend to become aligned, and their bodies tend to start moving in the same cadence. These interactional dynamics can take various forms, such as synchrony (simultaneous alignment of affect, physiology, or behavior), coregulation (time-lagged influences between partners), convergence (gradual reduction of differences), and congruence (stable correspondence in emotional states). Interpersonal dynamics occur across numerous relational contexts, including between children and their caregivers (e.g., Feldman, 2012), between romantic partners (e.g., Butler, 2015), and even among strangers (Cwir et al., 2011). Moreover, these biobehavioral linkages are associated with a wide range of meaningful outcomes, such as healthy development (e.g., Feldman, 2012) and overall relationship quality (e.g., Butler, 2015).

Many psychotherapy theories emphasize the importance of interpersonal dynamics between clients and therapists (e.g., Aron & Harris, 2014; Fosha, 2001). These theories suggest that for clients whose development may have lacked attuned interactions, therapy may provide a corrective emotional experience. Through such attuned interactions, the bond between client and therapist is thought to deepen, enabling clients to explore perceptions and process emotions more effectively. As clients and therapists dynamically attune to each other, the therapeutic relationship is hypothesized to strengthen, thereby enhancing regulation abilities and ultimately contributing to better therapeutic outcomes.

The pervasive, documented association between interpersonal dynamics and well-being across the life span has led our team to take a deeper interest in these dynamics to learn about the mechanisms of change in psychotherapy (Atzil-Slonim et al., 2023). For example, we examined the association between treatment outcomes and the congruence between client and therapist emotions as they co-fluctuated session by session (Atzil-Slonim et al., 2018). Clients and therapists were congruent in the emotions they experienced, but therapists experienced less intense positive (but not negative) emotions compared with their clients. Importantly, incongruence between clients and therapists in both positive and negative emotions predicted worsened symptoms in the next session.

In another study, we assessed therapists' ability to accurately infer clients' emotions and examined the associations between this empathic accuracy and treatment outcomes (Atzil-Slonim et al., 2019). We found that therapists accurately tracked their clients' negative (and, to a lesser extent, positive) emotions and tended to overestimate their clients' negative emotions and underestimate their clients' positive emotions. In addition, therapists' own emotions partially mediated the association between clients' emotions and therapists' assessments. Interestingly, therapists' inaccuracy in assessing positive emotions was associated with an increase in reported symptoms at the next session. These results demonstrate the importance of studying the emotional dynamics of both clients and therapists. The results also point to the risk on the part of therapists of neglecting clients' positive emotions and stress the importance of attending to these emotions.

This type of research gained momentum with the advent of methods that can handle the complexity of dense multimodal measurements during psychotherapy interactions. However, as research findings on interpersonal dynamics started to amass, it became clear that these dynamics are not always associated with favorable therapy outcomes (e.g., Reich et al., 2014; Schoenherr et al., 2021).[1] Our systematic review and meta-analysis (Atzil-Slonim et al., 2023) identified several directions that could contribute to a better understanding of the role of interpersonal dynamics in psychotherapy.

First, the context in which interpersonal dynamics occur is critical to understanding when a specific dynamic is beneficial and when it is not. For example, synchrony between dyads in situations of distress can lead to escalation and higher distress. In contrast, synchrony during situations of emotional pain or in the case of positive emotions may lead to feelings of shared experience and closeness. To investigate this, we measured physiological synchrony between clients and therapists, while considering the emotional context in which synchrony occurred (Bar-Kalifa et al., 2023). Synchrony was assessed by measuring respiratory sinus arrhythmia (RSA; an autonomic index associated with emotion regulation) from 28 client—therapist dyads in five preselected sessions during short-term dynamic therapy for depression. Compared with moments of unproductive emotional experience, we observed greater synchrony during moments of positive emotional experiences. Moreover, these patterns of synchrony were associated with clients' favorable evaluations of the session.

A second direction pointed out by our systematic review is that effective dyadic processes may depend on the therapists' ability to induce

[1] https://paperpile.com/c/W18ZHk/x4vd+o2bw

coregulation patterns, perhaps through self-regulating their own emotions in the session. To examine this idea, we used an automatic method of assessing arousal in vocal data and dynamic systems models to explore self-regulation and coregulation of affect dynamics within psychotherapy sessions and to determine whether these dynamics are associated with treatment outcomes (Paz et al., 2021; Paz et al., 2025). The data from 21,133 mean vocal arousal observations were extracted from 279 therapy sessions in a sample of 30 clients treated by 24 therapists (previously described in Paz et al., 2024). Clients self-reported their well-being level before and after each session using the ORS. Figure 8.3 illustrates the simultaneous effects of intra- and interpersonal pull forces of two kinds. In Panel A, affect dampening (downregulation) is depicted as resulting from the synergistic action of (a) the client's intrapersonal self-regulatory force toward homeostasis, and (b) an interpersonal coregulatory force in which the therapist's affect "pulls" the client's affect toward their baseline. In Panel B, affect amplification (upregulation) is depicted as resulting from the contrasting forces of (a) the client's intrapersonal self-regulatory force pulling toward homeostasis, compared with (b) an interpersonal coregulatory force in which the therapist's affect "pulls" the client's affect away from the baseline. The results indicated that clients' and the therapists' levels of arousal were "pulled" toward the other party's arousal level, and clients were "pulled" by their

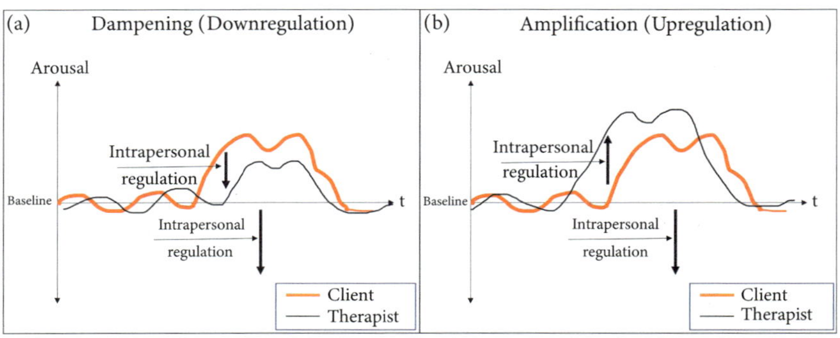

Figure 8.3 Illustration of Dampening and Amplification Models of Arousal Regulation

Note: Panel A represents the Dampening model in which the intrapersonal and interpersonal regulatory "pull forces" conjoin to dampen arousal toward the affective baseline. Panel B represents the Amplification model in which the intrapersonal regulatory force pulls toward the baseline while the interpersonal regulatory force pulls away from the affective baseline. Adapted from Paz et al., 2025.

therapists' vocal arousal toward their own baseline. Higher levels of interpersonal downregulation were associated with better session outcomes. The findings advance the idea that therapists who are synchronized with their clients, but at the same time downregulate their own and their client's affect, may be more successful in helping clients develop affective regulation capabilities.

In addition, our systematic review highlighted that most previous studies assessed dyadic processes in only one modality (e.g., movement, physiology, voice), but it is crucial to include a multimodal assessment of different dyadic processes to examine how these processes interact with each other throughout therapy. Furthermore, the systematic review suggested that differences in patterns of dyadic processes should be considered. Synchrony is commonly examined as a positive association between two persons' stream of bio-behavioral signals. One disadvantage of this approach is that it overlooks the fact that successful interpersonal coordination requires partners to dynamically move toward and away from each other (Mayo & Gordon, 2020). Recent models of synchrony suggest that people tend to move in and out of synchrony while they interact, and that these interpersonal dynamics are complementary and adaptive (Feldman, 2021; Mayo & Gordon, 2020).

We implemented these suggested directions in a study with a sample of 58 client–therapist dyads (the same sample as in Atzil-Slonim, Yehezkel, et al., 2024), where we examined whether flexibility in synchrony in five different modalities (i.e., body movement, facial expressions, heart rate, respiratory sinus arrhythmia, and electrodermal activity) is associated with session-level outcome (Sayda et al., 2024). Higher body movement flexibility in synchrony predicted better session outcomes. Facial expression flexibility in synchrony moderated the synchrony–outcome association, with higher synchrony predicting better outcomes when flexibility in synchrony was high, but poorer outcomes when flexibility in synchrony was low. No significant effects were found for physiological modalities. Multimodality and flexibility in synchrony may elucidate the mixed findings on when synchrony is beneficial and when it is not.

Many of our studies focused on the dialogue between clients and therapists and used advanced NLP techniques to first scale up psychotherapy data by automatically annotating key aspects of the therapeutic interaction and then drilling down to explore processes associated with improved therapeutic outcome. In one such study, we trained a logistic regression model to automatically detect the occurrence of a rupture from the text of the session, as rated by clients and therapists at the end of the session (Tsakalidis et al., 2021). The models achieved 83% accuracy in automatically identifying sessions in which both the client and the therapist reported a rupture. We were particularly interested in sessions where the client reported a rupture, but the therapist did not recognize its occurrence. Our models identified 40% of these instances. Interestingly, qualitative analysis revealed that it was easier for therapists in our sample to identify confrontational ruptures (i.e., the client moves against the therapist by expressing anger or dissatisfaction with the therapist or treatment, or by trying to apply pressure on the therapist) than to identify withdrawal ruptures (i.e., the client moves away from the therapist and the work of therapy). This finding is consistent with previous research (Eubanks et al., 2018) showing that therapists tend to better recognize confrontational ruptures and highlights the importance of using automated methods to capture ruptures that are challenging for therapists to detect.

We have also found that advanced deep-learning models can effectively identify client emotions and therapist interventions (Mayer et al., 2024). Using manually labeled transcripts of 196 therapy sessions—annotated speech turn by speech turn—we trained models to automatically label the remaining data. The models achieved 66% accuracy in detecting clients' emotions and 64% accuracy in detecting therapists' interventions. These scalings up of the data allow us to explore sequences of therapists' intervention and clients' emotional responses that are predictive of positive outcomes in the next steps.

Summary, Conclusions, and Implications for Practice and Training

This chapter was aimed at illustrating how adopting a practice-oriented research approach enabled our interdisciplinary team to identify some key challenges in mental health practice and research and to collaboratively discover ways to address them. Our focus has been on employing innovations in clinical science and technology to investigate the intrapersonal and interpersonal dynamics that underlie therapeutic change.

Several key insights emerged from our studies. Concerning intrapersonal dynamics, our findings highlight the central role of flexibility as a robust predictor of treatment outcome. Flexibility—in emotional experience, facial expressions, voice, cognitions, and even physiology—was associated with fewer symptoms and better treatment outcomes. Therapists may be encouraged to pay more attention to what occurs in both verbal and nonverbal channels to help their clients increase their psychological flexibility, helping them achieve better well-being. Our findings also revealed the importance of clients' experience of positive emotions and therapists' tendency to neglect these emotions in favor of a focus on negative emotions. By underestimating the importance of positive emotions, therapists may miss opportunities to draw on these emotions for constructive change. Our studies demonstrate the potential of advanced NLP methods to identify patterns in verbal communication, predictive of positive outcomes. For example, using computerized emotion recognition models, we demonstrated that coherence between emotional experience and expression is associated with favorable outcomes. Such computerized measures could be integrated into monitoring systems, providing a more precise assessment of individuals' progress over time.

At the interpersonal level, we found that synchrony between clients and therapists across multiple communication channels—such as movement, physiology, voice, and facial expression—was often linked to positive outcomes. However, our studies also suggested that the benefits of synchrony depend on additional factors, including therapists' ability to induce coregulation patterns and the emotional context in which synchrony occurs. Effective therapeutic outcomes appear to hinge on flexible movement between synchronized and unsynchronized states. Implementing a practice-oriented research approach, we have translated these insights back to the clinicians in our departmental clinic. For instance, based on our findings on the importance of empathic accuracy, our feedback system now visualizes the extent to which therapists were empathically accurate with clients, allowing therapists to enhance their attunement to their clients' fluctuating emotions from session to session.

Moreover, we demonstrated the ability of advanced NLP techniques to automatically detect important information about client states and therapeutic interactions. The models we developed automatically annotated nuanced elements within psychotherapy sessions, such as client emotions and therapist interventions. Model performance was comparable to human interrater reliability. This automatic annotation offers a cost-effective means of analyzing large data sets and yielding reliable insights into the processes driving therapeutic progress. Recent findings from our studies also highlight the usefulness of LLMs in generating clinically meaningful information, such as formulations of individuals' mental states.

These innovations can be integrated into session-by-session support tools, as well as in training and supervision to enhance therapy skills. For example, with the help of their supervisors, therapists in training can explore the feedback provided by the AI system and identify their clients' adaptive and maladaptive states as well as their own helpful and less helpful interventions. Ultimately, such feedback should facilitate the selection of the most appropriate interventions for a specific therapist to employ with a specific client at a specific time. We are currently developing an advanced feedback system that uses LLMs to generate clinically meaningful summaries, clients' formulation, and suggested sequences of interventions based on the session's verbal and nonverbal data. This development exemplifies the type of knowledge translation that practice-oriented research intentionally fosters, bridging innovative research with real-world clinical applications.

Despite these promising findings, several limitations must be acknowledged. The studies were conducted within the context of routine care in a training clinic, and some focused on specific client populations (e.g., individuals with MDD), which may restrict the generalizability of the results to other clinical settings and populations. Future research is needed to assess the extent to which these findings can be applied more broadly.

While AI and LLMs offer exciting opportunities to optimize mental health services, several challenges must be addressed to ensure their effective and ethical integration into clinical practice. LLMs are prone to factual errors, often called "hallucinations," and have known biases (Bang et al., 2023). As these systems continue to advance in their power and capabilities, there are concerns that they may pursue objectives that do not fully align with client needs. Additionally, the "black box" nature of AI models can hinder their adoption by mental health professionals, making it imperative that AI suggestions are explainable and transparent. These concerns underscore the importance of the practice-oriented research approach in fostering clinician–researcher collaboration for integrating AI-based monitoring and feedback systems into clinical routines. These systems must be developed with input from clinicians, guided by clients' preferences, and aligned with clinical knowledge. It is crucial that therapists are adequately trained to use these technologies, ensuring that AI systems augment rather than replace clinical decision-making. To address these challenges, our interdisciplinary team of clinicians and AI researchers is closely collaborating throughout the system's design, development, evaluation, and future real-world implementation, ensuring it prioritizes safety, ethics, and clients' well-being while meeting the needs of both clients and therapists.

Much work must be done to deepen our understanding of the mechanisms driving therapeutic change and refine our ability to tailor interventions to our clients' specific needs. By grounding our research questions in real-world practice and fostering interdisciplinary collaboration between psychotherapy researchers and AI experts, we can develop more appropriate methods to explore the dynamics that underlie therapeutic change. The ability to study these questions using large, naturalistic samples rich with multimodal data, capturing both verbal and nonverbal interactions between therapists and clients, brings us closer to uncovering more effective solutions to these pressing challenges.

References

Aafjes-van Doorn, K., Kamsteeg, C., Bate, J., & Aafjes, M. (2021). A scoping review of machine learning in psychotherapy research. *Psychotherapy Research, 31*(1), 92–116. https://doi.org/10.1080/10503307.2020.1808729

American Psychiatric Association. (2013). *Diagnostic and statistical manual of mental disorders* (5th ed.). https://doi.org/10.1176/appi.books.9780890425596

Arntz, A., & Jacob, G. (2013). *Schema therapy in practice: An introductory guide to the schema mode approach.* Wiley-Blackwell.

Aron, L., & Harris, A. (2014). *Relational psychoanalysis: Evolution of process* (Vol. 5). Routledge.

Atzil-Slonim, D. (2024). *Self-other dynamics: A transtheoretical coding manual.* PsyArXiv. https://doi.org/10.31234/osf.io/tk268

Atzil-Slonim, D., Bar-Kalifa, E., Fisher, H., Lazarus, G., Hasson-Ohayon, I., Lutz, W., & Rafaeli, E. (2019). Therapists' empathic accuracy toward their clients' emotions. *Journal of Consulting and Clinical Psychology, 87*(1), 33.

Atzil-Slonim, D., Bar-Kalifa, E., Fisher, H., Peri, T., Lutz, W., Rubel, J., & Rafaeli, E. (2018). Emotional congruence between clients and therapists and its effect on treatment outcome. *Journal of Counseling Psychology, 65*(1), 51.

Atzil-Slonim, D., Eliassaf, A., Warikoo, N., Paz, A., Haimovitz, S., Mayer, T., & Gurevych, I. (2024). Leveraging natural language processing to study emotional coherence in psychotherapy. *Psychotherapy, 61*(1), 82–92.

Atzil-Slonim, D., Soma, C. S., Zhang, X., Paz, A., & Imel, Z. E. (2023). Facilitating dyadic synchrony in psychotherapy sessions: Systematic review and meta-analysis. *Psychotherapy Research, 33*(7), 898–917.

Atzil-Slonim, D., & Tschacher, W. (2020). Dynamic dyadic processes in psychotherapy: Introduction to a special section. *Psychotherapy Research, 30*(5), 555–557.

Atzil-Slonim, D. A., Yehezkel, I., Paz, A., Bar-Kalifa, E., Wolff, M., Dar, A., & Gilboa-Schechtman, E. (2024). Facing change: Using automated facial expression analysis to examine emotional flexibility in the treatment of depression. *Administration and Policy in Mental Health and Mental Health Services Research, 51*(4), 501–508.

Bang, Y., Cahyawijaya, S., Lee, N., Dai, W., Su, D., Wilie, B., Lovenia, H., Ji, Z., Yu, T., Chung, W., Do, Q. V., Xu, Y., & Fung, P. (2023). *A multitask, multilingual, multi-modal evaluation of ChatGPT on reasoning, hallucination, and interactivity*. In J. C. Park, Y. Arase, B. Hu, W. Lu, D. Wijaya, A. Purwarianti et al. (Eds.), *Proceedings of the 13th International Joint Conference on Natural Language Processing and the 3rd Conference of the Asia-Pacific Chapter of the Association for Computational Linguistics (Volume 1: Long Papers)*. Association for Computational Linguistics. (pp. 675–718). https://aclanthology.org/2023.ijcnlp-main.45/

Bar-Kalifa, E., & Atzil-Slonim, D. (2020). Intrapersonal and interpersonal emotional networks and their associations with treatment outcome. *Journal of Counseling Psychology, 67*(5), 580–594.

Bar-Kalifa, E., Goren, O., Gilboa-Schechtman, E., Wolff, M., Rafael, D., Heimann, S., Yehezkel, I., Scheniuk, A., Feldman, R, & Atzil-Slonim, D. (2023). Clients' emotional experience as a dynamic context for client–therapist physiological synchrony. *Journal of Consulting and Clinical Psychology, 91*(6), 367.

Beck, A. T., Finkel, M. R., & Beck, J. S. (2021). The theory of modes: Applications to schizophrenia and other psychological conditions. *Cognitive Therapy and Research, 45*, 391–400. https://doi.org/10.1007/s10608-020-10098-0

Beck, A. T., Steer, R. A., & Brown, G. K. (1996). *Beck Depression Inventory* (BDI-II): *Manual and questionnaire*. The Psychological Corporation.

Bommasani, R., Hudson, D. A., Adeli, E., Altman, R., Arora, S., von Arx, S., Bernstein, M. S., Bohg, J., Bosselut, A., Brunskill, E., Brynjolfsson, E., Buch, S., Card, D., Castellon, R., Chatterji, N., Chen, A., Creel, K., Davis, J. Q., Demszky, D., & Liang, P. (2021). *On the opportunities and risks of foundation models*. arXiv preprint arXiv:2108.07258. https://arxiv.org/abs/2108.07258

Bromberg, P. M. (1998). *Standing in the spaces: Essays on clinical process, trauma, and dissociation*. Analytic Press.

Butler, E. A. (2015). Interpersonal affect dynamics: It takes two (and time) to tango. *Emotion Review, 7*(4), 336–341.

Castonguay, L. G. (2011). Psychotherapy, psychopathology, research and practice: Pathways of connections and integration. *Psychotherapy Research, 21*, 125–140, https://doi.org/10.1080/10503307.2011.563250

Castonguay, L. G., Barkham, M., Youn, S. J., & Page, A. C. (2021). Practice-based evidence-findings from routine clinical settings. In M. Barkham, W. Lutz, & L. G. Castonguay (Eds.), *Bergin and Garfield's handbook of psychotherapy and behavior change* (pp. 129–186). Wiley.

Chim, J., Tsakalidis, A., Gkoumas, D., Atzil-Slonim, D., Ophir, Y., Zirikly, A., Resnik, P., & Liakata, M. (2024). Overview of the clpsych 2024 shared task: Leveraging large language models to identify evidence of suicidality risk in online posts. In A. Yates, B. Desmet, E. Prud'hommeaux, A. Zirikly, S. Bedrick, S. MacAvaney, K. Bar, M. Ireland, & Y. Ophir (Eds.), *Proceedings of the 9th Workshop on Computational Linguistics and Clinical Psychology (CLPsych 2024)* (pp. 177–190). Association for Computational Linguistics. https://aclanthology.org/2024.clpsych-1.15

Cohn, J. F., Cummins, N., Epps, J., Goecke, R., Joshi, J., & Scherer, S. (2018). Multi-modal assessment of depression from behavioral signals. In S. Oviatt, B. Schuller, P. R. Cohen, D. Sonntag, G. Potamianos, & A. Krüger. (Eds.). *The handbook of multi-modal multisensory interfaces: Signal processing, architectures, and detection of emotion and cognition* (Vol. 2, pp. 375–417). https://doi.org/10.1145/3107990.3108004

Constantino, M. J., Boswell, J. F., & Coyne, A. E. (2021). Patient, therapist, and relational factors. In M. Barkham, W. Lutz, & L. G. Castonguay (Eds.), *Bergin and Garfield's handbook of psychotherapy and behavior change* (pp. 225–262). Wiley.

Crits-Christoph, P., & Gibbons, C. M. B. (2021). Psychotherapy process–outcome research: Advances in understanding causal connections. In M. Barkham, W. Lutz, & L. G. Castonguay (Eds.), *Bergin and Garfield's handbook of psychotherapy and behavior change*, (pp. 263–295). Wiley.

Cuijpers, P., Quero, S., Noma, H., Ciharova, M., Miguel, C., Karyotaki, E., Cipriani, A., Cristea, I. A.,. & Furukawa, T. A. (2021). Psychotherapies for depression: A network meta-analysis covering efficacy, acceptability and long-term outcomes of all main treatment types. *World Psychiatry*, *20*(2), 283–293. https://doi.org/10.1002/wps.20860

Cwir, D., Carr, P. B., Walton, G. M., & Spencer, S. J. (2011). Your heart makes my heart move: Cues of social connectedness cause shared emotions and physiological states among strangers. *Journal of Experimental Social Psychology*, *47*(3), 661–664.

Delgadillo, J., & Atzil-Slonim, D. (2022). Artificial intelligence and machine learning in psychotherapy. In H. S. Friedman & C. H. Markey (Eds.), *Encyclopedia of mental health* (3rd ed., Vol. 1, pp. V1-132–V1-142). Elsevier.

Devlin, J., Chang, M. W., Lee, K., & Toutanova, K. (2018). *BERT: Pre-training of deep bidirectional transformers for language understanding.* arXiv Preprint arXiv:1810.04805. https://doi.org/10.48550/arXiv.1810.04805

Eubanks, C. F., Muran, J. C., & Safran, J. D. (2018). Alliance rupture repair: A meta-analysis. *Psychotherapy*, *55*(4), 508–519.

Feldman, R. (2012). Bio-behavioral synchrony: A model for integrating biological and microsocial behavioral processes in the study of parenting. *Parenting*, *12*(2–3), 154–164. https://doi.org/10.1080/15295192.2012.683342

Feldman, R. (2021). Social behavior as a transdiagnostic marker of resilience. *Annual Review of Clinical Psychology*, *17*(1), 153–180. https://doi.org/10.1146/annurev-clinpsy-081219-102046

Flückiger, C., Rubel, J., Del Re, A. C., Horvath, A. O., Wampold, B. E., Crits-Christoph, P., Atzil-Slonim, D., Compare, A., Falkenström, F., Ekeblad, A., Errázuriz, P., Fisher, H., Hoffart, A., Huppert, J. D., Kivity, Y., Kumar, M., Lutz, W., Muran, J. C., Strunk, D. R., ... Barber, J. P. (2020). The reciprocal relationship between alliance and early treatment symptoms: A two-stage individual participant data meta-analysis. *Journal of Consulting and Clinical Psychology*, *88*(9), 829.

Fosha, D. (2001). The dyadic regulation of affect. *Journal of Clinical Psychology*, *57*(2), 227–242.

Gaines, A. N., & Goldfried, M. R. (2021). Consensus in psychotherapy: Are we there yet? *Clinical Psychology: Science and Practice*, *28*(3), 267.

Girard, J. M., Cohn, J. F., Jeni, L. A., Sayette, M. A., & De la Torre, F. (2015). Spontaneous facial expression in unscripted social interactions can be measured automatically. *Behavior Research Methods*, *47*(4), 1136–1147. https://doi.org/10.3758/s13428-014-0536-1

Hill, C. E., & Kellems, I. S. (2002). Development and use of the Session Evaluation Questionnaire. In G. S. Tryon (Ed.), *Counseling based on process research: Applying what we know* (pp. 235–246). Allyn & Bacon.

Hill, C. E., & Norcross, J. C. (Eds.). (2023). *Psychotherapy skills and methods that work.* Oxford University Press.

Höfling, T. T. A., Gerdes, A. B. M., Föhl, U., & Alpers, G. W. (2020). Read my face: Automatic facial coding versus psychophysiological indicators of emotional valence and arousal. *Frontiers in Psychology*, *11*. Article 1388. https://doi.org/10.3389/fpsyg.2020.01388

Hofmann, S. G., & Hayes, S. C. (2019). The future of intervention science: Process-based therapy. *Clinical Psychological Science*, *7*(1), 37–50. https://doi.org/10.1177/2167702618772296

Houben, M., Van Den Noortgate, W., & Kuppens, P. (2015). The relation between short-term emotion dynamics and psychological well-being: A meta-analysis. *Psychological Bulletin*, *141*(4), 901–930. http://dx.doi.org/10.1037/a0038822

Kazdin, A. E. (2008). Evidence-based treatment and practice: New opportunities to bridge clinical research and practice, enhance the knowledge base, and improve patient care. *American Psychologist*, *63*(3), 146–159. https://doi.org/10.1037/0003-066X.63.3.146

Kazdin, A. E. (2021). Extending the scalability and reach of psychosocial interventions. In M. Barkham, W. Lutz, & L. G. Castonguay (Eds.), *Bergin and Garfield's handbook of psychotherapy and behavior change* (pp. 763–790). Wiley.

Lazarus, G., & Rafaeli, E. (2023). Modes: Cohesive personality states and their interrelationships as organizing concepts in psychopathology. *Journal of Psychopathology and Clinical Science, 132*(3), 238–248. https://doi.org/10.1037/abn0000699

Luborsky, L., Mark, D., Hole, A. V., Popp, C., Goldsmith, B., & Cacciola, J. (1995). Supportive-expressive dynamic psychotherapy of depression: A time-limited version. In J. P. Barber & P. Crits-Christoph (Eds.), *Dynamic therapies for psychiatric disorders* (Axis I) (pp. 13–42). Basic Books.

Mayer, T., Warikoo, N., Eliassaf, A., Atzil-Slonim, D., & Gurevych, I. (2024). Predicting client emotions and therapist interventions in psychotherapy dialogues. In Y. Graham & M. Purver (Eds.), *Proceedings of the 18th Conference of the European Chapter of the Association for Computational Linguistics (Volume 1: Long Papers)* (pp. 1463–1477). Association for Computational Linguistics. https://doi.org/10.18653/v1/2024.eacl-long.88

Mayo, O., & Gordon, I. (2020). In and out of synchrony—Behavioral and physiological dynamics of dyadic interpersonal coordination. *Psychophysiology, 57*(6). https://doi.org/10.1111/psyp.13574

McCullough, L., Kuhn, N., Andrews, S., Valen, J., Hatch, D., & Osimo, F. (2003). The reliability of the Achievement of Therapeutic Objectives Scale (ATOS): A research and teaching tool for psychotherapy. *Journal of Brief Therapy, 2*, 75–90.

Miller, S. D., Duncan, B. L., Brown, J., Sparks, J. A., & Claud, D. A. (2003). The outcome rating scale: A preliminary study of the reliability, validity, and feasibility of a brief visual analog measure. *Journal of Brief Therapy, 2*(2), 91–100.

Pascual-Leone, A., & Greenberg, L. S. (2005). Classification of affective-meaning states (CAMS). In A. Pascual-Leone (Ed.), *Emotional processing in the therapeutic hour: Why the only way out is through* (pp. 289–367). York University.

Paz, A., Rafaeli, E., Bar-Kalifa, E., Gilboa-Schectman, E., Gannot, S., Laufer-Goldshtein, B., Narayanan, S., Keshet, J., & Atzil-Slonim, D. (2021). Intrapersonal and interpersonal vocal affect dynamics during psychotherapy. *Journal of Consulting and Clinical Psychology, 89*(3), 227–239.

Paz, A., Rafaeli, E., Bar-Kalifa, E., Gilboa-Schechtman, E., Gannot, S., Narayanan, S. S., & Atzil-Slonim, D. (2024). Multimodal analysis of temporal affective variability within treatment for depression. *Journal of Consulting and Clinical Psychology, 92*(9), 569–581. https://doi.org/10.1037/ccp0000901

Paz, A., Rafaeli, E., Bar-Kalifa, E., Gilboa-Schechtman, E., Gannot, S., Narayanan, S., & Atzil-Slonim, D. (2025). Dampening versus amplification: Intrapersonal and interpersonal vocal affect dynamics during psychotherapy for depression. *Psychotherapy Research*, 1–14. https://doi.org/10.1080/10503307.2025.2534973

Reich, C. M., Berman, J. S., Dale, R., & Levitt, H. M. (2014). Vocal synchrony in psychotherapy. *Journal of Social and Clinical Psychology, 33*(5), 481–494. https://doi.org/10.1521/jscp.2014.33.5.481

Revelle, W. (2007). Experimental approaches to the study of personality. In B. Robins, R. C. Fraley, & R. F. Krueger (Eds.), *Handbook of Research Methods in Personality Psychology* (pp. 37–61). Guilford Press.

Ringeval, F., Schuller, B., Valstar, M., Cummins, N., Cowie, R., Tavabi, L., Schmitt, M., Alisamir, S., Amiriparian, S., Messner, E.-M., Song, S., Liu, S., Zhao, Z., Mallol-Ragolta, A., Ren, Z., Soleymani, M. & Pantic, M. (2019). AVEC 2019 workshop and challenge: State-of-mind, detecting depression with AI, and cross-cultural affect recognition. In F. Ringeval, B. W. Schuller, M. F. Valstar, N. Cummins, R. Cowie, & M. Pantic (Eds.), *Proceedings of the 9th International on Audio/Visual Emotion Challenge and Workshop (AVEC@MM 2019)* (pp. 3–12). Association for Computing Machinery. https://doi.org/10.1145/3347320.3357688

Safran, J. D. (2012). Doublethinking or dialectical thinking: A critical appreciation of Hoffman's "doublethinking" critique. *Psychoanalytic Dialogues*, *22*(6), 710–720.

Sayda, D., Bar-Kalifa, E., & Atzil-Slonim, D., (2024). *Can multimodality and flexibility explain mixed findings on synchrony-outcome association?* [Paper] Israeli Society for Psychotherapy Research.

Schoenherr, D., Strauss, B., Stangier, U., & Altmann, U. (2021). The influence of vocal synchrony on outcome and attachment anxiety/avoidance in treatments of social anxiety disorder. *Psychotherapy*, *58*(4), 510–522.

Sheehan, D. V., Lecrubier, Y., Sheehan, K. H., Amorim, P., Janavs, J., Weiller, E., Hergueta, T., Baker, R., & Dunbar, G. C. (1998). The Mini-International Neuropsychiatric Interview (M.I.N.I.): The development and validation of a structured diagnostic psychiatric interview for DSM-IV and ICD-10. *The Journal of Clinical Psychiatry*, *59*(Suppl. 20), 22–57.

Stade, E., Stirman, S. W., Ungar, L. H., Yaden, D. B., Schwartz, H. A., Sedoc, J., DeRubeis, R., Willer, R., & Eichstaedt, J. C. (2023). *Artificial intelligence will change the future of psychotherapy: A proposal for responsible, psychologist-led development.* PsyArXiv (Center for Open Science). https://doi.org/10.31234/osf.io/cuzvr

Stiles, W. B. (2001). Assimilation of problematic experiences. *Psychotherapy: Theory, Research, Practice, Training*, *38*(4), Article 462. https://doi.org/10.1037/0033-3204.38.4.462

Summers, R. F., Barber, J. P., & Zilcha-Mano, S. (2024). *Psychodynamic therapy.* Guilford Publications.

Tsakalidis, A., Atzil-Slonim, D., Polakovski, A., Shapira, N., Tuval-Mashiach, R., & Liakata, M. (2021). Automatic identification of ruptures in transcribed psychotherapy sessions. In N. Goharian, P. Resnik, A. Yates, M. Ireland, K. Niederhoffer, & R. Resnik (Eds.), *Proceedings of the Seventh Workshop on Computational Linguistics and Clinical Psychology: Improving Access* (pp. 122–128). Association for Computational Linguistics. https://doi.org/10.18653/v1/2021.clpsych-1.15

Wampold, B. E., & Owen, J. (2021). Therapist effects: History, methods, magnitude, and characteristics of effective therapists. In M. Barkham, W. Lutz, & L. G. Castonguay (Eds.), *Bergin and Garfield's handbook of psychotherapy and behavior change: 50th anniversary edition* (7th ed., pp. 297–326). John Wiley & Sons, Inc.

World Health Organization. (2019). *International statistical classification of diseases and related health problems* (11th ed.). World Health Organization. https://icd.who.int/

9

Studying Processes and Mechanisms of Change in Practice-Oriented Research Using the Alliance–Outcome Relation as a Point of Departure

Fredrik Falkenström

Introduction

My practice-oriented research program has been dedicated to exploring mechanisms of change in therapy. These mechanisms are the key variables that clinicians target during therapy, aiming to improve client outcomes. Examples of mechanisms traditionally thought to be unique to various psychotherapy orientations are distorted cognitions in cognitive therapy, warded-off affects in psychodynamic or emotion-focused therapy, avoidance behaviors in behavior therapy, and biological factors in pharmacotherapy. These mechanisms, however, may not be as unique to specific schools of therapy as traditionally thought due to the terminologies used in the various therapy orientations. To the contrary, cognitions, affects, and behaviors are likely to be addressed in any effective therapy, and differences among orientations may just be differences in degrees and/or in jargon. Other mechanisms, traditionally referred to as nonspecific or common factors, may also act as mechanisms of change.[1] These include elements of the therapist–patient relationship, like the working alliance, and patient intrapsychic variables such as self-acceptance, self-criticism, and mentalization/meta-cognition.

[1] Some authors distinguish between mechanisms of change and change processes, with the former clearly situated within the patient while the latter are processes happening between therapist and patient within sessions (Doss, 2004).

Fredrik Falkenström, *Studying Processes and Mechanisms of Change in Practice-Oriented Research Using the Alliance–Outcome Relation as a Point of Departure*. In: *Practice-Based Evidence in the Psychological Therapies*. Edited by: Louis G. Castonguay et al., Oxford University Press.
DOI: 10.1093/9780197748336.003.0009

In this chapter, I outline my attempt to identify mechanisms that underlie therapeutic change across psychotherapy schools, cultures, and study designs. In doing so, I aim to demonstrate how practice-oriented research can provide informative solutions to issues that have been challenging to resolve through traditional experimental research. The chapter is structured around three main sections; in the first, called "point of departure," I describe my initial attempts to study the alliance–outcome relationship in Swedish primary care and specialist psychiatry. In the second section, I outline a practice-oriented research project in Nairobi, Kenya, which is still ongoing and ultimately aims to improve the mental health services in the East African region. This also meant a possibility to study the alliance–outcome relationship in a severely impoverished patient sample from a very different culture. Finally, the last section describes my current work on improving the design of practice-oriented research to address some of the limitations inherent in this framework. The theme of mechanisms of change, and especially the centrality of the working alliance, is present here, as well.

Point of Departure

Since practice-oriented research is largely about the integration of practice and research, I will begin this chapter by sharing a bit of my own clinical background and the experiences that sparked my interest in research. My career as a clinical psychologist started in adult psychiatry, and then after 2 years transitioning to a counseling center for young adults aged 16–23. At the young adults counseling center, I observed that particularly the younger clients, often those below 18 years of age, rarely returned for a second appointment unless a strong therapeutic alliance was established in our first meeting. This realization pushed me to diligently explore each young person's motivation for seeking therapy, their expectations, and hopes. Simultaneously, I had to balance this with the psychotherapy theories I had learned during my training, and the practical aspects of therapy I was acquiring through supervision—all within the confines of the very first session.

Alongside my training to become a psychologist, I became involved in a research project on the long-term follow-up of psychodynamic therapy and psychoanalysis. Our study primarily focused on how patients endeavored to improve their mental health post therapy, discovering that various forms of self-analysis were closely linked to symptom improvement during the follow-up period (Falkenström et al., 2007). Later, I received a PhD grant within my role as a clinical psychologist and psychotherapist in the Swedish healthcare system. I approached Professor Rolf Holmqvist at Linköping University, where I had initially trained, to supervise my doctoral research. My PhD research delved into conceptual and measurement issues related to self-observation capacities, encompassing concepts like mindfulness, psychological mindedness, and mentalization. During this period, I began to discern a theoretical and clinical connection between these capacities in both patients and therapists, and the development of the working alliance. I found particular inspiration in the work of Safran and Muran (2000). They integrated relational psychoanalytic concepts with ideas from Buddhist meditation practices, another significant interest of mine, to formulate a theory and method for addressing and repairing alliance ruptures.

As my PhD project was nearing completion, Rolf approached me with an interesting proposition. He asked if I was interested in collaborating on a data analysis project involving a recently acquired a data set from two primary care regions in Sweden. Reflecting core features of practice-oriented research (see Castonguay et al., 2021), the data were collected as part of the clinical routine, without research requirements imposed on the conduct of treatment provided by therapists. This data set comprised weekly collected therapy data, including two key variables: the Clinical Outcomes in Routine Evaluation—Outcome Measure (CORE-OM; Evans et al., 2002), and the Working Alliance Inventory (WAI-SR; Hatcher & Gillaspy, 2006). Analyses reported by Holmqvist et al. (2014) showed that for the very brief psychological treatments (median number of sessions = 6), 43% of the patients showed reliable improvement, and 34% recovered. Patients in psychotherapies (reflective or directive) had better outcomes than in supportive therapy. However, patients in supportive therapy were considered less motivated, less reflective, and with a worse alliance, according to the therapists. Thus, selection of patients with less favorable prognoses to supportive therapy may explain these outcome differences.

At that time, a heated debate was ongoing within psychotherapy research communities about whether or not the alliance played a mutative role in treatment outcomes. Proponents in one group emphasized the significance of numerous studies that demonstrated a correlation between the quality of the alliance, measured early in therapy, and the overall treatment outcome (Flückiger et al., 2018; Horvath et al., 2011). On the other side of the debate, some researchers dismissed the mutative effect of the alliance and supported their stance by referencing critiques of alliance research, such as those presented by DeRubeis et al. (2005). This critique highlighted the possibility that early symptom improvement could be responsible for both a strong alliance and a positive overall outcome, so that the alliance–outcome correlation would be merely a byproduct of early outcome.

I got inspired from reading a paper by Curran and Bauer (2011) about within- and between-person effects in longitudinal multilevel models[2] and wanted to apply these concepts to Rolf's primary care practice-oriented research data to analyze the alliance–outcome relationship as a within-person process. The approach involved dividing the alliance data into two components: a between-person part, consisting of the average level of a particular person's alliance (potentially also with a trend component capturing the person's change in alliance over time), and a within-person part that contains what cannot be explained by the between-person part. Thus, the within-person part contains fluctuations around each person's mean or general trend over time.

The results of this analysis offered a compelling middle ground in the ongoing alliance–outcome debate. The findings indicated that the quality of the alliance influenced subsequent psychological distress on a session-by-session basis, and conversely, the level of psychological distress also seemed to affect the alliance. If the alliance quality in a session was higher than usual for a particular therapist–patient dyad, more significant improvements in the patient's distress was observed by the following session than if the alliance was rated lower than usual. Similarly, if a patient's psychological distress in the preceding week was less severe than usual, a better-than-expected alliance rating was likely to follow.

Some of the critiques my colleagues and I received from reviewers of this paper pertained to common issues in practice-based data, such as the diverse backgrounds of patients and therapists, the variety and uncontrolled nature of interventions, and the significant amount of missing data. Indeed, while randomized controlled trials (RCTs) often grapple with missing data, practice-based studies typically have fewer restrictions regarding the number of sessions, or the range of patients included. In response to these criticisms, our paper (Falkenström et al., 2013) employed sophisticated

[2] I am indebted to Scott Baldwin for suggesting this paper as a potential solution to my struggle to find ways of analyzing alliance–outcome data using panel data models.

analyses to address missing data and explored moderators of the alliance–outcome relationship. It is important to acknowledge that no statistical method can completely compensate for lost data or fundamental design limitations. However, we utilized techniques recommended by Enders (2010) to assess the robustness of our findings against the impact of missing data. Additionally, we conducted moderator analyses to determine if certain subgroups within the study had a disproportionate influence on the results. Although previous studies had explored moderators of the alliance–outcome relationship, our use of random slopes was a key innovation. This approach allowed us to estimate the variance in alliance–outcome predictions across different patients, adding a novel dimension to our study.

In our study (Falkenström et al., 2013), we discovered considerable variability in the alliance–outcome relationship. Interestingly, the type of treatment and initial levels of distress did not significantly influence this relationship. However, we found that patients with personality problems had a more pronounced effect on the session-by-session alliance–outcome relationship. This could be due to their challenges in interpersonal relationships, which likely extend to their interactions with therapists. Our interpretation of these findings points to a dynamic of rupture and repair in the therapeutic relationship. Specifically, alliance ruptures appear to be linked with increased patient distress, whereas repairs predict improvements, perhaps serving as corrective experiences for clients experiencing particularly high levels of personality difficulties. These findings would have been much more challenging to obtain in experimental settings where patients are selected for homogeneity. The heterogeneity of practice-oriented research samples, though a limitation in the context of RCTs, can be considered a strength by enabling comparisons among subgroups that are not typically included in the same RCT.

These insights offer valuable guidance for clinical practice and training. Closely monitoring patient distress, and the quality of the therapeutic alliance in each session, might help therapists to identify and address alliance ruptures. This proactive approach may prevent detrimental cycles where alliance ruptures exacerbate distress, leading to further ruptures. This proactive approach can also be adopted even in the absence of a routine measurement of alliance, as worsening patient distress can, by itself, serve as a critical indicator of potential alliance ruptures. Thus, if a patient reports heightened symptoms or distress in a session, therapists should be alert to the possibility of ongoing and/or unaddressed alliance ruptures. As a whole, these findings underscore the importance of continuous monitoring and responsive intervention in the therapeutic process.

Later, we replicated these findings in an effectiveness trial headed by Annika Ekeblad, in specialist psychiatry (Ekeblad et al., 2016). The trial was conducted in a small Swedish town, focusing on patients with major depressive disorder. These patients, who had significant comorbidity (e.g., around 50% personality disorders) and had shown none or only partial responses to previous treatments, received 14 sessions of either cognitive-behavioral therapy (CBT) or interpersonal psychotherapy (IPT) in regular psychiatric care. The findings from this study showed that the reciprocal alliance–outcome model extended to patients with depression in psychiatric settings and applied to specific treatments like IPT and CBT (Falkenström et al., 2016).

Improving the Outcomes of Psychotherapy in Public Hospitals in Nairobi, Kenya

Between 2013 and 2015, I resided in Nairobi, Kenya, doing postdoctoral work supported by a grant from the Swedish Research Council for Work, Health, and Welfare. During this period, I collaborated with researchers from the University of Nairobi on a practice-oriented research project. Inspired by Rolf Holmqvist's work in Sweden, we wanted to conduct a study in primary care settings, but this time in two public hospitals affiliated with the University of Nairobi: Mathari National Teaching and Referral Hospital, and three outpatient clinics at Kenyatta National Hospital. These institutions are the primary psychiatric and mental health teaching and referral centers in Kenya.

Both hospitals provide free services to specific demographic groups: individuals impacted by gender-based violence or HIV, combat veterans and their families, unemployed or disabled persons, and youth under 24 years. These services are particularly crucial for patients from low socioeconomic backgrounds who cannot afford private healthcare. Many of these patients come from impoverished areas in Nairobi or rural regions outside the city. Being referral hospitals, Kenyatta and Mathari often see patients who travel long distances for treatment. Due to financial and time constraints, regular weekly therapy sessions are not feasible for many of these patients. Consequently, therapy attendance tends to be sporadic, with intervals between sessions extending to a month or more.

In this study, we observed a higher proportion of male participants (73%), which could likely be attributed to the large number of patients dealing with addiction issues (54%). This trend might be related to the presence of an addiction clinic at Mathari Hospital, which contributed significantly to our study data. Additionally, there was an atypically high, at least for psychotherapy research, percentage of patients with psychotic disorders (17%). This might be due to the study's inpatient setting at Mathari Hospital. In contrast to common demographics in European or American studies, the percentages of patients suffering from depression or anxiety disorders were relatively low in our sample, at 17% and 12%, respectively. Consequently, the sample represented in this study was markedly severe, both in terms of psychiatric and socioeconomic conditions, and was substantially different from the patient demographics we encountered in our studies in Sweden.

Our primary aim with this practice-oriented research project was to identify patient groups for whom the currently available treatments were less effective (Falkenström, Gee, et al., 2017). As a Western researcher with a limited understanding of Kenyan culture, I found the practice-oriented research approach particularly suitable due to its "bottom-up" strategy, which starts with observing the existing practices in regular care. This research strategy allowed us to explore which patient groups were benefiting from the current treatments and which were not. It was crucial for us not to disrupt treatments that were already effective, especially to avoid replacing them with approaches that, while successful in Sweden, might not be as effective in the Kenyan context. Our rationale was that by pinpointing patient groups who were not showing improvement, we could then direct resources more effectively toward developing more suitable treatments for them.

Due to constrained funding for this project, we were unable to fully achieve the more ambitious objectives of the study. However, we successfully gathered session-by-session data on distress (using CORE-OM) and alliance (using WAI-SR) from a substantial patient sample ($N = 345$). The results of these treatments were reported in one paper (Kumar et al., 2018), while another paper (Mbuthia et al., 2018) detailed qualitative analyses of interviews with patients from the youth clinic. The findings indicated that patients were showing improvement, even though they attended an average of only about three sessions. On average, improvement was about the same as in the primary care study in Sweden. Notably, adolescents in urban Nairobi expressed a preference for talking therapies, while also highlighting the need for more intensive therapy options.

In this project, we once again collected session-by-session data on the therapeutic alliance using the Session Alliance Inventory (Falkenström et al., 2015) and psychological distress using the CORE-OM. This provided us with an opportunity to replicate our previous alliance studies in a culturally distinct setting. After extensive discussions with political scientist and methodologist Stephen Finkel (Falkenström, Finkel, et al., 2017; Finkel, 1995), I decided to shift our methodology to structural equation modeling (Hamaker et al., 2015). Our analysis again supported the reciprocal effects model, with the alliance significantly predicting changes in distress by the next session. We observed that the influence of preceding symptoms on the alliance varied, but it was significant in 3 out of 5 sessions (Falkenström et al., 2019).

A unique challenge in this context was the high staff turnover at the clinics, often involving student therapists. This led to patients frequently seeing different therapists across sessions, necessitating the re-establishment of the alliance at each new encounter. Unfortunately, we lacked specific data on when therapist changes occurred, so we couldn't examine this aspect in detail. However, we hypothesize that this dynamic might place even greater emphasis on the therapeutic alliance for effective treatment outcomes.

Since then, we have initiated a smaller-scale practice-oriented research project focused on children and adolescents at the youth clinic of Kenyatta Hospital. This project is led by doctoral student Nduku Wambua, under the supervision of Pim Cuijpers, Manasi Kumar, and me (Wambua et al., 2020). The results have mirrored those from our previous project: We observed a significantly impaired patient group who, on average, showed improvement despite undergoing very brief treatments. However, the alliance–outcome study conducted as part of this project did not replicate our earlier findings. We observed null effects for both the influence of the therapeutic alliance on psychological distress and vice versa (Wambua et al., 2022). This discrepancy is likely attributable to a lack of statistical power, that is, the study's ability to detect an effect if there is one. The limited size of the sample, consisting of 98 patients and only three repeated measurements, probably contributed to this issue.

Improving the Design of Practice-Oriented Psychotherapy Research

In two ongoing practice-oriented research projects, in Swedish community-based psychiatric care, we are employing a quasi-experimental multiple baseline design (Falkenström et al., 2025). This design, originally developed for single-case studies, requires at least two baselines—periods without any intervention—of varying lengths for effective implementation (Kazdin, 2019). The design can be applied to either multiple behaviors within a single subject or across multiple subjects. Typically, even when used for multiple subjects, the design involves only a few participants. This design proves particularly persuasive in scenarios where baselines are expected to remain stable and intervention effects are immediately apparent, allowing for evaluation of results through straightforward visual inspection of graphs. However, in the context of psychotherapy research, these conditions often do not apply. Patients on waiting lists may experience changes in their condition, either improving or deteriorating, and the effects of treatments might be delayed. These factors present unique challenges when using the multiple baseline design in psychotherapy research settings.

However, at a group level, if the treatment is indeed effective, we would expect to see more improvement during the treatment phase than during the baseline period. Consequently, I believe a multiple baseline design, involving many subjects and comparing changes during treatment with those during baseline on a group level, possesses several appealing attributes for psychotherapy practice-oriented research. Firstly, this approach avoids the need to assign patients to an inactive control group, which may be ethically contentious and, in public healthcare systems like Sweden's, even legally prohibited. Secondly, it eliminates the necessity of randomizing patients between different active treatments, which could also raise ethical and/or legal issues, especially if it conflicts with the patient's or clinician's preferred treatment choice.

Christ (2007) recommends randomizing the duration of the baseline period in multiple baseline designs to reduce the likelihood of confounding the commencement of treatment with other factors. However, randomizing waiting times could introduce similar ethical and/or legal concerns to those of treatment randomization. To navigate these challenges, our studies have adopted a quasi-experimental version of this design. We leverage the natural variation in waiting times at clinics to establish different baseline lengths across subjects. While this approach may slightly compromise internal validity due to a higher potential for confounding, its key advantage is the minimal disruption it causes to clinical routines. This aspect is particularly beneficial for practice-oriented research studies, representing a third significant advantage of this design for practice-oriented research.

Child and Adolescent Psychiatry Treatment for Depressed Adolescents Using IPT in Norrköping (CAPTAIN)

In our first project employing this design, we are examining the effectiveness of interpersonal psychotherapy for adolescents (IPT-A; Mufson, 2004) in treating depressed adolescents aged 15–18 within child and adolescent psychiatry in Sweden. The project is led by Liselotte Lindegren, who works both as a clinician at the Norrköping Child and Adolescent Psychiatric Clinic, where the study is taking place, and as a part-time doctoral student at Linnaeus University. The study fulfills the three defining features of practice-oriented research as outlined by Castonguay et al. (2021) in that the IPT-A team (consisting of six therapists) is part of the clinic routine, reflecting everyday practice, and we do not impose any restrictions on the treatments over and above those included in the clinic routine. In addition, the research plan has been worked out in close collaboration between researchers and practitioners at the clinic.

After being included in the project, patients are placed on a waiting list until an IPT-A therapist becomes available. The waiting time typically ranges from a few weeks to 6 months, with a median duration of about 2 months. During this waiting period, patients rate their symptoms biweekly using the Patient Health Questionnaire-9 (PHQ-9; Kroenke & Spitzer, 2002). During therapy, they fill out the PHQ-9 before each session. This enables testing for differential growth curves (regression slopes by time) between the waiting- and treatment periods. In addition, four mechanisms of change are being studied in this project: working alliance, emotion regulation, social support, and symptom-specific reflective functioning. These factors may be seen as pan-theoretical mechanisms of change, although at the same time, all have been considered important for IPT (Lipsitz & Markowitz, 2013; Markowitz et al., 2019; Markowitz & Milrod, 2011). The relationship between mechanisms and depressive symptom change will be analyzed using cross-lagged panel models. As of this writing, 20 patients have been enrolled in the CAPTAIN project. Our power analysis, conducted before starting the study, indicated that a sample size of 60 patients is required to achieve an 80% chance (power) of detecting a statistically significant difference (with an alpha level of 5%) between the baseline and treatment phases. We anticipate completing data collection within the next few years.

So far, our experience suggests that IPT-A is being positively received by the adolescent participants. The patient group at the specialist child and adolescent psychiatric unit presents with considerable complexity in terms of comorbidity. Many of these patients have concurrent neuropsychiatric disorders and/or are facing challenging family situations. Additionally, it's noteworthy that most, if not all, patients were already receiving medication(s) prior to their assessment for inclusion in the project.

PRocess and Outcome Monitoring in Psychiatric Treatments (PROMPT)

The PROMPT project is a routine outcome monitoring initiative, which, as with the previous study, fulfills the three criteria of practice-oriented research (Castonguay et al., 2021) in that data are collected as part of clinical routine practice, what is assessed reflects everyday practice, and the researchers do not impose any constraints on practice at the clinics. In the project, patients at two psychiatric outpatient clinics in Stockholm are tracked from their initial assessment at the clinic, through their waiting period for treatment, and throughout their treatment journey. One of the clinics is a general psychiatric outpatient clinic, to which treatment-resistant patients are referred from primary care, and the other one is a specialist personality disorder clinic.

A battery of measures is employed at the initial evaluation and every 3rd month during treatment, including measures of borderline symptoms, depressive and anxiety symptoms, general functioning, and emotion regulation. In addition, each week, patients participating in the PROMPT project complete the Clinical Outcome in Routine Evaluation-10 (CORE-10; Barkham et al., 2013) using their smartphones. This tool is used to assess changes in psychological distress. To evaluate the quality of the therapeutic alliance, we use the Session Alliance Inventory (SAI; Falkenström et al., 2015). Moreover, we use the Multitheoretical List of Therapeutic

Interventions—30 (MULTI; Solomonov et al., 2019) to assess a variety of therapeutic interventions that are common across different therapy orientations. Therapists complete the MULTI every 3 months.

The natural waiting time due to therapist availability is utilized to establish multiple baselines for the CORE-10. The effectiveness of the treatment is evaluated by comparing the average change in the outcome measure during the treatment phase with its average change during the baseline period. Furthermore, we will study mechanisms of change using cross-lagged panel models. We will select a subset of interventions from the MULTI based on their frequency of use in the clinics, as determined by a preliminary survey, to use as predictors of processes and outcomes in analyses.

Discussion

As this chapter reflects, my journey in practice-oriented research has been both varied and enriching, traversing different cultures, treatment settings, and patient demographics. My work has aimed to unravel the intricacies of the therapeutic process and the factors that contribute to successful outcomes in psychotherapy. The exploration of mechanisms of change, particularly in the context of the therapeutic alliance, has been a central theme. I strongly believe that the study of mechanisms, whether specific to psychotherapy orientations or common across them, is central to understanding and improving psychotherapy effectiveness.

This practice-oriented research program has led to a number of clinical implications regarding the therapeutic relationship. For example, it suggests that when working with clients, especially those with a personality disorder, improving the alliance may have effects on outcome already by the following session. This is important to emphasize in the training of therapists by, for instance, including practice on collaboration on goal setting, negotiation of tasks, sensitization to rupture markers, and practicing resolution strategies (Safran & Muran, 2000). Alliance-focused training (Eubanks-Carter et al., 2015) may be used as a framework for developing self-awareness, affect regulation, and interpersonal sensitivity of therapists in training, so that they can more effectively facilitate alliance development during treatment. Moreover, knowing that symptom deterioration predicts deterioration in alliance is important to emphasize in therapist training, as another potential marker of alliance ruptures.

In our studies in Kenya, we were impressed that the young clients expressed a preference for talking therapy and that the effect of the alliance on outcome seemed to be similar to what studies have found in Western countries. This was observed in a severely distressed sample in terms of both psychiatric and socioeconomic conditions, most of whom would have been unlikely to be included in any RCT. Thus, this exemplifies one of the strengths of practice-oriented research: reaching underserved populations that are hard to study in controlled experimental research. We also believe that this underscores the importance of establishing a therapeutic relationship with clients, which should not be ignored in our attempt to address the treatment gap and provide mental health services at scale.

The range of projects I have been involved in, from investigating the alliance–outcome relationship in primary care and specialist psychiatry to studying processes and outcomes of psychotherapy in diverse cultural settings, has enriched my understanding of the complexity of psychotherapy research. These experiences have also highlighted the importance of considering the unique challenges and needs of patients in diverse socioeconomic situations. The shift in methodologies, from multilevel modeling to structural equation modeling, and the use of multiple baseline designs, has been instrumental in addressing the complexities of conducting practice-oriented research.

The research implications of my practice-oriented research program include my strong belief that advanced statistical methods are often needed to accommodate the complexities of practice-oriented research data. This is not just a way of handling problems in the data (such as missing data) but also a way of more fully making use of the richness of practice-oriented research data. As mentioned, the moderator analyses in my alliance studies might not have been possible on more homogeneous RCT data, which highlights the complementarity between practice-oriented research and RCT frameworks.

Limitations

Although a unique strength of the practice-oriented research paradigm includes the possibility of collecting large data sets, restrictions in some settings combined with complex statistical models means that statistical power can still be an issue in practice-oriented research studies. This was most likely the case in the alliance–outcome analysis of the Kenyan youth clinic study (Wambua et al., 2020). Moreover, complex statistical models should be used cautiously since errors in model specification are easily made and can have serious consequences. Additionally, it is crucial to carefully check model assumptions and acknowledge any assumptions that are untestable.

On a broader level, while we took great care not to impose our cultural values on the study in Kenya, completely avoiding this is challenging since culture is an integral part of who we are. Collaborating with researchers born and raised in Kenya was essential in this work.

Summary and Conclusions

In summary, the field of psychotherapy research is continually evolving, with new challenges and opportunities emerging. As we move forward, I believe that the integration of practice-oriented research with innovative methodologies will be crucial in enhancing our understanding of psychotherapy processes. This understanding, in turn, will guide us in tailoring therapeutic interventions more effectively to meet the diverse needs of patients. Improved methods will enhance the internal validity of practice-oriented research, bringing it closer to the rigor of controlled experiments. Together with the superior ecological validity of practice-oriented research, this may be instrumental in bridging the gap between science and practice. My hope is that the insights gained from these studies will contribute to the ongoing development of psychotherapy as a dynamic and responsive field, one that continues to evolve in its quest to alleviate psychological distress and enhance well-being.

References

Barkham, M., Bewick, B., Mullin, T., Gilbody, S., Connell, J., Cahill, J., Mellor-Clark, J., Richards, D., Unsworth, G., & Evans, C. (2013). The CORE-10: A short measure of psychological distress for routine use in the psychological therapies. *Counselling and Psychotherapy Research*, *13*(1), 3–13. https://doi.org/10.1080/14733145.2012.729069

Castonguay, L. G., Barkham, M., Youn, S. J., & Page, A. (2021). Practice-based evidence—Findings from routine clinical settings. In M. Barkham, W. Lutz, & L. G. Castonguay (Eds.), *Bergin and Garfield's handbook of psychotherapy and behavior change* (pp. 191–222). Wiley.

Christ, T. J. (2007). Experimental control and threats to internal validity of concurrent and nonconcurrent multiple baseline designs. *Psychology in the Schools*, *44*(5), 451–459. https://doi.org/10.1002/pits.20237

Curran, P. J., & Bauer, D. J. (2011). The disaggregation of within-person and between-person effects in longitudinal models of change. *Annual Review of Psychology, 62*, 583–619. https://doi.org/10.1146/annurev.psych.093008.100356

DeRubeis, R. J., Brotman, M. A., & Gibbons, C. J. (2005). A conceptual and methodological analysis of the nonspecifics argument. *Clinical Psychology: Science and Practice, 12*, 174–183. https://doi.org/http://dx.doi.org/10.1093/clipsy/bpi022

Doss, B. D. (2004). Changing the way we study change in psychotherapy. *Clinical Psychology: Science and Practice, 11*(4), 368–386. https://doi.org/10.1093/clipsy.bph094

Ekeblad, A., Falkenström, F., Andersson, G., Vestberg, R., & Holmqvist, R. (2016). Randomized trial of Interpersonal Psychotherapy and Cognitive Behavioral Therapy for Major Depressive Disorder in a community-based psychiatric outpatient clinic. *Depression and Anxiety, 33*(12), 1090–1098. https://doi.org/10.1002/da.22495

Enders, C. K. (2010). *Applied missing data analysis*. Guilford Press.

Eubanks-Carter, C., Muran, J. C., & Safran, J. D. (2015). Alliance-focused training. *Psychotherapy, 52*(2), 169–173. https://doi.org/10.1037/a0037596

Evans, C., Connell, J., Barkham, M., Margison, F., McGrath, G., Mellor-Clark, J., & Audin, K. (2002). Towards a standardised brief outcome measure: Psychometric properties and utility of the CORE-OM. *British Journal of Psychiatry, 180*, 51–60. https://doi.org/10.1192/bjp.180.1.51

Falkenström, F., Ekeblad, A., & Holmqvist, R. (2016). Improvement of the working alliance in one treatment session predicts improvement of depressive symptoms by the next session. *Journal of Consulting and Clinical Psychology, 84*(8), 738–751. https://doi.org/10.1037/ccp0000119

Falkenström, F., Finkel, S., Sandell, R., Rubel, J. A., & Holmqvist, R. (2017). Dynamic models of individual change in psychotherapy process research. *Journal of Consulting and Clinical Psychology, 85*(6), 537–549. https://doi.org/10.1037/ccp0000203

Falkenström, F., Fjällström, R., & Bengtsson, D. (2025). The quasi-experimental multiple baseline panel design: A suitable design for psychotherapy outcome research in clinical practice. *Journal of Consulting and Clinical Psychology, 93*(12). https://doi.org/10.1037/ccp0000973

Falkenström, F., Gee, M. D., Kuria, M. W., Othieno, C. J., & Kumar, M. (2017). Improving the effectiveness of psychotherapy in two public hospitals in Nairobi. *BJPsych International, 14*(3), 64–66. https://doi.org/10.1192/s2056474000001938

Falkenström, F., Granström, F., & Holmqvist, R. (2013). Therapeutic alliance predicts symptomatic improvement session by session. *Journal of Counseling Psychology, 60*(3), 317–328. https://doi.org/10.1037/a0032258

Falkenström, F., Grant, J., Broberg, J., & Sandell, R. (2007). Self-analysis and post-termination improvement after psychoanalysis and long-term psychotherapy. *Journal of the American Psychoanalytic Association, 55*(2), 629–674. https://doi.org/10.1177/00030651070550020401

Falkenström, F., Hatcher, R. L., Skjulsvik, T., Larsson, M. H., & Holmqvist, R. (2015). Development and validation of a 6-item working alliance questionnaire for repeated administrations during psychotherapy. *Psychological Assessment, 27*(1), 169–183. https://doi.org/10.1037/pas0000038

Falkenström, F., Kuria, M., Othieno, C., & Kumar, M. (2019). Working alliance predicts symptomatic improvement in public hospital-delivered psychotherapy in Nairobi, Kenya. *Journal of Consulting and Clinical Psychology, 87*(1), 46–55. https://doi.org/10.1037/ccp0000363

Finkel, S. (1995). *Causal analysis with panel data*. Sage Publications.

Flückiger, C., Del Re, A. C., Wampold, B. E., & Horvath, A. O. (2018). The alliance in adult psychotherapy: A meta-analytic synthesis. *Psychotherapy, 55*(4), 316–340. https://doi.org/10.1037/pst0000172

Hamaker, E. L., Kuiper, R. M., & Grasman, R. P. P. P. (2015). A critique of the cross-lagged panel model. *Psychological Methods, 20*, 102–116. https://doi.org/10.1037/a0038889

Hatcher, R. L., & Gillaspy, J. A. (2006). Development and validation of a revised short version of the Working Alliance Inventory. *Psychotherapy Research, 16*, 12–25. https://doi.org/10.1080/10503300500352500

Holmqvist, R., Ström, T., & Foldemo, A. (2014). The effects of psychological treatment in primary care in Sweden—A practice-based study. *Nordic Journal of Psychiatry, 68*, 204–212. https://doi.org/10.3109/08039488.2013.797023

Horvath, A. O., Del Re, A., Flückiger, C., & Symonds, D. (2011). Alliance in individual psychotherapy. *Psychotherapy, 48*, 9–16. https://doi.org/http://dx.doi.org/10.1037/a0022186

Kazdin, A. E. (2019). Single-case experimental designs. Evaluating interventions in research and clinical practice. *Behaviour Research and Therapy, 117*, 3–17. https://doi.org/https://doi.org/10.1016/j.brat.2018.11.015

Kroenke, K., & Spitzer, R. L. (2002). The PHQ-9: A new depression diagnostic and severity measure. *Psychiatric Annals, 32*, 509–515. https://doi.org/10.3928/0048-5713-20020901-06

Kumar, M., Kuria, M. W., Othieno, C. J., & Falkenström, F. (2018). Improving psychotherapies offered in public hospitals in Nairobi, Kenya: Extending practice-based research model for LMICs. *International Journal of Mental Health Systems, 12*(1), 76. https://doi.org/10.1186/s13033-018-0254-7

Lipsitz, J. D., & Markowitz, J. C. (2013). Mechanisms of change in interpersonal therapy (IPT). *Clinical Psychology Review, 33*, 1134–1147. https://doi.org/10.1016/j.cpr.2013.09.002

Markowitz, J. C., Milrod, B., Luyten, P., & Holmqvist, R. (2019). Mentalizing in interpersonal psychotherapy. *American Journal of Psychotherapy, 72*(4), 95–100. https://doi.org/10.1176/appi.psychotherapy.20190021

Markowitz, J. C., & Milrod, B. L. (2011). The importance of responding to negative affect in psychotherapies. *American Journal of Psychiatry, 168*, 124–128. https://doi.org/10.1176/appi.ajp.2010.10040636

Mbuthia, J. W., Kumar, M., Falkenström, F., Kuria, M. W., & Othieno, C. J. (2018). Attributions and private theories of mental illness among young adults seeking psychiatric treatment in Nairobi: An interpretive phenomenological analysis. *Child and Adolescent Psychiatry and Mental Health, 12*, 28. https://doi.org/10.1186/s13034-018-0229-0

Mufson, L. (2004). *Interpersonal psychotherapy for depressed adolescents*. Guilford Press.

Safran, J. D., & Muran, J. C. (2000). *Negotiating the therapeutic alliance: A relational treatment guide*. Guilford Press.

Solomonov, N., McCarthy, K. S., Gorman, B. S., & Barber, J. P. (2019). The Multitheoretical List of Therapeutic Interventions - 30 items (MULTI-30). *Psychotherapy Research, 29*(5), 565–580. https://doi.org/10.1080/10503307.2017.1422216

Wambua, G. N., Falkenström, F., Kumar, M., & Cuijpers, P. (2022). Outcome evaluation of psychological interventions offered to adolescents seeking mental health services at the national referral and teaching hospital in Nairobi, Kenya. *SSM - Mental Health, 2*, Article 100137. https://doi.org/10.1016/j.ssmmh.2022.100137

Wambua, G. N., Kumar, M., Falkenström, F., & Cuijpers, P. (2020). Process and outcome of child psychotherapies offered in Kenya: A mixed methods study protocol on improving child mental health. *BMC Psychiatry, 20*(1), 263. https://doi.org/10.1186/s12888-020-02611-2

SECTION IV

EXTENDING TO SPECIFIC POPULATIONS

10

Researchers and Clinicians Employing Rigorous Methods to Understand and Improve Community-Based Care for Children With Significant Behavioral Challenges

Ann F. Garland and Yesenia Mejia

Introduction

The United States Surgeon General and other health policy experts have declared a current crisis in youth mental health (Office of the Surgeon General, 2021). The prevalence of mental health problems has increased dramatically among youth (Centers for Disease Control and Prevention [CDC], 2021). This increase was apparent prior to the COVID-19 pandemic, and many speculate that the social isolation and trauma associated with the pandemic have exacerbated the crisis. Unfortunately, the majority of youth who need mental health care do not receive care, and many of those who do receive care do not receive effective care (Garland et al., 2017). Over decades, research has identified effective interventions to improve service access, engagement, and clinical outcomes, but the integration of research and community-based practice has been grossly insufficient. Practice-oriented research conducted in partnership with community representatives can improve research–practice integration through bidirectional knowledge exchange. As exemplified throughout this book, these approaches boost the ecological validity, contextual relevance, and clinical utility of research while also building providers' research capacity.

Ann F. Garland and Yesenia Mejia, *Researchers and Clinicians Employing Rigorous Methods to Understand and Improve Community-Based Care for Children With Significant Behavioral Challenges*. In: *Practice-Based Evidence in the Psychological Therapies*. Edited by: Louis G. Castonguay et al., Oxford University Press. © Oxford University Press (2026). DOI: 10.1093/9780197748336.003.0010

Practice-oriented research is driven by values that are not necessarily common in all types of research. These values include balanced and reciprocal respect for empirically derived knowledge and clinically derived knowledge, as well as genuine interest in understanding routine practice contexts and processes prior to implementing interventions to change practices. Consistent with these values, practice-oriented research is often conducted in collaboration with key practice partners, potentially including funders, administrators, direct service providers, and/or clients and their families.

Our chapter will focus on how and why collaboration between researchers and community practice partners is beneficial for successful practice-oriented research. We will highlight the partnerships that have driven several research studies of children's mental health care in our research group. These studies all address publicly funded mental health care for children with behavioral needs and their families, including children diagnosed with disruptive behavior disorders (e.g., conduct disorder and oppositional defiant disorder) and autism spectrum disorder, who are commonly seen in public mental health care.

We will provide contextual information about our multidisciplinary research group and the partnering provider organizations as background for the research study case examples. In addition, we will summarize research identifying factors that facilitate or inhibit successful research–practice partnerships. We will share participants' perspectives on the benefits and challenges of practice-oriented research experience and conclude with recommendations for advancing practice-oriented research on children's mental health care. These advances are essential for addressing the youth mental health crisis not only in the United States but also in other countries around the world.

Background Information on Research and Practice Contexts

Research Group

All the studies described in this chapter have been conducted through the Child and Adolescent Services Research Center (CASRC), based in San Diego, California. CASRC was established in the early 1990s as a multidisciplinary, multi-institutional research group devoted to understanding and improving public sector mental health and child welfare services for children and families. A small group of health services and applied clinical researchers founded the group, which has grown exponentially over the years (Landsverk et al., 2011). This growth is reflected in millions of US dollars in grant funding from a variety of sources including National Institutes of Health (NIH), CDC, private foundations such as MacArthur Foundation, and state and local government entities. Affiliated investigators and students represent a range of disciplines including psychology, social work, public health, anthropology, biostatistics, psychiatry, nursing, sociology, pediatrics, and education.

CASRC is physically located at San Diego's Rady Children's Hospital, and a few members are hospital employees, but the majority of investigators, staff, and trainees have appointments across a variety of universities and health centers in Southern California, including University of California San Diego, San Diego State University, University of San Diego, University of Southern California, and Cal State San Marcos. Investigators contribute toward infrastructure administrative support through a small portion of grant funding; NIH center grants have also provided essential infrastructure support and funding for research innovations.

Most of the research and research training conducted through CASRC is practice oriented, with an emphasis on publicly funded mental health and child welfare services. CASRC investigators have worked hard to build and sustain community partnerships over three decades. Administrators in leadership positions in the county's department of health and human services have partnered with investigators to prioritize the most relevant research questions to inform policy decisions. As noted in the case studies shared later, practice partners also help to shape research methods to maximize both feasibility and rigor; they often offer complementary perspectives on the interpretation of data and assist with dissemination of research findings, particularly in venues and publications more frequently accessed by practitioners (as opposed to traditional academic publications). Likewise, investigators have partnered with front-line mental health providers to ensure that research proposals are relevant to the real challenges of community-based practice. In addition, families with lived experience in the child welfare and mental health systems have partnered with investigators to share their perspectives on services, research methods, and recruitment strategies, as well as interpretation of research findings.

One of the themes of this chapter will be the value of building genuine partnerships that are mutually respectful and beneficial. Developing and sustaining such partnerships is not necessarily easy, but we and our colleagues have found this work to be particularly rewarding, both professionally and personally. The first author of this chapter (A. F. G.) was drawn to practice-oriented research before even knowing that such a specialization existed. As a pragmatist, she sought to pursue applied research in naturalistic contexts. Building sustained collaborative relationships with practice partners became a valued "perk." Similarly, the second author (Y. M.) was drawn to practice-oriented research through her work addressing mental health disparities in underserved communities, where she recognized the need to actively include the communities being studied in the research itself.

Practice Partners

CASRC researchers have built partnerships with public sector service providers in specialty mental health clinics, primary care clinics, schools, child welfare, and developmental services agencies. Initially, researchers met with leaders of service agencies to build trust by transparently discussing aims, and allocation of potential funding. Partnership building often included vetting through ethics panels and often formal memoranda of understanding (MOUs). Fiscal support has been discussed prior to beginning any particular study to ensure fair resource allocation. As will be noted, depending on the study, partners may include administrators, managers/supervisors, front-line clinicians, teachers, or client (youth and family) representatives.

Research on Factors That Affect Research–Practice Partnership Effectiveness

Federal agencies including the National Institute of Mental Health (NIMH), Centers for Disease Control and Prevention, and the Institute of Medicine have all called for improved collaboration between researchers and practice partners to strengthen the integration of research and practice (Brookman-Frazee et al., 2016). There are many different models of research–practice partnerships. One of the most well-established models is community-based participatory research (CBPR) developed originally in public health but now used and adapted in other disciplines (Israel et al., 1998). Many other models exist including participatory action research, community–academic partnerships, research–practice partnerships, practice research networks, and so on. All differ on mission and goals, structure, membership selection, administrative support, and resource allocation but share the goal of improving the integration of research and community care.

Unfortunately, there is limited research available on effective partnership models or strategies to inform successful partnership development. In a systematic literature review of 50 studies of a variety of community–academic partnerships, Drahota and colleagues (2016) found that the vast majority (96%) of published studies were case studies utilizing qualitative methods (82%). Thus, quantitative empirical evaluation of the impact of such partnerships on research or practice is particularly sparse.

Drahota and colleagues' (2016) review identified 12 factors frequently cited as facilitating partnership success and 11 factors that hinder success. A review of these factors reflects the prominence of facilitating interpersonal processes such as building positive, trusting, mutually beneficial relationships. Historically, relationships between researchers and practitioners in mental health have not necessarily been characterized in these positive terms. In fact, according to some writers, relationships between researchers and mental health practitioners have been fraught with a lack of mutual respect and even antagonism (Lilienfeld et al., 2013; Tavris, 2003). More recent efforts to develop genuine collaborations with mutual respect and benefit, such as those described next and throughout this book, are hopefully changing this historical dynamic.

Description of Studies Supported by Partnership

Study Example 1: Practice and Research: Advancing Collaboration (PRAC)

The PRAC study was funded by NIMH. The aims were to (a) to identify common elements of evidence-based practice (EBP) for children (ages 4–13) with disruptive behavior problems and their families; (b) to examine the extent to which psychotherapists in community-based clinics were delivering care consistent with common elements of EBP, and (c) to identify practice-based evidence of practice elements (EBP and others) associated with differential outcomes. The study was conducted in partnership with a

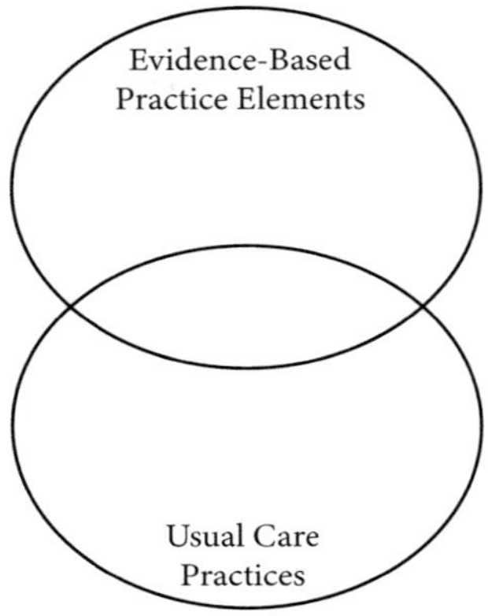

Figure 10.1 Conceptual Model for PRAC Study

Note: PRAC = practice and research: advancing collaboration

group of clinicians who represented different disciplines (e.g., psychology, marriage/couples & family therapy (MFT), social work). These clinician partners were nominated as leaders in each of the six outpatient mental health clinics participating in the study (for more details see Garland et al., 2006).

The conceptual model for the study is partially illustrated in Figure 10.1. We were interested in the extent of overlap between elements of EBP for this clinical population and practice elements actually delivered in "usual" community-based care. In Phase One, the researchers conducted a Delphi study, culling out essential practice elements from the eight treatments designated as effective for this clinical population. The team reviewed the cumulated practice elements and identified those present in at least half the individual treatment models. This list of common elements of evidence-based treatments was then reviewed by a panel of experts (including the treatment developers of the reviewed models) to validate the list (Garland et al., 2008).

Phase Two required extensive data collection on psychotherapy practices and was the first observational study characterizing community-based psychotherapists' practices with this clinical population. As reflected in this book, there are multiple methodological challenges and decisions to be made in measuring psychotherapy practice processes. These include ethical challenges due to the privacy of the endeavor, and methodological decisions regarding data source or informant (i.e., therapist or client self-report vs. observational coding vs. record review, etc.). In addition, it can be challenging to decide on the level of detail for capturing practice process elements.

This can range from broad categories such as theoretical orientation all the way to micro details on each participants' verbal and nonverbal behavior.

Decisions about how to measure practice processes for this study were made in partnership with the team of clinicians. The research and clinician representatives had lively discussions about how to capture essential elements of practice in a way that would be rigorous and reliable from a research perspective, as well as ecologically valid and feasible from a clinician perspective. The final measure of practice elements (referred to as the PRAC-Therapy Process Observational Coding System [PRAC-TPOCS]) reflected mutually agreed-upon practice elements that included both the common elements of EBP identified in Phase One and additional practice elements contributed by the clinician partners.

The clinician partners were essential for operationally defining the practice elements based on their clinical experience. This is an important example of how a practice-oriented research approach, pursued in collaboration with practice partners, may differ from other approaches where the research team would decide on measurement methods on their own.

Phase Three of the study was the most ambitious, requiring collection of video recordings for thousands of psychotherapy sessions across six community-based clinics. The clinician partner leaders were also essential for clinician recruitment in this phase. Participation in the study required video recording of all sessions (with the clients who consented) and was thus potentially somewhat arduous. Prior to launching the study, many of us worried that clinicians would not agree to participate. Fortunately, our worries were allayed as we successfully recruited 96 clinicians (80% of those who were eligible); this success is primarily attributed to the clinician partner leaders.

Approximately 200 child clients aged 4–13 years who were referred to outpatient care for disruptive behavior problems and their parents participated in the PRAC study. (Details on the clinician and client participants can be found in Garland et al., 2010.) We collected video recordings of 3,241 sessions and randomly selected (by random number generation) 1,215 for coding. Coders rated occurrence and intensity of the 27 practice elements jointly identified by research and practice partners. A subset of 379 sessions (31%) was randomly selected for double coding to test for inter-rater reliability. The interclass correlation coefficient (ICC) assessing reliability on the full measure across the 27 practice element codes was .78 representing good reliability.

Results of the practice observation and coding stage of this study provide a rare glimpse of "usual" psychotherapy practice in typical public community outpatient clinics. Overall, the data suggested that therapists were delivering care consistent with several elements of EBP (such as use of positive reinforcement with children), but they were infrequently delivering other elements (such as use of behavioral rehearsal/role-playing). Therapists were observed to deliver many different practice elements within a session (mean > 10), but the average intensity of each element was relatively low. Thus, therapists practiced with more breadth than depth.

The descriptive nature of this study provided a great deal of data on service use patterns, client attendance and engagement (Garland et al., 2012; Haine-Schlagel et al., 2012), client satisfaction and perceived effectiveness (Haine-Schlagel et al., 2014), therapist- and client-perceived therapeutic alliance (Accurso & Garland, 2015), and factors associated with therapist use of EBP practice elements (Brookman-Frazee et al., 2010). Some of the notable findings included the fact that clients whose therapists delivered practice elements common in EBPs with greater frequency attended more sessions and reported significantly stronger therapeutic alliances.

The final aim of the study was to examine the association between practice elements and clinical outcome trajectories assessed longitudinally every 4 months of treatment. Thus, this can be characterized as an attempt to identify practice-based evidence regarding therapeutic elements linked to better or worse clinical outcomes. The outcomes that were assessed included clients' perceptions of treatment effectiveness, as well as changes in symptom severity, functional impairment, family functioning, and parental discipline strategies.

Results indicated that when therapists delivered elements of EBPs with greater intensity, parental disciplinary strategies showed greater improvement (Garland et al., 2014). We tested for many other client characteristics, therapist characteristics, and practice elements that could have been associated with outcome trajectories and found no other significant effects.

Results of the PRAC study were presented to the broader community of researchers and providers in a "Research–Practice Expo" with each session co-led by a clinician leader and a researcher. This partnership resulted in sessions that emphasized clinical applications of research findings over details of research design and data analysis. The presenters worked on finding a mutually acceptable compromise between traditional academic presentation expectations and clinical training expectations. In many ways, this reflects the aims of practice-oriented research to find balance in optimizing both research rigor and clinical relevance.

Almost 20 years later, some of the participants in this PRAC study research–practice partnership group are still collaborating on new projects, as will be described. Participants have reported that this experience greatly impacted their career trajectories going forward.

Study Example 2: Clinical Supervision Study

Upon completion of the PRAC study, the partnership group of researchers and clinicians discussed priorities for a follow-up study. The clinician partners advocated strongly for a study of clinical supervision practices, given the essential role of clinical supervision in training therapists and the limited available research on clinical supervision. The partnership group wrote a grant proposal for a pilot study and successfully received funding from a local university. The goal was to learn more about supervision practices in the community-based clinics that had participated in the PRAC study.

Most of the clinician leaders on the partnership team were clinical supervisors, and thus they were extraordinarily influential in crafting the study's self-report measure of supervision processes and content. They piloted and refined the measure in their own practice. The resulting measure included two parts: (a) The *Supervision Process* section assessed supervision structure (e.g., duration, format, data source, and functions), and (b) the *Treatment Strategy* section of the questionnaire asked participants to indicate which psychotherapeutic treatment strategies (or practice elements) were discussed in supervision and the extent to which they were discussed (on a 1–4 scale). More details about the study are available in Accurso et al. (2011).

This two-part survey was administered to seven participating supervisors and 12 supervisees via online access. Data on 130 supervision sessions were collected. Results indicated that the majority (83%) of supervision sessions utilized progress notes as the data source. Only 13% utilized video or audio recordings. Supervisors and supervisees concurred that about 25% of the supervision session time was devoted to therapy interventions with another 25% devoted to case conceptualization. Additional time was reportedly devoted to administrative tasks and crisis intervention. Very little time was reportedly devoted to the supervisory relationship.

Results of the treatment strategies data collection indicated that treatment elements common to EBP were discussed fairly frequently in clinical supervision, but not very thoroughly. For example, according to supervisors, the use of positive reinforcement was discussed in 70% of supervision sessions, but it was discussed thoroughly in only 5% of sessions.

This study would not have been launched without the initiative of the clinician leader partners who wanted to learn more about what their peers were doing in supervision sessions. They were instrumental in working with the research team to develop a measure of supervision processes and content. This study represents a great example of practitioner initiated, practice-based research that was highly relevant to the community providers. They made subsequent policy decisions based on the results. For example, they required more use of video or audio recording, which is consistent with the research on effective supervision practice.

Study Example 3: The Southern California BRIDGE Collaborative

The Southern California BRIDGE Collaborative (see Brookman-Frazee et al., 2012) for a review) is a research–community partnership that was established in 2007, due to community identified needs, and was developed based on the principles of CBPR (Viswanathan et al., 2004) and community-partnered participatory research (CPPR; Jones & Wells, 2007). Conversations between researchers, community providers, and early-intervention funding agencies highlighted the common challenges they were encountering in providing services for young children with an increased likelihood of being identified with autism. An informal group of eight members began meeting monthly, with an initial goal of applying for NIH funding to support a larger goal of improving early intervention services for young children with an increased likelihood of being identified with autism.

During Phase I of the project, the aim was to collaboratively develop a group mission statement, formalize a leadership structure, and establish communication methods. Through an iterative process the group crafted the mission statement "To build a community dedicated to improving the earliest intervention for children with challenges in relating and communicating" and "named themselves the SoCal BRIDGE Collaborative (to signify the bridge they are building between research and practice, and to stand for their early intervention values: *B*ond-*R*egulate-*I*nteract-*D*evelop-*G*uide-*E*ngage;" Brookman-Frazee, Stahmer, et al., 2012, p. 718). Uniquely, the leadership structure was formalized to include a joint-leadership operations group, which included a researcher, community provider, and a parent, and worked to ensure joint decision-making. Additionally, collaborative workgroups for specific tasks were created, as well as a Collaborative Process Committee that was responsible for evaluating the collaborative itself, reporting findings, and recommending changes, if necessary. The group communicated via monthly meetings, email, and Google Sites, and promoted attendance by offering virtual meeting options and providing lunch during meetings.

During Phase II, the group focused on identifying a specific target population and obtaining funding to build community capacity. Together, the group members reviewed relevant literature while considering clinician and family experiences, and they elected to focus on building capacity of evidence-based interventions for children ages 12–24 months with increased likelihood of being identified with autism.

The group received funding from NIH to develop a coalition for community and research collaboration, to identify and adapt a sustainable intervention model for infants and toddlers with increased likelihood of being identified with autism and their families, and to test the feasibility of the adapted intervention (Brookman-Frazee, Stahmer, et al., 2012). In true CBPR and CPPR spirit, group members worked together to outline the procedures and select the outcome measures to be used. The group elected to collect data on proximal (process) outcomes, such as partnership synergy, intermediate goal attainment, and creation of tangible products, and distal outcomes, such as sustainability of partnership infrastructure, including rates of participation in monthly meetings and retention of members.

Overall, the collaborative trust, satisfaction, and perceptions of the research team were rated highly across the 4 years of partnership (Brookman-Frazee, Stahmer, et al., 2012). Participants reported feeling that researchers and community members had equal decision-making power, with 22% reporting that decision-making lay with community members guided by the researchers. Members also noted the importance of in-kind contributions from all members/organizations in the sustainability of the collaborative. Using participatory research methods (outlined in Stahmer et al., 2011), the collaborative selected the Ingersoll and Dvortcsak (2010) Teaching Social Communication (TSC) curriculum for community implementation. Results from the pilot study demonstrated it was feasible to implement TSC in the community, supervisors and therapists reached fidelity, and therapists and families were satisfied with the intervention (Brookman-Frazee, Stahmer, et al., 2012). Preliminary analyses of child outcomes also found increases in child communication and engagement, and in parent skills to facilitate child social communication skills.

The group's success was also measured in terms of tangible products, including a number of publications, presentations, community awards, grants, and trainings. Lastly, in terms of sustainability of partnership infrastructure, attendance in meetings increased to 85% by Year 4, and 100% of members remained with the group (Brookman-Frazee, Stahmer, et al., 2012).

In sum, the BRIDGE collaborative demonstrated the feasibility of developing and sustaining highly effective and productive community-partnered research projects. A quote from one of the BRIDGE group members sums it up best: "We are building, have built, a committed community, that is actively seeding other communities and providing enrichment to the revision and improvement of an intervention. It is bigger than most of us, and the loss of one person would not stop its growth" (Brookman-Frazee, Stahmer, et al., 2012, p. 722).

Study Example 4: AIM HI Study

Like the other studies highlighted in this chapter, An Individualized Mental Health Intervention for Autism Spectrum Disorder (AIM HI) was developed because of a community-identified need to better support the mental health of autistic children in community care. Through a community-needs assessment, Brookman-Frazee, Drahota, and colleagues (2012) found that autistic school-age children often present for mental health services due to interfering behaviors and often have co-occurring mental health needs. Further, they found therapists working in community mental health reported needing more specialized training to effectively address the mental health needs of this population. In response, researchers worked collaboratively with agency leaders, therapists, and parents to develop AIM HI to fill this training and service gap. AIM HI is a package of evidence-based, parent-mediated, and child-focused strategies aimed at reducing interfering behaviors in autistic children ages 5–13 years (Brookman-Frazee et al., 2016). Uniquely, AIM HI is both a clinical intervention protocol and a therapist training model that was tailored for therapists with limited autism and behavioral training.

The development of AIM HI was initiated by key community partners, and the community-research partnership was essential in informing adaptations made to AIM HI over time. Agency leaders, therapists, and parents were active participants in ensuring the AIM HI protocol was developed to be a good "fit" for implementation within a community mental health context. They collaborated to provide content expertise, data on the clinical needs of autistic children, and therapist training needs, and they actively provided feedback during the community trials. For example, qualitative data from therapists and families elucidated a need to increase information about autism for Latino/a/x parents (over 50% of participants) and highlighted the importance of the parent–therapist relationship for engaging these families (Chlebowski et al., 2018). As a result, researchers, in collaboration with therapists and parents, developed a cultural enhancement to AIM HI, "EQUIPO," which includes an additional collaborative psychoeducation session and additional training for therapists in culturally informed strategies for parent engagement (Chlebowski et al., 2020).

AIM HI training proved to be successful, as results from a randomized controlled community effectiveness trial of 29 community mental health programs, including 202 children (60% Latino/a/x), found that children whose therapists were trained in AIM HI had greater reductions in parent-reported challenging behaviors (over 18 months) compared with children who received usual care (Brookman-Frazee et al., 2019). These intervention effects on child clinical outcomes were mediated by therapist fidelity (observer-rated) to AIM HI strategies within their sessions. Additionally, children whose therapists participated in AIM HI training received significantly higher session structure and continuity across sessions, which was in turn associated with fewer challenging behaviors, compared with the usual care group (Brookman-Frazee et al., 2019). Further, caregivers reported significant increases in sense of competence at 6 months, which were in turn associated with improved child behavior outcomes (Brookman-Frazee et al., 2021).

Consistent and continuous collaboration with key community partners during the effectiveness trials helped elucidate another area of need in the implementation of AIM HI in community mental health systems. Results showed variability in AIM HI training completion and fidelity to the intervention. Given the importance of therapist fidelity and its association with child outcomes, researchers collaborated with agency leaders to test the impact of two implementation strategies: leadership training [TEAMS

Leadership Institute (TLI)] and provider training [TEAMS Individualized Provider Strategy for Training (TIPS)], to improve training completion and fidelity to AIM HI, and in turn improve child outcomes (see Brookman-Frazee & Stahmer, 2018, for study protocol). Results show that the leadership training (TLI) was associated with significantly higher therapist fidelity to AIM HI and a significant improvement in child clinical outcomes across time, compared with the control group (Brookman-Frazee et al., 2023).

The success of AIM HI in training therapists and meeting the mental health needs of children with autism in community care is an exemplary model of the type of work that can be accomplished through community-partnered, practice-oriented research. AIM HI provides therapists with tools and strategies they can use to adapt and augment ongoing psychotherapy for autistic children. Community collaboration has been at the core for this research from the initial development of AIM HI through the various iterations, and as it continues to be adapted to meet the needs of autistic children via telehealth settings. This approach has facilitated the engagement and commitment from community organizations, leaders, therapists, and families necessary to continue to effectively implement AIM HI to improve mental health outcomes for autistic children.

Benefits and Challenges of Participating in Practice-Oriented Research

The four case example studies described earlier addressed different research aims and utilized different research methods, but all relied upon strong genuine partnerships between researchers and community partners. As measured by traditional academic indicators such as academic publications, each of these studies was a success. Beyond these traditional indicators, participants in these efforts have reported that the partnership experience in and of itself has been particularly impactful, both personally and professionally. As noted by a researcher,

> Practice oriented research can be rewarding as you often get to see first-hand the impact on families of your research. For example, when doing intervention research, you may get to see first-hand a client's progress or hear about a client's progress through participant post intervention interviews. You may even get some words of appreciation or validation.

As is often the case, the benefits of a particular approach also present the significant challenges. For example, researchers and clinicians who have participated in partnered research have told us that sustainable relationship building has helped them to expand their knowledge and skills, as well as challenge preconceived assumptions about research and practice (and likewise researchers and practitioners). Clinicians have reported that they were surprised to gain insights about effective practice techniques after discussions with researchers. Some clinicians expressed initial concern that partnership invitations would be superficial or transactional (i.e., just to facilitate researchers' completion of a study), but they were pleasantly surprised to find that their input on relevant research questions, feasibility of research design issues, and interpretation of data was genuinely respected and valued by researchers.

Researchers have reported that they have gained renewed respect for the realities and responsibilities of clinical practice. Research trainees have said that they appreciate the direct and timely public health impact of partnered research in a community. For example, a researcher noted, "[. . .] I have learned the importance of conducting focus groups and participant interviews to gain direct feedback on intervention materials, and then incorporating this feedback into the intervention delivery in order to increase community satisfaction and engagement."

Despite all the perceived benefits of partnered research, participants also unanimously express that relationship building is "really tough work and because of that it's important to have a strong understanding of context and a relationship with folks in that context" (as noted by a researcher). With further elaboration, this researcher noted the importance of "knowing the ask for providers," knowing how things work on the back end, and how you are going to help make it easier for participants to integrate the study requirements into what they already do. Additionally, it takes considerable time to build trusting relationships, and most research-funding mechanisms and practice agency budgets do not include support for relationship building. We find that there are no shortcuts to building genuine partnerships.

Numerous additional challenges of partnered practice-oriented research include the fact that academic researchers are neither necessarily trained nor rewarded for community partnership building. And most practice contexts don't have any infrastructure supports to implement research projects, including research methods expertise among staff. Practice-oriented research also presents ethical challenges in participant recruitment and tracking based on national privacy regulations. The very issues that make practice-oriented research more ecologically valid present the thorniest challenges because the complexity of community-based practice is quite difficult to "control" in terms of research design. For example, another researcher notes,

> Some of the aspects that may be challenging about this type of work are that you are interacting with real people not just numbers; thus, participants may have obstacles that prevent them from coming to your session or interviews as planned, which can make data collection and retention challenging. Similarly, humans are complex and don't always fit into a box captured by your data.

Given all these challenges, to what do we attribute our group's relative success in sustaining research–practice partnerships? As noted earlier, infrastructure support and specific research study support have been essential to providing some limited compensation to community partners for their time. Beyond practical resources, we attribute success to all participants' patience and sincere motivation to build mutually trusting relationships where everyone recognizes they can learn from each other and any potential conflicts are discussed openly; likewise, participants frequently remind each other of the shared purpose of improving care for vulnerable families.

The following quote reflects our experience, noting that the benefits of partnerships outweigh the frustrations: "True partnerships between researchers and practitioners and associated stakeholders are likely to be instructive, humbling, fun and only occasionally frustrating" (Olswang & Goldstein, 2017, p. 70).

Conclusions and Call to Action

Practice-oriented research conducted in partnership with community representatives is essential for bridging the ubiquitous gap between science and community-based practice. Research and practice generate complementary knowledge about how to improve access to care and outcomes of care. Older models that relied upon the unidirectional application of research to practice have only limited effectiveness in improving care. Successful integration of research and practice requires bidirectional, or multidirectional, efforts. Community practice representatives (leaders, providers, clients/families, etc.) need to influence and inform research just as we hope research informs practice.

The practice oriented research (POR) described in this chapter significantly influenced the participating individuals and the institutions. Researchers gained greater understanding of the realities and challenges of practice, as well as practitioners' highest priority research questions, which influenced their research focuses going forward. Clinicians learned more about how to identify and integrate evidence-based practice elements into treatment and clinical supervision, thus influencing practice and training approaches in the multiple clinics participating in these studies. Lessons learned from the studies also reinforced the value of conducting research with traditionally underserved community representatives and modeled how to do that.

Unfortunately, there are few national structures in place to facilitate multidirectional communication and research–practice partnership models. Thus, most efforts are local initiatives as described throughout this book. We need broader state and federal initiatives to provide fiscal support to build and sustain partnerships. For example, calls to include community partners in research as well as resources and timelines that account for the additional time it can take to foster such collaborations are essential. Such support is critical to operationally support partnership efforts, and also to reinforce the value of such efforts.

More research on practice-oriented research methods and partnership models is also needed; gaining greater clarity and consistency in nomenclature will be an important first step (as noted by Drahota and colleagues, 2016). Research on partnership processes and outcomes could benefit from input from a variety of disciplines including public health, business management, nursing, and perhaps even political science. While there is general consensus about the importance of building mutually trusting and respectful partnerships for success, there is minimal research on how to operationalize and measure these constructs. Too often partnership building has relied on tacit knowledge. Projects that include explicit study of partnership processes and outcomes, such as the BRIDGE project (Study Example 3), are needed to generate more explicit and generalizable knowledge to guide future partnership development.

Throughout this chapter we have emphasized the importance of building truly equitable partnerships where decision-making, resource allocation, knowledge dissemination, and leadership are shared equitably. This requires explicit attention to, and discussion about, power dynamics, including potentially dismantling traditional hierarchical structures in academic research and/or healthcare organizations. Our partnership examples described in this chapter have aimed toward but not always achieved truly equitable collaboration. It is a goal requiring continuous learning and adaptation. Essential ingredients for equitable collaboration and implementation include taking time to build trusting partnerships, practicing transparent decision-making, engaging the community in interpreting and using the data collected, and distributing information and decision-making authority to the community who is most affected by the research (Metz et al., 2021).

Toward this end, it is also essential to continue examining ways to disrupt power dynamics at the intervention implementation level (see Stanton et al., 2022, for a review). They propose a call to action to examine and disrupt three types of intervention implementation power: discursive power, epistemic power, and material power. Practice-oriented research seems to be an approach that can lend itself to doing this very work. Discursive power refers to ways in which dominant perspectives become what is implemented in the real world and shape the actions and capabilities of others. This includes defining the health problems to be addressed and developing health narratives about communities (e.g., hard to reach). The antidote here is to include the community in these definitions and in developing/correcting the narrative. Epistemic power refers to being able to assert one's knowledge as essential to a collective set of beliefs or truths. We can interrogate this power by examining whose knowledge is valued in decision-making and ensuring the community's knowledge is valued and used to inform intervention implementation decisions. Material power refers to the distribution of and patterns of access to critical resources. The key consideration here is to ensure community members can equitably access the resources and truly benefit from the intervention being implemented.

Those of us who have participated in genuine partnership efforts recognize the empowering synergy that can be achieved when the combined effects of partners are stronger than separate effects. We need the synergy of all types of complementary knowledge and skills to tackle the serious challenges of the youth mental health crisis. Mutually respectful and trusting relationships built across academic research and community practice contexts provide an essential foundation for improving mental health care.

References

Accurso, E. C., & Garland, A. F. (2015). Child, caregiver, and therapist perspectives on therapeutic alliance in usual care child psychotherapy. *Psychological Assessment*, *27*(1), 347–352. http://doi.org/10.1037/pas0000031

Accurso, E. C., Taylor, R. M., & Garland, A. F. (2011). Evidence-based practices addressed in community-based children's mental health clinical supervision. *Training and Education in Professional Psychology*, *5*(2), 88–96. https://doi.org/10.1037/a0023537

Brookman-Frazee, L., Chlebowski, C., Villodas, M., Roesch, S., & Martinez, K. (2021). Training community therapists to deliver an individualized mental health intervention for autism spectrum disorder: Changes in caregiver outcomes and mediating role on child outcomes. *Journal of the American Academy of Child & Adolescent Psychiatry*, *60*(3), 355–366. https://doi.org/10.1016/j.jaac.2020.07.896

Brookman-Frazee, L., Drahota, A., Stadnick, N., & Palinkas, L. A. (2012). Therapist perspectives on community mental health services for children with autism spectrum disorders. *Administration and Policy in Mental Health and Mental Health Services Research*, *39*, 365–373. https://doi.org/10.1007/s10488-011-0355-y

Brookman-Frazee, L., Haine, R. A., Baker-Ericzén, M., Zoffness, R., & Garland, A. F. (2010). Factors associated with use of evidence-based practice strategies in usual care youth psychotherapy. *Administration and Policy in Mental Health and Mental Health Services*, *37*, 254–269. https://doi.org/10.1007/s10488-009-0244-9

Brookman-Frazee, L., Lau, A., Roesch, S., Jobin A., Chlebowski, C., Mello, M., Caplan, B., Naar, S., Aarons, G. A., & Stahmer, A. C. (2023). *Effectiveness of multi-level implementation strategies for autism interventions: Outcomes of two linked implementation trials* [Manuscript in preparation]. Department of Psychiatry, University of California, San Diego.

Brookman-Frazee, L., Roesch, S., Chlebowski, C., Baker-Ericzen, M., & Ganger, W. (2019). Effectiveness of training therapists to deliver an individualized mental health intervention for children with ASD in publicly funded mental health services: A cluster randomized clinical trial. *JAMA Psychiatry*, *76*(6), 574–583. https://doi.org/10.1001/jamapsychiatry.2019.0011

Brookman-Frazee, L., & Stahmer, A. C. (2018). Effectiveness of a multi-level implementation strategy for ASD interventions: Study protocol for two linked cluster randomized trials. *Implementation Science*, *13*, Article 66. https://doi.org/10.1186/s13012-018-0757-2

Brookman-Frazee, L., Stahmer, A. C., Lewis, K., Feder, J. D., & Reed, S. (2012). Building a research-community collaborative to improve community care for infants and toddlers at-risk for autism spectrum disorders. *Journal of Community Psychology*, *40*(6), 715–734. https://doi.org/10.1002/jcop.21501

Brookman-Frazee, L., Stahmer, A., Stadnick, N., Chlebowski, C., Herschell, A., & Garland, A. F. (2016). Characterizing the use of research-community partnerships in studies of evidence-based interventions in children's community services. *Administration and Policy in Mental Health and Mental Health Services Research*, *43*, 93–104. https://doi.org/10.1007/s10488-014-0622-9

Centers for Disease Control and Prevention. (2021). *Youth risk behavior survey: Data summary and trend report 2009–2019*. https://www.cdc.gov/healthyyouth/data/yrbs/pdf/YRBSDataSummaryTrendsReport2019-508.pdf

Chlebowski, C., Hurwich-Reiss, E., Wright, B., & Brookman-Frazee, L. (2020). Using stakeholder perspectives to guide systematic adaptation of an autism mental health intervention for Latinx families: A qualitative study. *Journal of Community Psychology*, *48*(4), 1194–1214. https://doi.org/10.1002/jcop.22296

Chlebowski, C., Magaña, S., Wright, B., & Brookman-Frazee, L. (2018). Implementing an intervention to address challenging behaviors for autism spectrum disorder in publicly-funded mental health services: Therapist and parent perceptions of delivery with Latinx families.

Cultural Diversity and Ethnic Minority Psychology, *24*(4), 552–563. https://doi.org/10.1037/cdp0000215

Drahota, A., Meza, R. D., Brikho, B., Naaf, M., Estabillo, J. A., Gomez, E. D., Vejnoska, S. F., Dufek, S., Stahmer, A. C., & Aarons, G. A. (2016). Community-academic partnerships: A systematic review of the state of the literature and recommendations for future research. *The Milbank Quarterly*, *94*(1), 163–214. https://doi.org/10.1111/1468-0009.12184

Garland, A. F., Accurso, E. C., Haine-Schlagel, R., Brookman-Frazee, L., Roesch, S., & Zhang, J. J. (2014). Searching for elements of evidence-based practices in children's usual care and examining their impact. *Journal of Clinical Child and Adolescent Psychology*, *43*(2), 201–215. https://doi.org/10.1080/15374416.2013.869750

Garland, A. F., Brookman-Frazee, L., Hurlburt, M. S., Accurso, E. C., Zoffness, R. J., Haine-Schlagel, R., & Ganger, W. (2010). Mental health care for children with disruptive behavior problems: A view inside therapists' offices. *Psychiatric Services*, *61*(8), 788–795. https://doi.org/10.1176/ps.2010.61.8.788

Garland, A. F., Haine-Schlagel, R, Accurso, E. C., Baker-Ericzén, M. J., & Brookman-Frazee, L. (2012). Exploring the effect of therapists' treatment practices on client attendance in community-based care for children. *Psychological Services*, *9*(1), 74–88. https://doi.org/10.1037/a0027098

Garland, A. F., Hawley, K. M., Brookman-Frazee, L., & Hurlburt, M. S. (2008). Identifying common elements of evidence-based psychosocial treatments for children's disruptive behavior problems. *Journal of the American Academy of Child and Adolescent Psychiatry*, *47*(5), 505–514. https://doi.org/10.1097/CHI.0b013e31816765c2

Garland, A. F., Lebensohn-Chialvo, F., Hall, K. G., & Cameron, E. R. N. (2017). Capitalizing on scientific advances to improve access and quality of children's mental health care. *Behavioral Sciences & the Law*, *35*(4), 337–352. https://doi.org/10.1002/bsl.2296

Garland, A. F., Plemmons, D., & Koontz, L. (2006). Research-practice partnership in mental health: Lessons from participants. *Administration and Policy in Mental Health and Mental Health Services*, *33*, 517–528. https://doi.org/10.1007/s10488-006-0062-2

Haine-Schlagel, R., Brookman-Frazee, L., Fettes, D. L., Baker-Ericzén, M., & Garland, A. F. (2012). Therapist focus on parent involvement in community-based youth psychotherapy. *Journal of Child and Family Studies*, *21*, 646–656. https://doi.org/10.1007/s10826-011-9517-5

Haine-Schlagel, R., Fettes, D. L., Garcia, A. R., Brookman-Frazee, L., & Garland, A. F. (2014). Consistency with evidence-based treatments and perceived effectiveness of children's community-based care. *Community Mental Health Journal*, *50*, 158–163. https://doi.org/10.1007/s10597-012-9583-1

Ingersoll, B., & Dvortcsak, A. (2010). *Teaching social communication to children with autism: A practitioner's guide to parent training*. The Guilford Press.

Israel, B. A., Schulz, A. J., Parker, E. A., & Becker, A. B. (1998). Review of community-based research: Assessing partnership approaches to improve public health. *Annual Review of Public Health*, *19*, 173–202. https://doi.org/10.1146/annurev.publhealth.19.1.173

Jones, L., & Wells, K. (2007). Strategies for academic and clinician engagement in community-participatory partnered research. *JAMA*, *297*(4), 407–410. https://doi.org/10.1001/jama.297.4.407

Landsverk, J., Garland, A., Rolls Reutz, J., & Davis, I. (2011). Bridging science and practice in child welfare and children's mental health service systems through a two-decade research center trajectory. *Journal of Social Work*, *11*(1), 80–98. https://doi.org/10.1177/1468017310381816

Lilienfeld, S. O., Ritschel, L. A., Lynn, S. J., Cautin, R. L., & Latzman, R. D. (2013). Why many clinical psychologists are resistant to evidence-based practice: Root causes and constructive remedies. *Clinical Psychology Review*, *33*(7), 883–900. https://doi.org/10.1016/j.cpr.2012.09.008

Metz, A., Woo, B., & Loper, A. (2021, December 14–16). Equitable implementation at work [Conference presentation]. In *14th Annual Conference on the Science of Dissemination and Implementation in Health*. Academy Health. https://doi.org/10.1186/s13012-022-01210-x

Office of the Surgeon General. (2021). *Protecting youth mental health: The U.S. Surgeon General's advisory*. U.S. Department of Health and Human Services. https://pubmed.ncbi.nlm.nih.gov/34982518/

Olswang, L. B., & Goldstein, H. (2017). Collaborating on the development and implementation of evidence-based practices: Advancing science and practice. *Evidence-Based Communication Assessment and Intervention, 11*(3–4), 61–71. https://doi.org/10.1080/17489539.2017.1386404

Stahmer, A. C., Brookman-Frazee, L., Lee, E., Searcy, K., & Reed, S. (2011). Parent and multidisciplinary provider perspectives on earliest intervention for children at risk for autism spectrum disorders. *Infants & Young Children, 24*(4), 344–363. https://doi.org/10.1097/IYC.0b013e31822cf700

Stanton, M. C., Ali, S. B., & the SUSTAIN Center Team. (2022). A typology of power in implementation: Building on the exploration, preparation, implementation, sustainment (EPIS) framework to advance mental health and HIV health equity. *Implementation Research and Practice*, 3. https://doi.org/10.1177/26334895211064250

Tavris, C. (2003). Mind games: Psychological warfare between therapists and scientists. *The Chronicle of Higher Education, 49*(25), B7.

Viswanathan, M., Ammerman, A., Eng, E., Garlehner, G., Lohr, K. N., Griffith, D., Rhodes, S., Samuel-Hodge, C., Maty, S., Lux, L., Webb, L., Sutton, S. F., Swinson, T., Jackman, A., & Whitener, L. (2004). Community-based participatory research: Assessing the evidence. *Evidence Report/Technology Assessment (Summary)*, (99), 1–8.

11

The Seamless Integration of Science and Practice in College Student Mental Health

Building Relationships Among Stakeholders to Better Understand and Improve Services

Jeffrey A. Hayes and Louis G. Castonguay

Historical Context

Across the globe, more than 230 million individuals are enrolled in institutions of higher education. Post-secondary education typically invokes both excitement and trepidation for students. At the outset, one's college years lie shrouded in the future, with normative developmental challenges ahead, such as establishing an identity, solidifying values, forming meaningful relationships with peers, and preparing for a career (Chickering & Reisser, 1993). This transition is all the more difficult when a student is encumbered with mental health problems. A number of psychological disorders first appear between the ages of 18 and 25, ages that include most undergraduate and many graduate students. Even in the absence of psychological disorders, college students' mental health affects their academic performance, social functioning, risk of dropping out of school, time to graduation, and prospects for employment after graduating (National Academies of Sciences, Engineering and Medicine, 2021). In short, the potential impact of tomorrow's likely societal leaders will be greatly undermined by untreated mental health challenges during the college years.

Until the beginning of the 21st century, scientific knowledge about college students' mental health was largely based on studies that were conducted at a single university. Imagine conducting a study at Cairo University and then generalizing the findings to students at Florida A&M University, the University of the Andes, and Padova University. Although it may seem like a stretch

Jeffrey A. Hayes and Louis G. Castonguay, *The Seamless Integration of Science and Practice in College Student Mental Health*. In: *Practice-Based Evidence in the Psychological Therapies*. Edited by: Louis G. Castonguay et al., Oxford University Press. © Oxford University Press (2026). DOI: 10.1093/9780197748336.003.0011 to think that findings from one university would apply to students at all schools, that was, with noteworthy exceptions (e.g., Silverman et al., 1997), the general state of affairs until a few years after the turn of the 21st century. Even when studies were conducted on the same or similar topics, they typically used different measures, which made results difficult to synthesize.

Shortly after the turn of the century, an opportunity fell out of the sky and into the lives of this chapter's authors that would revolutionize the field of college student mental health and its treatment. Dr. Ben Locke, a colleague of the authors at Penn State's counseling center, envisioned building a practice research network of counseling centers in higher education throughout the United States, and he invited us along for the ride. As psychotherapy researchers already invested in the generation and dissemination of process outcome findings, we (and a succession of graduate students in our respective labs) enthusiastically embarked on a career-changing journey devoted to the gathering of practice-based evidence regarding the utilization, effectiveness, and improvement of mental health services in university counseling centers (UCCs). Because these centers are the primary source of psychological treatment for college students, we viewed this large practice research network (PRN) infrastructure as an optimal conduit for collecting data that would be generalizable at a national level. Furthermore, as university professors and psychologists, we have naturally been interested in the well-being of college students throughout our careers. In addition, because our respective mentors (Charlie Gelso and Marv Goldfried) had instilled in each of us the value of scientific collaboration, the involvement in a PRN allowed us to maintain a meaningful link with our academic roots while providing us with an optimal pathway for our professional and scientific actualization.

It should be pointed out that Dr. Locke's vision of a national PRN was born out of a very practical need, in response to the threat of UCCs being eliminated. That threat still exists. A large community college in the United States, with an enrollment of greater than 17,000 students, closed its 20-person counseling center in 2019. Some years previously, in the early 2000s, the "perfect storm" was present: Many universities sought to trim their budgets, and little evidence existed that UCCs contributed in a critical way to the mission of their institutions. There was not even compelling evidence that UCCs effectively reduced students' distress or improved their functioning (Locke et al., 2012; Sharkin, 2004). This should not be interpreted as a criticism of the effectiveness of UCCs or their staff. It is simply a real-world, long-standing reflection of priorities at virtually all UCCs. Research is not of paramount importance in these settings, and the time required for research has been limited by the high demand for therapy and psychiatric services (Cooper & Archer, 2002). Further contributing to this challenging situation, concerns had been raised near the turn of the century about the validity of popular instruments that were used for clinical purposes to measure distress among college students (Hayes, 1997; Kim et al., 2010).

In the face of these challenges, Dr. Locke invited the two of us to a series of breakfast meetings in 2005 at a local restaurant. The scale of Dr. Locke's vision, which was almost incomprehensible to us, generated an instant, contagious enthusiasm. In our prior research experience, we had become painfully aware of the hurdles and headaches associated with collecting naturalistic psychotherapy data. As Dr. Locke described his vision, the possibility of building a network capable of gathering ecologically valid data on a national scale was a formidable challenge whose benefits we simply could not ignore. Our excitement and ambition and naiveté hooked us; from the first cup of coffee, we were in.

The Center for Collegiate Mental Health

After three or four breakfast meetings, Dr. Locke organized a conference in 2006 that was attended by psychologists from 55 UCCs. The Center for Collegiate Mental Health (CCMH; ccmh.psu.edu) was born out of this conference. CCMH now comprises more than 825 counseling centers in higher education, primarily in the United States and also in Canada, the United Kingdom, and the Caribbean (Hayes, Locke et al., 2011). CCMH has an advisory board with members from a dozen counseling centers, as well as a research team of counseling center psychologists, faculty members, and graduate students at Penn State. This infrastructure is the result of a collaborative, multidisciplinary effort that incorporates the expertise of mental health treatment providers, psychology and psychotherapy researchers, graduate students, administrators, information science and technology experts, industry partners, and funding agencies. Several goals were paramount from the outset: assess and describe the state of college student mental health on a large-scale basis; develop clinical tools to inform and enhance therapists' day-to-day practice; provide UCCs with scientifically based information for advocacy purposes; conduct clinically relevant, rigorous, client-oriented research; and improve mental health and its measurement in higher education settings. The ultimate aim of CCMH was, and remains, to create and sustain reciprocally advantageous relationships among a wide array of collaborators who are invested in research that will enhance mental health services provided to college students.

CCMH Instruments

One of the first tasks faced by CCMH was to decide on common measures that would be administered to college students who received counseling on campus. Two primary instruments were selected. The first one is called the Standardized Data Set (SDS; Hayes, Locke et al., 2011). The SDS, which has evolved over time, now measures variables including client and counselor cultural demographics; students' employment, housing, experiences of discrimination, extracurricular involvement, and mental health history (e.g., previous suicide attempts); the type of services provided to students, such as individual or group counseling, crisis appointments, or psychiatric evaluations; the number of sessions attended; and why treatment concluded. The client version is filled out only once, during the intake session.

In addition to the SDS, the other instrument that CCMH uses is the Counseling Center Assessment of Psychological Symptoms-62 (CCAPS-62; Locke et al., 2011). At the 2006 conference, there were a number of contenders as to which instrument ought to be selected to measure distress among college students. At the time, the CCAPS was in use at the University of Michigan's counseling center. Although it consisted originally of more than 100 items, it was chosen over other instruments because it was developed specifically for college students, it was multidimensional, and there were promising signs that CCMH would not face insurmountable financial or legal difficulties using the CCAPS (Castonguay et al., 2011; Locke et al., 2012). Through a series of factor analyses, the CCAPS was narrowed to 70 items and eventually to 62 items, which measure distress on eight dimensions: depression, generalized anxiety, eating concerns, social anxiety, academic distress, substance use, family concerns, and hostility/frustration (Locke et al., 2011). In studies of its psychometric properties, the CCAPS-62 has generally evidenced solid reliability and validity. For instance, McAleavey et al. (2012) found strong correlations (greater than .55) between each of the CCAPS-62 subscales and established measures of similar constructs. Evidence has been found supporting the subscales' retest reliability, proposed factor structure, lack of socially desirable responding, sensitivity, and convergent validity (Locke et al., 2011; McAleavey et al., 2012; Youn et al., 2020). In addition, strong evidence has been found regarding the internal consistency of 7 of the 8 CCAPS-62 subscales. Internal consistency estimates range from α = .64 (Family Distress) to α = .91 (Depression). Collectively, a rather convincing body of findings suggests that the CCAPS-62 can reliably and accurately assess psychological distress in college students.

It should be noted, however, that to date very little evidence exists regarding the cultural validity of the CCAPS-62. Locke et al. (2011) reported the internal consistency estimates of each subscale for various ethnoracial groups but did not examine validity data for these groups. It is important to determine the validity of CCAPS-62 scores for students from a variety of ethnoracial backgrounds, especially given the widespread use of the CCAPS-62 among students of color. For example, more than 50,000 students of color were assessed with the CCAPS-62 in the 2021–2022 academic year (CCMH, 2025). Given the potential for a client's culture to affect how they interpret and respond to test items, Zhao et al. (202) examined CCAPS-62 data from more than 300,000 clients at 137 counseling centers. Factor analyses were conducted for five ethnoracial groups (Asian Americans, Blacks / African Americans, Hispanic/Latinx, Native Americans, and Whites). Evidence of factor invariance across groups was generally strong, although several items did not load on expected subscales for multiple ethnoracial groups. Differential item functioning revealed that many of these same items did not perform in a similar manner across ethnoracial groups. At the factor level, the CCAPS-62 seems to accurately measure its intended constructs for students of various ethnic and racial backgrounds. At the item level, however, clinicians and researchers should exercise caution in assigning meaning to clients' scores on particular items, depending on clients' ethnoracial identity.

As CCMH grew during its early years, it became evident that a briefer version of the CCAPS-62 would be needed to assess how well clients were improving during treatment. As a result, a 34-item version of the CCAPS was generated (Locke et al., 2012). All of the items on the CCAPS-34 are contained within the CCAPS-62. Both the CCAPS-62 and CCAPS-34 also contain an overall Distress Index, which is composed of 20 items drawn from five CCAPS subscales (Nordberg et al., 2018). These 20 items are identical on the CCAPS-34 and the CCAPS-62. The Distress Index often is used by researchers as a general measure of treatment progress and outcome, although clinicians typically rely on session-to-session changes on specific scales to determine the progress and success of treatment (Hayes et al., 2016; Isadore et al., 2024).

Despite the many strengths of the CCAPS, it is important to note that the CCAPS is problem focused; it measures distress, or the lack thereof, but it does not measure students' joy, interpersonal intelligence, coping skills, goals, self-awareness, aspirations, values, or life satisfaction. Furthermore, low scores on any, or even all, of the CCAPS subscales cannot be interpreted to mean that a student feels fulfilled or is functioning optimally. The absence of distress is not synonymous with psychological well-being.

Early Growth of CCMH

To determine the feasibility of its infrastructure, CCMH conducted a pilot study in 2009, gathering data from more than 28,000 students at 66 universities. After this initial pilot study, a series of technological, legal, logistical and practical challenges were addressed by CCMH, such as securely storing large amounts of data, allowing students who did not want to contribute their information to CCMH to easily opt out of doing so, encrypting data to ensure its anonymity, and settling copyright agreements for the CCAPS (see McAleavey et al., 2015, for a description of obstacles faced by CCMH at organizational, scientific, clinical, and funding levels).

Imagine spending several years lining up dominoes that stretch out to the horizon. This metaphor describes the preparatory work undertaken by CCMH following the conference in 2006. In 2010, the first domino was tipped. Full-time data collection began, and the dominoes have been colliding recursively and dynamically ever since, with new dominoes added in response to emerging challenges and opportunities. In the 2010–2011 academic year, data were gathered from more than 82,000 college students seeking help at nearly 100 UCCs. In 2013–2014, data were collected from more than 100,000 college student clients. The following year, that number topped 150,000 clients, and it has done so every year since. As of 2023, CCMH had gathered data from more than 1.7 million college students seeking help at UCCs and, based on those data, had published scores of empirical articles, trained thousands of mental health professionals, and helped shape policies and practices at UCCs on a multinational level.

In 2021, Dr. Brett Scofield from Penn State's counseling center became the executive director of CCMH, and it has continued to thrive under his leadership. Perhaps the most critical component to the success of CCMH has been the integration of the SDS and CCAPS into routine clinical practice at hundreds of UCCs. This integration was made possible by technology that allowed for data to be collected as part of everyday procedures rather than as an additional burden at UCCs. By embedding the SDS and CCAPS directly into a client's electronic medical record, UCCs were able to gather data with ease. This represented an enormous culture shift within counseling centers. Previously, data collection had been conducted by researchers located outside the counseling center, and these efforts were often met with apathy or opposition. As a result of CCMH and its 800+ member institutions, UCCs now have at their disposal data that can be used for research, training, monitoring clients' improvements, and examining in-house policies and practices. Based on years of collaborative engagement among multiple stakeholders, reliance on a diversity of complementary expertise, and shared ownership of standardized data collected as part of clinical routine, CCMH has been able to accomplish the very difficult task of seamlessly and simultaneously balancing the interests of UCCs (e.g., minimizing burden to staff, protecting client confidentiality) with the needs of researchers (e.g., obtaining high-quality, large-scale, and ecologically valid data).

Empirical Studies

Scores of studies, including graduate student theses and dissertations, have now been conducted based on CCMH data. While many of these studies are the fruits of collaborative efforts between the two authors' respective labs and their colleagues at Penn State University, the CCMH data is accessible for researchers around the world 2 years after being aggregated. Examples of studies will be briefly described (additional CCMH publications are available at ccmh.psu.edu/publications).

Effectiveness

Addressing a top priority for CCMH stakeholders, McAleavey and colleagues (2019) examined the effectiveness of psychological therapies as delivered in routine clinical practice at 108 UCCs. Based on the subscales of the CAPS-34 and an overall sample of 9,895 clients treated by 1,454 therapists, the results showed pre-post treatment reliable improvement (percentage of clients who show positive change that is not likely to be due to chance) ranging from 8.0% (for Alcohol Use) to 28.8% (for Depression). The study also assessed how the symptomatic improvement observed in these UCCs compared with "gold standard" criteria. Benchmark comparisons were conducted with randomized clinical trial (RCT) findings and revealed that, for highly distressed clients (those who were most similar to individuals included in RCTs), the pre-post effect sizes were equivalent for all CCAPS-34 subscales except Alcohol Use. What made these results particularly significant was the fact that the average length of treatment in the UCCs was shorter than that of the RCTs used as benchmarks. On the less positive side, however, the findings also indicated that, at the end of treatment, clients who had been highly distressed at intake tended to not be in the range of normative distress on any of the CCAPS subscales. Clients who were moderately distressed at intake, on the other hand, tended to have normative distress scores on all domains at termination.

The use of a multidimensional measure of outcome has allowed CCMH to provide further support to, and expand the breadth of, two well-known models of change in therapy. These two models are the dose–effect model (Howard et al., 1986), which postulates that lengthier treatment leads to greater change, albeit with less change occurring as therapy progresses, and the good enough model (Barkham et al., 2006), postulating that clients receiving shorter treatment show a faster rate of change. Based on a sample of 64,319 clients treated by 3,102 therapists in 147 UCCs, Niilekela et al. (2021) found support for both models. More sessions were associated with greater client improvement, including reliable and clinically significant change, with diminished improvement in later sessions. The results also showed that clients who attended fewer sessions tended to change at a faster rate than clients who had more sessions. These findings held for not only a global measure of outcome (i.e., the CCAPS Distress Index) but also the specific subscales of the CCAPS-34, each of them assessing clinically meaningful domains of symptomatology.

The effectiveness studies presented earlier suggest that a substantial number of clients benefit from psychological treatment they receive in UCCs in terms of symptom improvement, and that some of the patterns of symptomatic change they experienced are similar to those observed in other settings. Other studies, however, have focused on impacts of counseling that are particularly relevant to college students. For example, Lockard et al. (2019) highlighted the relevance of monitoring academic distress during treatment. Collected within one counseling center, data from 404 students who received psychotherapy indicated that clients who decreased their academic distress during treatment had a higher rate of retention, one semester after the treatment began, than students whose academic distress did not decrease during treatment. The findings also showed that clients who, at the end of treatment, were both academically distressed and depressed were particularly at risk of not being retained.

Client Variables

Several CCMH studies have focused on a range of client variables to predict the utilization, course, and impact of psychotherapy at UCCs. For example, in a study involving more than 50,000 clients, Nordberg et al. (2016) conducted latent profile analyses on pretreatment CCAPS scores that led to the identification of 16 distinct and reliable types of clients. These profiles differed in terms of not only client symptoms but also demographics, psychological history, diagnoses, risk severity (e.g., suicide, hostility toward others), and eventual treatment length and outcome. These profiles were then rationally grouped into nine types of clinical problems. For instance, four profiles of eating concerns were identified, based on the extent of mood symptoms and substance abuse. The clients with substance abuse concerns did not respond well to treatment; mood symptoms did not predict treatment outcomes.

The previous study illustrates how complex analyses of several client variables can lead to information that may be relied upon to build an individualized case formulation and treatment plan early in therapy. Similarly complex analyses, especially when conducted on large samples, can reliably serve other functions. Predicting who will return to therapy, for instance, can be useful in informing case dispositions in the context of limited resources. This is particularly relevant to UCCs, not only because the length of treatment is typically short but because, as we mentioned before, a counseling center is, for a number of years, the primary source of mental health services for many members of a campus community. In a study of 8,329 students receiving treatment at 52 UCCs, Kilcullen et al. (2021) found that 30% of clients returned for more than one course of treatment. Using machine learning (advanced statistical methods allowing the analysis of a large number of variables), the researchers predicted which clients were likely to return for additional therapy after their first treatment had concluded. A substantial number of client variables failed to predict a return to treatment, including some that may, intuitively, make clinical sense such as problem chronicity, prior utilization of mental health services, and changes on the subscales of the CCAPS. Results also indicated, however, that clients' pretreatment social anxiety and perceived social support were directly associated with likelihood of returning for further therapy, whereas academic distress and alcohol use at intake were inversely related to the probability of additional treatment.

While the investigations of a wide range of client variables have shed light on the delivery and impact of services provided in UCCs, clinicians and administrators would benefit from additional data regarding specific groups of clients. For example, the past half-century has witnessed a substantial growth in the cultural diversity of students enrolled in higher education. Correspondingly, UCCs are providing treatment to students with a broad array of cultural characteristics, where culture is conceptualized as including ethnicity, sexual orientation, disability status, race, religion, age, gender, and socioeconomic status. For instance, nearly 5% of students receiving treatment at UCCs identify as transgender or non-binary; one-third describe their sexual orientation as other than heterosexual; approximately 40% are students of color; and 12% have a documented disability (CCMH, 2023). Studies conducted with CCMH data have yielded a host of interesting findings pertaining to culture. In terms of mental health, it is generally the case that minoritized students have worse mental health than their counterparts. For example, Native American students in counseling have more distress related to academics than White students (Isadore et al., 2024). In fact, ethnoracial minority students tend to have more psychological distress than do White students, though effect sizes generally are not large and exceptions do exist (Hayes, Chun-Kennedy, et al., 2011). White student clients, for instance, tend to have more problems related to alcohol than do clients of color (Hayes, Chun-Kennedy et al., 2011). Clients with physical and learning disabilities struggle more with their mental health, including suicidal thoughts and behaviors, than do clients without disabilities (Eissenstat et al., 2023; Fleming et al., 2018). This same pattern of findings extends to gender minority clients (Lefevor et al., 2019), non-domestic clients (Kawamoto et al., 2018), and lesbian, gay, and bisexual clients (Drinane et al., 2025; Hayes et al., 2011).

Many of the studies cited in the previous paragraph also have examined treatment utilization and therapy outcomes among culturally marginalized groups. Findings indicate that, for starters, UCC services are utilized by students of color at rates that are consistent with what would be predicted based on enrollment data at individual schools (Hayes, Youn, et al., 2011).

Students who identify as gay, bisexual, or lesbian are slightly overrepresented among counseling center clients, as are women (CCMH, 2023). In terms of therapy outcomes, research has demonstrated the welcome, if not slightly surprising, finding that racial and ethnic minority clients benefit comparably from therapy, as do White students (Hayes et al., 2016; Isadore et al., 2024). Because of the scope of the data set that CCMH has accumulated since its inception, it has been possible to conduct studies with large statistical power on other particular subgroups of student clients, including women who are pregnant (Markin et al., 2021), military veterans (Fredman et al., 2019; Johnson et al., 2014), those with suicidal ideation (Hayes et al., 2020), and student athletes (Kilcullen et al., 2021).

Therapist Effects

The role that providers play in treatment outcome has been a major theme of practice-based evidence (Barkham et al., 2010; Barkham & Margison, 2007). How therapists differ in terms of effectiveness and with whom have indeed been investigated in many clinical settings (see, for example, Barkham et al.; Constantino & Boswell; Nissen-Lie in this volume). In conducting such investigations, members of CCMH have given priority to issues of particular relevance to UCC communities. For example, Hayes et al. (2016) conducted a study to determine whether UCC therapists differed in their treatment effectiveness as a function of clients' ethnoracial identity. They examined treatment outcomes for 3,825 clients seen by 251 therapists (64% of them identified themselves as White/Caucasian) at 45 counseling centers. Results indicated that, as expected, there were disparities within therapists' caseloads in their effectiveness with ethnoracial minority clients compared with White clients, although effect sizes tended to be small. None of the therapist variables for which CCMH collected data (e.g., gender, race, experience) predicted clinicians' differential effectiveness. On the positive side, treatment success (i.e., reductions in clients' overall distress) was comparable for ethnoracial minority and White clients.

Other studies have investigated the impact that therapists may have on issues that potentially hinder the optimal functioning of clinical routine in UCC. One such issue is premature termination. Based on a large sample of clients (N = 10,147) and therapists (N = 481), Xiao, Castonguay, et al. (2017) found that 9.5% of the variance in dropout rates could be attributed to therapists. Given the substantial percentage of clients in the study who dropped out of treatment (15.9%), understanding such therapist variability could provide insight toward improving the delivery of adequate and efficient care in UCCs. Similar to Hayes et al.'s (2016) study on clients' ethnoracial identity, however, none of the provider variables that were assessed (e.g., age, gender, professional background, experience) explained the observed therapist differences. In a study involving 5,253 treatment-seeking students at 22 universities, Xiao, Hayes, et al. (2017) showed that therapist differences accounted for a large part of the variance in clients' nonattendance to therapy sessions late in treatment. One noteworthy finding was that 16 therapists from one counseling center had no nonattendance, suggesting that specific, though unknown, strategies to enhance client attendance might have been utilized by these therapists.

Dyadic Processes

In addition to investigating clients and therapists, CCMH collaborators have examined specific processes involving both of them, both before and during treatment. For example, Pottschmidt et al. (2022) assessed the consequences of similarity between clients' and therapists' views regarding clients' presenting concerns. Specifically, the authors assessed the convergence of clients' (N = 47,023) and therapists' (N = 2419) views at intake regarding clients' sleep difficulties—a transdiagnostic issue frequently associated with life in college. Based on data collected in 99 UCCs, the findings showed that sleep difficulties were frequently reported at intake by clients (i.e., by 49.3% of clients). In contrast, fewer than 20% of clients were identified by therapists as having sleep problems. Nonetheless, when clients and therapists agreed that sleep concerns were present, clients tended to rate their sleep difficulties as worse than clients whose therapist did not think they had a sleep problem. Furthermore, lack of convergence mattered: Therapists' identification of sleep problems at intake was predictive of greater sleep difficulty and other psychological symptoms at the end of therapy, particularly for clients who reported fewer sleep problems at intake.

A key to success in virtually any form of treatment is the therapy relationship (Gelso & Hayes, 1998; Norcross & Lambert, 2019). CCMH stakeholders, fortunately, also view the therapy relationship as a priority for further research (Youn et al., 2019). To ensure its relevance to the rapidly changing field of mental health, the therapy relationship needs to be understood in various modes of service delivery. Toward this end, Davis et al. (2024) compared the quality of the working alliance assessed on a session-by-session basis in two cohorts of clients: one that received treatment in person (before the onset of the COVID-19 pandemic) and one that received treatment via teletherapy (after the onset of the pandemic). Non-inferiority analyses (which are more stringent methods to assess the potential equivalence of two conditions than null-hypothesis significant testing) conducted with clients ($N = 958$) matched across cohorts in terms of gender, race/ethnicity, and financial stress found that the working alliance and the outcome (as measured by the Distress Index of the CCAPS) were non-inferior in teletherapy to in-person therapy.

Center Effects

Dyadic processes within therapy take place in the context of many variables. One of the most significant of them, for all stakeholders of college student mental health, is the specific center where treatment is delivered. Based on data from 116 UCCs, encompassing 58,423 clients treated by 2,362 therapists, Carney et al. (2021) examined the amount of outcome variance explained by centers, in terms of magnitude and rate of change. With regard to magnitude of change, the average center effect across the seven specific scales of the CCAPS and the Distress Index was 1.93%. In terms of rate of change, the average center effect was 3.2%. While these are small effects, Pybis et al. (2017) demonstrated that center effects of 1.8% found in a study involving 103 sites within the United Kingdom national health system reflected non-negligible differences in terms of client's recovery rates: a mean of 59% for clinics that were reliably more effective than others, compared with 43% for clinics that were less reliably effective than others. Carney et al. (2021) also identified a number of factors that explained the center effects they observed, including session limits, session frequency, number of clients served annually, and the availability of services other than counseling (e.g., psychiatric treatment). With regard to the overall outcome variance, however, these variables did not make a significant difference, with the exception of session frequency: Centers where clients received more frequent sessions had better outcomes.

Methodological Contributions

Given its yearly growing data set, and its good fortune in collaborating with colleagues and graduate students who are knowledgeable and passionate about cutting-edge statistics, CCMH has been the source of several studies devoted to research design and methodology. For example, in a previously described study, McAleavey et al. (2019) demonstrated that different methods of assessing the effectiveness of routine care can yield different results. One method, change-based benchmarking, revealed that the effect sizes of pre-post change for clinically distressed clients were similar to those achieved by clients treated in RCTs. In contrast, another method, end-state normative comparisons, showed that highly distressed clients tended not to reach normative levels of functioning at the end of therapy. Taken together, the findings suggest not only that these statistical methods are complementary but also that relying only on one of them is insufficient to provide a nuanced and comprehensive view of the impact and limitations of mental health services.

Another study showed that methods make a difference and, in doing so, shed light on discrepancies across previous studies regarding rates of dropout in psychological treatments. Xiao et al (2023) simultaneously compared three definitions of dropout: clients' failure to attend their last scheduled appointment; treatment judged by therapists as having ended prematurely; and treatment that ended while clients had deteriorated on the CCAPS. With a sample of 2,977 clients treated by 234 therapists at 17 UCCs, the researchers found that 27.3% of clients met at least one definition of dropout. Furthermore, there was little overlap among the three definitions; very few clients (less than 1%) met all three of them. Therapist and center effects were also observed for the three definitions, but their respective magnitude was considerably smaller for the symptom deterioration definition of dropout relative to the other two. These findings suggest that rather than attempting to identify one overarching definition of dropout, the field should recognize that different operationalizations capture distinct types of clients and that future attempts to estimate and predict the rate of dropout (including in meta-analyses) should be specifically tied to a particular operationalization rather than assuming that dropout is a uniform construct.

In yet another methodological paper, McAleavey et al. (2020) examined a crucial issue regarding the validity of self-reported assessment of psychological distress, namely, whether an instrument developed to assess differences between individuals (traitlike factors) can adequately capture change within one individual across time (statelike factors). To address this question, they conducted multilevel factor analysis, which, in contrast with traditional or single-level factor analyses, separates between- and within-person levels of measurement. Using treatment-seeking (N = 757) and nonclinical (N = 1,223) samples, the authors demonstrated that the factor structure of the CCAPS is simpler (characterized by broad factors) at the between-person level than at the within-person level (characterized by narrow factors). In other words, how one client changes across time is more complex than how clients differ between one another. These findings suggest that when monitoring outcomes of a client during therapy, therapists should pay attention to specific aspects of change that may or may not be captured by general measures of distress.

Conclusion

For close to 20 years, CCMH has generated practice-based evidence by fostering studies that meet the defining criteria of practice-oriented research: These studies have been conducted in naturalistic settings, they reflect mental health care services as they are provided in day-to-day practice, and they do not impose constraints or additions to clinical routine (Castonguay et al., 2021). In addition, and embodying the core definition of a PRN, these studies have been designed, implemented, and disseminated utilizing an active collaboration among various stakeholders in the domain of college student mental health. Stemming from the shared values underlying such a collaboration, many of the studies conducted within CCMH are more than clinically relevant—they simply needed to be done. They were, and still are, necessary to better understand the factors related to the psychological distress experienced by college students, to overcome problems that plague day-to-day clinical services (e.g., attendance, dropout), and to enhance the treatment provided to students. These studies also needed to be done to provide scientifically useful information for lobbying purposes, such as demonstrating the quality and academic relevance of services provided at UCCs.

The delineation of research that was and still is needed has not been dictated by the funding priorities of grant agencies. Instead, studies based on CCMH data have been driven largely by clinical observations, practical challenges experienced by UCCs, and unfolding clinician training needs, all of which are identified via regular meetings within the CCMH infrastructure, as well as by a survey of clinicians and administrators across our PRN (Youn et al., 2019).

The CCMH infrastructure embodies a guiding recommendation of practice-oriented research: work locally, collaborate globally (Castonguay, 2011). Because they own their data, each center can make use of it (often with the help of the core research group at Penn State) to conduct research they are interested in or to address policy-driven questions. Given that data collected by the UCCs is aggregated in a central repository, stakeholders within one or across multiple sites also have access to the large data set to which they have contributed. This large data set allows researchers to overcome a common obstacle in the field of psychotherapy research, particularly when studying specific types of clients: sufficient statistical power. As statistical advances often require researchers to use larger and larger samples to adequately investigate their questions, CCMH has kept pace, allowing researchers to examine complex questions about mental health and its treatment, even without an exorbitant amount of money from a grant agency. While it would be inconceivable, for example, to have a government agency (such as the National Institute of Mental Health) fund an RCT involving more than 47,000 clients, this was the sample size in a master's thesis previously described (Pottschmidt et al., 2022).

In addition to the limited sample sizes, comparatively speaking, that characterize most RCTs, an experimental design with random assignment to conditions is not an appropriate design to investigate many of the questions that are central to CCMH stakeholders (e.g., What are the treatment outcomes associated with various types of dropout? Which clients are likely to need more than one treatment modality? Why are some counseling centers more effective than others?).

The studies conducted within CCMH have yet another advantage over RCTs: external validity. Since these studies have been conducted as part of standard clinical routine, the generalizability of the results tends to be strong within UCC settings. Practitioners working in a UCC are less likely to ask themselves, "Are these findings applicable to my practice?," when they read about findings derived from a CCMH study than from an RCT conducted in an academic setting, or even from a study conducted in a UCC setting but testing the effectiveness of therapies that are not part of clinical routine (e.g., manualized treatments implemented for a limited period of time, under specific conditions of training, supervision, adherence, and competence).

While the findings may not be generalized to other client populations, the external validity of most CCMH studies within UCC settings tends to make the clinical, social, and policy implications of their results particularly noteworthy. For example, by demonstrating that counseling services can facilitate retention of students who suffer from psychological distress, Lockard et al. (2019) have shown that UCCs can help fulfill students' and parents' aspirations, as well as the university's academic mission. They also argued that these academic outcomes can potentially benefit colleges by avoiding disruption of tuition revenues from their students. Niilekela et al.'s (2021) study demonstrated that many clients can experience a diminution of a wide range of symptoms even if they are receiving a short treatment. While their findings show that more change is associated with longer treatment (supporting the dose–effect model), faster rate of change is linked with shorter treatment (supporting the good-enough model). McAleavey et al.'s (2019) findings, however, warn us that brief treatments may not be sufficient for all students seeking psychological help, as clients with very high distress at intake often did not reach a normative level of functioning at the end of therapy. As a whole, the practice-based evidence derived from these effectiveness studies suggests that the psychotherapy routinely provided by UCCs is a worthwhile investment (in terms of time, expectations, and resources) for all stakeholders in the area of college mental health. At the same time, the evidence should also encourage administrators to work toward implementing longer, more comprehensive, and still more effective services than those currently provided for students.

Some of the studies described earlier also suggest that the consideration of a large number of client variables at intake, including symptomatic distress, demographic, and risk factors, could be useful for case formulation, treatment planning, and case management practices and policies. For example, a counseling center that assessed the fit of incoming clients with profiles that have been derived from latent analyses by Nordberg et al. (2016) could potentially identify clients who are likely to require long treatment. Using machine learning algorithms delineated by Kilcullen et al. (2021) could also help the same center to predict clients who they might be able to help, and at what cost, based on who is likely to require more than one treatment episode. Yet another study (Pottschmidt et al., 2022) suggested that a center could increase its effectiveness by adopting a simpler and hands-on practice guideline: encouraging providers to assess sleep problems at intake and to pay attention to such difficulties during treatment—especially if sleep is not viewed as problematic by the client before treatment begins.

Furthermore, perhaps the ultimate implication of the studies described earlier on therapist effects is that clinicians who are experts in working with particular clients (e.g., culturally diverse clients) or in preventing problems such as dropout should be identified so that other therapists could learn from them. In reality, however, because of the highly sensitive nature of collecting data from some agencies with very few practitioners, it has proven to be challenging on a practical and ethical level to determine the identity of these expert therapists within the CCMH database.

Whereas many implications can be drawn from studies conducted on the CCMH data so far, what is needed in the future are studies that assess psychotherapy process. We know virtually nothing from CCMH data about the mechanisms of change in individual or group therapy. In addition, while we reported earlier a study on the alliance conducted in one UCC, large-scale data on the therapy relationship (and other process variables) have yet to be gathered. Future studies could also profitably address how practice and policy changes are being implemented based on prior research, and the effects of such implementation. This is in line with the concept of "closing clinical and empirical loops" (Castonguay et al., 2021), where (1) clinical data obtained in one (or many) setting(s) is used to modify the delivery of care in this/these setting(s); (2) the effects of such modification are examined in the same setting(s); and (3) the findings of this examination is used as clinical data to further modify and improve care delivery. For instance, future studies could investigate the consequences on outcome of allowing longer treatments for highly distressed clients. Another possibility would be to investigate the effects on session attendance of policies that discourage cancellations and no-shows. On a basic level are questions about how readily these changes can be implemented and sustained in day-to-day practice.

Limitations and Cautions

There are several noteworthy limitations to the CCMH data set. Preeminent among them is the fact that students who seek psychological help at UCCs are different in important ways from their classmates who do not. Scores on 7 of the 8 CCAPS subscales are elevated for students who receive services at UCCs; only scores on the Substance Use subscale are similar for students who do and do not seek counseling. This limits the external validity of CCMH findings in terms of the general college student population.

Another limitation is that CCMH has disproportionately low membership from community colleges; the same holds for low representation from historically Black colleges and universities, tribal colleges, and Hispanic-serving institutions. Also, the size of CCMH is both a strength and a hindrance. In its early days, CCMH periodically collected data on variables such as college student resilience, self-compassion, and perfectionism. Although multi-site data collection using newly introduced instruments was still a challenge, CCMH was nimble enough to accomplish these projects. Today, however, it would be very difficult to add new measures to a network that has more than 800 members. For instance, although CCMH gathers information on students' religion (including categories such as "agnostic" and "atheistic"), it does not measure the deeper construct of faith (Parker, 2010). To do so would require agreement from more than 800 UCCs about the best definitions and measures of faith, as well as new institutional review board approval from every UCC. CCMH began like a small speedboat that could accelerate rather quickly and make fairly precise turns; now it is like a large cargo ship carrying a sizable load that does not easily change course.

Despite these limitations, CCMH has had a tremendous effect on the study and treatment of college student mental health, largely due to its use of standardized instruments that are incorporated into routine clinical care with a large number of clients, therapists, and counseling centers. We believe that it is not an exaggeration to say that CCMH has changed the field of college student counseling. It is now standard for UCCs to collect data to monitor the progress of their clients; that standard of accountability was far less common prior to 2005. Furthermore, by pooling data together, CCMH has made it possible for UCCs to compare themselves with other similar schools on any number of dimensions. For example, the director of the counseling center at Oxnard College, which is designated as a Hispanic-serving institution, might wonder what the average ratio is of mental health professionals to students at other Hispanic-serving institutions and how Oxnard College compares. CCMH data make it possible to answer such questions. In fact, one study examined CCMH data and determined that ethnic minority students across the country sought psychological help on campus in direct proportion to the number of clinicians at their counseling center who shared students' ethnicity (Hayes, Locke, et al., 2011). The results of this study helped counseling centers advocate for hiring more staff members of color.

From a personal perspective, the achievements of CCMH—past, present, and future—operate and are dependent on the currency of relationship.

CCMH, which began over breakfast among a UCC staff member and two academics, has grown enormously since its inception, not only in terms of institutional membership but also in terms of the size of its staff and the number of relevant stakeholders. In some ways, that growth both reflects the success of CCMH and creates challenges to maintaining high-quality relationships in the face of their increasing volume. Like all worthwhile relationships, those among CCMH stakeholders occasionally experience periods of rupture that need attention and repair. Furthermore, CCMH will need to contend with how it will function as a PRN, rather than as simply a practice network, after the authors of this chapter have retired, given that we and our students have been responsible for most of the research impetus within CCMH since it began. This will require the development, maintenance, and nurturance of relationships that currently do not exist. As has been the case since its inception, CCMH is likely to overcome these and other challenges it will face in the future.

References

Barkham, M., Connell, J., Stiles, W. B., Miles, J. N. V., Margison, F., Evans, C., & Mellor-Clark, J. (2006). Dose-effect relations and responsive regulation of treatment duration: The good enough level. *Journal of Consulting and Clinical Psychology, 74*, 160–167. https://doi.org/10.1037/0022-006X.74.1.160

Barkham, M., Hardy, G. E., & Mellor-Clark, J. (Eds.). (2010). *Developing and delivering practice-based evidence. A guide for the psychological therapies*. Wiley-Blackwell.

Barkham, M., & Margison, F. (2007). Practice-based evidence as a complement to evidence-based practice: From dichotomy to chiasmus. In C. Freeman & M. Power (Eds.), *Handbook of evidence-based psychotherapies: A guide for research and practice* (pp. 443–476). John Wiley & Sons.

Carney, D., Castonguay, L. G., Janis, R. A., Scofield, B. E, Hayes, J. A., & Locke, B. D. (2021). Center effects: Counseling center variables as predictors of psychotherapy outcomes. *The Counseling Psychologist, 49*, 1013–1037. https://doi.org/10.1177/00110000211029271

Castonguay, L. G. (2011). Psychotherapy, psychopathology, research and practice: Pathways of connections and integration. *Psychotherapy Research, 21*, 125–140. https://doi.org/10.1080/10503307.2011.563250

Castonguay, L. G., Barkham, M., Youn, S., & Page, A. C. (2021). Practice-based evidence—Findings from routine clinical settings. In M. Barkham, W. Lutz, & L. G. Castonguay (Eds.), *Bergin and Garfield's handbook of psychotherapy and behavior change* (pp. 191–222). John Wiley & Sons.

Castonguay, L. G., Locke, B. D., & Hayes, J. A. (2011). The Center for Collegiate Mental Health: An example of a practice-research network in university counseling centers. *Journal of College Student Psychotherapy, 25*, 105–119. https://doi.org/10.1080/87568225.2011.556929

Center for Collegiate Mental Health (CCMH). (2023). *2022 annual report* (Publication No. STA 23-168).

Chickering, A., & Reisser, L. (1993). *Education and identity* (2nd ed.). Jossey-Bass.

Cooper, S. E., & Archer, J. A. (2002). Evaluation and research in college counseling center contexts. *Journal of College Counseling, 5*, 50–59. https://doi.org/10.1002/j.2161-1882.2002.tb00206.x

Davis, K. A., Zhao, F., Janis, R. A., Castonguay, L. G., Hayes, J. A., & Scofield., B. E. (2024). Therapeutic alliance and clinical outcome in in-person psychotherapy and teletherapy: A non-inferiority study. *Psychotherapy Research, 34*, 589–600. https://doi.org/10.1080/10503307.2023.2229505

Drinane, J. M., Cassells, R. C., Hayes, J. A., Park, J., & Foster, E. (2025). Queer in college? Sexual orientation disparities in therapist effectiveness in a national sample of university counseling center clients. *Psychotherapy, 62*, 173–179.

Eissenstat, S., Coduti, W., & Hayes, J. A. (2023). Predictors of self-harming behavior among college students with disabilities seeking counseling services. *Journal for Postsecondary Education and Disability, 36*, 167–178.

Fleming, A. R., Edwin, M., Hayes, J. A., Locke, B. D., & Lockard, A. J. (2018). Treatment-seeking college students with disabilities: Presenting concerns, protective factors, and academic distress. *Rehabilitation Psychology, 63*(1), 55–67. https://doi.org/10.1037/rep0000193

Fredman, S. J., Marshall, A. D., Le, Y., Aronson, K. R., Perkins, D. F., & Hayes, J. A. (2019). Interpersonal relationship quality mediates the association between military-related post-traumatic stress and academic dysfunction among student veterans. *Psychological Trauma: Theory, Research, Practice, and Policy, 11*, 415–423. https://doi.org/10.1037/tra0000363

Gelso, C. J., & Hayes, J. A. (1998). *The psychotherapy relationship: Theory, research, and practice.* Wiley.

Hayes, J. A. (1997). What does the Brief Symptom Inventory measure in college and university counseling center clients? *Journal of Counseling Psychology, 44*, 360–367. https://doi.org/10.1037/0022-0167.44.4.360

Hayes, J. A., Chun-Kennedy, C., Edens, A., & Locke, B. D. (2011). Do double minority students face double jeopardy? Testing minority stress theory. *Journal of College Counseling, 14*, 117–126. https://doi.org/10.1002/j.2161-1882.2011.tb00267.x

Hayes, J. A., Locke, B. D., & Castonguay, L. G. (2011). The Center for Collegiate Mental Health: Practice and research working together. *Journal of College Counseling, 14*, 101–104. https://doi.org/10.1002/j.2161-1882.2011.tb00265.x

Hayes, J. A., McAleavey, A. A., Castonguay, L. G., & Locke, B. D. (2016). Psychotherapist effects with White and racial/ethnic minority clients: First, the good news. *Journal of Counseling Psychology, 63*, 261–268. https://doi.org/10.1037/cou0000098

Hayes, J. A., Petrovich, J., Janis, R. A., Yang, Y., Castonguay, L. G., & Locke, B. D. (2020). Suicide among college students in psychotherapy: Individual predictors and latent classes. *Journal of Counseling Psychology, 67*, 104–114. https://doi.org/10.1037/cou0000384

Hayes, J. A., Youn, S. J., Castonguay, L. G., Locke, B. D., McAleavey, A. A., & Nordberg, S. (2011). Rates and predictors of counseling center use among college students of color. *Journal of College Counseling, 14*, 105–116. https://doi.org/10.1002/j.2161-1882.2011.tb00266.x

Howard, K. I., Kopta, S. M., Krause, M. S., & Orlinsky, D. E. (1986). The dose–effect relationship in psychotherapy. *American Psychologist, 41*, 159–164. https://doi.org/10.1037/0003-066X.41.2.159

Isadore, K., Hayes, J. A., Beitel, M., & Cutter, C. (2024). Native American college students in counseling: Results from a large scale, multisite effectiveness study. *Psychotherapy, 61*, 173–183. https://doi.org/10.1037/pst0000526

Johnson, M. C., Graceffo, J. M., Hayes, J. A., & Locke, B. D. (2014). Examining treatment-seeking college students with and without military experience and trauma histories. *Journal of College Counseling, 17*, 260–270. https://doi.org/10.1002/j.2161-1882.2014.00062.x

Kawamoto, A., Youn, S., Bartholomew, T. T., Castonguay, L. G., & Locke, B. D. (2018). Inter- and intra-group differences in psychological concerns among international students. *Counselling Psychology Quarterly, 31*(2), 186–204. doi.org/10.1080/09515070.2016.1274962

Kilcullen, J. R., Castonguay, L. C., Janis, R. A., Hallquist, M. N., Hayes, J. A., & Locke, B. D. (2021). Predicting future courses of psychotherapy within a grouped LASSO framework. *Psychotherapy Research, 31*, 63–77. https://doi.org/10.1080/10503307.2020.1762948

Kim, S., Beretvas, S. N., & Sherry, A. R. (2010). A validation of the factor structure of OQ-45 scores using factor mixture modeling. *Measurement and Evaluation in Counseling and Development, 42*, 275–295. https://doi.org/10.1177/0748175609354616

Lockard, A. J., Hayes, J. A., Locke, B. D., Bieschke, K. J., & Castonguay, L. G. (2019). Helping those who help themselves: Does counseling enhance retention? *Journal of Counseling & Development, 97*(2), 128–139. https://doi.org/10.1002/jcad.12244

Locke, B. D., Bieschke, K. J., Castonguay, L. G., & Hayes, J. A. (2012). The Center for Collegiate Mental Health: Studying college student mental health through an innovative research infrastructure that brings science and practice together. *Harvard Psychiatric Review, 20*, 233–245. https://doi.org/10.3109/10673229.2012.712837

Locke, B. D., Buzolitz, J., Lei, P., Boswell, J. F., McAleavey, A. A., Sevig, T., Dowis, J., & Hayes, J. A. (2011). Development of the Counseling Center Assessment of Psychological Symptoms-62 (CCAPS-62). *Journal of Counseling Psychology, 58*, 97–109.

Markin, R., McCarthy, K., & Hayes, J. A. (2021). Young pregnant clients in college or university counseling centers: Environmental and symptom experiences. *Counselling and Psychotherapy Research, 21*, 768–780. https://doi.org/10.1002/capr.12445

McAleavey, A. A, Castonguay, L. G., Hayes, J. A., & Locke, B. D. (2020). Multilevel vs single level factor analysis. Differentiating within-person and between-person variability using the CCAPS-34. *Journal of Consulting and Clinical Psychology, 88*, 907–922. https://doi.org/10.1037/ccp0000529

McAleavey, A. A., Lockard, A. J., Castonguay, L. G., Hayes, J. A., & Locke, B. D. (2015). Building a practice research network: Obstacles faced and lessons learned at the Center for Collegiate Mental Health. *Psychotherapy Research, 25*, 134–151. https://doi.org/10.1080/10503307.2014.883652

McAleavey, A. A., Nordberg, S. S., Hayes, J. A., Castonguay, L. G., Locke, B. D., & Lockard, A. J. (2012). Clinical validity of the Counseling Center Assessment of Psychological Symptoms-62 (CCAPS-62): Further evaluation and clinical applications. *Journal of Counseling Psychology, 59*, 575–590. https://doi.org/10.1037/a0029855

McAleavey, A. A., Youn, S., Xiao, H., Castonguay, L. G., Hayes, J. A., & Locke, B. D. (2019). Effectiveness of routine psychotherapy: Method matters. *Psychotherapy Research, 29*(2), 139–156. https://doi.org/10.1080/10503307.2017.1395921

National Academies of Sciences, Engineering, and Medicine (US). (2021). *Mental health, substance use, and wellbeing in higher education: Supporting the whole student.* The National Academies Press (US). https://doi.org/10.17226/26015

Niileksela, C. R., Ghosh, A., & Janis, R. (2021). The dose effect and good enough level models of change for specific psychological concerns. *The Journal of Consulting and Clinical Psychology, 89*, 200–213. https://doi.org/10.1037/ccp0000635

Norcross, J. C., & Lambert, M. J. (Eds.). (2019). *Psychotherapy relationships that work: Volume 1: Evidence-based therapist contributions.* Oxford University Press.

Nordberg, S. S., Castonguay, L. G., McAleavey, A. A., Locke, B. D., & Hayes, J. A. (2016). Enhancing feedback for clinical use: Creating and evaluating profiles of clients seeking counseling. *Journal of Counseling Psychology, 63*, 278–293. https://doi.org/10.1037/cou0000147

Nordberg, S. S., McAleavey, A. A., Duszak, E., Locke, B. D., Hayes, J. A., & Castonguay, L. G. (2018). The Counseling Center Assessment of Psychological Symptoms Distress Index: A

pragmatic exploration of general factors to enhance a multidimensional scale *Counselling Psychology Quarterly*, *31*, 25–41. https://doi.org/10.1080/09515070.2016.1202809
Parker, S. (2010). Research in Fowler's faith development theory: A review article. *Review of Religious Research*, *51*, 233–252.
Pottschmidt, N. R., Castonguay, L. G., Janis, R. A., Carney, D. M., Kilcullen, J. R., Davis, K. A., & Scofield, B. E. (2022). Client-therapist convergence on sleep difficulty and its impact on treatment outcomes. *Psychotherapy Research*, *32*, 663–677. https://doi.org/10.1080/10503307.2021.1995068
Pybis, J., Saxon, D., Hill, A., & Barkham, M. (2017). The comparative effectiveness and efficiency of cognitive behaviour therapy and generic counselling in the treatment of depression: Evidence from the 2nd UK National Audit of psychological therapies. *BMC Psychiatry*, *17*(1), 215. https://doi.org/10.1186/s12888-017-1370-7
Sharkin, B. (2004). College counseling and student retention: Research findings and implications for counseling centers. *Journal of College Counseling*, *7*, 99–108. https://doi.org/10.1002/j.2161-1882.2004.tb00241.x
Silverman, M. M., Meyer P. M., Sloane, F., Raffel, M., & Pratt, D. M. (1997). The Big Ten student suicide study: A 10-year study of suicides on midwestern university campuses. *Suicide and Life Threatening Behavior*, *27*, 285–303. https://doi.org/10.1111/j.1943-278X.1997.tb00411.x
Xiao, H., Castonguay, L. G., Hayes, J. A., Janis, R. A., & Locke, B. D. (2023). Reconstructing dropout: Building from multiple definitions, therapist effects, and center effects. *Psychotherapy Research*, *33*, 146–157. https://doi.org/10.1080/10503307.2022.2082897
Xiao, H., Castonguay, L. G., Janis, R. A., Youn, S., Hayes, J. A., & Locke, B. D. (2017). Therapist effects on dropout from a college counseling center practice research network. *Journal of Counseling Psychology*, *64*(4), 424–431. https://doi.org/10.1037/cou0000208
Xiao, H., Hayes, J. A., Castonguay, L. G., McAleavey, A. A., & Locke, B. D. (2017). Therapist effects and the impacts of therapy nonattendance. *Psychotherapy*, *54*, 58–65. https://doi.org/10.1037/pst0000103
Youn, S., Xiao, H., McAleavey, A. A., Scofield, B. E., Pedersen, T. R., Castonguay, L. G., Hayes, J. A., & Locke, B. D. (2019). Assessing and investigating clinicians' research interests: Lessons on expanding practices and data collection in a large practice research network. *Psychotherapy*, *56*(1), 67–82. https://doi.org/10.1037/pst0000192
Youn, S. J., Castonguay, L. G., McAleavey, A. A., Nordberg, S. S., Hayes, J. A., & Locke, B. D. (2020). Sensitivity to change of the Counseling Center Assessment of Psychological Symptoms-34. *Measurement and Evaluation in Counseling and Development*, *52*, 75–88.
Zhao, F., Hayes, J. A., Janis, R. A., Lei, P., McClain, J. M., Panlilio, C., Castonguay, L. G., & Scofield, B. E. (2025). How full is the glass? Examining the validity of the Counseling Center Assessment of Psychological Symptoms-62 across five ethnoracial groups. *Journal of Counseling Psychology*, *72*, 240–257.

12

Practice-Based Evidence Approaches Extend the Benefits of Routine Outcome Monitoring

Andrew C. Page, Geoff R. Hooke, Ashleigh G. Cameron, and Ruby J. Ross

Practice-based evidence involves the systematic collection of patient-related data that are relevant to treatment goals. The definition identifies the purpose of the data collection: namely, to support achievement and evaluation of the treatment goal. Additionally, the definition describes the process whereby practice-based evidence achieves its goal, in that the choice of data and the application of these data are informed by the treatment context and relevant stakeholders. As such, practice-based evidence gives privilege to the wisdom and perspectives of key stakeholders in framing the research questions (i.e., patients, their friends and families, as well as healthcare staff and volunteers). In addition, privilege is granted to the potential for impact within the sphere of clinical practice. The present chapter illustrates this broader point by describing why routine outcome monitoring (ROM) was selected as a focus of practice-based evidence at a particular mental health service. It describes how ROM evolved in this service, to integrate new learnings that have moved the service toward their overall goal of improving the mental health outcomes for patients and sharing these new insights with the wider community. The steps taken in the journey are summarized, beginning with a discussion of the processes whereby ROM was adopted. The chapter then provides a review of the ways in which the clinic has explored adaptations of ROM, to ensure that the data collected are aligned with the clinical goals. These adaptations include changes to the way monitoring is delivered, the tracking of risks for therapy-interfering behaviors such as patient self-harm and dropout from group psychotherapy. The chapter concludes with a discussion of how ROM can be extended to novel areas, such as readmission to treatment.

Andrew C. Page et al., *Practice-Based Evidence Approaches Extend the Benefits of Routine Outcome Monitoring*. In: *Practice-Based Evidence in the Psychological Therapies*. Edited by: Louis G. Castonguay et al., Oxford University Press. © Oxford University Press (2026). DOI: 10.1093/9780197748336.003.0012

Why Routine Outcome Monitoring?

Perth Clinic is a 100-bed private psychiatric hospital in Western Australia with a long tradition of innovation using evidence-based psychotherapy and was the first local facility to receive insurance rebates for cognitive-behavioral therapy (CBT) for diagnostically heterogeneous groups (Manning et al., 1994). It was against this backdrop that the hospital's leadership encouraged a practice base evidence collaboration whereby academic researchers and clinicians came together to decide what projects to focus on. The framework for the first research project began with the academics from a nearby university meeting with the therapists running the CBT groups and having a conversation that asked the question, "as therapists, what do you know that is as yet unknown by the research community?" The answer provided by the therapists was that for patients who began the group CBT program as inpatients, they believed that the outcomes were better for those who were discharged during the program when compared with those who remained inpatients for the duration of the program. The logic was that discharging a patient allowed them to practice homework assignments in real-world contexts and allowed troubleshooting of the issues and obstacles that were not present in the hospital environment. Thus, the research focus and the potential impact could be mutually beneficial. That is, not only was there the prospect of a publishable outcome, but there was also potential for information that could be used in a tangible way to positively impact practice (Andrews & Page, 2005).

The resulting research broadly confirmed the hypothesis formulated from clinical observation, but it did add nuance in that patterns were not the same across different diagnostic groups (Page & Hooke, 2003). The research also had direct clinical impact; the results could be used by staff as part of the narrative around planning for discharge. Patients can experience an apprehension about discharge, and being able to describe the potential benefits facilitated those conversations. Additionally, the research outcomes cemented in the minds of the team a culture of mutual respect—hospital staff and patients were seen as a legitimate source of hypotheses, and the hospital could see the impact of independent analyses.

One step to formalize these principles of research co-design was the creation of the hospital's *Clinical Improvement Team*. To ensure a broad representative membership, it drew from patient-facing staff (i.e., nurses and therapists), key leaders (including the hospital's CEO, as well as the heads of nursing, therapy teams, and the medical advisory committee), as well as university representatives. The engagement of the hospital staff also allowed a two-way dialogue with the hospital's patient liaison/advisory group. Importantly, the group was not called a "research committee," but the committee was named in terms of its function, which had the mission to improve clinical outcomes. This Clinical Improvement Committee serves an approval function to indicate support for research projects, but it also serves to provide direction to the research activities, thereby ensuring that potential outcomes are aligned with positive health benefits and the clinic's mission.

The decision for the hospital to consider incorporating ROM as part of routine practice arose because of the Clinical Improvement Team's oversight. The hospital had taken a leading role in a national collaboration to collect and share outcome data as part of a national benchmarking exercise. Benefits from participation included greater understanding of the extent of positive change as well as being able to benchmark outcomes for specific patient groups. However, while these reports summarized the average pre- to post-treatment change, they did not communicate the percentage of patients who showed clinically significant change. Furthermore, the reports did not provide real-time feedback on patient progress so that treatment could be reviewed and adapted for those who were not demonstrating the desired progress.

Concurrent with these observations, some of the initial publications from Michael Lambert's group, on the use of the 45-item Outcomes Questionnaire (OQ) to provide feedback regarding progress in weekly psychotherapy, were being published (Lambert, 2015; Shimokawa et al., 2010). Additionally, our researchers had implemented a project to identify the clinical significance of the outcomes (Newnham et al., 2007; Ronk et al., 2012, 2013). That is, the pre- to post-treatment changes were divided into those patients who were "recovered" (i.e., statistically reliable change plus a return to the healthy range on a scale), "improved" (i.e., a reliable change but not yet in the healthy range), "unchanged" (i.e., no statistically reliable change), or "deteriorated" (i.e., a statistically reliable deterioration in symptoms or well-being). The supplementation of data showed that even though there was a very large pre–post treatment effect, there was a sizable portion of patients who terminated treatment with a score similar to or worse than their intake score. That is, the shift from presenting just the grouped data of a mean (and standard deviation) change to presenting the individual data highlighted that the generally positive outcomes for the group did not capture the treatment journey of every patient. Since the goal of the Clinical Improvement Team was to maximize the positive outcomes for every single patient, the presentation provided a focal point for the Team. Specifically, it allowed the Team to develop greater understanding as to which patients had symptom levels that were unchanged or deteriorated, and the reasons why they were not progressing as well as others.

The shift in focus whereby an evaluation of the average outcomes of patients was supplemented by a focus upon individuals with non-optimal outcomes aligned with the hospital's mission—to maximize the benefits for each patient. To this end, we embarked on a program to translate the model of ROM, which had been developed by Lambert and colleagues in an outpatient setting (with weekly data collection, i.e., the OQ Analyst; Lambert, 2012), to an inpatient setting. Some key principles of the OQ Analyst are that (i) prior data are used to identify the expected trajectory of patient progress, (ii) each trajectory identifies points at which progress would be "on track" and "not on track" during treatment and an identification of returning to the "healthy" range, and (iii) each patient is matched to a personalized trajectory based on their intake profile. The consequence is that feedback can be provided to patients and therapists regarding progress so that the data can be interpreted both against the group-based expected trajectory and against the person's earlier scores. Based on the feedback, the therapist and patient can reflect upon the pattern of change and decide if an adaptation to the treatment plan is desirable.

To translate to an inpatient setting, we noted that a key problem was that since the average duration of a hospital stay was measured in days, instruments like the OQ-45 were unsuitable given their length and time frame. To this end, the World Health Organization's 5-item well-being index (WHO-5; Topp et al., 2015) was used, as it is suitable for daily administration (Newnham et al., 2010a) and offered patients the opportunity to complete it every second day. Interestingly, patient feedback indicated that the frequency was not sufficient. They asked, "Why are you not interested in me on alternate days?" Therefore, we changed the protocol so that the questionnaire was available every day. In addition, patients asked why we were focusing only on well-being, and so we developed a companion daily measure of symptoms/distress (DI-5; Dyer et al., 2014). Dyer and colleagues demonstrated that the DI-5 has a unidimensional factor structure that correlates positively and highly with measures of affective psychological distress and strong negative correlations with measures of subjective well-being. We examined the benefits of including these measures in CBT groups delivered in inpatient settings to determine if the use of ROM improved outcomes. We found that we replicated, with similar effect sizes, the benefits of feedback that had been published with the OQ-45 (Shimokawa et al., 2010) and demonstrated that the beneficial effects were greater when therapists and patients received the combined symptom and well-being feedback (Dyer et al., 2016), compared with the well-being feedback alone (see Figure 12.1). The patient depicted demonstrated a period where symptoms were off track but were as expected by the end of treatment. However, the well-being remained below the expected trajectory of improvement and so would remain a target for follow-up care.

Buoyed by the apparent successes by translating the ROM approach to inpatient versions of outpatient psychotherapy, we took our scales and rolled them out across the whole inpatient setting. Unlike the closed CBT group program that has a uniform duration, inpatient admissions have variable lengths, so we created an expected trajectory of improvement based around the average length of stay. With the benefit of hindsight, this is a point when it would have been prudent to consult more closely with patients and staff.

The Clinical Improvement Team started to receive feedback from hospital staff that we must have gotten things wrong because too many people were being identified as "Not on Track." We checked our calculations and found that the algorithms categorized patients correctly. However, since patients were discharged when improved, at any moment in time, the wards hosted a higher proportion of patients who were not yet improving as they were not ready for discharge. This build-up created the perception that the algorithm was too strict, and staff found it demoralizing to be giving daily feedback about a lack of progress to this challenging group of patients.

We, belatedly, consulted with staff and patients to re-design feedback for inpatients, and in response to discussions we implemented a "traffic light" system for current inpatients. That is, the four clinical significance categories are used to form a color-coded graph where the amber "unchanged" grouping is assigned based on the patient's admission score. Red signals deterioration, green is healthy, and blue is return to the normal range. This signaling is depicted in the left-hand side of Figure 12.2 during the inpatient admission, but the CBT trajectories (similar to Figure 12.1) began when the person began the CBT group and was discharged to day patient care.

This approach has been nuanced so that defined patient groups receiving particular treatment programs can receive bespoke feedback. For example,

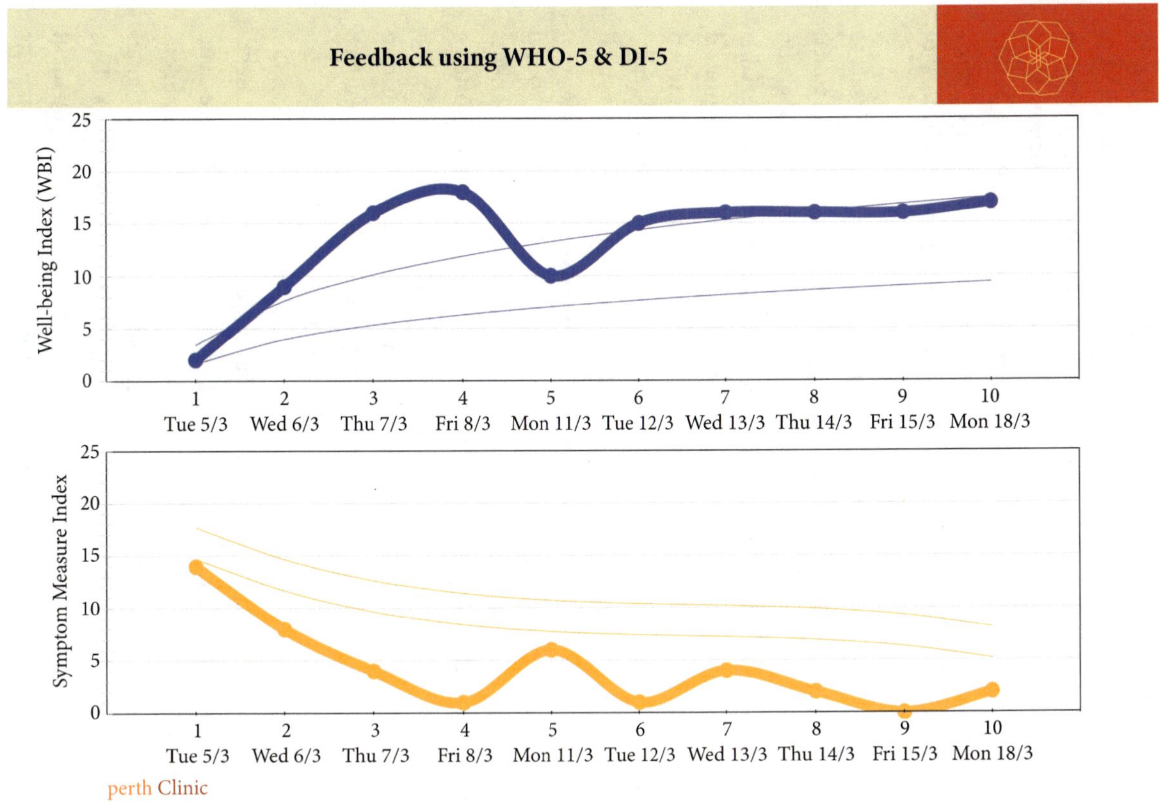

Figure 12.1 Individual Patient Well-Being (WHO-5) and Symptom (DI-5) Progress Mapped Against Group-Based Expected Treatment Trajectories

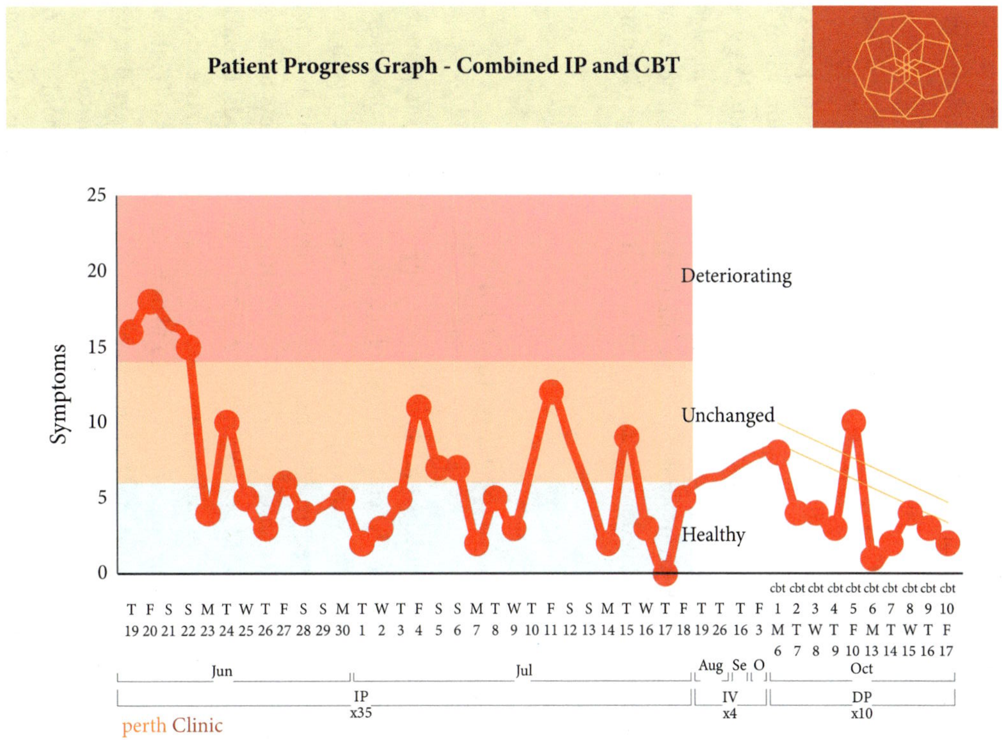

Figure 12.2 Individual Symptom Outcomes During an Inpatient Stay (Plotted Against Color-Coded Clinical Significance Categories) and Relative to the Group Trajectory as the Person Transitioned From Inpatient to Day Patient Status

patients receiving electroconvulsive therapy (ECT) or repetitive transcranial magnetic stimulation (rTMS) for treatment-resistant depression complete symptom and well-being questionnaires each day and now receive tailored feedback indicating the probability that they are going to complete a standard course of the treatment with symptoms that could be classified as "recovered" (Gill et al., 2023). The treating doctors can evaluate progress early within a course of treatment to decide if the treatment warrants change or adaptation (e.g., a change of dose or electrode placement). Hospital staff receive feedback each day not only on the absolute level of symptoms, but also on the level relative to their admission score. Following common practice in the psychiatric literature of classifying a 50% or greater reduction in symptoms as "recovered," staff receive an indication when a patient's symptoms have decreased by more than a half. This feedback gives staff the opportunity to consider if a change in treatment focus is needed (e.g., should a switch from symptom remediation to maintenance and relapse prevention be considered? At what point should discharge planning begin?).

Adaptations to ROM

The uses of ROM described so far highlight the application of the general principles that had been developed in the literature, in which deviations from an expected trajectory of improvement are used to guide treatment implementation. However, in keeping with the practice-based evidence approach adopted at the clinic, we engaged with staff and patients to identify adaptations of the ROM approach that might meet other needs. In part, this was driven by our observations that staff were less inclined to use ROM feedback with more severe patients, who stood to benefit the most (Hutson et al., 2020). Thus, the remainder of the chapter will describe ways that we have engaged with staff and patients to identify adaptations of ROM that meet the local needs. The first of the identified needs was patient risk of self-harm to better target treatment resources. We visited nursing stations to discuss with staff what was and was not working with the ROM feedback systems. The nurses commented that one of the key pieces of information that they used was responses to the item about suicidal thoughts. Therefore, we began to investigate ways that we could improve this feedback to address self-harm and suicide risks, as potential therapy-interfering behaviors.

Current Practice-Based Evidence Initiatives

Therapy-Interfering Behaviors: Self-Harm and Suicide Risk

Our meetings with nurses resulted in a request to adapt the graphical feedback system to include the current and recent scores on the item "I have thoughts about killing myself." The importance of this feedback to their practice led us to investigate what information to deliver, and our research revealed that the highest self-harm risk was associated with a patient who had elevated scores on two consecutive days (Kashyap et al., 2015; Restifo et al., 2015). It suggested that ward-based interventions delivered when a patient expressed suicidal thoughts might reduce the risk of imminent self-harm by de-escalating the ideation. One problem with delivering such "just-in-time" interventions is the challenge of responding quickly in the context of a busy hospital ward. Helping us to address this issue, subsequent projects have demonstrated that changes in the suicidal ideation followed from changes in feelings of burdensomeness and belongingness (Kyron et al., 2018). Elevations in these constructs could be identified in the two days prior to a self-harm event. The clinical value of this information is the additional time within which to deliver an intervention. In addition, this information could provide the possibility of targeting an intervention at the specific variable that appears to be responsible for the elevated suicidal ideation. Machine learning (ML) and network modeling have since been used to refine the risk profile using many more potential factors (Kyron et al., 2021, 2023, 2024). The next step in the clinical improvement journey will be to adapt the ROM feedback system so that in addition to providing staff with an indication of when a patient's risk of self-harm is increased (based on the ML algorithm), bespoke interventions can also be recommended based on the pattern of factors that are relevant for that patient. For instance, the intervention might be different if the immediate risk is being predicted by disrupted sleep rather than a decline in a person feeling like they belong within relationships that are important to them.

Therapy-Interfering Behaviors: Dropout Risk in CBT

While ROM is able to identify patients not improving as expected, it is possible that it could also identify those who are likely to prematurely withdraw from treatment. This clinical hypothesis could complement research demonstrating that severity of patient presentation at the start of treatment is a predictor of dropout (Davis et al., 2006; Zimmermann et al., 2016), but the dynamic nature of ROM assessments during treatment could refine treatment protocols to identify the intake profile that clinicians should focus on, as well as within-treatment changes that predict dropout.

Estimates suggest that approximately 1 in every 5 patients commencing therapy fails to complete the course of treatment in full (Swift & Greenberg, 2012), most commonly disengaging early—prior to the fifth therapy session (Bados et al., 2007). While it is conceivable that patients may terminate treatment prematurely because they have improved rapidly, it is prudent for dropout to be considered a negative outcome. It interferes with therapy because dropout undermines the overall effectiveness of treatment, contributes to therapist burdens and burnout, and, in group therapy settings, can have adverse impacts on the progress of other group members by disrupting group cohesion (Fernandez et al., 2015; Goetter et al., 2015).

The Clinical Improvement Team was keen to explore the degree to which intake data (e.g., patient demographic, diagnostic, and baseline characteristics) could be supplemented by symptom and well-being data collected each day of treatment with their ROM system. Thus, using these data, we aimed to understand the process of dropout, by considering baseline risk factors for early termination and investigating whether patients' progress *during* therapy had a bearing on dropout risk. This research gave rise to several important insights.

The first insight was that comorbidity predicted dropout in CBT. We developed prediction algorithms for dropout that prioritized a balance of sensitivity and simplicity in best model selection. Models were developed for two group CBT programs delivered in different formats: a Weekly CBT program, in which sessions are delivered once per week for 10 weeks, and an intensive Daily CBT program, in which 10 sessions are delivered over consecutive days (two weeks). The resulting models were simple, classifying dropouts from completers based only on one intake variable: degree of comorbidity, indicated by the number of secondary diagnoses patients held. Highly comorbid patients—that is, those with more than three secondary diagnoses, additional to the primary diagnosis assigned at intake assessment—were the most at risk for dropout. These patients, representing 27% of the overall patient sample, had a 65% chance of dropping out of treatment at some point during therapy. The secondary diagnosis itself did not appear relevant—rather, the *extent* of comorbidity was important.

This observation suggested that diagnostic complexity is the active driver of dropout rather than the specific diagnosis.

Given that the prediction of adverse therapeutic events, such as self-injury and suicidality, have been bolstered by monitoring the dynamic change of symptoms and well-being during treatment (e.g., Kyron et al., 2021), we had speculated a similar benefit for predicting dropout. Despite our preconception that a patient's decision to drop out chiefly reflected something to do with their immediate experience during treatment, this speculative hypothesis was not supported. In contrast to our expectations, the second insight was that dropout risk for CBT was better predicted by pre-treatment rather than within-treatment variables. The addition of patients' trajectories (whether increases or decreases) of symptom and well-being change throughout treatment into our algorithms did not improve our prediction of dropout for CBT. If this finding is replicated, it does suggest that efforts to reduce dropout need to focus on the characteristics that are present at intake, especially those reflecting symptom severity and diagnostic complexity.

Survival analyses of our data gave rise to a third insight. When dropout is destined to occur, it tends to do so early in therapy. Specifically, plotting the percentage of patients remaining in treatment at each session revealed that approximately half of the total dropout recorded in that group had already occurred by the third treatment session. By the sixth (out of 10) session, all dropouts had occurred. This finding is consistent with the broader literature on the time course of dropout (see Delgadillo et al., 2014; Gonzales Salas Duhne et al., 2022), and it encouraged reflection on the structure of the therapy where, like many programs, foundational material is introduced after a few sessions.

Our reflection on this attempt to use ROM to improve the prediction of dropout has led to consideration of a revision of the structure and content of the treatment. Conceivably, patients with a more diverse symptom profile due to extensive comorbidity could be harder to monitor and manage within a manualized format of CBT relative to patients with only one diagnosis or presenting issue (Kuyken & Tsivrikos, 2009; Olatunji et al., 2010). If acknowledging and addressing comorbidity was sufficient for dropout prevention, however, we would expect dropout to be lower in transdiagnostic CBT programs compared with focused or single-diagnosis treatments. The *Unified Protocol (UP) for Transdiagnostic Treatment of Emotional Disorders* is a prime example of a CBT transdiagnostic program; the UP aims to address the underlying common or latent features that are shared across mood and anxiety disorders, by providing a generalized toolkit for adaptive emotional processing. It has been argued that UP may deal more effectively with comorbidity than single-disorder treatments (Farchione et al., 2012), streamlines clinical decision-making, and has equivalent outcomes for patients in terms of symptom reduction (Steele et al., 2018). However, despite this, UP appears equally as poor in handling dropouts, yielding dropout rates equivalent to single-disorder CBT programs (Titov et al., 2015).

We now know that patients' experiences in treatment are not key in whether they ultimately decide to continue attending—therefore, attempting to indirectly reduce dropout via improving CBT's ability to treat comorbidity may not prove fruitful. Instead, if dropout is a therapy-interfering behavior that can be pre-identified, we are considering that CBT should include a clear protocol for targeting and treating dropout risk prior to treating symptoms. This could involve a bespoke set of interventions for patients at risk for dropout prior to the beginning of therapy and (while currently unknown) would target the *mechanisms* linking comorbidity and dropout risk. Dialectical behavior therapy (DBT) is an exemplar as to how this protocol may function clinically; DBT prioritizes treating behaviors that threaten a patient's life and physical safety first, followed by behaviors that may interfere with their engagement in therapy or ability to derive therapy's full benefit prior to treating their symptoms. If CBT practitioners were to adopt this protocol, self-injury and suicidality (as well as key predictors of these behaviors) would be treated first, followed by mechanisms driving dropout risk, all before a patient even begins the treatment for their symptoms.

Also, reflecting on this observation about dropout in the context of the clinic's engagement with ROM, it does highlight the value of practice-oriented research. Drawing on the existing literature and clinical expertise, we generated hypotheses that we then investigated and ended up refining. In this instance, some of our clinical insights required revision, and it has allowed us to review the structure of the CBT program and to consider whether different delivery models for people at risk of dropout may improve outcomes. Importantly, it indicates that research and evaluation can be informed by clinical wisdom, but there is also a requirement to be open to testing these hypotheses, and the result will allow an evidence-based review of clinical practices.

Extending the ROM Paradigm to Predict Recurrent Use of Treatment Services

While the clinic's use of ROM sought to improve patients' engagement with treatment, the Clinical Improvement Team continues to have questions regarding the optimal pathway through treatment. That is, while the standard application of ROM is within a particular episode of care, for many patients attendance at a therapy group or an inpatient admission is but one chapter in a longer story. For this reason, Perth Clinic and the health insurance companies are keen to leverage the value of psychotherapy (and CBT in particular) delivered in an inpatient context as a possible protection against future readmissions (Byrne et al., 2010, 2012; Newnham et al., 2010b). Page and Hooke (2009) noted that when attendance at psychotherapy groups during an inpatient admission was more strongly encouraged (and so increased from an average of 16 to 27 sessions per admission), the percentage of patients readmitted within one month halved from 10% to 5%. Discussions led the Clinical Improvement Team to examine the degree to which a within-episode ROM approach might be adapted to view progress across episodes of care. That is, rather than considering the trajectory of relevant symptom improvement within a single episode of care, we shifted our focus to examine changes in the pattern of readmission across time. This shared goal arose because preventable inpatient readmissions can have far-reaching consequences for patients and service providers (Duhig et al., 2017; Goldman, 1988; Williams et al., 2014), they are financially costly (Heslin & Weiss, 2015), and they can exacerbate waiting lists.

Thus, it was important to reflect on what may be required to understand and address the different patterns of readmission and develop a better understanding of the factors that predict or protect against future admissions. The hospital had access to inpatient readmission rates (e.g., approximately 40% of inpatients readmit). However, without an understanding of the various factors that may be driving the readmission, clinicians must rely on "one-size-fits-all" interventions to reduce the likelihood of future admissions, as it is not yet possible to implement specific interventions that target the unique causes underlying a readmission. To target treatments more efficiently and effectively with a goal of reducing a need for future readmissions, it is necessary to (1) accurately identify patients who are likely to readmit in future; (2) have an adequate understanding of the key factors driving the readmission; and (3) introduce preventative interventions that target these specific causal factors for each given patient. This must all be achievable during the earliest possible stages of the treatment journey.

Existing research typically aimed to predict the likelihood of any subsequent admission. In so doing, the focus was on predicting a "universal" risk of readmission, which implicitly assumes that all instances of readmission are driven by the same set of underlying causes. However, patients may exhibit different patterns of readmissions that could be driven by distinct underlying causes, and hence, they may respond differently to interventions that seek to prevent future readmissions. For example, two closely spaced admissions might be a consequence of the same episode of a mental disorder, while two widely spaced admissions could reflect two separate mental disorders. Therefore, using ROM, we sought to model our approach after two studies that deviated from the typical literature by examining inpatients' sets of admissions across extended time frames. These studies found that patients can be grouped according to distinct profiles of readmissions that are uniquely associated with several variables (Hudson, 2005; Shafer, 2019).

Extending this methodology, we have been able to demonstrate that a 5-year window is adequate to understand the different profiles of readmissions (when compared with 10- and 15-year time windows). We identified five distinct profiles of readmissions that appear to arise from different causal processes. These profiles are characterized (and named) according to the relative frequency of admissions (being either mild, moderate, or intense) and whether these admissions occurred episodically or maintained a stable pattern over time. To illustrate this point, line graphs depict patients' patterns of admissions across time for 2 of the 5 profiles, named "Mild Episodic" and "Intense Stable" (Figure 12.3a and 12.3b, respectively). Each patient is depicted by an individually colored line, depicting the durations (days; y-axis) between each of their consecutive inpatient admissions (x-axis). "Mild Episodic" patients had few admissions (3.7 on average) that occurred episodically (illustrated by the sharp peaks and slopes in Figure 12.3a), fluctuating between having short durations (approximately 74 days) and long durations (approximately 1,197 days) between their admissions. On the other hand, "Intense Stable" patients had a high number of admissions (12.5 on average) and exhibited a stable pattern (illustrated by the relatively flat lines in Figure 12.3b) of consistently short durations between these admissions (approximately 113 days).

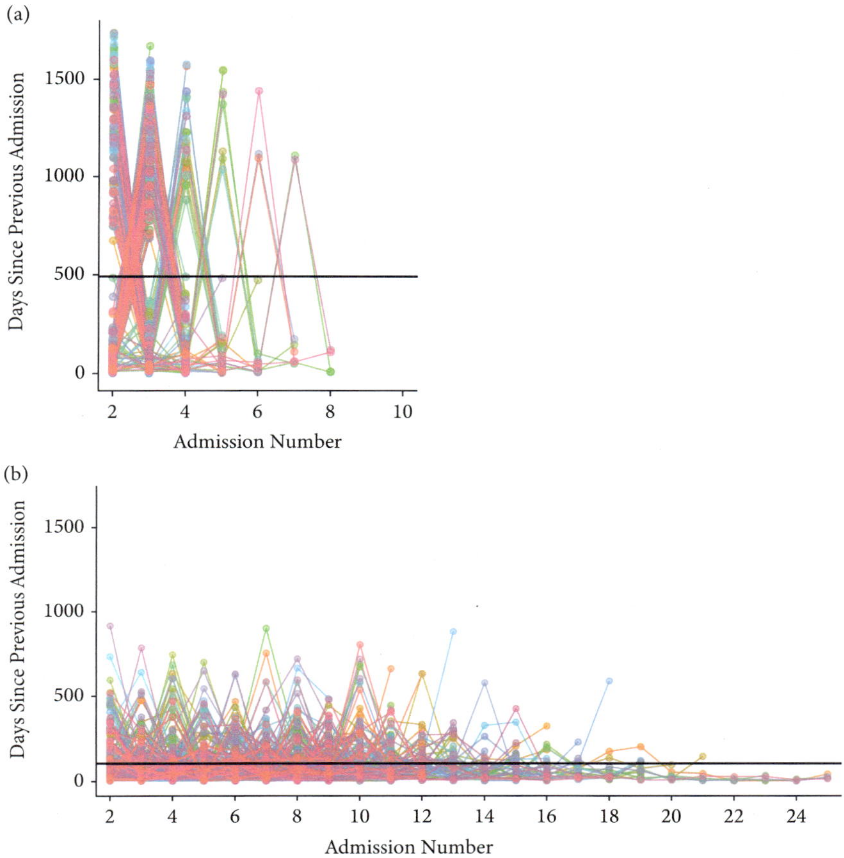

Figure 12.3 Readmission Patterns of Each Patient for the "Mild Episodic" and "Intense Stable" Readmission Profiles.

Thus, we are now identifying whether there are particular characteristics or treatment experiences associated with admission patterns that involve rapid readmissions (e.g., do these patients have less engagement with psychotherapy early in their patient journeys?). The goal is to provide staff with the tools to identify patients who are likely to readmit and an adequate understanding of the risk and protective factors associated with these specific readmissions. This again illustrates how an approach adopting ROM can be adapted to focus both within admissions and across admissions, and how practices can benefit from a combined implementation of these processes. Identifying variables (and patterns of changes in variables) that are associated with points across the five readmission patterns will allow for a greater understanding of the distinct factors that likely underlie individual instances of readmission across different patients. This research would allow the clinic to predict patients' readmission patterns from an early point in treatment, potentially from the very first admission (before any readmission), and could assist clinicians' treatment planning and decision-making by highlighting the factors that may lead certain patients to readmit. Furthermore, this practice-based evidence approach could enable the development of interventions that target the patients' specific needs that, if not addressed, would increase their risk of readmitting. Such patient-specific interventions allow resources to be allocated more efficiently and are expected to be more effective at preventing unnecessary readmissions and improving patients' treatment outcomes.

Conclusions

The challenge faced by all psychotherapists, including CBT practitioners, is that despite many years of research and development, the effect sizes for treatment (despite being large) have remained relatively constant across decades and similar across therapy variants. The potential value of ROM is that it takes a different approach to quality improvement, and rather than seeking to find a superior treatment, it focuses attention on patients who are not responding as expected. The journey that the Perth Clinic's Team has been on illustrates, at a local level, the journey being taken by the field more generally. That is, while the initial studies showed that the provision of progress feedback to patients and therapists was beneficial to outcomes for those who were "Not on Track," those studies did not prescribe interventions or propose programs that were tailored to be delivered in a "just-in-time" manner. This real-time progress-relevant feedback is a core concept of ROM that answers the questions posed by Gordon Paul (1967) when he asked, "What treatment, by whom, is most effective for this individual with that specific problem, and under which set of circumstances?" The value of adopting a practice-based evidence approach is that it guides the ROM journey. Practice-based evidence provides this guidance because of the privileged status that it gives to the patient and therapist wisdom as well as the privilege given to outcomes that have therapeutic impact. For researchers, the twin dangers—akin to Scylla and Charybdis—are findings that restate what people already knew or findings that no one cares about. These two practice-based evidence principles serve to guide the process of clinical improvement as researchers learn from and deliver impactful learnings to the clinical setting and in so doing ensure that the process of knowledge generation improves the mental health outcomes for all.

References

Andrews, G., & Page, A. C. (2005). Outcome measurement, outcome management, and monitoring. *Australian and New Zealand Journal of Psychiatry, 39*(8), 649–651. https://doi.org/10.1080/j.1440-1614.2005.01648.x

Bados, A., Balaguer, G., & Saldaña, C. (2007). The efficacy of cognitive–behavioral therapy and the problem of drop-out. *Journal of Clinical Psychology, 63*(6), 585–592. https://doi.org/10.1080/10503307.2013.775528

Byrne, S. L., Hooke, G. R., Fieldhouse, B., De Felice, C. N., & Page, A. C. (2012). Readmission to psychiatric hospital following treatment for depression with electroconvulsive therapy: The effect of planned readmissions. *The Journal of Electroconvulsive Therapy, 28*(2), e12–e13. https://doi.org/10.1097/YCT.0b013e31823fbb13

Byrne, S. L., Hooke, G. R., & Page, A. C. (2010). Readmission: A useful indicator of the quality of inpatient psychiatric care. *Journal of Affective Disorders, 126* (1–2), 206–213. https://doi.org/10.1016/j.jad.2010.02.135

Davis, S., Hooke, G. R., & Page, A. C. (2006). Identifying and targeting predictors of drop-out from group cognitive behaviour therapy. *Australian Journal of Psychology, 58*(1), 48–56. https://doi.org/10.1080/00049530500504096

Delgadillo, J., McMillan, D., Lucock, M., Leach, C., Ali, S., & Gilbody, S. (2014). Early changes, attrition, and dose-response in low intensity psychological interventions. *British Journal of Clinical Psychology, 53*(1), 114–130. https://doi.org/10.1111/bjc.12031

Duhig, M., Gunasekara, I., & Patterson, S. (2017). Understanding readmission to psychiatric hospital in Australia from the service users' perspective: A qualitative study. *Health & Social Care in the Community, 25*(1), 75–82. https://doi.org/10.1111/hsc.12269

Dyer, K., Hooke, G., & Page, A. C. (2014). Development and psychometrics of the five item daily index in a psychiatric sample. *Journal of Affective Disorders, 152–154*, 409–415. https://doi.org/10.1016/j.jad.2013.10.003

Dyer, K., Hooke, G. R., & Page, A. C. (2016). Effects of providing domain specific progress monitoring and feedback to therapists and patients on outcome. *Psychotherapy Research, 26*(3), 297–306. https://doi.org/10.1080/10503307.2014.983207

Farchione, T., Fairholme, C. P., Ellard, K. K., Boisseau, C. L., Thompson-Hollands, J., Carl, J. R., Gallagher, M. W., & Barlow, D. H. (2012). Unified Protocol for Transdiagnostic Treatment of Emotional Disorders: A randomized controlled trial. *Behavior Therapy, 43*(3), 666–678. https://doi.org/10.1016/j.beth.2012.01.001

Fernandez, E., Salem, D., Swift, J. K., & Ramtahal, N. (2015). Meta-analysis of dropout from cognitive behavioral therapy: Magnitude, timing, and moderators. *Journal of Consulting and Clinical Psychology, 83*(6), 1108–1122. https://doi.org/10.1037/ccp0000044

Gill, J., De Felice, N., Gill, J., Page, A. C., & Hooke, G. R. (2023). Repetitive transcranial magnetic stimulation: Course and early prediction of response in depression. *Journal of Psychiatric Research, 157*, 108–111. https://doi.org/10.1016/j.jpsychires.2022.11.018

Goetter, E. M., Bui, E., Ojserkis, R. A., Zakarian, R. J., Brendel, R. W., & Simon, N. M. (2015). A systematic review of dropout from psychotherapy for posttraumatic stress disorder among Iraq and Afghanistan combat veterans. *Journal of Traumatic Stress, 28*(5), 401–409. https://doi.org/10.1002/jts.22038

Goldman, S. K. (1988). *Series on community-based services for children & adolescents who are severely emotionally disturbed: Volume II: Crisis services.* CASSP Technical Assistance Center, Georgetown University.

Gonzalez Salas Duhne, P., Delgadillo, J., & Lutz, W. (2022). Predicting early dropout in online versus face-to-face guided self-help: A machine learning approach. *Behaviour Research and Therapy, 159,* Article 104200. https://doi.org/10.1016/j.brat.2022.104200

Heslin, K. C., & Weiss, A. J. (2015). Hospital readmissions involving psychiatric disorders, 2012 (Statistical Brief No. 189). In *Healthcare Cost and Utilization Project (HCUP) Statistical Briefs.* Agency for Healthcare Research and Quality (US). https://hcup-us.ahrq.gov/reports/statbriefs/sb189-Hospital-Readmissions-Psychiatric-Disorders-2012.pdf

Hudson, C. G. (2005). Patterns of acute psychiatric hospitalization in Massachusetts. *Administration and Policy in Mental Health and Mental Health Services Research, 32*(3), 221–240. https://doi.org/10.1007/s10488-004-0842-5

Hutson, J., Hooke, G. R., & Page, A. C. (2020). Progress monitoring and feedback delivered in routine psychiatric care: Beneficial but not reaching those thought to need it most. *Psychotherapy Research, 30*(7), 843–856. https://doi.org/10.1080/10503307.2019.1710305

Kashyap, S., Hooke, G. R., & Page, A. C. (2015). Identifying risk of deliberate self-harm through longitudinal monitoring of psychological distress in an inpatient psychiatric population. *BMC Psychiatry, 15,* Article 81. https://doi.org/10.1186/s12888-015-0464-3

Kuyken, W., & Tsivrikos, D. (2009). Therapist competence, comorbidity and cognitive-behavioural therapy for depression. *Psychotherapy and Psychosomatics, 78*(1), 42–48. https://doi.org/10.1159/000172619

Kyron, M. J., Hooke, G. R., Bryan, C. J., Kiekens, G., Chen, W., Hasking, P., & Page, A. C. (2023). Daily prediction of non-suicidal self-injury among inpatients: The roles of suicidal thoughts, interpersonal difficulties, hopelessness, and affect. *Journal of Consulting and Clinical Psychology, 91*(6), 323–336. https://doi.org/10.1037/ccp0000812

Kyron, M. J., Hooke, G. R., Bryan, C. J., Kiekens, G., Chen, W., Udupa, N., Joiner, T., & Page, A. C. (2024). Daily prediction of inpatient suicide attempts using routinely collected theory-driven data. *The Journal of Psychopathology and Clinical Science.* https://doi.org/10.1037/abn0000880

Kyron, M. J., Hooke, G. R., & Page, A. C. (2018). Daily assessment of interpersonal factors to predict suicidal ideation and non-suicidal self-injury in psychiatric inpatients. *Journal of Consulting and Clinical Psychology, 86*(6), 556–567. http://doi.org/10.1037/ccp0000305

Kyron, M. J., Hooke, G. R., & Page, A. C. (2021). Prediction and network modelling of self-harm through daily self-report and history of self-injury. *Psychological Medicine, 51*(12), 1992–2002. https://doi.org/10.1017/S0033291720000744

Lambert, M. J. (2012). Helping clinicians to use and learn from research-based systems: The OQ-analyst. *Psychotherapy, 49*(2), 109–114. https://doi.org/10.1037/a0027110

Lambert, M. J. (2015). Progress feedback and the OQ-system: The past and the future. *Psychotherapy, 52*(4), 381–390. https://doi.org/10.1037/pst0000027

Manning, J. J., Hooke, G. R., Tannenbaum, D. A., Blythe, T. H., & Clarke, T. M. (1994). Intensive cognitive-behaviour group therapy for diagnostically heterogeneous groups of patients with psychiatric disorder. *Australian & New Zealand Journal of Psychiatry, 28*(4), 667–674. https://doi.org/10.1080/00048679409080790

Newnham, E. A., Harwood, K. E., & Page, A. C. (2007). Evaluating the clinical significance of responses by psychiatric inpatients to the mental health subscales of the SF-36. *Journal of Affective Disorders, 98*(1–2), 91–97. https://doi.org/10.1016/j.jad.2006.07.001

Newnham, E. A., Hooke, G. R., & Page, A. C. (2010a). Monitoring treatment response and outcomes using the World Health Organization's Wellbeing Index in psychiatric care. *Journal of Affective Disorders, 122*(1–2), 133–138. https://doi.org/10.1016/j.jad.2009.06.005

Newnham, E. A., Hooke, G. R., & Page, A. C. (2010b). Progress monitoring and feedback in psychiatric care reduces depressive symptoms. *Journal of Affective Disorders, 127*(1–3), 139–146. https://doi.org/10.1016/j.jad.2010.05.003

Olatunji, B. O., Cisler, J. M., & Deacon, B. J. (2010). Efficacy of cognitive behavioral therapy for anxiety disorders: A review of meta-analytic findings. *Psychiatric Clinics of North America, 33*(3), 557–577. https://doi.org/10.1016/j.psc.2010.04.002

Page, A. C., & Hooke, G. R. (2003). Outcomes for depressed and anxious inpatients discharged before or after group cognitive behavior therapy: A naturalistic comparison. *The Journal of Nervous and Mental Disease, 191*(10), 653–659. https://doi.org/10.1097/01.nmd.0000092174.38770.e9

Page, A. C., & Hooke, G. R. (2009). Best practices: Increased attendance in inpatient group psychotherapy improves patient outcomes. *Psychiatric Services, 60(4)*, 426–428. https://doi.org/10.1176/ps.2009.60.4.426

Paul, G. L. (1967). Strategy of outcome research in psychotherapy. *Journal of Consulting Psychology, 31*(2), 109–118. https://doi.org/10.1037/h0024436

Restifo, E., Kashyap, S., Hooke, G. R., & Page, A. C. (2015). Daily monitoring of temporal trajectories of suicidal ideation predict self-injury: A novel application of patient progress monitoring. *Psychotherapy Research, 25*(6), 705–713. http://doi.org/10.1080/10503307.2015.1006707

Ronk, F. R., Hooke, G. R., & Page, A. C. (2012). How consistent are clinical significance classifications when calculation methods and outcome measures differ? *Clinical Psychology: Science and Practice, 19*(2), 167–179. https://doi.org/10.1111/j.1468-2850.2012.01281.x

Ronk, F. R., Korman, J. R., Hooke, G. R., & Page, A. C. (2013). Assessing clinical significance of treatment outcomes using the DASS-21. *Psychological Assessment, 25*(4), 1103–1110. https://doi.org/10.1037/a0033100

Shafer, A. (2019). Hospitalization patterns over 30 years across a statewide system of public mental health hospitals: Readmission predictors, optimal follow-up period, readmission clusters and individuals with statistically significant high healthcare utilization. *Psychiatric Quarterly, 90*, 263–273. https://doi.org/10.1007/s11126-019-9626-7

Shimokawa, K., Lambert, M. J., & Smart, D. W. (2010). Enhancing treatment outcome of patients at risk of treatment failure: Meta-analytic and mega-analytic review of a psychotherapy quality assurance system. *Journal of Consulting and Clinical Psychology, 78*(3), 298–311. https://doi.org/10.1037/a0019247

Steele, S. J., Farchione, T. J., Cassiello-Robbins, C., Ametaj, A., Sbi, S., Sauer-Zavala, S., & Barlow, D. H. (2018). Efficacy of the Unified Protocol for transdiagnostic treatment of comorbid psychopathology accompanying emotional disorders compared to treatments targeting single disorders. *Journal of Psychiatric Research, 104*, 211–216. https://doi.org/10.1016/j.jpsychires.2018.08.005

Swift, J. K., & Greenberg, R. P. (2012). Premature discontinuation in adult psychotherapy: A meta-analysis. *Journal of Consulting and Clinical Psychology, 80*(4), 547–559. https://doi.org/10.1037/a0028226

Titov, N., Dear, B. F., Staples, L. G., Terides, M. D., Karin, E., Sheehan, J., Johnston, L., Gandy, M., Fogliati, V. J., Wootton, B. M., & McEvoy, P. M. (2015). Disorder-specific versus transdiagnostic and clinician-guided versus self-guided treatment for major depressive disorder and comorbid anxiety disorders: A randomized controlled trial. *Journal of Anxiety Disorders, 35*, 88–102. https://doi.org/10.1016/j.janxdis.2015.08.002

Topp, C. W., Østergaard, S. D., Søndergaard, S., & Bech, P. (2015). The WHO-5 Well-Being Index: A systematic review of the literature. *Psychotherapy and Psychosomatics, 84*(3), 167–176. https://doi.org/10.1159/000376585

Williams, P., Csipke, E., Rose, D., Koeser, L., McCrone, P., Tulloch, A. D., Salaminios, G., Wykes, T., & Craig, T. (2014). Efficacy of a triage system to reduce length of hospital stay. *The British Journal of Psychiatry, 204*(6), 480–485. https://doi.org/10.1192/bjp.bp.113.141051

Zimmermann, D., Rubel, J., Page, A. C., & Lutz, W. (2016). Therapist effects on and predictors of non-consensual dropout in psychotherapy. *Clinical Psychology and Psychotherapy, 24*(2), 312–321. https://doi.org/10.1002/cpp.2022

SECTION V
INTEGRATION AND DISSEMINATION

13

Psychotherapists Can Improve Their Outcomes and Contribute to Research Using Data They Collect When Providing Measurement-Based Care

Jacqueline B. Persons, Garret G. Zieve, Caroline J. Harris, and Letian Li

We describe here a strategy for conducting research in a clinical practice setting that relies on data the psychotherapist collects as part of measurement-based care, defined as "the systematic evaluation of patient symptoms before or during each clinical encounter to inform behavioral health treatment" (Lewis et al., 2018, p. E1). Measurement-based care (MBC) is a boon to the scientist-practitioner in two ways. First, therapists who use it can improve their outcomes. Large numbers of randomized controlled trials show that MBC improves outcomes and reduces dropout in psychotherapy (de Jong et al., 2021; Lewis et al., 2018). Second, as we will show here, data collected while providing MBC can make important contributions to research. The research strategy we describe here exemplifies the defining characteristics of practice-based evidence (PBE), in that studies are conducted by clinicians in naturalistic settings as they provide routine care (Castonguay et al., 2021, pp. 192–193).

We begin the chapter by describing a large database created by the first author and her colleagues as they provided MBC. We offer a personal account of how the database came to be created and how the research enterprise using the database was initiated. Next, we identify three research questions that can be addressed using data collected during MBC: *implementation studies* examining the generalizability to routine practice of treatments, assessments, and other practices shown effective in research settings; *studies of innovations* developed by clinicians in the course of their daily

Jacqueline B. Persons et al., *Psychotherapists Can Improve Their Outcomes and Contribute to Research Using Data They Collect When Providing Measurement-Based Care*. In: *Practice-Based Evidence in the Psychological Therapies*. Edited by: Louis G. Castonguay et al., Oxford University Press.
DOI: 10.1093/9780197748336.003.0013

work; and *studies of change processes* during psychotherapy. We describe studies addressing these areas that we and others have published based on data collected for clinical purposes. Next, we briefly describe strategies we use to conduct research using our database in our clinical practice setting. We conclude by describing our plans for the future.

The Personal and Professional Story of the Construction of Our Archival Database

The database comprised of the data we collected as we provided MBC from 1981 through 2008 is formally named the Naturalistic CBT Archival Database, and we usually refer to it as the Archival Database. It includes data from 1,470 adults who received outpatient cognitive behavior therapy (CBT) provided by the first author and 19 of her trainees and colleagues from 1981 through 2008. The database includes item-by-item scores from 18,602 administrations of the Beck Depression Inventory (BDI), for a total of 18,602 × 21 items in the BDI = 390,642 BDI item scores. However, we would like to highlight here (and will demonstrate) that important contributions to science are possible with less data collected over a shorter time period. The Archival Database includes information from four main sources: (1) intake data, including demographics, diagnosis, scores on screening measures, and information about background factors such as trauma history; (2) item-by-item scores on symptom measures completed by patients at each therapy session (the primary measures were the version of the BDI published in Beck et al. (1979) and the Burns Anxiety Inventory (Burns & Eidelson, 1998)); (3) clinician-rated items indicating whether the termination of treatment was premature and/or uncollaborative and ratings of two reasons for the termination; and (4) some information about the treatment. Information about the treatment included dates of therapy sessions, identity of the therapist, whether the patient received pharmacotherapy or other adjunctive treatment, and ratings by the research team of the presence of three decision support tools in the clinical record (a written case formulation, a list of treatment goals, and a plot of progress monitoring data with at least one score on it). Persons et al. (2023) provides additional information about the database and the procedures involved in creating it.

The earliest version of the database resulted from the fact that Persons was trained as a student clinician to collect data to monitor her patients' progress in treatment. She learned as a graduate student during her practicum experience in Aaron Beck's Mood Clinic at the University of Pennsylvania to administer the BDI to all the depressed patients she was treating, score the measure before the session, plot the score, and use the data to guide treatment. (Beck and his colleagues may have used these data for research, but Persons did not participate in the research.) As she finished her training and moved into clinical practice, Persons continued to use this process with most of her cases, selecting measures other than the BDI when the patient had another problem, and teaching this method to clinicians she worked with and trained.

Dr. Persons amassed her MBC data into a database gradually over time. The first version of the Archival Database included only data from her patients, as in the study of predictors of dropout and outcome that was based on data collected from 23 patients treated by Persons and 47 treated by Burns (Persons et al., 1988). Later data were added from patients treated by colleagues in Persons's group practice. However, samples were still small at first. For example, the study of changes in anxiety and depression over time (Persons et al., 2003) examined a sample of 58 patients. Although the data set included 439 patients at that point, the selection for study of patients who provided at least four sessions of data monitoring both anxiety and depression, received individual treatment (not group or couple), and were aged 19 to 65 years reduced the sample to 58. This study illustrated the potential of the database, and yet the *N* was not sufficient to carry out studies of the change process, studies of therapist effects, and other studies that the first author and her colleague Cannon Thomas, a local colleague who was also a research-minded clinical psychologist, had in mind to carry out. Another limitation was that most of the data came from Persons's patients, which limited the generalizability of findings based on the data set.

To address these issues, in 2005, Cannon Thomas suggested to Persons that they create a research database made up of all the progress-monitoring data collected by Persons over the course of her career and the data collected by all the clinicians in Persons's group practice since the beginning of the practice 10 years earlier. We describe here the factors that helped us create the Archival Database with the hope of assisting and inspiring others to create their own research databases based on data they collect for clinical purposes.

Of course, the collaboration of Persons's colleagues in her practice was essential; we tried to limit the data that we needed to obtain directly from them, and to focus primarily on culling data from their patients' clinical records. Another helpful factor was the availability of volunteer research assistants, usually advanced undergraduate students at University of California at Berkeley who wanted research experience to strengthen their applications to graduate school in clinical psychology. Persons and Thomas worked with several volunteer research assistants, led by Corey Pallatto Hughan, to create a research database made up of all the data from all the (paper) clinical records of all the patients treated by all the clinicians in Persons's group practice. We worked on Fridays, a day we allocated to research, for more than 2 years, beginning in 2005 and ending in the summer of 2007 when we began our final push to clean the data set, a project that itself lasted 6 months, although we had done proofreading as we went. As a result of our hard work and systematic methods, the error rate analysis for the project revealed an error rate of only 1.75%.

Creating the database was only possible because the clinicians in the practice routinely obtained consent from their patients for the use of data in their clinical record for research purposes as part of the Treatment Agreement they obtained from all their patients; Persons had learned to ask for research consent in her Treatment Agreement from David Burns, who was one of her first clinical supervisors.

Creating this database was a huge amount of work. Why do it? Many factors facilitated the development of the Archival Database. A major factor is that Persons loves doing research. One of her favorite things in the world is to sit alone in a room and plan and implement research studies. She especially loves developing hypotheses drawn from her clinical work that can be tested with our database and writing up the studies. She doesn't love data analysis, and her data analytic skills are weak; to address that deficit, she has relied on talented collaborators, including Cannon Thomas and coauthor Garret Zieve. Working with talented collaborators, including graduate students at UC Berkeley, is part of the fun of the work. In addition, Persons finds research rewarding because it allows her to participate in the international scientific community and contribute to science, not just to the lives of her patients. And once her papers began being accepted for publication, she enjoyed the recognition she received, including the recognition as a unique psychologist who conducts research in a clinical practice setting.

The Archival Database also has its origins in Persons's research training as a clinical psychologist at the University of Pennsylvania. Her dissertation work (Persons & Baron, 1985) examined cognitive mechanisms underpinning symptoms of formal thought disorder, and as part of that work she learned to think about relationships between symptoms and maintaining mechanisms, thinking that led her to ideas about case formulation (which we will describe) and to questions about the change process during treatment that are well suited to research investigations using data collected in MBC. Another element of Persons's training that proved to be important to her practice-based research success was the fact that she was not trained in a large laboratory but instead worked primarily alone, guided by faculty mentors (especially Jonathan Baron and Henry Gleitman, both cognitive psychologists), and so developed the skills to work independently to carry out research. Another formative element of her training was the fact that David Burns, one of her first clinical supervisors, modeled the professional identity of a clinician who conducted research in his clinical practice (e.g., Burns & Eidelson, 1998). Another seminal training event was Persons's experience during her internship, when she worked with an advanced undergraduate student, Peter Rao, to test a hypothesis about belief change during treatment based on longitudinal data collected in the inpatient psychiatric unit at the Hospital of the University of Pennsylvania (Persons & Rao, 1985). This experience taught two things: the scientific value of longitudinal data, and the importance of having complete control over the data collection rather than relying on others to accomplish this essential research task.

Postdoctoral training at the Behavior Therapy Unit at the Eastern Pennsylvania Psychiatric Institute by noted clinical scientists Joseph Wolpe, Edna Foa, and Ralph M. Turner, who taught a course in single-case experimental design, also showed how research and clinical work could be tightly integrated. Persons's learning single-case experimental design led to a publication (Persons, 1986) based on a patient she treated during her postdoctoral fellowship, and her training with Edna Foa led to a study Persons initiated of cognitive processes in OCD that was published as Persons & Foa (1984).

Persons's choice to pursue a career as a clinician rather than an academic also contributed to the development of the Archival Database. When her husband, an economist, received a job offer at University of California at Berkeley, she elected to follow him to California where he had family, rather than go on the academic job market herself. She used her clinical skills and interests to make a living and found, especially in the beginning days when she had few patients, that she had time to write up for publication the data from her dissertation (Persons & Baron, 1985) and a handful of small-scale studies she had initiated as a graduate student and postdoctoral fellow (Persons, 1986; Persons & Burns, 1985; Persons & Rao, 1985; Persons & Foa, 1984; Persons, 1991).

Persons and Thomas closed the Archival Database to new cases in 2008, primarily because it became clear that we needed to transition from paper and pencil assessment to use of an online tool. That decision meant that we needed to abandon the primary symptom-tracking measures we had relied on (the BDI and the Burns Anxiety Inventory [AI]) to use a public domain measure that was available at no cost (we selected the Depression Anxiety Stress Scales; DASS; Lovibond & Lovibond, 1995). As we describe in our "Plans for the Future" section, we are now embarked on creating a second database based on the DASS.

Research Studies Based on Data Collected During Measurement-Based Care

MBC offers an unprecedented opportunity to harness the creativity, innovation, and insights of clinicians working outside academia to answer foundational questions in our field, including: How effective are our treatments when they leave the controlled settings of randomized controlled trials (RCTs) and are implemented in real-world clinical settings? What might totally new approaches to psychotherapy look like? How and why does therapeutic change take place? We describe here studies addressing these questions that we and others have conducted using data collected for clinical purposes.

Implementation of Evidence-Based Practices

A central question in implementation science is whether interventions, assessments, and other practices developed and tested in research and academic settings are effective when implemented in practice settings (Bauer & Kirchner, 2020). In a study of this sort, Persons et al. (1999) compared the outcomes of cognitive therapy for depression delivered in a private practice setting with outcomes of patients treated in RCTs of the same treatment in academic settings. Data for the study were drawn from 45 adult patients treated by the first author who completed the BDI (Beck et al., 1979) at each session as she provided MBC. Persons et al. (1999) found that outcomes of patients she treated in private practice were similar to outcomes of patients treated in RCTs even though the private practice sample included patients who would have been screened out of the trials due to mental health comorbidities.

It is important to highlight that the treatment provided to patients in this study was CBT provided by the clinician (and researcher) in her routine practice. That is, the clinician did not change her day-to-day practice to adhere to a treatment manual that was created by researchers who wanted to know whether such a treatment manual was effective in a naturalistic setting. Nor did the study design require that only clients who met strict inclusion and exclusion criteria be treated. This investigation of cognitive therapy as conducted in routine clinical practice thus fits the definition of practice-based evidence (Castonguay et al., 2021, pp. 192–193), which is not necessarily the case for traditional effectiveness studies—which are driven by the theoretical interests of researchers and generally impose constraints on clinicians' behaviors.

The study of the effects of implementing EBPs in routine practice can also go beyond treatment to include assessment tools. For example, Moore et al. (2015) studied the clinical utility of the Overall Anxiety Severity and Impairment Scale (OASIS; Norman et al., 2006) when administered for MBC in a private practice anxiety treatment center. This measure is often used as an outcome assessment in RCTs of anxiety treatments conducted in academic settings. Findings from the study showed that the OASIS was valid and reliable as a measure of change during treatment across a range of anxiety disorders (Moore et al., 2015). Additional opportunities for implementation research using data collected for MBC might include a study comparing outcomes before and after receiving training in a new EBP (Goldberg et al., 2016) or evaluating an EBP delivered to a novel clinical or demographic population.

Clinicians frequently adapt EBPs to their unique settings and patient populations in ways that are worthy of empirical study. These adaptations can include integrating ideas from different treatments; adding, removing, or reordering elements of a protocol; shortening or lengthening treatment or modules within a protocol; or loosening the structure of a protocol (Stirman et al., 2013). One particularly important opportunity for adaptation is modifications intended to increase fit of EBPs with diverse populations, for example, by integrating culturally relevant metaphors, symbols, teachings, and values (Hong, 2013), or by addressing stigma. To identify a potential contribution in this area, clinicians are invited to reflect if and how their practice differs from documented EBPs.

Implementation studies play an important role in exploring whether EBPs are robust given the complexities of real-world settings. A common complexity is more heterogeneous patient populations in practice settings compared with samples in RCTs, particularly with regard to comorbidity and severity. Other complexities include limitations in the amount of time clinicians can devote to training and supervision, or larger caseloads. The studies reviewed earlier reflect good generalizability of EBPs from research to practice settings. However, it is equally possible to find an "implementation cliff," or a drop in benefit that occurs when EBPs move from research to practice settings (Weisz et al., 2014). One factor that may contribute to these cliffs is a lack of fit between practices developed in academic contexts and the settings where most mental health treatments are delivered. Thus, clinicians may find it is necessary to innovate, modify, or adapt existing practices to meet the needs of their practice setting or patient population, as we describe in the next section.

Innovation

Clinicians who provide MBC can use the data they collect to evaluate innovations they develop in the course of their clinical work. An example is the case formulation approach to CBT developed by Persons (1989, 2008). The case formulation approach to CBT is not a new treatment; it is best viewed as a systematic approach to personalizing CBT to meet the unique needs of each patient. The case formulation approach calls for the therapist to use the nomothetic evidence-based cognitive behavioral theories (e.g., Beck's cognitive theory and therapy, and learning theories) to develop an idiographic model of the psychological factors that maintain all of a particular patient's problems and disorders, to use the model to guide intervention, and to collect progress-monitoring data to evaluate whether the treatment helps the patient accomplish their goals and produces change in the maintaining mechanisms (Persons, 2008). This innovation exemplifies how practice-oriented research (Castonguay et al., 2021) contributes not only to the understanding of clinical routine, but also to its improvement (from bottom up [i.e., by clinicians] as opposed to top to bottom [i.e., from researchers to clinicians]), as in the "two-way bridge" between science and practice described by Goldfried (2010).

The process Persons used to develop a case formulation approach to CBT (Persons, 2008) relied on a model of treatment development that John Weisz and his colleagues (Weisz et al., 2015) described as the deployment-focused model, that is, a model of developing treatment in the setting in which it will be deployed. Persons's innovation flowed directly from her clinical work. She was using protocols for empirically supported treatments (e.g., Beck's cognitive therapy for depression (Beck et al., 1979) to guide her work. As she did so, she experienced several bumps in the road. One was the case of a woman who lived out of town but was here in the Bay Area staying in a motel and spending all her time in the hospital where her father was dying of cancer. She sought help from Persons because she was extremely uncomfortable using the public bathrooms in the hospital, fearing that others would hear noises she made when she urinated or defecated. Persons approached this case using the empirically supported treatments she had been trained to provide, which called for her to make a diagnosis and offer the patient a treatment guided by an empirically supported treatment protocol for that disorder. This patient met criteria for social phobia. However, very reasonably, given the strain she was experiencing, she was not willing to undertake treatment of her social phobia at that time. Persons had been trained to refuse treatment to patients who did not want to complete the treatment for their disorder, and so she turned this patient away and did not offer her any treatment.

This painful error was one of many experiences that led Persons to develop a case formulation approach to clinical work that calls for the therapist to identify and consider offering treatment that addresses *the patient's idiographic goals*, which frequently do not include treating a patient's disorder to remission. In this particular case, the therapist could have provided the patient with the information that she met criteria for social anxiety disorder, provided information about the evidence-based treatment of social phobia, and, if the therapist felt comfortable doing this, offered an alternative treatment option of a few sessions to help the patient accomplish her goal of reducing her distress (e. g., perhaps by helping the patient assert herself to get help locating a private bathroom in the hospital). This approach to treatment might fit the definition of harm reduction (Logan & Marlatt, 2010). In a formal process of informed consent for treatment, the therapist could let the patient know that the option of solving her problem using the harm reduction approach, which in this case entailed avoidance of distressing situations, could help her achieve her goal of reducing distress but might in the long run worsen her social anxiety disorder. The therapist could recommend that, when her situation permitted it, the patient undertake treatment of her social anxiety disorder. The question of when it is ethical and clinically indicated to offer non-optimal treatments is an important one that therapists confront daily and that deserves more attention in the literature (Gruber and Persons (2010) discuss strategies for approaching this problem).

The case formulation model also had its origins in Persons's experiences training cognitive behavioral therapists at Ricardo Munoz's Depression Clinic at San Francisco General Hospital, where she was called on to help therapists provide treatment to depressed patients who had multiple psychiatric, medical, and psychosocial difficulties that meant that these patients were not represented in the RCTs and that strategies to address these comorbidities were not described in the treatment protocols. The writings of behavior analysts, especially Ira Turkat (1985), offered guidance in using the idiographic conceptualization to personalize the treatment and solve problems like homework noncompliance and lack of progress.

To evaluate the effectiveness of her innovation, Persons et al. (2006) published an uncontrolled trial based on data collected during MBC of 58 patients treated in her own office and by clinicians she supervised (these are the same 58 patients mentioned previously in the description of Persons et al., 2003). The study showed that the use of a case formulation approach to cognitive therapy for depression, implemented in routine practice (as opposed to being added for research purposes), produced outcomes comparable to those seen in the RCTs studying CBT for depression guided by a standardized protocol. Studies of single cases (e. g., Persons & Mikami, 2002; Persons et al., 2013) illustrated the way the case formulation can help the therapist address treatment failure.

Change Process

Both clinicians and psychotherapy researchers are intensely interested in understanding the change process in psychotherapy, and this confluence of interests increases the potential for psychotherapists to contribute to the science of our field. Moreover, MBC provides intensive longitudinal data that are not commonly collected by researchers—at least not during RCTs—and that are ideally suited to studying the change process. Another advantage of practice-oriented research studying change processes is that studies address questions clinicians encounter in their daily work and can have immediate clinical application.

Several of our studies based on the Archival Database take up questions about the change process in CBT. For example, following up on the implementation study of the case formulation approach to CBT described earlier (Persons et al., 2006), Gates et al. (2021) conducted a study to learn something about the change process in case formulation–driven CBT. Gates et al. (2021) asked whether the decision support tools used in the case formulation approach to CBT (that is, the case formulation, list of treatment goals, and plot of progress-monitoring data) were related to outcome and dropout. Gates et al. (2021) analyzed data from 845 patients selected from the complete Archival Database of 1,470 cases. Patients were excluded from the study if they (a) sought consultation rather than treatment, (b) had incorrect or missing data describing the total number of sessions, or (c) had fewer than three sessions in the database. We excluded these cases in order to study treatment, not consultation; to ensure that the imputation strategy we used to interpolate missing data could be carried out in a reasonable length of time; and to ensure that we could use the same patient sample for all the analyses we conducted. We studied three decision support tools: the written case formulation, the list of treatment goals, and the progress plot. The independent variable was the presence of the tool in the clinical record, based on a rating the research team made when culling the data from the clinical record. Dependent variables were end-of-treatment score on the BDI (Beck et al., 1979) or Burns AI (Burns & Eidelson, 1998), and therapist-rated premature and uncollaborative dropout.

Results showed that the therapist's use of a written case formulation was associated with a lower rate of premature and uncollaborative dropouts but did not predict end-of-treatment symptom scores. Therapist use of a list of treatment goals was associated with lower end-of-treatment symptom scores and less uncollaborative dropout but, contrary to prediction, with a higher rate of premature termination. Therapist use of a progress-monitoring plot with at least one score on it predicted lower end-of-treatment symptom scores and fewer premature and uncollaborative terminations. A weakness of this study is that we do not have direct evidence of the therapist's use of these decision support tools in treatment; we just know that they were present in the clinical record. These findings have direct implications for clinical work.

They remind clinicians of the value of developing a written formulation of the case to reduce dropout, a list of treatment goals to improve symptom outcomes, and a plot of progress-monitoring scores to reduce dropout and improve symptom outcomes.

The case formulation approach to CBT calls for the therapist to personalize the treatment based on many factors, including information about patient pretreatment characteristics. In support of this approach to personalizing treatment, Jiyoung Song led a study (Song et al., 2024) of the Archival Dataset that shows that higher pretreatment interpersonal sensitivity predicts a slower rate of change in anxiety and less change in anxiety but not depression symptoms during CBT and also predicts premature but not early or uncollaborative termination. The clinical implication of this finding is that assessing interpersonal sensitivity before treatment begins can inform the therapist to be alert to the potential for patients who are high in interpersonal sensitivity to show a slow rate of change in anxiety symptoms and to terminate treatment prematurely.

A common question we confront in our clinical work is how long to persist with the current treatment plan when the patient is not responding to treatment. In a study tackling this question, Persons and Thomas (2019) showed that patients who report a BDI score in the severe range after four sessions of treatment for depression are very unlikely to remit after 20 sessions, a number we selected because it is the number of sessions in the empirically supported protocols for depression. This study examined 82 patients in the Archival Database[1] and 158 patients who received protocol therapy in a research setting. We also tested the hypothesis that early symptom severity was as predictive of outcome as early change, a widely studied construct in the literature. We showed that in both our naturalistic sample and the research samples, a simple model based on BDI score after four sessions was as predictive of remission as more complex models that required calculation of change scores. These findings have direct clinical implications, namely: Monitor your depressed patients' progress in every session, and if your depressed patient scores in the severe range on the BDI or another measure of depression after four sessions of treatment, your patient is unlikely to fully recover from depression, and it is a good idea to discuss the issue with your patient and consider making a change in the treatment plan. Our

[1] Selection criteria: patients (a) were ages 18 or over, (b) received individual therapy, (c) completed a BDI at the intake session, (d) had a BDI score of 20 or greater at intake, (e) provided a BDI score at Week 4 (28 +/− 3 days post intake), and (f) provided at least one BDI score after Week 4.

findings are consistent with those of other studies showing that early change is a predictor of outcome (Lutz et al., 2009; Vittengl et al., 2019).

A clinical question we confronted that we found had received very little attention in the research literature was: What is the relationship between outcome and dropout in cognitive behavioral therapy? We predicted that dropout would be more likely when patients were not making progress in treatment. Zieve et al. (2019) studied the relationship between dropout and outcome in naturalistic CBT in a sample of 1,092 cases from the Archival Database and found, as predicted, that dropouts had higher symptom severity at the end of treatment than completers. However, contrary to prediction, they found that dropouts did not show a slower rate of change during treatment, indicating that the dropouts' higher symptom severity at the end of their treatment was a result of the patient staying in treatment for fewer sessions and thus receiving less benefit than the completers. The investigators also found that cases rated as dropouts, as compared with completers, were more likely to be coded by the therapist as having termination reasons related to poor outcome or process of treatment, including patient dissatisfaction with the treatment plan. These findings point to the importance of the therapist's monitoring of the patient's satisfaction with the treatment outcome and process to identify and address any dissatisfaction that might cause the patient to terminate treatment before they had gained the full benefit from the treatment.

Based on results of this study, our own clinical experience, and many other findings in the psychotherapy literature (e.g., Lambert & Shimokawa, 2011), we now collect feedback at every session from our patients to monitor their experience during treatment using a scale we and our colleagues developed, the Session Assignment and Feedback Scale (SAFF) (Persons et al., 2012). Jensen et al. (2020) carried out a qualitative and quantitative analysis of the content of the SAFF completed in 541 sessions of individual CBT by 41 patients. This study showed that homework compliance was higher when the therapist and patient agreed on a homework assignment that was congruent with the content of the take home message the patient reported was most helpful from the session. This study has a direct clinical implication: To maximize homework compliance, ask your patient what they found most useful and memorable about the session and use that information to guide the content of the homework assignment.

Finally, we used the Archival Database to study the mechanism of action of Beck's cognitive therapy in a study that has a title that states its result:

Changes in affective and cognitive distortion symptoms of depression are reciprocally related during cognitive behavior therapy (Persons et al., 2023). This study is particularly important because surprisingly little data supports Beck's proposal that cognitive change produces change in emotions (Lorenzo-Luaces et al., 2015), and of course it's vitally important both to theoreticians and to clinicians to know if Beck's proposal is true. Our study design capitalized on the fact that the Archival Database includes item-by-item scores on the BDI at each session for a large sample of patients. Coaüthor Craig Marker used bivariate latent difference score modeling to show that change in the cognitive distortion symptoms of depression preceded and predicted change in the affective symptoms of depression, as predicted by Beck's theory. The results of the study also support Beck's secondary prediction about the relationship between cognitive distortion and affective symptoms, namely, that change in the affective symptoms predicts changes in the cognitive distortion symptoms.

From Measurement-Based Care to Published Empirical Papers

Data alone do not contribute to the research literature. Here we briefly describe some of the steps we take to get from MBC data to published empirical papers. Persons (2018, 2023) provides additional detail.

A key step along the way from MBC data to published paper is the process of organizing the data into a database. Persons and Thomas made the first pass at the database structure for the Archival Database and created a coding manual. As we began working on larger-scale studies, we discovered errors and problems in the organization of the database. Fortunately, Garret Zieve, who first worked with Persons when he was a graduate student at UC Berkeley and later joined her practice and is a coauthor of this chapter, has excellent skills in database organization, and he carried out a substantial piece of work in 2021 to clean (again) and strengthen the organization of the Archival Database.

Knowledge about ethical principles in research and access to an institutional review board are also important elements of the research enterprise. Persons was fortunate to be invited to join a group of private practitioners who developed their own institutional review board (IRB), the Behavioral Health Research Collective (BHRC), described in Osborne and Luoma (2018). Although IRB review of research is not legally required unless it is federally funded or similar (Persons et al., 2021), it is always a good ethical practice to obtain some sort of review of your research.

Informed consent for research from patients who contribute data is another essential element of the research process. We have always included in our routine Treatment Agreement a paragraph asking our patients to provide consent for research; the paragraph is posted at https://oaklandcbt.com/resources-for-clinician-researchers and has been reviewed by the BHRC. In recent years we made research participation optional. Patients can also withdraw from research participation, and their data will be deleted from the database, although we let patients know that if the data have already been used in a study or publication, we may not be able to delete their data from the database used for those projects.

Research collaborators are an essential element of research for all investigators, and especially for those of us working in clinical settings. Persons has a clinical faculty title in the Department of Psychology that connects her to faculty and graduate student collaborators. Participation in national and international professional associations also provides a source of research collaborators and an invaluable source of collegial and scholarly support. The two groups most important to us are the Association for Behavioral and Cognitive Therapies (ABCT) and the Society for Psychotherapy Research.

Another key element of the research process is library access, which Persons receives via her UC Berkeley clinical faculty title. Patience and persistence are also essential elements to research success in a clinical setting. Many of the studies of the Archival Database we described earlier required many years of work. The database was completed in 2007, and yet we published the first study based on the complete database (Thomas & Persons, 2013) many years later. Freedom from the time pressure of the academic tenure clock gives the clinician-scientist the leisure to conduct research at a pace that works for them.

Intrinsic interest is essential to the enterprise. The work is only sustainable if it is intrinsically rewarding, as it requires many hours of uncompensated work. Other rewards include the opportunity to make a larger contribution, one that will live after us, than we can do with our clinical work, and the privilege and collegial rewards of being part of the international scientific community. Finally, to return to the place we started, the fact that the research is woven tightly into the clinical work via our use of MBC contributes to its intrinsic interest and means that many of the research tasks (e.g., identifying useful measures) are clinical tasks that we would be doing even if we were not conducting research.

Plans for the Future

We are planning several additional studies based on the Archival Database, including studies of deterioration, therapist effects, lack of progress, and session frequency. We also hope to carry out studies of clinical supervision. We are working on a longitudinal study of Persons's outcomes over the course of her career, examining the relationship of outcomes and caseload to years of experience, events in the therapist's life, and the therapist's use of decision support tools (Coe-Odess et al., 2020; Haft et al., 2023).

We are also working to build a second research database. Our new database includes the same types of data that we collected for the archival database described earlier, with a few changes, including the adoption of the DASS (Lovibond & Lovibond, 1995) as our primary symptom-monitoring measure. We have been hampered in building our new database because even though the tool we are now using, PsychSurveys, has many desirable features, it does not include an electronic medical record, and so we do not have a way to capture session dates without the clinician hand-entering this information, which has so far proved to be not feasible in our group practice.

As we create our new database, we are taking steps to increase the diversity of our sample, at least as represented in our database. Our sample is not very diverse, largely because we are setting relatively high fees (in part to support the research) and we do not accept insurance, with the result that our sample consists primarily of well educated and financially successful White people. That said, because we live in the San Francisco Bay area, our patients do represent considerable diversity in gender identity, sexual orientation, and marital status. However, our original demographic coding in the database did not reflect that diversity. To capture more of the diversity in our sample, we have updated our intake questionnaire to include more options for patients to report their gender, sexual orientation, and marital status. For example, the previous version of the intake questionnaire only had two options for gender, "male" and "female." In the updated version, we expanded the possibilities to "male," "female," "transgender," and "other." In the Archival Database, we did not code for sexual orientation at all; we now ask patients on their intake questionnaire to self-report their sexual orientation as heterosexual, homosexual, or other. We have also strengthened our coding of diversity by coding for neurodiversity, by including diagnoses of attention-deficit hyperactivity disorder and autism spectrum disorder. By updating our assessment scales, we might even be able to increase the diversity of our sample by helping diverse individuals feel more welcome to seek treatment in our practice. Collecting more information about our sample's diversity will also allow us to examine research questions about the effects of diversity on outcome, dropout, and the change process.

We plan to add measures of psychological mechanisms that maintain symptoms of psychopathology to our routine progress monitoring to increase our ability to study change processes in treatment. We already collect measures of perfectionism and intolerance of uncertainty, overestimation of threat and inflated responsibility, and overimportance of thoughts using the Obsessive Beliefs Questionnaire 44 (Obsessive Compulsive Cognitions Working Group, 2005) and aspects of emotion regulation difficulties using the Difficulties in Emotion Regulation Scale (Ritschel et al., 2015), but we would like to add more measures of transdiagnostic maintaining mechanisms, including anxiety sensitivity, repetitive negative thinking, self-criticism, and others.

We plan to increase our participation in and support of Open Science. We recently increased our dissemination efforts by posting our work on ResearchGate and PsyArXiv. We are considering sharing a deidentified version of our Archival Database.[2] We hope to move toward preregistering our analyses for future studies. We recently experimented for the first time with preregistering one of our studies, a study of symptom deterioration during treatment. However, after preregistering the study, we decided to change the definitions of the independent variables, and this meant we needed to abandon our preregistration for this study.

We plan to learn more about single-case experimental design (SCED) and make greater use of that methodology. SCED is an underappreciated methodology that is ideally suited for the integration of practice and research. It aligns with the practitioner's intensive focus on one individual (see the classic paper on this topic by Hayes, 1981), and a carefully designed SCED allows the test of causal hypotheses about change processes in therapy.

[2] We are not quite ready to post the database. However, we will be happy to entertain requests to use it from individual investigators, who can reach out to the first author at persons@oaklandcbt.com.

Conducting research in a clinical practice setting is often lonely and challenging. To provide an intellectual home and supportive community for clinician-researchers, the first author created and chairs the Research in Clinical Practice Special Interest Group at the Association for Behavioral and Cognitive Therapies. The first author and colleagues at her practice, including coauthor Zieve, participate in this group to facilitate research in clinical practice and generate practice-based evidence. Related to this, we will continue to work to promote the adoption of MBC (Barkham et al., 2023; Jensen-Doss et al., 2016; Persons, 2022), which is used by too few clinicians.

Conclusion

Data collected by clinicians in the course of their routine work can lead to published papers that contribute to the scientific study of psychotherapy. We described here a strategy for conducting practice-oriented research that has as its foundation the use of MBC, which calls for the clinician to collect symptom data at the beginning of every therapy session and use it to guide the clinical work. We described a large database of data we collected using MBC and several of the studies we have published based on the database. The research questions we tackled flowed out of our clinical interests and the results inform our clinical work.

References

Barkham, M., de Jong, K., Delgadillo, J., & Lutz, W. (2023). Routine Outcome Monitoring (ROM) and feedback: Research review and recommendations. *Psychotherapy Research*, *33*(7), 841–855. https://doi.org/10.1080/10503307.2023.2181114

Bauer, M. S., & Kirchner, J. (2020). Implementation science: What is it and why should I care? *Psychiatry Research*, *283*, Article 112376. https://doi.org/10.1016/j.psychres.2019.04.025

Beck, A. T., Rush, J. A., Shaw, B. F., & Emery, G. (1979). *Cognitive therapy for depression*. Guilford Press.

Burns, D. D., & Eidelson, R. J. (1998). Why are depression and anxiety correlated? A test of the tripartite model. *Journal of Consulting and Clinical Psychology*, *66*(3), 461. https://doi.org/10.1037//0022-006x.66.3.461

Castonguay, L. G., Barkham, M., Youn, S. J., & Page, A. C. (2021). Practice-based evidence—Findings from routine clinical settings. In *Bergin and Garfield's handbook of psychotherapy and behavior change* (50th anniversary edition, pp. 192–193). Wiley.

Coe-Odess, S., Thomas, C., & Persons, J. B. (2020, November 17–22). *A longitudinal analysis of the performance of one evidence-based psychotherapist* [Conference presentation]. Association for Behavioral and Cognitive Therapies 54th Annual Convention, Virtual.

de Jong, K., Conijn, J. M., Gallagher, R. A. V., Reshetnikova, A. S., Heij, M., & Lutz, M. C. (2021). Using progress feedback to improve outcomes and reduce drop-out, treatment duration, and deterioration: A multilevel meta-analysis. *Clinical Psychology Review*, Article 102002. https://doi.org/10.1016/j.cpr.2021.102002

Gates, V., Hsiao, M., Zieve, G. G., Courry, R., & Persons, J. B. (2021). Relationship to CBT outcome and dropout of decision support tools of the written case formulation, list of treatment goals, and plot of symptom scores. *Behaviour Research and Therapy, 142*, Article 103874. https://doi.org/10.1016/j.brat.2021.103874.

Goldberg, S. B., Babins-Wagner, R., Rousmaniere, T., Berzins, S., Hoyt, W. T., Whipple, J. L., Miller, S. D., & Wampold, B. E. (2016). Creating a climate for therapist improvement: A case study of an agency focused on outcomes and deliberate practice. *Psychotherapy, 53*(3), 367–375. https://doi.org/10.1037/pst0000060

Goldfried, M. R. (2010). Building a two-way bridge between practice and research. *The Clinical Psychologist, 63*(1), pp. 1–3.

Gruber, J. L., & Persons, J. B. (2010). Unquiet treatment: Handling treatment refusal in bipolar disorder. *Journal of Cognitive Psychotherapy, 24*, 16–25. https://doi.org/10.1891/0889-8391.24.1.16

Haft, S. L., Thomas, C., Harris, C., Li, L., & Persons, J. B. (2023, November 16–19). *A single therapist case study of associations between therapist experience and patient outcomes and use of decision support tools* [Poster presentation]. Association for Behavioral and Cognitive Therapies 58th Annual Convention, Seattle, WA, United States.

Hayes, S. C. (1981). Single case experimental design and empirical clinical practice. *Journal of Consulting and Clinical Psychology, 49*(2), 193–211. https://doi.org/10.1037/0022-006X.49.2.193

Hong, J. J. (2013). An idiographic evidence-based approach to addressing cultural factors in treatment: A case example. *The Behavior Therapist, 36*(6), 143–146.

Jensen, A. S., Fee, C., Miles, A. L., Beckner, V. L., Owen, D., & Persons, J. B. (2020). Congruence of patient takeaways and homework assignment content predicts homework compliance in psychotherapy. *Behavior Therapy, 51*(3), 424–433. https://doi.org/10.1016/j.beth.2019.07.005

Jensen-Doss, A., Haimes, E. M. B., Smith, A. M., Lyon, A. R., Lewis, C. C., Stanick, C. F., & Hawley, K. M. (2016). Monitoring treatment progress and providing feedback is viewed favorably but rarely used in practice. *Administration and Policy in Mental Health and Mental Health Services Research, 45*, 48–61. https://doi.org/10.1007/s10488-016-0763-0

Lambert, M. J., & Shimokawa, K. (2011). Collecting client feedback. *Psychotherapy, 48*(1), 72–79. https://doi.org/10.1037/a0022238

Lewis, C. C., Boyd, M., Puspitasari, A., Navarro, E., Howard, J., Kassab, H., Hoffman, M., Scott, K., Lyon, A., & Douglas, S. (2018). Implementing measurement-based care in behavioral health: A review. *JAMA Psychiatry, 76*(3), 324–335. https://doi.org/10.1001/jamapsychiatry.2018.3329

Logan, D. E., & Marlatt, G. A. (2010). Harm reduction therapy: A practice-friendly review of research. *Journal of Clinical Psychology, 66*(2), 201–214. https://doi.org/10.1002/jclp.20669

Lorenzo-Luaces, L., German, R. E., & DeRubeis, R. J. (2015). It's complicated: The relation between cognitive change procedures, cognitive change, and symptom change in cognitive therapy for depression. *Clinical Psychology Review, 41*, 3–15. https://doi.org/10.1016/j.cpr.2014.12.003

Lovibond, S. H., & Lovibond, P. F. (1995). *Manual for the Depression Anxiety Stress Scales* (2nd ed.). Psychology Foundation.

Lutz, W., Stulz, N., & Köck, K. (2009). Patterns of early change and their relationship to outcome and follow-up among patients with major depressive disorders. *Journal of Affective Disorders, 118*(1–3), 60–68. https://doi.org/10.1016/j.jad.2009.01.019

Moore, S. A., Welch, S. S., Michonski, J., Poquiz, J., Osborne, T. L., Sayrs, J., & Spanos, A. (2015). Psychometric evaluation of the Overall Anxiety Severity and Impairment Scale (OASIS) in

individuals seeking outpatient specialty treatment for anxiety-related disorders. *Journal of Affective Disorders*, *175*, 463–470. https://doi.org/10.1016/j.jad.2015.01.041
Norman, S. B., Hami Cissell, S., Means-Christensen, A. J., & Stein, M. B. (2006). Development and validation of an overall anxiety severity and impairment scale (OASIS). *Depression and Anxiety*, *23*(4), 245–249. https://doi.org/10.1002/da.20182
Obsessive Compulsive Cognitions Working Group. (2005). Psychometric validation of the obsessive belief questionnaire and interpretation of intrusions inventory—Part 2: Factor analyses and testing of a brief version. *Behaviour Research and Therapy*, *43*(11), 1527–1542. https://doi.org/10.1016/j.brat.2004.07.010
Osborne, T. L., & Luoma, J. B. (2018). Overcoming a primary barrier to practice-based research: Access to an institutional review board (IRB) for independent ethics review. *Psychotherapy*, *55*(3), 255. http://doi.org/10.1037/pst0000166
Persons, J. B. (1986). Generalization of the effects of exposure treatments for phobias: A single case study. *Psychotherapy*, *23*(1), 160–166. http://doi.org/10.1037/h0085583
Persons, J. B. (1989). *Cognitive therapy in practice: A case formulation approach*. W. W. Norton.
Persons, J. B. (1991). Psychotherapy outcome studies do not accurately represent current models of psychotherapy: A proposed remedy. *American Psychologist*, *46*(2), 99–106. https://doi.org/10.1037/0003-066X.46.2.99
Persons, J. B. (2008). *The case formulation approach to cognitive-behavior therapy*. Guilford Press.
Persons, J. B. (2018). Simultaneous practice and research: A model for conducting research in private practice. In R. Trent Codd III (Ed.), *Practice-based research: A guide for clinicians* (pp. 153–169). Taylor & Francis/Routledge. http://dx.doi.org/10.4324/9781315524610-9
Persons, J. B. (2022, October 28). *Measurement-based care* [Webinar]. Association for Behavioral and Cognitive Therapies. https://elearning.abct.org/products/jacqueline-persons-recorded-webinar-measurement-based-care-october-28-2022
Persons, J. B. (2023). How to conduct research in your private practice. *Cognitive and Behavioral Practice*, *30*(2), 195–207. https://doi.org/10.1016/j.cbpra.2021.11.004
Persons, J. B., & Baron, J. (1985). Processes underlying formal thought disorder in psychiatric inpatients. *Journal of Nervous and Mental Disorders*, *173*, 667–676.
Persons, J. B., Burns, D. D., & Perloff, J. M. (1988). Predictors of dropout and outcome in cognitive therapy for depression in a private practice setting. *Cognitive Therapy and Research*, *12*, 557–575.
Persons, J. B., Beckner, V. L., & Tompkins, M. A. (2013). Testing case formulation hypotheses in psychotherapy: Two case examples. *Cognitive and Behavioral Practice*, *20*, 399–409.
Persons, J. B., Bostrom, A., & Bertagnolli, A. (1999). Results of randomized controlled trials of cognitive therapy for depression generalize to private practice. *Cognitive Therapy and Research*, *23*, 535–548. https://doi.org/10.1023/A:1018724505659
Persons, J. B., & Burns, D. D. (1985). Mechanisms of action of cognitive therapy: The relative contributions of technical and interpersonal interventions. *Cognitive Therapy and Research*, *9*, 539–551. https://doi.org/10.1007/BF01173007
Persons, J. B., & Foa, E. B. (1984). Processing of fearful and neutral information by obsessive-compulsives. *Behaviour Research and Therapy*, *22*, 259–265.
Persons, J. B., Hong, J., Beckner, V. L., Owen, D. J., & Eidelman, P. (2012, November 15–18). *Monitoring therapy process at every session: Development of a new tool and clinical examples of its utility* [Conference presentation]. Association for Behavioral and Cognitive Therapies 46th Annual Convention, National Harbor, MD, United States.
Persons, J. B., Marker, C. D., & Bailey, E. N. (2023). Change in affective and cognitive distortion symptoms of depression is reciprocal during cognitive behavior therapy. *Behaviour Research and Therapy*, *166*, Article 104338. https://doi.org/10.1016/j.brat.2023.104338
Persons, J. B., & Mikami, A. Y. (2002). Strategies for handling treatment failure successfully. *Psychotherapy: Theory/Research/Practice/Training*, *39*, 139–151. http://doi.org/10.1037/0033-3204.39.2.139

Persons, J. B., Osborne, T. L., & Codd, III, R. T. (2021). Ethical and legal guidance for mental health practitioners who wish to conduct research in a private practice setting. *Behavior Therapy, 51*(3), 313–323. https://doi.org/10.1016/j.beth.2020.04.012

Persons, J. B., & Rao, P. A. (1985). Longitudinal study of cognitions, life events, and depression in psychiatric patients. *Journal of Abnormal Psychology, 94*, 51–63. https://doi.org/10.1037//0021-843x.94.1.51

Persons, J. B., Roberts, N. A., & Zalecki, C. A. (2003). Anxiety and depression change together during treatment. *Behavior Therapy, 34*, 149–163. https://doi.org/10.1016/S0005-7894(03)80010-2

Persons, J. B., Roberts, N. A., Zalecki, C. A., & Brechwald, W. A. G. (2006). Naturalistic outcome of case formulation-driven cognitive-behavior therapy for anxious depressed outpatients. *Behaviour Research and Therapy, 44*, 1041–1051. https://doi.org/10.1016/j.brat.2005.08.005

Persons, J. B., & Thomas, C. (2019). Symptom severity at week four of cognitive behavior therapy predicts depression remission. *Behavior Therapy, 50*, 791–802. https://doi.org/10.1016/j.beth.2018.12.002

Persons, J. B., Thomas, C., Hsiao, M., & Courry, R. (2023). How to build a research database from data you collect to guide your clinical work. *Cognitive and Behavioral Practice, 30*(1), 35–44. http://doi.org/10.1016/j.cbpra.2021.10.002

Ritschel, L. A., Tone, E. B., Schoemann, A. M., & Lim, N. E. (2015). Psychometric properties of the Difficulties in Emotion Regulation Scale across demographic groups. *Psychological Assessment, 27*(3), 944–954. https://doi.org/10.1037/pas0000099

Song, J., Freedman, G., Li, L., & Persons, J. B. (2024). Interpersonal sensitivity predicts slower change and less change in anxiety symptoms in Cognitive Behavioural Therapy. *The British Journal of Clinical Psychology, 63*(3), 416–430. https://doi-org.libproxy.berkeley.edu/10.1111/bjc.12470

Stirman, S. W., Miller, C. J., Toder, K., & Calloway, A. (2013). Development of a framework and coding system for modifications and adaptations of evidence-based interventions. *Implementation Science, 8*(1), Article 65. https://doi.org/10.1186/1748-5908-8-65

Thomas, C., & Persons, J. B. (2013). Sudden gains can occur in psychotherapy even when the pattern of change is gradual. *Clinical Psychology: Science and Practice, 20*, 127–142. http://dx.doi.org/10.1111/cpsp.12029

Turkat, I. D. (Ed.). (1985). *Behavioral case formulation*. Plenum Press.

Vittengl, J. R., Clark, L. A., Thase, M. E., & Jarrett, R. B. (2019). Partner criticism during acute-phase cognitive therapy for recurrent major depressive disorder. *Behaviour Research and Therapy, 113*, 48–56. https://doi.org/10.1016/j.brat.2018.12.010

Weisz, J. R., Krumholz, L. S., Santucci, L., Thomassin, K., & Ng, M. Y. (2015). Shrinking the gap between research and practice: Tailoring and testing youth psychotherapies in clinical care contexts. *Annual Review of Clinical Psychology, 11*(1), 139–163. https://doi.org/10.1146/annurev-clinpsy-032814-112820

Weisz, J. R., Ng, M. Y., & Bearman, S. K. (2014). Odd couple? Re-envisioning the relation between science and practice in the dissemination-implementation era. *Clinical Psychological Science, 2*(1), 58–74. https://doi.org/10.1177/2167702613501307

Zieve, G. G., Persons, J. B., & Yu, L. A. D. (2019). Relationship between dropout and outcome of naturalistic cognitive behavior therapy. *Behavior Therapy, 50*, 189–199. http://dx.doi.org/10.1016/j.beth.2018.05.004

14

A Clinician-Researcher's Journey Through Routine Outcome Monitoring and Practice-Based Research

Robbie Babins-Wagner

Introduction

I am a practicing clinician, researcher, educator, and chief executive officer of Calgary Counselling Centre (CCC). This agency is a large community-based nonprofit/charity in Calgary, Canada, focused on routine outcome monitoring (ROM) with an internal research center dedicated to the collection of practice-based evidence. ROM incorporates three fundamental characteristics (1) a counselor collects client data on a routine basis; (2) the data collected is fed back to the counselor and to the client; and (3) where there is a lack of improvement in client well-being, the process and/or focus of counseling is adapted in response to the data collected from the client (feedback). In other words, ROM enables CCC staff and students to respond to clients' needs and objectives if and where required. In this context, ROM should be viewed as practice-based evidence, as it refers to data that is routinely collected in "real-world" or naturalistic counseling settings rather than in a controlled context like a clinical trial.

When I joined CCC in 1992, it served between 600 and 750 clients per year. Today, it serves an average of 10,000 new clients each year, trains 120 practicum and postgraduate students each year, and has integrated practice-based evidence and ROM into every aspect of its business. The center is well known as a center of excellence in counseling and has developed the first research Center for practice-based evidence in Canada. With over 40 years of experience as a practicing clinician,

Robbie Babins-Wagner, *A Clinician-Researcher's Journey Through Routine Outcome Monitoring and Practice-Based Research*. In: *Practice-Based Evidence in the Psychological Therapies*. Edited by: Louis G. Castonguay et al., Oxford University Press. © Oxford University Press (2026). DOI: 10.1093/9780197748336.003.0014 clinical supervisor, and educator, this chapter details how I became interested in ROM as well as my motivation to use and then scale it across all programs at our Calgary office and more recently across our provincial programs.

Background Experience and Training

At the beginning of my career, I had no specific plan in mind and had not even planned to become a social worker. It was all a happy accident. While pursuing my Bachelor of Arts in Psychology at McGill University in Montreal, I happened to stumble into a lecture about social work practice with seniors, and I was intrigued about what I was hearing about the individual in context, as it provided a different lens to life's challenges. From that day, I was drawn to social work after being inspired by the profession's focus on clinical practice and a philosophy of understanding people's problems, including mental health problems in their personal context or environment, including family, community, health status, employment, lived experience, and more. After completing my Bachelor of Arts in Psychology, I applied to and completed the post-degree Bachelor of Social Work and subsequently completed a Master of Social Work (MSW) from Carleton University in Ottawa. I started my MSW in the clinical program and moved to the policy program, as the clinical program did not meet my needs. My education in the social policy arm of the program initiated my interest in social policy that influences my work to this day.

Over the course of my career, I have worked in child protection, family services, health systems, and a community-based nonprofit organization. When I first moved to Calgary, I was employed as a social worker in the mental health department of a community hospital where I was introduced to outpatient and inpatient mental health and further developed my clinical skills working with clients referred to our programs. In mid-1982, I began teaching social work at the University of Calgary. I joined the CCC 10 years later as director of counselling in June 1992 and was given the opportunity to professionalize services. The center, then called the Pastoral Institute, had provided services to residents of Calgary and surrounding communities for 30 years. I joined a team of five clinicians, each of whom had already been with the organization for several years. I was assigned the responsibility of improving the quality of the institute's clinical work and to determine ways to improve programs and services. This was a challenging task, as I was "the new kid on the block" and there was internal resistance to change. Resistance to change is a theme that I have encountered throughout my career. In June 1996, I was appointed executive director, following a 2-year evaluation of the institute's Family Violence Program. Though I didn't know it at the time, this marked the beginning of a 25-year journey to embrace and integrate ROM and practice-based evidence into every aspect of the organization's activities.

The Journey to Routine Outcome Monitoring: Evaluation of the Men's Domestic Violence Program

My interest in clinical research began in 1994 at CCC, when I engaged an external evaluator to conduct both a formative and summative evaluation of the men's family violence program at the center. At the time, the program was designed to operate in a two-step process. New referrals began with an assessment that sought to understand the degree of abuse that had been perpetrated against their intimate partner. Following the assessment, clients proceeded to begin the group program where they would receive counseling to address the abusive behavior. The primary objective of the evaluation was to understand why 70% of clients were dropping out after the assessment. This was a problem for CCC, but also for the community, as these men were at risk of being abusive to their partner again. The evaluation took 2 years and included the addition of standardized surveys on the first and last sessions of the group program to assess the short-term impact of the intervention. We learned immediately that participants were making progress in the program and that the primary barrier to success was the difficulty retaining clients after the assessment.

The conclusion came to us in an unexpected way. One of the clinicians consulted with me during an assessment session with a new client. She reported that the man she was meeting with had disclosed that he had been sexually abused as a child. The clinician wanted to know whether or not she should complete the assessment or if she should work with his disclosure. When I asked how she wanted to proceed, she elected to work with the disclosure—which I supported. Over time it became clear to everyone that the assessment process prevented a counselor from building a relationship with a new client. We responded by changing the focus of the assessment to a new framework that allowed the counselor to build a relationship with the client. We believed (and later confirmed in research) that this early relationship was a fundamental component to achieving a positive outcome in counseling.

The decision to change the assessment process based on the results of the evaluation was not well received. Internally, there were concerns that we were making changes to a program that had existed since 1982. Counselors were reluctant to eliminate the assessment and fought the changes every step of the way. This included deliberate attempts by counselors employed by CCC to undermine the findings of the evaluation both within the CCC and with colleagues in the community. The general theme of their message was that "we didn't need to fix something that was already in place and was working," But it wasn't. Despite the pressure being put on me and the center, we were clear that the results of the evaluation were sufficiently robust and provided direction as to what changes we needed to make. It did not take long for participation and completion in the family violence group program to increase from 30% of referrals to 80%—a number which has remained unchanged to this day. While this part of the story does not involve ROM, it was the first time the CCC modified the design of a program based on learning from research. It would not be the last.

The Heroic Client

The results of the family violence evaluation and the subsequent changes to the family violence program were stronger than we had originally thought. A second finding from our evaluation was that the changes led to results that surpassed those that we had found in the published peer-reviewed literature at that time. It was clear that another key determinant of a program's success was our ability to measure and manage it. Between 1996 and 2000, we made the decision to expand the use of pre- and post-measures to CCC's other programs. The purpose of this data collection was simple. We wanted to use it to ensure that stated program goals were being achieved through a process of continuous evaluation and quality improvement.

It was around June 2000 that the organization's name was changed to Calgary Counselling Centre. With the changes to the results and impact of the group programs, we conducted a year-long multicultural organizational change assessment of the center to ensure that they were meeting the needs of a more ethnically and culturally diverse community. The successes and the future-oriented work that I was doing resulted in changes to my title and role and I became chief executive officer.

In mid-2000, one of the staff recommended that I read a newly published book, *The Heroic Client* (Duncan & Miller, 2000)—which challenged several conventional counseling practices of that time. The authors argued that the emphasis on diagnosis, formulaic interventions, and a focus on solutions were of limited benefit to clients. Their suggestion was that clinicians consider working with clients differently to explore the client's own internal capacity for healing and growth, their strengths, experiences, and ideas of how best to improve their lives. They also proposed that counseling become more of a collaborative endeavor.

The Heroic Client clearly outlined several universal challenges experienced by therapists. The authors proposed that clinicians become outcome informed, which required the implementation of a systematic method for evaluating the outcome of individual cases and/or programs using a relatively new outcome measure, the Outcome Questionnaire–45 (OQ-45) (Lambert et al., 2003). The key strategies were directly aligned with the ones we implemented in response to the findings of the evaluation of the center's family violence group program. The strategies included the use of two measures, the OQ-45 prior to the start of a counseling session to track whether a client is making changes from session to session, and the Session Rating Scale (SRS v2.1; Johnson, 2000), an alliance measure, toward the end of a counseling session to obtain client feedback if they perceived that the counselling was on track or not. The use of both measures had the potential to assist counselors in improving the client's response to counseling.

What we were doing at the center was moving from pre-post evaluation of group programs to session-by-session understanding of whether or not clients were benefiting from the service, and if not, exploring what was or was not working for the client. The question I had was whether the center and its staff were ready to implement this type of strategy in every other service offered to clients. I reached out randomly to one of the authors to see if training was available for agencies. One year later, we held our first daylong training session with one of the book's authors, focused on ROM with CCC staff.

The Conference That Changed Everything

In June 2002, I travelled to Toronto, Canada, to attend the Heart and Soul of Change Conference. This conference was organized around the ideas presented in the recently published book titled *The Heart and Soul of Change—What Works in Therapy* (Hubble et al., 1999). I was thrilled by the prospect of learning from the authors, who were all in attendance. I read the book and wanted to learn more about research in counseling practice and what we could do at the CCC to improve our practice. The presentations were practical and relevant for the clinicians in attendance. Many relevant topics were covered over the 2-day conference. I fondly remember those that focused on outcomes, the common factors in therapy, hope in therapy, the therapeutic relationship, client self-healing, models and technique, the ways clients change, and placebo effects. The complementary nature of each session provided me with a sense that I needed to go back and learn more about the individual topic areas and about their interrelationships. I was excited about the possibilities of using some of these ideas at the center, but first I had to brief my team and engage them in learning more about some of these new ideas. Specifically, I wanted to focus our learning on the science and practice of building and enhancing the therapeutic relationship between client and counselor and explore the implementation of an outcome measure at the CCC.

On the flight back to Calgary, I decided that the center should conduct a pilot project focused on outcomes. Pilot projects are one way to test ideas before a final decision is made about a project or program. A pilot project could help us prevent some of the challenges we experienced during and after the family violence evaluation. It could help us understand the warning signs we might encounter as we went through the introduction of using outcomes in the pilot project. On my return, I discussed the ideas shared at the conference with my academic research partners, who enthusiastically suggested that I pursue a PhD concurrent with the implementation of outcomes at the center. I was interested in focusing on understanding the theory and practice strategies in areas such as the common factors in therapy, the role of hope and expectancy in the early stage of counseling, and placebo effects. Many of these ideas became topics in our counseling team meetings with a goal of broadening our thinking about people and change.

However, in order to enter a PhD program, I needed a further qualification. And so, more than 25 years after completing my MSW, I completed a Certificate in Social Work Research at the University of Calgary, which provided direct entry into the PhD Program. My doctoral work was focused on understanding the research on outcome monitoring, practice-based evidence, and learning the skills to conduct a naturalistic study. In the fall of 2011, I completed the PhD (Babins-Wagner, 2011).

The Pilot Project

During the planning of the pilot project, I was confident that reorienting the counseling service around outcomes had the potential to be transformational. It was also directly aligned with the center's goal to provide the best possible counseling to the community. However, I knew a gentler hand was needed to implement this type of change within the organization. The resistance and pushback following the earlier changes to the family violence program showed me how counselors might be resistant to change. This time, I wanted to engage with them in a more constructive manner—so that they could feel like they were partners and felt a sense of ownership around the work.

The pilot project had its roots in the training we held at the center, *The Heroic Client*, *The Heart and Soul of Change*, and our own experience at the CCC. Counselors seemed enthusiastic and curious about the project, but none of us understood the impact of using new measures with our clients. In developing the project, I thought it might be useful to compare two outcome measures so that we had a broader view of the utility in counseling. This allowed counselors to not only engage in outcome monitoring but also determine if they had any preferences for either tool. The plan was to track the scores in a spreadsheet. The pilot project ran between September 2002 and June 2004. In the first year, counselors used the OQ-45 (Lambert et al., 2003), and in the second year they used the Outcome Rating Scale (ORS), a briefer measure (Duncan et al., 2003). The outcome measures were provided to clients, in the waiting room, prior to the beginning of the counseling session. We also used the SRS v2.1 to assess the alliance about 10 minutes before the counseling session ended. With 2 years of data in hand and feedback from counselors, they recommended the use of the OQ-45 and SRS. The counselors perceived that the questions on the OQ-45 reflected their experiences with their clients. I supported the decision to move forward with the OQ-45 as our primary outcome measure, as it had the support of the counselors and met the need for our client base.

Following the recommendation that we move forward with the OQ-45, we acquired a license for the measure, provided training for use of the measure to the counselors, and set a start date of September 2004 for implementation to begin. We were completely transparent about the next steps with the counselors, and we did not overtly experience any resistance. We spent time in training sessions exploring challenges and barriers to a successful implementation and more. As we proceeded with a more widespread implementation of ROM, I was not anticipating as much resistance as we actually ended up receiving.

Implementation of Routine Outcome Monitoring (2004–2008)

The center's implementation of outcome measures was designed for clinical use and client benefit. This change required that counselors use the measures on a session-by-session basis. At that time, there were no external requirements to undertake this endeavor, nor were there any requirements from external funders. From the outset, we made a commitment to the counselors that client outcomes, based on the use of the measures, would not be used for performance management.

Initial implementation occurred between September 2004 and September 2008. Clinicians were required to offer the OQ-45 to their clients at the beginning of each counseling session and SRS in the last 10 minutes of each session. This included the completion of a graph of the OQ-45 scores, which would be presented to the client at the start of each session to give them feedback on their progress to date. While clients could decline the use of the outcome measure, few did, as they seemed interested in the information and how they could use it to further their progress. To ensure consistency, counselors were reminded of these requirements at every counseling team meeting. A few raised some challenges, which we worked through, but no one directly raised questions about the use of the measures on a session-by-session basis. We had heard about some grumbling and rumors about the use of the OQ-45, and when we asked the counselors directly about the questions, rumors, and complaints, we thought the issues were put to rest. The plan was to do an initial analysis of the data in the summer of 2008. At that point in time, we had been using the measure for 4 years and thought we would have sufficient data to understand progress, or lack thereof, at the center.

This analysis was pivotal to the future direction of the CCC. It became clear that there was compliance from more than 50% of counselors. We learned the clients liked using the measures and appreciated the feedback from the graphs. For those clients who did complete the measures, we learned that the results were promising and supported our moving forward with our plan for the integration of the measures into client care. We also discovered that that we only had data for 40% of all clients—meaning more than half had no data at all! On further investigation, we learned that some counselors were not offering the questionnaires to their clients in a consistent manner, if at all. There was no single factor that contributed to this situation. Some counselors saw the outcome measure as interfering with their counseling practice. Others were indifferent to knowing whether their clients were making progress. Another group simply did not want to use the measures. This lack of engagement was a risk to our strategy of using outcomes to support the community we served. The poor compliance prevented every client from receiving benefit from counseling.

While outcome monitoring was a requirement of all counselors working or training at the center, the message was not getting through. The next step was clear—we had to enforce the policy that outcome and SRS data were to be collected from *all* clients at *every* counseling session. This message was delivered at the September 2008 counseling team meeting. Three months later, more than 40% of clinicians had resigned. While these resignations were upsetting, they did not shake my confidence. The group of counselors who resigned were the ones who were not completing the measures.

I recall one specific afternoon when the director of counselling came to talk through everything we were dealing with. She was eager to discuss why I was so confident that mandating session-by-session monitoring was the right thing to do. First, I wanted to alleviate her concerns regarding the recent resignations. While it was certainly upsetting, I saw it as an opportunity to cement our organizational culture around ROM, practice-based evidence, and continuous quality improvement. I shared that this was an opportunity we could leverage to recruit new counselors who were more aligned with our objectives. Second, I saw many similarities to the changes made in response to the family violence program evaluation 8 years earlier. From the data we had analyzed, it was clear to me that this initiative was in everyone's best interests. We discussed how we both were committed to the plan and how it provided us with a tangible means to support the community more effectively.

Concurrent to the policy change, we knew we had to actively support the counselors' use of outcome measures. We began to provide monthly clinical consultations, with the support of an external consultant, Dr. Scott Miller, to discuss non-improving cases and help integrate the use of the measures. Counselors were required to provide an anonymized client graph for case discussion. The goal for this intervention was to demonstrate the use of the graphs in clinical practice and to build a culture of openness and sharing through which counselors could ask for and receive feedback. The expectation was that counselors would present a non-progressing case that provided an opportunity to prevent treatment failure. However, counselors only brought cases that were progressing, and it became apparent quite quickly that they were uncomfortable discussing and sharing client graphs for cases that were not progressing. After a year of presenting primarily graphs that were progressing well, we asked the counselors to bring graphs that were not going well. To ease this process, we identified themes for the consultation session when graphs were presented. Themes included presenting problems such as depression or anxiety, or consultations could be focused on the type of counseling, such as couples, individuals, or working with men or women. We were trying to demonstrate the universality of problems and contexts. In these new consultations, we also asked counselors to provide a follow-up on cases we had seen at the previous consultations. The follow-ups provided a way for counselors to share the progress they had made with a case that had previously been stuck. As supervisors, we deliberately didn't comment about the progress and let the counselors provide that feedback to their peers. This change provided strong support to the counselors individually and collectively. Over time, as the center built its culture of feedback within the team, case consultations became more focused on exploring strategies to change the client's trajectory of change. As counselors took risks and implemented suggestions from consultations, client scores began to improve. This process was very slow and deliberate and continues to this day. It's important to note that the culture of sharing and trust building has developed over time to the point where current consultations run smoothly, difficult cases are brought to consultations, and feedback provided to counselors is integrated into client care.

Progress in the Years 2008–2023

In 2008, with the requirement for the use of the measures in counseling, we saw increased compliance in data collection, and the data itself was more stable with fewer errors. Table 14.1 highlights the stages of our outcome journey.

Between 2008 and the beginning of the COVID pandemic in early March 2020, the counseling program grew in line with the growth of the population in Calgary, and our outcomes improved year-on-year in small and deliberate steps. The counseling team built their confidence in using the measures, developed strategies to train new counselors and practicum students, and counselors' use of the clinical consultations improved and became more strategic and effective. As counseling leaders, we also became more confident in the center's outcomes and began using this data to position the center in the community and in the media and other presentations. We also started using outcome data for decision-making in both specialized programs such as family violence and depression, and for the general counseling services.

Table 14.1 Key Stages of Session-by-Session Monitoring and Beyond Across 15 Years

Phase 1 2004–2008	Initial implementation	Staff trained to use the measures. Initial guidelines put in place to use measures on a session-by-session basis. Data collection begins.
Phase 2 2008–2011	Implementation with specific guidelines	Structures and polices added to implementation to support 100% use of measures. External ROM-based clinical consultations begin.
Phase 3 2011–2015	Becoming more deliberate	Clinical consultations are used to focus on deteriorating cases.
Phase 4 2015–2021	Growth of CCC requires changes to new staff and student orientation	Systematic protocols used for orientation and training new counselors, practicum students, and those licensing in the use of measures.
Phase 5 2022–present	Focusing on supervision	Focusing on the standardized and consistent framework for supervision to support the use of measures and improving outcomes (in process).

Note: CCC = Calgary Counselling Centre.

At the start of the COVID pandemic, the center transitioned its counseling services online within 36 hours and used Microsoft Teams to provide counseling services. We continued to collect outcome data via fax, via electronic means, and orally so that we could continue to track client outcomes but also to help understand the impact of the pandemic on our clients and the community. One of our successes during this time was that we provided over 100,000 counseling sessions online during lockdown.

In 2020, in response to our success during the pandemic, the center was invited by the Provincial Ministry of Mental Health and Addictions to expand our services provincially. We were asked, and received significant funding, to provide online/virtual counseling to residents of Alberta. Our outcome measures were key to this invitation, as we could track who was benefiting and who wasn't, and we would develop strategies to respond to non-progressing clients. Many of these individuals lived in smaller urban areas, rural areas, farm communities, and more remote areas of the province. That funding continues to this day. The training that we offer has also expanded whereby we have received a number of contracts to help others implement outcomes in their own local settings and had a contract to national services with offices in every province in Canada. It is not an understatement to say that the impact of all this work has been transformational in the way we do our work and, most importantly, to the community we serve.

The Impact of Using Routine Outcome Measures to Monitor Clients' Progress at CCC

The collection of ROM provided a way to determine if clients were benefiting from care and to intervene on a session-by-session basis when clients' outcome scores either did not improve or they deteriorated. The practice of ROM also gave counselors a standard method of talking about progress or lack thereof and strategies for responding to non-progressing cases. Over time, this became fundamental in developing strategies for training counselors and students. Year-on-year, we have seen small changes in our outcomes for each counselor, for each program, and for the center as a whole.

The use of practice-based evidence provided a common language for our team and methodology of conducting research at the center. We primarily conduct practice-based studies and use the findings to improve individual counselor results, program results, or center level results. We produce reports every trimester that allows us to track progress, and, where required, we explore differences in outcomes between trimesters. Anyone within the center can submit a request to our research team, and the responses are provided to the person requesting the information as well as others who may have an interest in the topic area. As of this date, we have 24 research questions in the queue, and they include topics such as: Do low-income clients benefit from counseling? How can we retain clients with high OQ-45 scores who only attend one session? What can we learn from our follow-up data? What is the impact of high inflation on the mental health of clients across income levels? and more. Many of these research questions result in partnerships with other researchers, as well as manuscripts prepared for publication. We can often simply ask the data questions that will be of interest to the leadership team, a group of counselors, and/or researchers.

Both ROM and practice-based evidence have impacted my academic work. I continue to have an appointment as an adjunct professor and sessional instructor where I teach advanced social policy, clinical research, and advanced practice skills. I also teach Innovation and Establishing Credibility in the Social Work Leadership Program. I typically teach the courses that I avoided in my bachelor's and master's programs, such as research and policy. At that time, I didn't see how they were relevant to clinical practice. Based on my own experience as a practicing clinician, I want to ensure that social workers understand the importance of research, data, and outcomes to their practice. I also want to ensure clinicians in all disciplines understand the ways in which social policy impacts our practice as well as ways we can influence policy development.

Practice-Based Evidence

When I was carrying out my PhD and trying to define the type of research I was interested in, I came upon ideas that aligned with my interest in outcomes. Practice-based evidence, a paradigm to explore counseling outcome, was defined by Barkham and Margison (2007) as the conscientious, explicit, and judicious use of current evidence drawn from practice settings in making decisions about the care of individual clients. Practice-based means integrating both individual clinical expertise and service-level parameters with the best available evidence drawn from rigorous research activity carried out in routine clinical settings. The emphasis is on acquiring evidence via rigorous research carried out in routine clinical practice. Barkham and Margison (2007) suggest that the concept of practice-based evidence is crucial in three ways. First, the focus of the research originates with the counselor; second, the paradigm is complementary to evidence-based practice; and lastly, it provides the opportunity for generating research questions that are grounded in practice and are relevant to counselors in the routine delivery of counseling services. These questions may be pragmatic or theory driven but have in common a fundamental relevance to practice. This approach contrasts with questions arising from academia that contribute to an advanced understanding but may not directly inform practitioners on the delivery and implementation of clinical interventions.

Practice-based evidence provided a clear, strategic way for me and the small research team at the center to frame our research and determine our focus and objectives. It gave us "permission" to focus on real-world research instead of more traditional academic research. The center was able to keep research projects and funding focused on maintaining the client and their benefit at the front of every research project. The focus on practice-based evidence also aligned with my clinical interest and attention, which was to utilize client and program-based data, data that was relevant to counselors, program managers, and leaders to understand real-time outcome data as a means to improving practice and the quality of client data. Over the last 20 years, the center has been engaged in or conducted its own studies with the paradigm and principles of practice-based evidence in mind. My experience with this way of working developed naturally through my interest in client and program outcomes. Once I started my doctoral studies I learned about the science, practice, and art of practice-based evidence and thought it was a strong fit for moving forward in my work.

The First Phase of Outcome Data Analysis

Our strategy was to use the framework provided by the OQ manual for reporting outcomes (Lambert et al., 2003). Cases closed during the calendar year were eligible for inclusion. In 2008, there were 1,255 closed cases, 43.5% of which improved or recovered, 48% were stable, and 8.5% had deteriorated. Four years later (2012; n = 1,277), 49% of cases had improved or recovered, 43.5% were stable, and 7.5% had deteriorated. In the most recent year with data (2023; n = 3,568), 50.7% of cases had improved or recovered, 44.6% were stable, and 4.6% of cases had deteriorated. I am proud that our outcomes have continued to improve even as the number of closed cases has almost tripled since 2008. These results suggest that the rate of client successes is growing while the deterioration rate is decreasing. We attribute these improvements to our strategy to use ROM to support our work with the communities we serve.

The Calgary Centre for Counselling Research

Based on the efforts described earlier, we have now assembled one of the world's largest outcomes databases in a community-based setting. A description follows of the ways by which my colleagues and I have attempted to leverage such data to promote meaningful contributions to the literature supporting practice-based evidence.

As stated previously, my early research experience was in family violence, which in turn introduced me to the paradigm of practice-based evidence. I was mentored by two academic colleagues who brought decades of traditional academic research experience to this endeavor, and I brought my experience with outcome research. We used data being routinely collected at the center in the family violence program. This partnership spanned over 15 years and produced a series of publications (e.g., Tutty & Babins-Wagner, 2016, Tutty, Rothery & Babins-Wagner, 2017, 2019).

A second phase began after I defended my doctoral dissertation in the fall of 2011, as the research focus expanded to include our work on improving care for the CCC clients and seeking solutions to "real-world" clinical problems. In late 2012, the CCC announced the establishment of the Calgary Centre for Counselling Research (CCCR), which was assigned the dual role of analyzing our data for the purpose of continuous improvement and using those analyses as a starting point for more comprehensive research to explore in collaboration with our academic colleagues. In addition to the family violence studies referenced earlier, the CCCR has been involved in 14 studies, 7 of which have been published in peer reviewed publications to date. Much of the research has been conducted by and with external research partners whose interests align with those of the CCCR. Many longstanding research collaborations have been built in the spirit of inquiry with the center's goal of trying to solve real-world clinical problems.

The first such project began in 2011 after discussions with a colleague at an outcome conference. The colleague was interested in understanding whether client treatment outcomes (as measured by the OQ-45.2) differed depending on who was providing the supervision. This study used a 5-year archival data set of psychotherapy outcome from the CCC. In total, 6,521 clients were seen by 175 trainee therapists who were supervised by 23 supervisors. The study explored whether client treatment outcomes (as measured by the OQ-45.2) differed depending on who was providing the supervision. Results suggested supervisors explained less than 1% of the variance in client psychotherapy outcomes (Rousmaniere et al., 2016). The findings of this study prompted a number of questions including: What was the practice of supervision being used at the center? What might explain the small contribution of supervision to client outcomes? Given the small contribution to client outcomes, should we continue to provide clinical supervision into the future? Internal conversations about the findings of the study suggested that we had more work to do.

Following discussions both internally with our team and externally with colleagues and mentors, the center launched a new phase of the supervision project in 2023 whereby with the support of two experts in counseling and supervision, we began a naturalistic RCT where we divided the supervisors into three groups and provided each group with a year of specialized supervision training. The conditions included competency-based, experiential supervision, and outcome-based supervision, which served as the treatment-as-usual condition. The initial findings of the RCT suggest that there was no difference in group outcomes based on the supervision condition. Based on these findings, the center is continuing the study as a naturalistic study and having the groups rotate conditions so that over the next year and a half each supervisor will have been trained in all three conditions. The study will continue to track the impact of the training on client outcomes and develop a model of supervision for the center.

In 2014, I was approached by another external researcher who was interested in using the center's data to replicate an earlier study that was conducted in a different setting. This study examined changes in psychotherapists' effectiveness within an agency making a concerted effort to improve outcomes through the use of ROM coupled with ongoing consultation and the planful application of feedback including the use of deliberate practice. In contrast with previous reports, psychotherapists in this study's sample showed improvements within their own caseloads across time of a 3.4%

increase each year over 3 years (Goldberg et al., 2016). This study brought some interest to the center and this author's work due to the significant positive changes reported in the findings. People were trying to understand what we were doing at the center and how we were so successful at improving both client and counselor outcomes.

A few months later I was approached by a researcher who was writing an article on outcome-based work for the *Atlantic Magazine*. The article was published in April 2017. The article was titled "What Your Therapist Doesn't Know," and the author was Dr. Tony Rousmaniere (*What Your Therapist Doesn't Know—The Atlantic*[1]). The publication clearly shared some of the center's experiences and brought even more attention to the center's work. A few weeks after the publication of this story, I received a phone call from a reporter from the *Globe and Mail*, Canada's national newspaper. She was interested in my opinion about a new phenomenon whereby some corporations in Canada were increasing employee mental health benefits from $500 per year to $5,000 per year and wondered if this was a good idea. I suggested that it could be a good idea if the increase was accompanied by a requirement that the provider of care used outcome monitoring so that both the employee and the payer could be confident that the investment in mental health would be more likely to make a difference in the lives of people dealing with mental health problems. This interview resulted in an almost yearlong engagement with the writer, which resulted in a publication in the *Globe and Mail* on April 8, 2018, and had a profound impact on the center (*Rethinking Therapy: How 45 Questions Can Revolutionize Mental Health Care in Canada—The Globe and Mail*[2]). This publication in a national newspaper resulted in over 150 emails and calls to the CCC where citizens, researchers, and counseling providers and leaders wanted to understand how we had achieved the ability to collect outcomes in a counseling setting. Many individuals had interests in developing similar programs. We heard from many citizens who were looking for a service in their own city or region where the measures were being used. We were struck by the broad range of interest, and it provided further support to continue on the path we were on. Additionally, it helped bring national attention to our work.

[1] https://www.theatlantic.com/magazine/archive/2017/04/what-your-therapist-doesnt-know/517797/

[2] https://www.theglobeandmail.com/canada/article-rethinking-therapy-how-45-questions-can-revolutionize-mental-health/

In 2017, the center was approached by a PhD student who had heard about the center's data set and wondered if he could use the center's Indigenous data for his dissertation. The aim of his study was to determine whether client therapeutic alliance ratings and client symptom severity were predictors of counseling outcomes among Canadian Indigenous clients. Results indicated that higher client alliance ratings at Sessions 2 and 3 and baseline client symptom severity were significant predictors of outcomes (Shaw et al., 2019).

In 2018 the city of Calgary was in the midst of an economic recession, the fourth financial crisis in a decade. The impact of the financial crisis on the center's clients was visible, and the team decided it was important to conduct a study on the impact of recession on mental health. The research question was: During a recession with high regional unemployment levels, can therapists expect the same improvements from therapy as they could in good economic times? The results suggested that less improvement was gained from counseling during the recession period than during good economic times, and that outcomes were affected by age, gender, and income level differentially for employed and unemployed clients (Berzins et al., 2018).

In 2019, the center participated in a publication that was focused on outcomes of couples counseling. This study utilized a benchmarking approach to compare the effectiveness of couples therapy in a community-based setting (CCC) with findings from efficacy treatments, such as treatment within randomized clinical trials. The archival sample of 3,347 couples in couples counseling provided weekly OQ-45 data as part of their counseling. The study found that treatment effect sizes found at community clinics were smaller than efficacy studies (i.e., the benchmark). However, when taking monitoring reactivity into account, the effect sizes were comparable. (Quirk et al., 2020).

In 2020, the COVID-19 pandemic impacted the center, and on March 11, counselors transitioned from face-to-face services at the center's office to virtual or online work from home. As the weeks and months of virtual/online care continued, we began considering what might happen when it was deemed safe enough to return to in-person work. In particular, we were interested in knowing what our client data could tell us about client outcomes during the pandemic when services were provided online. The team tested whether online or telemental health services delivered during the pandemic were inferior to face-to-face services delivered prior to the pandemic. What the team found was that telemental health services were found not to be inferior to in-person services, allaying concerns about the effectiveness of telemental health services delivered during the COVID-19 pandemic (Gurm et al., 2023). This result provided the evidence to support the use of either in-person or online services coming out of the pandemic and to the current day.

Conclusion

This chapter has detailed how I became interested in ROM and practice-based research as well as my motivation to use and scale ROM across the center. I initially became interested in ROM as it provided a way to measure and track client progress in counseling. The center has come a long way since the time when counselors were unwilling learn about ROM and some even thought that it was unethical to collect this type of data and use it in clinical practice. My motivation to use ROM was always focused on ensuring that we did our best at the center to ensure that clients could benefit from counseling.

I am pleased to share that year-on-year we see the lives of our clients change. We have the tools to quantify these results, which is important to our clients and to those who fund or invest in our services. We now have counselors wanting to join our team, as they want to use ROM, to understand its benefit to them and to their clients. Our recent expansion of our services provincially is a testament to our work with ROM. We never chose to use ROM for the needs of an external funder, but its use has provided advantages that could not have been predicted almost 20 years ago when we began this journey.

The use of ROM as part of our clinical routine has also allowed the research program at CCC to provide unique contributions that practice-based evidence offers to the scientific foundations of psychotherapy. Many of our studies at CCC have investigated topics that have not and, in some cases, could not have been examined in studies conducted in controlled settings. For example, we have learned that mandated family violence treatment for men can lead to lower rates of recidivism and, at the same time, improve their mental health and well-being (Tutty & Babins-Wagner 2016). In another study, we found that for clients presenting with depression and anxiety, the combination of individual and group counseling leads to more successful outcomes than either one of them alone (Babins-Wagner, 2022). Both of these examples illustrate that the work we do can support public policy and training of the next generation of clinicians.

Implementing ROM and practice-based research is no guarantee of the successes described in this chapter. It has taken over 20 years to get to our current state. In that time, we have faced staff revolt, had recruitment challenges, and changed our operating and business models on a number of occasions. Other organizations might not have access to the same level of support from their board, a leadership team as aligned as mine has been, and access to a variety of grants and philanthropy to support the long-term vision needed to make this transition.

I am proud of the work we have been doing and the lack of fear to try new things and move in new directions. This past year we have been sharing outcome data with funders who aren't wanting or requesting this type of information and are thrilled when they receive more detailed information and can better understand what we are doing at the center. We continue to achieve an early goal of growing as an organization only if the quality of our work produces strong results for the community. I can report that we are accomplishing that goal. CCC has scaled from a small local nonprofit to a large provincial Counselling Centre meeting the needs of individuals and families who are able to access counseling services without a waiting list and without financial barriers.

Acknowledgments

When my career started, I would not have believed that I would be doing anything other than clinical practice. I never envisioned that I would do a PhD, nor did I ever think that I would be involved in clinical research in my work setting. I have had the pleasure of meeting with and working with leaders in our field, in social work, in practice-based research, and more. Many people have given their time to mentor me, respond to my many questions, and to partner with me and with my team at CCC. Thank you for giving your time and efforts on behalf of my and my team's learning and CCC's clients. I want to thank the following people who have greatly influenced by own work as well as the work of CCC. This listing is alphabetical and recognizes individuals in Canada, the United States, the United Kingdom, and Europe. I apologize if I left anyone off this list: Michael Barkham, Gary Burlingame, Louis Castonguay, Kim DeJong, Jamie Delgadillo, Michael Ellis, David Este, Simon Goldberg, Michael Lambert, Wolfgang Lutz, Scott Miller, Jessie Owen, William Pelech, Michael Rothery, Tony Rousmaniere, Jackie Sieppert, Joshua Swift, Leslie Tutty, Daniel Wagner, Bruce Wampold, and Michael Yapko.

References

Babins-Wagner, R. (2022). *The impact of differential dose of individual and group counselling in depression treatment outcomes* [Unpublished manuscript]. Calgary Counselling Centre.

Babins-Wagner, R. (2011). *Understanding the predictors of counselling outcomes* [Unpublished doctoral dissertation]. University of Calgary. https://doi.org/10.11575/PRISM/3762

Barkham, M., & Margison, F. (2007). Practice-based evidence as a complement to evidence-based practice: From dichotomy to chiasmus. In C. Freeman & M. Power (Eds.), *Handbook of evidence-based psychotherapies* (pp. 443–476). Wiley.

Berzins, S., Babins-Wagner, R., & Hyland, K. (2018). Relationship of employment status and socio-economic factors with distress levels and counselling outcomes during a recession. *Counselling & Psychotherapy Research, 18*(2), 122–132. https://doi.org/10.1002/capr.12164

Duncan, B., & Miller, S. D. (2000). *The heroic client* (1st edition). Jossey-Bass.

Duncan, B., Miller, S., Sparks, J., Claud, D., Reynolds, L., Brown, J., & Johnson, L. (2003). The Session Rating Scale: Preliminary psychometric properties of a "working" alliance measurement. *Journal of Brief Therapy, 3*(1), 3–12.

Goldberg, S. B., Babins-Wagner, R., & Miller, S. D. (2017). Nurturing expertise at mental health agencies. In T. Rousmaniere, R. K. Goodyear, S. D. Miller, & B. E. Wampold (Eds.), *The cycle of excellence: Using deliberate practice to improve supervision and training* (pp. 199–217). Wiley Blackwell. https://doi.org/10.1002/9781119165590

Goldberg, S. B., Babins-Wagner, R., Rousmaniere, T., Berzins, S., Hoyt, W. T., Whipple, J. L., Miller, S. D., & Wampold, B. E. (2016). Creating a climate for therapist improvement: A case study of an agency focused on outcomes and deliberate practice. *Psychotherapy, 53*(3), 367–375. https://doi.org/10.1037/pst0000060

Gurm, K., Wampold, B. E., Piatt, C., Jagodzinski, R., Caperton, D. D., & Babins-Wagner, R. (2023). Effectiveness of telemental health during the COVID-19 pandemic: A propensity score noninferiority analysis of outcomes. *Psychotherapy, 60*(2), 231–236. https://doi.org/10.1037/pst0000472

Hubble, M., Duncan, B., & Miller, S. (Eds.). (1999). *The heart and soul of change* (1st ed.). American Psychological Association.

Johnson, L. D. (2000). *The session rating scale manual: A practical approach to improving psychotherapy*. The Brief Therapy Center.

Lambert, M. J., Hansen, N. B., Umpress, V., Lunned, K., Okoishi, J., & Burlingame, G. M., (2003). *Administration and scoring manual for the OQ-45.2*. American Professional Credentialing Services.

Quirk, K., Owen, J., Reese, R. J., Babins-Wagner, R., & Berzins, S. (2020). Benchmarking community-based couple therapy: Considering measurement reactivity. *Family Process, 59*(4), 1423–1433. https://doi.org/10.1111/famp.12513

Rousmaniere, T. G., Swift, J. K., Babins-Wagner, R., Whipple, J. L., & Berzins, S. (2016). Supervisor variance in psychotherapy outcome in routine practice. *Psychotherapy Research, 26*(2), 196–205. https://doi.org/10.1080/10503307.2014.963730

Shaw, S. L., Lombardero, A., Babins-Wagner, R., & Sommers-Flanagan, J. (2019). Counseling Canadian indigenous peoples: The therapeutic alliance and outcome. *Journal of Multicultural Counseling and Development, 47*(1), 49–68. https://doi.org/10.1002/jmcd.12120

Tutty, L. M., & Babins-Wagner, R. (2016). Outcomes and recidivism in mandated batterer intervention before and after introducing a specialized domestic violence court. *Journal of Interpersonal Violence, 34*(5), 1039–1062. https://doi.org/10.1177/0886260516647005

Tutty, L. M., Babins-Wagner, R., & Rothery, M. A. (2017). Women in IPV treatment for abusers and women in IPV survivor groups: Different or two sides of the same coin? *Journal of Family Violence, 32*(4), https://doi.org/10.1007/s10896-017-9927-2

Tutty, L. M., Babins-Wagner, R., & Rothery, M. A. (2019). The responsible choices for Men IPV Offender Program: Outcomes and a comparison of court-mandated to non-court-mandated men. *Journal of Aggression, Maltreatment and Trauma, 29*(3), 292–313. https://doi.org/10.1080/10926771.2019.1578316

15

Expanding the Borders of Practice-Based Evidence

Meeting Clinical and Population Health Needs in Emerging Economies

Paula Errázuriz

Chile is an interesting case to observe regarding mental health treatments and research. It is also a country where practice-oriented research is needed and feasible. In this chapter, I will tell you about Chile, our mental health challenges and treatment reality, and how my research team and I have conducted practice-oriented research effectively in this far-from-ideal context.

I will share a personal experience to exemplify what I mean by far-from-ideal context. In 2022, I was supposed to present some of the research findings I wrote about in this chapter in an online panel at the Society for Psychotherapy Research (SPR) international conference. That day, I was working from home and locked my door to avoid being interrupted by my kids. While waiting with the other researchers for the panel to be "on the air," I heard a scream. A few seconds later, a man I had never seen punched his arm through the door, and before I could understand what was happening, he brusquely covered my mouth, shut my laptop and dragged me to the room where my partner was tied on the floor. Moments later, I found myself face down next to him on the floor, blindfolded and with my wrists tied behind my back. I started screaming to find out where my children and nanny were and realized they were being held hostage by a woman in the bathroom. What followed was about 90 minutes of horror and ended with everyone traumatized and my partner with several broken ribs and a busted eardrum.

Paula Errázuriz, *Expanding the Borders of Practice-Based Evidence*. In: *Practice-Based Evidence in the Psychological Therapies*. Edited by: Louis G. Castonguay et al., Oxford University Press. © Oxford University Press (2026).
DOI: 10.1093/9780197748336.003.0015

The rising violence in Chile in recent years can be attributed to a complex interplay of factors, including our deeply entrenched economic inequality, increase in drug trafficking, and pervasive social and mental health challenges. Given our financial situation, my family, our nanny, and I had access to high-quality psychotherapy that played a crucial role in helping us recover from this traumatic experience. Unfortunately, this is not the reality for many others in Chile who suffer psychological trauma—whether due to violence, natural disasters, or other causes—or other mental health challenges and who lack access to the necessary treatment.

Chile: Challenges of a Developing Country

Chile is classified as a high-income country by the World Bank Group (2024), consistent with its rapid economic growth and positive quality-of-life indicators. Between 1990 and 2013, our GDP grew by an impressive 5%–6% annually. However, this growth has slowed significantly in the last decade, averaging just 2%. As a result, opportunities for employment and the provision of public goods have been narrower, sharpening social, economic, and political problems and making various inequalities more visible.

Chile presents high inequality in relation to income, wealth, and education (Lecaros et al., 2023). According to the World Inequality Report (Chancel et al., 2022) the top 1% of Chileans earn a quarter of total (pre-tax) income and own almost 50% of the country's wealth, making Chile one of the most unequal countries in Latin America.

Despite Chile's classification as a high-income country, the lack of access to mental health treatment for most of our population underscores the critical nature of our mental health challenges. Therefore, the proposals I put forth in this chapter could apply to other developing countries, middle-income countries, and disadvantaged areas within developed nations, particularly those grappling with high inequality.

Chile's healthcare system, restructured during the military dictatorship, has seen improvements under subsequent democratic governments yet remains highly unequal. The public healthcare system, which serves 82% of the population (Fondo Nacional de Salud, 2024), is underfunded and often delivers lower-quality care, while the private system, catering to the wealthiest 18%, offers significantly higher standards (Jiménez & Marinho, 2013). Research consistently highlights these deep inequalities in healthcare access and quality (Busta, 2017; Mieres, 2020; Vukusic & Bravo, 2020).

Mental Health in Chile and Inequality in Treatment Access

According to Chile's Health Ministry (Ministerio de Salud de Chile [MINSAL], 2017), "mental problems and disorders constitute the main source of disease burden in Chile" (p. 12). A nationwide prevalence study revealed that 36% of individuals over 15 years old have experienced some mental health disorder during their lifetime, and only 38% of them have received treatment for it (Vicente et al., 2016). Despite these alarming figures, the budget allocated to mental health in Chile represents only 1.7% of Chile's public health expenditure (Aguilera Correa & Arenas Gómez, 2023), a low percentage compared with other high-income countries.

Inequality extends to mental health service delivery, with significant differences in treatment duration and session frequency between the public and private sectors (De la Parra et al., 2019; Mathus, 2023). In the public system, mental health care is severely under-resourced, with long waiting times and inadequate treatment availability (Schönsteiner, 2022; Errázuriz et al., 2023), resulting in self-medication and chronicity of disorders (Vukusic & Bravo, 2020). Mental health providers interviewed by our team (Fischer et al., 2019) described their professional situation in the public system as having work overload (i.e., requirement to treat an excessive number of clients per day and clients with mental health problems of high severity), working in contexts with scarce resources (i.e., lack of medications, and/or inadequate treatment facilities), and not being able to offer adequate treatment due to low frequency of sessions and insufficient time allotted for each session, among other factors. As in many other countries, mental health problems in Chile are also unequally distributed, with higher prevalence in populations with low socioeconomic conditions (Alvarado & Encina, 2021), who are also the least likely to access treatment. Hopefully, the Comprehensive Mental Health Bill, recently signed (Gobierno de Chile, 2024), will overcome some of our mental health challenges by enhancing access to mental health services nationwide.

I have briefly explained the context in which my team and I have conducted research and the specific mental health challenges we face as a country because the personal and socioeconomic factors surrounding mental health treatment and research are crucial. Thus, before sharing my experiences and thoughts about practice-oriented research I feel the need to comment on an issue that I believe has contributed to the illusion that psychotherapy research findings apply across frontiers: the fact that most psychotherapy research publications do not adequately describe the clients and psychotherapists that participated in the studies, nor the context in which they took place.

Who Are We Studying in Psychotherapy Research?

With Stephanie Vaccarezza, Sebastián Opazo, Candice Fischer, and other colleagues, I am conducting a study titled "Who Are We Studying?" to describe how psychotherapy research participants (clients and therapists) are characterized in researcher publications. To do this, we are analyzing 100 recently published research articles. Our preliminary findings show that almost no information is published about clients' socioeconomic status, work status, and educational level; 75% of samples are from the United States and Europe; there is insufficient information about age, but it is evident that children and older adults are underrepresented; that most studies take place at university clinics and don't report session frequency or type of treatment; and that information about therapists' socioeconomic characteristics, theoretical orientation, years of training, and experience is almost nonexistent.

Our preliminary conclusion is that it is important to report more comprehensive information than is frequently done about patient demographics, therapists' characteristics, treatment provided, and the setting where it took place. This is very important as we can't assume that our accumulated research knowledge applies to clients of diverse socioeconomic conditions and different demographic characteristics, readers need to know what populations are being represented when they read a specific paper. Of course, systematic reviews, meta-analyses, and clinical guidelines should also consider these variables.

Psychotherapy Research in Chile

In addition to the difficulties mentioned in the previous sections, it is worth noting that many of the decisions made for mental health public policies in Chile are not based on scientific knowledge (Zitko et al., 2017), let alone scientific knowledge properly contextualized to the local reality. In Chile, as in most countries, there is almost no information available about what treatment variants are practiced in routine mental health care, nor the short- or long-term results that these treatments have. The lack of local evidence is particularly relevant, as it has been documented that one of the determining factors in mental health research is the context in which it is conducted. It has been argued that Chile "does not have an established periodical process to identify and prioritize health research needs" (Zitko et al., 2017, p. 2).

The World Health Organization (2013) proposes that scientific evidence is a fundamental tool for making informed health policy decisions—especially in contexts with very limited resources—as it has been shown that it decreases the disease burden and helps achieve universal coverage. The scarcity of mental health research in the Chilean context has practical consequences. For example, the national practice guidelines of the Chilean Ministry of Health, for depression (Ministerio de Salud de Chile, 2013) are mostly based on international research and we do not know whether it applies to our country. Due to the scarcity of research in Chile and similar contexts, the clinical guidelines used to treat mental health problems in Chile may not be appropriate for our cultural context and the needs and characteristics of our population.

This potential "disconnection" between established knowledge and local reality has had a deep personal meaning for me. After volunteering during high school and college in *campamentos* (human settlements associated with poverty and housing precariousness) in Chile and receiving my title as a psychologist in my home country, I continued my doctoral training in clinical psychology in the United States. At that time, I started reading rigorous international research and attending the SPR international conferences. While I felt deep admiration for the work of my mentors and colleagues, I usually had a nagging question: "I wonder if this would work in Chile?" When I returned to Chile in 2010, I wanted to conduct similar research in my country with vulnerable populations, but I couldn't. That's why when in 2019 I received the SPR's Outstanding Early Career Award, I shared some of my growing frustration:

> (. . .) I am very proud to be recognized for my research, and even more motivated to continue doing it. (. . .) But I also feel disappointed. I feel disappointed about not having been able to study the population of patients that need the most attention. (. . .) I believe our research has to consider patients who are not receiving optimal care because they represent most of the world's population. But the challenge is that *the same conditions that make patient care less than ideal are the conditions that make it very hard to conduct rigorous research in those settings.*

At the time of writing this chapter, I continue to struggle with this challenge, but learning that the research I have been conducting since 2010 is considered practice-oriented research (and is not just a mediocre copy of research done in controlled research settings) has inspired me and has validated the efforts I was making without knowing that my empirical work has been in line with a growing research paradigm.

I also want to acknowledge that even though conducting research in Chile is difficult, we have a thriving and committed community of psychotherapy researchers who have been inspired and trained by Mariane Krause, Guillermo de la Parra, and Juan Pablo Jiménez. In addition to actively participating in the international SPR and its Latin American Chapter, researchers in Chile and other Latin American countries have recently created a Latin American Consortium (Society for Psychotherapy Research, n.d.) in order to promote collaboration in practice-oriented research.

Why Is Practice-Oriented Research Relevant in Contexts like Chile?

Practice-oriented research can be understood as a form of research that aims to construct knowledge *from* professional practice *for* professional practice (Hermans & Schoeman, 2015). This approach distinguishes itself from others in that the value of the research resides in its contribution to the practice itself (Hermans & Schoeman, 2015). It doesn't remain confined to academic circles, where the primary objective of research often is to contribute to building more knowledge—whether or not such knowledge has a direct and actionable impact on professional practice.

In the specific case of psychotherapy, practice-oriented research stands as a viable strategy to address the documented gap between scientific knowledge and clinical practice (Castonguay & Muran, 2015). Many clinicians consider research in psychotherapy not only as irrelevant but also foreign to their work (Castonguay et al., 2011), as traditional research tends to be conducted in controlled settings, and the objects of study often align primarily with academic interests (Castonguay & Muran, 2015). In contrast, practice-oriented research enables clinicians themselves, not just researchers and academics, to participate in the design and implementation of studies, thereby ensuring that the results are informed by and applicable to the specific contexts, needs, and issues that define their professional practice.

This is particularly relevant in countries where economic resources are limited, but the demand for quality mental health care becomes increasingly pressing given the high prevalence of psychological disorders in the population. Research that assesses the effectiveness of psychotherapeutic treatments, specifically in Chile, is scarce, and studies show the absence of a "measurement culture" in the Latin American region, both in the public and private sectors (Trujillo & Paz, 2020). While many countries in the region subscribed to the mental health recommendations outlined by WHO in 1990, Trujillo and Paz (2020) have argued that "it is unknown whether they are being applied, if they have been implemented appropriately, and if they have contributed to improving the mental health of the populations in which they have been carried out" (p. 7).

Cultural values and practices, which differ in different regions of the world, play an important role in shaping how individuals conceptualize and experience mental or emotional health (Markus & Kitayama, 2010). With colleagues (Fernández-Alvarez et al., 2024), we have argued that this is particularly relevant for underserved populations, who often face material deprivation and multiple layers of discrimination based on identities such as race, ethnicity, gender, and socioeconomic status. These individuals experience more frequent and severe daily stressors, making their living situations a constant risk factor for mental health difficulties. Additionally, they face greater obstacles in accessing mental health services, such as transportation and child care barriers. We have also argued that practice-oriented research aims to address these challenges by generating practice-based evidence in real-world clinical settings; evidence that can be relevant and beneficial for the diverse and often marginalized populations who need mental health care the most. For example, it has been demonstrated that evidence-based public policies can improve efficiency and effectiveness regarding resource utilization and outcomes (Chaverri & Arguedas, 2020). This is because the entire policy design, decision-making, implementation, and evaluation process is supported by context-sensitive evidence, which determines beforehand and throughout the process what works and what doesn't in addressing a specific issue. In the absence of such contextualized research, it is very difficult to make adequate public policy decisions that maximize the yield from the few resources that are available to treat mental health disorders.

As a source of practice-based evidence, practice-oriented research emerges as a promising, cost-effective proposition to help clinicians and researchers gain knowledge about treatment currently used in Chile and to support large-scale policy-making processes aimed at improving the country's mental health problems. In addition, it can assist institutions and professionals, enabling them to receive feedback tailored to their practice and organization, benefiting both practitioners and their clients.

My Experience Conducting Practice-Oriented Research in Chile

With the hope of improving treatments provided to the Chilean population, I designed in 2009 a large-scale study—which I will refer to as the "Feedback Study"—to evaluate whether providing therapists with feedback about clients' psychological dysfunction and perception of alliance could enhance treatment adherence and outcome. While previous research had shown that providing therapists with real-time feedback can improve treatment outcome (e.g., Harmon et al., 2007), these findings had not been implemented globally—including in our country. I also thought that it would be highly relevant to assess the impact of feedback on adherence, as a vast literature has demonstrated that client therapy dropout and absenteeism represent not only an economic resource drain but also a barrier to timely access to mental health care and symptomatic improvement (Errázuriz, 2011).

Conducted in an outpatient clinic in Santiago, the study began in 2010, before phone apps were common and when data collection in Chile was seen with skepticism and fear. In case I found something helpful, I designed a study with feedback conditions that could be replicated inexpensively. The study also included a more expensive feedback condition, namely, the use of Lambert's OQ Progress Feedback Report, which provided a progress graph with all the patient's Outcomes Questionnaire (OQ) scores until that time and a message about the status of patient progress based on the OQ general scores that signals whether the patient is "on track" or not (Lambert, 2015b). This condition served as a control gold standard.

Main Findings of the Feedback Study

The Feedback Study (Errázuriz & Zilcha-Mano, 2018) comprised 547 clients, 28 therapists, and five conditions: (1) no feedback; (2) feedback on symptomatology; (3) feedback on the alliance; (4) feedback on both symptomatology and alliance; and (5) Lambert's OQ Progress Feedback

Report. The main results revealed that the feedback provided to therapists did not affect treatment outcomes, session attendance, or alliance quality. Nevertheless, clients' previous psychiatric history, as well as their baseline severity combined with lack of progress, significantly moderated the impact of feedback. For this more dysfunctional population, positive feedback given to therapists (i.e., providing feedback about their clients presenting low symptomatology) positively impacted treatment outcomes, while negative feedback (i.e., feedback to therapists about their clients presenting high symptomatology) had a negative effect.

The most significant conclusion of this study was that providing feedback to therapists without supporting them to improve their work with their clients can be ineffective and even detrimental. This is even more relevant for clients suffering from more severe mental health issues, whose therapists mostly receive discouraging news as feedback. This study has significant clinical implications, as it suggests that not all types of feedback are suitable for all clients and that "negative feedback" to therapists may harm treatment. We also concluded that the impact of any feedback system must be studied in the targeted context before implementing it on a large scale (Errázuriz & Zilcha-Mano, 2018).

Additional Findings of the Feedback Study

The data obtained in the Feedback Study was also used to identify subgroups of clients showing different *therapeutic change trajectories* during psychotherapy, given that evidence indicates studying responses to treatment in clinical routine contexts is important to develop personalized and, therefore, effective therapeutic processes for clients. Data analysis (Fuentes et al., 2023) identified three change trajectories: (a) moderate initial dysfunction followed by slight deterioration, (b) mild initial dysfunction with favorable change, and (c) severe initial dysfunction with rapid favorable change. Our results show that these three trajectories predicted the outcome of the psychotherapeutic process, where therapies that begin with moderate initial dysfunction followed by slight deterioration, Trajectory a, will be more likely to maintain poor psychotherapy outcomes than the other two trajectories, regardless of the duration of the treatment. Furthermore, we observed that the probability of belonging to Trajectory a increases with the client's age, suggesting a poorer prognosis for older clients. We also found that 20% of therapies in our sample fell into Trajectory a. This finding is worrisome, not only because clients increase their level of dysfunction throughout therapy, but also because this percentage is higher than those obtained for this type of trajectory (between 5% and 10%) in previous studies (Lambert, 2015a; Lutz et al., 2014). This alerts us to the fact that clients in this Chilean clinic are doing worse than would be expected by international research. While it is necessary to know if this worse outcome represents what is generally happening in Chile, and if it may be explained by our specific definition of change pattern, it reminds us that we cannot rely solely on international studies to guide our clinical decision-making, and that local research is required.

Also, as part of the Feedback Study, we examined the *relationship between family income, changes in symptomatic burden, and changes in life satisfaction* (Behn et al. 2017). Overall, the results show that initial levels and improvement in life satisfaction are related to initial levels and improvement in psychological distress. Furthermore, our results show that family income level significantly affects the relationship between symptom improvement and life satisfaction during psychotherapy. For high-income clients, situational improvements in psychological distress appear to produce prospective improvements in life satisfaction and not the other way around. For low-income clients, however, the opposite is true, and only previous situational levels of life satisfaction predict subsequent effects on psychological distress. This may mean that, particularly for low-income clients, psychotherapy may benefit clients by fostering situational improvements in life satisfaction to promote a reduction in psychological distress. For high-income clients, it appears that a standard therapeutic focus on the reduction of psychological distress may be enough to improve life satisfaction. This finding illustrates the clinical, training, and social implications that can emerge from practice-oriented research, highlighting its particular value in the scientific foundations of psychotherapy.

We also used data from the Feedback Study to explore *therapeutic alliance trajectories* (Zilcha-Mano & Errázuriz, 2017). We identified three distinct early alliance development patterns within the first four sessions of therapy: (a) early gradual strengthening, (b) early repaired rupture, and (c) early unrepaired rupture. Our results showed that the gradual strengthening and the repaired rupture patterns early in treatment predicted alliance strengthening later in treatment, whereas the unrepaired rupture pattern early in treatment predicted alliance stability later in treatment. In addition, early alliance trajectories significantly predicted treatment outcomes, with different patterns appearing to be more beneficial for different subgroups of patients based on their pretreatment interpersonal functioning. Specifically, the early gradual strengthening and early repaired rupture patterns were associated with better treatment outcomes, especially for patients with better interpersonal functioning at intake.

The *predictive power of the alliance* was further investigated in another secondary study (Zilcha-Mano et al., 2017). Our results first confirmed that the therapeutic alliance precedes symptomatic change, providing support to the causal role of the alliance in improving treatment outcomes. The study also differentiated between the traitlike component, which reflects a general tendency to form strong alliances, and the statelike component, which captures changes in the alliance during treatment. Both components were found to significantly predict treatment outcomes, with statelike changes showing immediate effects on subsequent session outcomes. Additionally, life satisfaction was identified as a critical moderator, enhancing the positive impact of statelike changes in the alliance on treatment progress. These findings underscore the importance of the alliance's stable and dynamic aspects and highlight the role of client well-being in the therapeutic process.

Another important use of the Feedback Study data was our study on the phenomenon of *sudden gains* (Zilcha-Mano et al., 2019). This study revealed that clients who experienced "sudden gains" were also more likely to show subsequent strengthening of the therapeutic alliance, which in turn predicted further improvements in life satisfaction and reductions in psychological dysfunction. These findings support the proposed theoretical framework, suggesting that the alliance plays a crucial role in an upward spiral leading to sustained sudden gains.

Continuing with our interest in understanding the impact of the therapeutic alliance on the effectiveness of a therapeutic process, we assessed whether a *match within the therapeutic dyad regarding gender, age, and income* predicted early growth in the therapeutic alliance (Behn et al., 2018). Our results indicated that the matching type did not appear to significantly impact how clients rate the quality of the therapeutic relationship at the beginning of treatment. Additionally, it was observed that across all levels of attribute matching, clients tended to rate the alliance positively, and dyads in which the therapist is younger than the client, and/or comes from a higher income level than the client, showed additional growth in the alliance beyond initial positive ratings.

In addition to the previous uses of our Feedback Study data by our team and international collaborators, it's important to note that our data also contributed to a larger international study (Flückiger et al., 2020) that aimed to better understand the *relationship between alliance and symptoms in the early stages of therapy*. The results showed that symptoms and alliances were reciprocally related to each other in the early phase of treatment, often reflecting the connection between a stronger alliance and lower symptoms, which in turn predicted even stronger alliances and even lower symptoms in the subsequent sessions.

The data of the Feedback Study was also included in the multilevel meta-analysis by de Jong and colleagues (2021) that assessed the effectiveness of progress feedback in psychological treatments. The authors reported that overall, feedback on patient's progress in psychotherapy significantly improves symptom reduction and reduces dropout, but it does not impact treatment duration or diminish the percentage of clients who deteriorate. They also found that the effects of feedback were moderated by country—among other variables—and that some feedback instruments appear to have specific effects in certain subsamples. The latter confirms the importance of presenting information about participants when reporting research and the need to study psychotherapy in diverse contexts.

Along with the various findings related to outcome, process, and participant characteristics summarized earlier, the Feedback Study allowed for the adaptation to Spanish and validation of two instruments for the Chilean population: the Outcome Questionnaire OQ-30.2 (Errázuriz et al., 2017) and the Self-Concealment Scale (Letelier & Errázuriz, 2020), facilitating psychotherapy research in Chile.

Some Thoughts About the Feedback Study and Its Methodology

Looking back at all the research questions we could answer with the Feedback Study data makes me conclude that even though clients and therapists in Chile are not accustomed to data collection, and it can be very challenging (this will be discussed further), practice-oriented research is possible and worth the effort in a context like Chile. Our practice-oriented research was highly productive in answering questions regarding therapy in our country. In addition, it contributed to building important global psychotherapy knowledge with participants who are often underrepresented in international studies and where manualized treatments typically investigated in controlled settings are not likely to be generalizable to clinical practice—which requires a lot of flexibility to be responsive to the needs of its population.

I can also conclude that even though as researchers we are used to reading about RCT studies that take place in controlled research settings, some aspects of RCTs can be implemented successfully using practice-oriented research. In the case of the Feedback Study, even though treatments were therapy as usual—we did not interfere with how each therapeutic dyad worked—and took place in a naturalistic setting, the feedback component did meet some of the RCT requirements, such as random assignment to feedback and a control group, as well as clients being blinded to the feedback condition to which they were assigned. Thus, I believe this study may be considered a hybrid design that exemplifies how research can simultaneously meet certain criteria for both RCT methodology and also practice-oriented research in terms of the hallmarks as described by Castonguay and colleagues (2021).

Some practice-oriented research (e.g., practice research networks) involves a collaborative approach between researchers and clinicians (Castonguay et al., 2021). While our team comprises researchers who are also experienced psychotherapists and clinical supervisors, we did not collaborate with the clinicians included in this study as participants, which is an aspect I would like to improve in future research projects. Despite this shortcoming, I consider that we successfully integrated elements of both RCT and practice-oriented methodologies. For the feedback that therapists received, we maintained the rigorous structure and control of an RCT while *embedding* the research within routine clinical practice, making it highly relevant to clinicians and clients.

New Directions

Since completing the Feedback study and considering its conclusions, I have been engaged in two projects aimed at collecting and using practice-based evidence. These projects are still in progress, and what I will describe is how they were started and the twists and turns that have marked their development. Thus, this section is not about research findings but, rather, the challenges and opportunities that can come with the desire to collect data and provide psychological services within the mental health care routine in countries like Chile. I should also mention that these projects are team efforts, which is crucial for conducting research in complex environments like Chile. As such, I am naming some of the members of these research projects to acknowledge their invaluable contributions.

Alliance Study

The first project is another extensive practice-oriented research study—which I will refer to as the "Alliance Study"—this time with the main goal of proposing a comprehensive empirical model regarding the therapeutic alliance's role in treating depression. This ongoing study, which I am conducting with Candice Fischer, Mariane Krause, Alex Behn, Sebastián Opazo, and Stephany Vaccarezza, includes client and therapist demographic and psychological baseline characteristics, characteristics of the client–therapist relationship (alliance's average, trajectory, and ruptures), other process variables (e.g., psychotherapy techniques and session frequency), and treatment outcomes (change in depression, change in psychological functioning, and treatment termination status).

To carry out this investigation, we started collecting data at the same institution as the Feedback Study. This outpatient clinic offers psychological and psychiatric services to middle- and low-income adults in downtown Santiago de Chile. During this new data collection process (as well as during the Feedback Study), we have encountered several challenges in our research task, primarily due to the short duration of many treatments, discontinuity from clients not having sessions for months, and irregular therapy frequencies. Moreover, overburdened professionals have often been reluctant to engage in research tasks, and it has been difficult to track clients' session schedules, attendance, and reasons for absences. To address these challenges, research assistants have covered the clinic's schedule extensively and used their social skills to gather crucial information from the front desk staff, piecing together data despite limited access to administrative records.

In this already challenging context, Chile's 2019 "Social Outburst"[1] with massive social demonstrations and violent riots and the COVID pandemic, which reached Chile in March of 2020, were both critical threats to research and an opportunity (I can only say this in retrospect) to develop a more promising practice-oriented study. The clinic was only a few blocks away

[1] https://en.wikipedia.org/wiki/2019%E2%80%932022_Chilean_protests

from the main city riots—and several burned subway stations—during the Social Outburst, forcing the staff to close it unexpectedly and without us having any idea of when it would reopen, although this was not a priority, considering that the city was burning, democracy was at risk, and human rights were violated. Once the clinic reopened, it was not clear if it was safe for our research assistants to go there and how this traumatic social situation had impacted the mental health and treatments of the clients in our study, a new variable that we had to start measuring.

We were trying to recover from the Social Outburst as a research team, a challenge in itself, considering that many aspects of everyone's lives had been affected, when the pandemic started to impact Chile and the data collection process. I won't provide details about this since I imagined most research projects worldwide had similar struggles. The major impact on our study was trying to quickly switch from a face-to-face data collection process to an online collection process. While we were able to manage this, the clinic restricted the data collection to protect their staff and clients who were overwhelmed by the pandemic and had to learn to do online psychotherapy for the first time. Because of this, we reached out to other public and private mental health centers, starting data collection in five new mental health centers, in addition to clinicians working independently. Some unique challenges we faced included investigating psychotherapy in places that had never done research or used questionnaires for clinical purposes. Thus, no data collection culture or administrative practices could help this process. In addition, we observed that therapists feared being evaluated, worrying that the results could negatively impact their careers. Since there is not a research culture in clinical settings in Chile, some professionals did not believe or understand the confidentiality of research, even though we took the informed consent process very seriously. We even faced ideological resistance against research.

Because of practical, historical, organizational, and cultural factors, the efforts that we devoted to the alliance study yielded mostly frustrations and little data for several years. However, as I am writing this chapter, we are still collecting data for this and another study as part of the day-to-day practice of the clinic that we have created, which I will refer to in the following section.

Promoting and Improving Mental Health Care

The second project arose during the course of the Alliance Study, which was progressing slowly and with difficulty such that the members of our team became disappointed and tired, and we were running out of research funds. Fortunately, in 2019, with Candice Fischer and Sebastián Opazo we had created PsiConecta,[2] a nonprofit mental health nongovernmental organization (NGO) that promotes mental health in Spanish-speaking countries. In the first years, we had two main aims: (1) psycho-educating the general public to take better care of their mental health and seek professional help when needed, and (2) training young therapists in practical therapeutic skills, which we were mainly doing through our online HAP program.[3] Nevertheless, we had been getting many requests for psychotherapy treatments. Considering our need to collect good quality data and our desire as an NGO to provide low-cost mental health treatments, in 2023, we created the PsiConecta Online Clinic.[4] We currently have 12 therapists and can treat up to 72 clients at a time. Clinicians receive weekly supervision and attend our online courses[5] with psychotherapy experts. We also sell these courses to Spanish-speaking therapists around the globe to help fund our NGO.

Initially, we only collected data from the psychotherapies delivered at the PsiConecta Clinic. Now, we are in the process of incorporating feedback for therapists and automated therapeutic training as needed. For example, we send automatic alerts to therapists whose patients report early life maltreatment and adversity (ELMA) at intake, providing information about how this early adversity may be related to the client's presenting problems and how to work effectively with these potentially traumatic experiences in psychotherapy. In addition to written information, we provide short videos showing the skills and interventions we suggest and handouts that can be downloaded to use with clients in sessions. For clients who report ELMA, we give them short, automated feedback about why discussing these experiences with their therapists may be useful for their treatment. We are testing if feedback for therapists and clients, and online training for therapists, positively impacts treatment outcomes. We are also assessing the acceptability of the automated feedback and training for clients and therapists.

If our ELMA feedback and training are positively accepted and improve treatment outcomes, we will build and test more feedback and training modules for therapists. We hope this will help therapists do their jobs better and provide an additional incentive for them to participate in our research since

[2] https://psiconecta.org/
[3] https://hap.psiconecta.org/material-hap/
[4] https://www.agenda.psiconecta.org/atencion-bajo-costo/
[5] https://hap.psiconecta.org/cursos/

they will receive a direct benefit. We also want to test providing automatized feedback and psychoeducational materials to patients based on their symptoms and needs.

Conclusions

Practice-oriented research is crucial and necessary in developing countries, as research conducted in more advantaged contexts cannot be assumed to generalize to these realities. One of the unique contributions of this research paradigm is its ability to investigate in real-life clinical settings, assessing the applicability of therapeutic interventions across diverse settings and populations. This being said, in order for practice-oriented research, and any clinical research, to contribute to local and global knowledge, publications must include demographic and clinically relevant information about its participants, which is the only way to know to which client, therapist, treatment type, and context the findings may generalize to.

From our experience conducting practice-oriented research studies in Chile, I would like to suggest a number of additional recommendations: (a) continuous training and incentives for therapists, supervisors, and clinic administrators to effectively use feedback; (b) training clinicians and administrators to integrate research into clinical practice; and (c) developing public policies that support the implementation of practice-oriented research, that will in turn provide contextually relevant research findings to inform public policies.

Moreover, for ethical, clinical, motivational, and practical reasons, I believe participants in practice-oriented research need to benefit directly from having their therapy process be part of a research project. This benefit can be offered by providing feedback to clinicians about how the process is evolving and, at the same time, providing them with knowledge and skills to help them deal more effectively with the challenges they encounter. In the case of clients, in addition to informing them about how the feedback to therapists may benefit treatment, providing them with direct feedback about their process, as well as psychoeducational material relevant to their case, should also be explored as a way to improve treatment outcomes and motivate clients to participate in research.

While I hope that these recommendations will help foster both the quantity and the quality of future practice-oriented research, I believe that by conducting this type of research in Chile, we have demonstrated its feasibility and necessity, providing valuable insights into real-life therapeutic processes and outcomes. In doing so, our research has highlighted the need for local data to inform public policy and clinical practice, ensuring that therapeutic interventions are effective and relevant in specific settings.

References

Aguilera Correa, I., & Arenas Gómez, A. (2023). Estimated spending on mental health in Chile 2014–2021. *Boletín Economía y Salud, 17*(1), 2–11. Ministry of Health, Chile. Retrieved from https://docs.bvsalud.org/biblioref/2024/12/1552319/boletin-economia-y-salud-vol-17-n1-2023.pdf

Alvarado, R., & Encina, E. (2021, October 8). Inequidades en Salud Mental: ¿Qué podemos hacer? *Escuela de Salud Pública*. Universidad de Chile. https://saludpublica.uchile.cl/noticias/180484/inequidades-en-salud-mental-que-podemos-hacer

Behn, A. J., Errázuriz, P. A., Cottin, M., & Fischer, C. (2017). Change in symptomatic burden and life satisfaction during short-term psychotherapy: Focusing on the role of family income. *Counselling and Psychotherapy Research, 18*(2), 133–142. https://doi.org/10.1002/capr.12158

Behn, A., Davanzo, A., & Errázuriz, P. (2018). Client and therapist match on gender, age, and income: Does match within the therapeutic dyad predict early growth in the therapeutic alliance? *Journal of Clinical Psychology, 74*(9), 1403–1421. https://doi.org/10.1002/jclp.22616

Busta, C. (2017). La medicalización del malestar como proceso generador de desigualdad en el sistema de salud chileno. *Castalia, 28*(4), 19–29. https://doi.org/10.25074/07198051.4.591

Castonguay, L. G., Barkham, M., Youn, S. J., & Page, A. C. (2021). Practice-based evidence—Findings from routine clinical settings. In M. Barkham, W. Lutz, & L. G. Castonguay (Eds.), *Bergin and Garfield's handbook of psychotherapy and behavior change* (6th ed., pp. 191–222). Wiley.

Castonguay, L. G., Locke, B. D., & Hayes, J. A. (2011). The Center for Collegiate Mental Health: An example of a practice research network in university counseling centers. *Journal of College Student Psychotherapy, 25*(2), 105–119. https://doi.org/10.1080/87568225.2011.556929

Castonguay, L. G., & Muran, J. C. (2015). Fostering collaboration between researchers and clinicians through building practice-oriented research: An introduction. *Psychotherapy Research, 25*(1), 1–5. https://doi.org/10.1080/10503307.2014.966348

Chancel, L., Piketty, T., Saez, E., & Zucman, G. (2022). *World inequality report 2022*. World Inequality Lab. Retrieved from https://wir2022.wid.world/www-site/uploads/2021/12/WorldInequalityReport2022_Full_Report.pdf

Chaverri, P., & Arguedas, A. (2020). Políticas Públicas Basadas en Evidencia: Una revisión del concepto y sus características. *Revista ABRA, 40*(60), 49–76. https://doi.org/10.15359/abra.40-60.2

de Jong, K., Conijn, J. M., Gallagher, R. A. V., Reshetnikova, A. S., Heij, M., & Lutz, M. C. (2021). Using progress feedback to improve outcomes and reduce drop-out, treatment duration, and deterioration: A multilevel meta-analysis. *Clinical Psychology Review, 85*, 102002. https://doi.org/10.1016/j.cpr.2021.102002

De la Parra, G., Errázuriz, P., Gómez-Barris, E., & Zúñiga, A. K. (2019). *Propuesta para una psicoterapia efectiva en atención primaria: Un modelo basado en la experiencia y la evidencia empírica*. Centro de Políticas Públicas UC. https://medicina.uc.cl/wp-content/

uploads/2019/06/Art%C3%ADculo-Propuesta-para-una-psicoterapia_G-de-la-Parra-y-otros_CPoliP%C3%BAblicas-UC_junio2019.pdf

Errázuriz, P. (2011). *To know or not to know: Does therapists' access to feedback about patients' psychological dysfunction and alliance perception affect treatment adherence, alliance, and outcome?* Research proposal submitted to the FONDECYT. National Research Funding Competition.

Errázuriz, P., Jiménez, J. P., Olhaberry, M., Altimir, C., & Dagnino, P. (2023). Epílogo: Salud mental en Chile: urgencias, desafíos y silencios. In MIDAP (Ed.), *Salud Mental y Sociedad en Tiempos de Crisis* (pp. 134–139), MIDAP. Festina Lente Ediciones.

Errázuriz, P., Opazo, S., Behn, A., Silva, O., & Gloger, S. (2017). Spanish adaptation and validation of the Outcome Questionnaire OQ-30.2. *Frontiers in Psychology*, *8*, Article 673. https://doi.org/10.3389/fpsyg.2017.00673

Errázuriz, P., & Zilcha-Mano, S. (2018). In psychotherapy with severe clients discouraging news may be worse than no news: The impact of providing feedback to therapists on psychotherapy outcome, session attendance, and the alliance. *Journal of Consulting and Clinical Psychology*, *86*(2), 125–139. https://doi.org/10.1037/ccp0000277

Fernández-Alvarez, J., Molinari, G., Kilcullen, R., Delgadillo, J., Drill, R., Errázuriz, P., Falkenstrom, F., Firth, N., O'Shea, A., Paz, C., Jeong Youn, S., & Castonguay, L. G. (2024). The importance of conducting practice-oriented research with underserved populations. *Administration and Policy in Mental Health and Mental Health Services Research*, *51*(3), 358–375. https://doi.org/10.1007/s10488-023-01337-z

Fischer, C., Cottin, M., Behn, A., Errázuriz, P., & Díaz, R. (2019). What makes a difficult patient so difficult? Examining the therapist's experience beyond patient characteristics. *Journal of Clinical Psychology*, *75*(5), 898–911. https://doi.org/10.1002/jclp.22765

Flückiger, C., Rubel, J., Del Re, A. C., Horvath, A. O., Wampold, B. E., Crits-Christoph, P., Atzil-Slonim, D., Compare, A., Falkenström, F., Ekeblad, A., Errázuriz, P., Fisher, H., Hoffart, A., Huppert, J. D., Kivity, Y., Kumar, M., Lutz, W., Muran, J. C., Strunk, D. R., . . . Barber, J. P. (2020). The reciprocal relationship between alliance and early treatment symptoms: A two-stage individual participant data meta-analysis. *Journal of Consulting and Clinical Psychology*, *88*(9), 829–843. https://doi.org/10.1037/ccp00005

Fondo Nacional de Salud. (2024, April). *Cuenta pública de FONASA 2024*. FONASA. https://www.fonasa.cl/sites/fonasa/noticia/cuenta_publica_2024

Fuentes, V., Errázuriz, P., Campos, S., & Miranda, D. (2023). Identificando las trayectorias de cambio terapéutico en psicoterapia breve en pacientes chilenos. *Terapia Psicológica 41*(1), 1–18. https://doi.org/10.4067/s0718-48082023000100001

Gobierno de Chile. (2024, July 18). *Proyecto de Ley Integral de Salud Mental: Detalles de la iniciativa del gobierno.* https://www.gob.cl/noticias/proyecto-ley-integral-salud-mental-detalles-iniciativa-gobierno/#:~:text=Establece%20deberes%20intersectoriales%20que%20promuevan,de%20la%20vida%20en%20comunidad.

Harmon, S. C., Lambert, M. J., Smart, D. M., Hawkins, E., Nielsen, S. L., Slade, K., & Lutz, W. (2007). Enhancing outcome for potential treatment failures: Therapist–client feedback and clinical support tools. *Psychotherapy Research*, *17*(4), 379–392. https://doi.org/10.1080/10503300600702331

Hermans, C., & Schoeman, W. J. (2015). Practice-oriented research in service of designing interventions. *Acta Theologica*, *22*, 26–44. https://doi.org/10.4314/actat.v21i1.4S

Jiménez, A., & Marinho, M. (2013). El sistema de salud en Chile: ¿Qué puede significar hoy protección social? *CIPER Chile*. Retrieved from https://www.ciperchile.cl/2013/09/10/el-sistema-de-salud-en-chile-que-puede-significar-hoy-proteccion-social/#:~:text=Nuestro%20actual%20sistema%20sanitario%2C%20altamente,no%20puede%20pagar%20por%20protecci%C3%B3n.

Lambert, M. J. (2015a). Effectiveness of psychotherapeutic treatment. *Resonanzen–E-Journal für biopsychosoziale Dialoge in Psychosomatischer Medizin, Psychotherapie, Supervision und Beratung*, *3*(2), 87–100.

Lambert, M. J. (2015b). Progress feedback and the OQ-system: The past and the future. *Psychotherapy*, *52*(4), 381–390. https://doi.org/10.1037/pst0000027

Lecaros, I., Cruzat, D. P., Pommer Muñoz, R., Tillan, P., Walton, M., López, R., Figueroa, E., & Gutiérrez, P. (2023). *Inequality in Chile: An overview* (Working Paper No. 436). Harvard University, Center for International Development. Retrieved from https://www.hks.harvard.edu/sites/default/files/centers/cid/files/publications/faculty-working-papers/436_Inequality_in_Chile.pdf

Letelier, C., & Errázuriz, P. (2020). Adaptación y validación en español de la self-concealment scale. *Psykhe*, *29*(2). https://doi.org/10.7764/psykhe.29.2.1220

Lutz, W., Deisenhofer, A.-K., Weinmann-Lutz, B., & Barkham, M. (2023). Data-informed clinical training and practice. In L. G. Castonguay & C. E. Hill (Eds.), *Becoming better psychotherapists: Advancing training and supervision* (pp. 191–213). American Psychological Association. https://doi.org/10.1037/0000364-010

Lutz, W., Hofmann, S. G., Rubel, J., Boswell, J. F., Shear, M. K., Gorman, J. M., Woods, S. W., & Barlow, D. H. (2014). Patterns of early change and their relationship to outcome and early treatment termination in patients with panic disorder. *Journal of Consulting and Clinical Psychology*, *82*(2), 287–297. https://doi.org/10.1037/a0035535

Markus, H. R., & Kitayama, S. (2010). Cultures and selves: A cycle of mutual constitution. *Perspectives on Psychological Science*, *5*(4), 420–430. https://doi.org/10.1177/1745691610375557

Mathus, C. (2023, March 21). Listas de espera y la crisis en salud mental en jóvenes en Chile. *Revista Ya, El Mercurio*, 14–17.

Mieres, M. (2020). La dinámica de la desigualdad en Chile: una mirada regional. *Revista de Análisis Económico*, *35*(2), 91–133. https://doi.org/10.4067/S0718-88702020000200091

Ministerio de Salud de Chile. (2013). Guía Clínica AUGE. Depresión en personas de 15 años y más. . Ministerio de Salud de Chile.

Ministerio de Salud de Chile. (2017). *Plan Nacional de Salud Mental 2017–2025*. Ministerio de Salud de Chile.

Schönsteiner, J. (2022). *Informe Anual sobre Derechos Humanos en Chile 2022*. Universidad Diego Portales. https://derechoshumanos.udp.cl/cms/wp-content/uploads/2022/11/DDHH2022_MG4.pdf

Society for Psychotherapy Research. (n.d.). *Consorcio Latinoamericano de Investigación en Psicoterapia (CLIP)*. Society for Psychotherapy Research. Retrieved October 29, 2024, from https://www.psychotherapyresearch.org/page/CLIP-About_engl

Trujillo, A., & Paz, C. (2020). Evidencia basada en la práctica en psicoterapia: El reto en Latinoamérica. *CES Psicología*, *13*(3), 1–14. https://doi.org/10.21615/cesp.13.3.1

Vicente, B., Saldivia, S., & Pihán, R. (2016). Prevalencias y brechas hoy; salud mental mañana. *Acta bioethica*, *22*(1), 51–61. https://doi.org/10.4067/S1726-569X2016000100006

Vukusic, V., & Bravo, P. (2020). Salud mental en Chile, determinantes sociales de la salud y desigualdad: ¿Cuáles son los alcances de la ley de protección a la salud mental? Entrevista al Diputado Gabriel Boric Font. *Vincularte. Revista Clínica y Psicosocial*, *5*(5), 100–108.

World Bank Group. (2024). *Chile - Prosperity Data 360*. Retrieved January 24, 2025, from https://prosperitydata360.worldbank.org/en/economy/CHL.

World Health Organization. (2013, August). *World health report 2013: Research for universal health coverage*. https://www.afro.who.int/publications/world-health-report-2013-research-universal-health-coverage#:~:text=The%20World%20health%20report%202013,evidence%20provided%20by%20scientific%20research.

Zilcha-Mano, S., & Errázuriz, P. (2017). Early development of mechanisms of change as a predictor of subsequent change and treatment outcome: The case of working alliance. *Journal of Consulting and Clinical Psychology*, *85*(5), 508–520. https://doi.org/10.1037/ccp0000192

Zilcha-Mano, S., Errázuriz, P., Yaffe-Herbst, L., German, R. E., & DeRubeis, R. J. (2019). Are there any robust predictors of "sudden gainers," and how is sustained improvement in treatment outcome achieved following a gain? *Journal of Consulting and Clinical Psychology, 87*(6), 491–500. https://doi.org/10.1037/ccp0000401

Zilcha-Mano, S., Lipsitz, I., & Errázuriz, P. (2017). When is it effective to focus on the alliance? Analysis of a within-client moderator. *Cognitive Therapy and Research, 42*(2), 159–171. https://doi.org/10.1007/s10608-017-9867-4

Zitko, P., Borghero, F., Zavala, C., Markkula, N., Santelices, E., Libuy, N., & Pemjean, A. (2017). Priority setting for mental health research in Chile. *International Journal of Mental Health Systems, 11*, Article 61. https://doi.org/10.1186/s13033-017-0168-9

16

Aligning Person-Centered and Systemic Perspectives to Strengthen Measurement-Based Care

Susan Douglas and Amanda Jensen-Doss

With this chapter, we close the section on the integration and dissemination of practice-based evidence. We propose a conceptual model that was inspired by Peter Senge's seminal writing on learning organizations, where he stated:

> Sharing knowledge is not about giving people something or getting something from them. That is only valid for information sharing. Sharing knowledge occurs when people are genuinely interested in helping one another develop new capacities for action; it is about creating learning processes (Senge, 1998, p. 11).

Our model is founded in 30 years of collective experience, intended to foster "new capacities for action" with the implementation of measurement-based care (MBC) and feedback as part of clinical routine. First, we frame our partnership in our respective professional narratives arising from practice-based evidence (Douglas) and evidence-based practice (Jensen-Doss). We then describe when and why we determined that a new conceptual model was needed that aligns mechanisms of action with outcomes and implementation. Next, we present our two-part model, called the Golden Thread Feedback Framework, which continues to evolve.

We start from the "inside-out" with a focus on how people who use MBC and clinical feedback interact with the intervention and each other. This incorporates mechanisms of action, including patient engagement and understanding, and the use of MBC data to inform behaviors and

Susan Douglas and Amanda Jensen-Doss, *Aligning Person-Centered and Systemic Perspectives to Strengthen Measurement-Based Care*. In: *Practice-Based Evidence in the Psychological Therapies*. Edited by: Louis G. Castonguay et al., Oxford University Press.
DOI: 10.1093/9780197748336.003.0016

conversations in the session. The second part of our model expands the focus from the "outside-in" to the larger system, which includes internal organizational structures and supports, and external characteristics of the healthcare system. The framework aligns MBC and clinical feedback to organizational learning and leadership as facilitators of care quality and health system improvement efforts. The chapter concludes with a call to action for the field of practice-based evidence to develop new capabilities for collaborative action and mutually beneficial learning processes.

When Happy Circumstance Brings You Together

This is a story of two people who followed different pathways that eventually converged in 2014 around supporting clinicians to use MBC. Early in our professional careers, both of us were highly influenced by the notion that a chasm existed between practice and research that needed to be bridged if we were ever to be successful at improving mental health outcomes (IOM, 2001). For Susan Douglas, she left graduate school identifying as a clinician and as a researcher, which at the time felt like polar opposites. To try to find her place along the bridge between practice and research, she completed two postdoctoral fellowships simultaneously, one in clinical practice and one in program evaluation research, setting her on a career grounded in the methods and theories of practice-based evidence. For Amanda Jensen-Doss, her academic journey started with a focus on evidence-based practice, working with John Weisz[1] on his effectiveness trials testing manualized cognitive-behavioral interventions in community mental health settings.

Susan's journey toward becoming an MBC researcher and consultant started in 2001. As a practitioner and clinic director in an academic medical setting, she applied evaluation research strategies to identify patterns in referrals and length of treatment (Kelley et al., 2001[2]) but felt hampered by an inability to use practice-based data in real time to shape program direction. In 2005, she joined Len Bickman[3] on a large-scale evaluation of

[1] John Weisz was my graduate advisor and was among the early voices in clinical psychology pointing out discrepancies between research and clinical practice (e.g., Weisz et al., 1995). He taught me that every child deserves the very best care, that rigorous science can help us get there, and that we need to test drive our practices under real-world conditions to make sure they work outside of the lab.

[2] Formerly published as Susan Douglas Kelley.

[3] Leonard Bickman is a seminal contributor to the development of program theory (Bickman, 1987), which is critical to learning how a program works rather than simply whether it works.

MBC in 28 sites across 10 states (Bickman et al., 2011). At the time, there were few measures available to inform treatment progress in youth mental health, so they partnered with clinicians to develop the Peabody Treatment Progress Battery (Riemer, Athay, et al., 2012), a collection of treatment outcome (e.g., symptom) and process (e.g., alliance, motivation for treatment) measures. They also partnered with a software company to develop feedback technology to increase ease of use. As the director of training and implementation, Susan worked side by side with their practice partners to develop an approach to ensure clinical staff and agency leaders had the knowledge, skills, and tools they needed to use MBC effectively.

In this role, she quickly realized the challenges associated with MBC training and ongoing implementation support. The perception at first was that training on the measures and a software operations manual were all that was needed. This blind spot was both simple and vast—the team assumed everyone would *value* data as a welcome addition to practice and therefore *use* the MBC feedback in practice. They quickly learned they were wrong as successful implementation varied drastically across the United States. Implementation seemed to depend on the luck of the draw as to whether a site had a visionary leader or a technology-savvy clinician.

Through strong practice–research partnerships (Riemer, Kelley, et al., 2012) and additional trials (Bickman et al., 2016), Susan and her collaborators developed a train-the-trainer approach with support for site-level readiness assessment, launch training, and ongoing coaching with clinicians. As Susan learned more about the value of a coaching approach as an effective workforce development strategy (Cannon et al., 2021; Hernandez & Douglas, 2022), she also sought her own training in coaching mindsets and methodologies. In 2014, she received her first certification in professional coaching and is currently a credentialed executive and team coach, coach supervisor, and coach educator. In 2016, she also began consulting for a behavioral health technology start-up called Mirah, where she continues today as an advisor. For several years, she was actively involved in leading dozens of MBC launches across the United States, ranging from small practice settings to large integrated healthcare systems to third-party payer solutions.

Len was also my graduate school advisor and taught me that system-level change is hard to connect to individual-level outcome improvement (Bickman, 1996). He also taught me that scientific rigor and compassion can and should coexist (Douglas, 2020).

Amanda's journey toward becoming an MBC researcher started with her thesis work, which utilized a sample of youth being treated in community mental health clinics to compare diagnoses generated via standardized diagnostic interviews with youths' chart diagnoses. Analyses revealed that agreement did not exceed chance agreement for most diagnoses and was "poor" across the board (Jensen & Weisz, 2002). These findings, which have been replicated across numerous samples and diagnostic categories (Rettew et al., 2009), spoke to a core challenge in bridging the research–practice gap: researchers and clinicians are not speaking a common language when it comes to characterizing the disorders that many evidence-based treatments (EBTs) are designed to treat, presenting a challenge to using EBTs.

She spent the next few years of her career focused on trying to understand this diagnostic gap and how to address it, including examining the implications of diagnostic disagreement for youth treatment (Jensen-Doss & Weisz, 2008), surveying clinicians to understand their attitudes toward the clinical utility of generating diagnoses as a part of care (Jensen-Doss & Hawley, 2011) and toward standardized assessment tools (Jensen-Doss & Hawley, 2010), and seeking to replicate her original findings under a broader range of clinical contexts (Jensen-Doss et al., 2014). From these studies, she concluded that (a) accurately identifying the problem to work on in treatment is important for youth outcomes, (b) many tools exist to help with this assessment process, but (c) clinicians find them impractical for use in routine care. At the same time, her own experiences as a clinician and clinical supervisor helped her realize that even gold standard diagnostic assessments typically generate a "best guess" of a youth's diagnosis that has some degree of uncertainty. Furthermore, the emergence of common elements (e.g., Chorpita et al., 2005) and transdiagnostic (e.g., Barlow et al., 2010) treatment approaches raised questions about how much diagnostic precision is even needed for effective care. The rise of these approaches, which are often modular in format, also struck her as requiring several assessment-relevant decisions across the course of treatment as clinicians decide which treatment modules to use with which clients and how to move between them.

These realizations are what led her to MBC. The notion of being able to use pragmatic measures throughout treatment to assist in identifying target problems at the beginning of treatment and modifying the treatment plan over time seemed to address many of the challenges to utilizing EBTs identified in her previous work. This is also where Amanda and Susan began to collaborate. Amanda's first grant that focused on MBC was the COMET Trial

(Jensen-Doss, Ehrenreich-May, et al., 2018), a randomized effectiveness trial comparing treatment as usual (TAU), TAU plus MBC (TAU+), and MBC plus the Unified Protocol for Adolescent Emotional Disorders (UP-A). The study design involved randomizing community mental health clinicians and adolescent clients with emotional disorders to one of the three conditions to test their effectiveness in community mental health clinics. Susan came on board the COMET trial as a consultant to train and provide consultation to the TAU+ clinicians, and our lines of work on practice-based evidence and evidence-based practice began to converge.

Convergence and Emerging Understanding of MBC as a Practice, Not Just a Tool

As we reflected on our separate and collective experiences in MBC research and development over the previous decade (2005–2017), we recognized there was a fundamental shift in how we perceived MBC. We had grown from seeing feedback as a simple tool or strategy to influence clinicians' thinking and behavior in response to data, to its being a complex practice that has the potential to influence how behavioral health care is delivered, reimbursed, and improved. In this section, we propose that MBC is a complex set of behaviors and mindsets that involve both practice competencies and developmental capabilities. We then talk about our exploration of MBC from multiple perspectives and with several collaborators. After summarizing the continued lack of progress in achieving successful and sustained MBC implementation, we detail our current research as a series of three studies that explore MBC intervention characteristics, mechanisms of action, and implementation factors.

MBC Practice Competencies and Developmental Capabilities

From 2015 to 2017, we co-led monthly consultation calls with clinicians to interpret feedback reports for their youth clients and integrate the resulting questions into case conceptualization, session planning, and treatment planning. We began conceptualizing the application of MBC as a combination of practice competencies (e.g., knowledge and skills) and developmental capabilities (e.g., qualities and behaviors that influence the proficiency of how competencies are applied) (Elias, 2016; Fouad et al., 2009).

Practice competencies can be seen and experienced and thus are readily measured as present or absent, while developmental capabilities are often related to an inner cognitive or emotional experience, and thus are more difficult to measure. Table 16.1 presents a list of MBC practice competencies and developmental capabilities we first generated during those initial consultation calls and have expanded upon since. We don't think this list is exhaustive but is indicative of the complexity of MBC practice. In addition, we believe these competencies and capabilities are role agnostic. For example, being able to articulate the "why" of MBC and motivate use is relevant to clinicians (with clients, peers), supervisors (with clinicians, clinical leaders), clinical leaders (with clinical and support staff), and executive leaders (with finance and policy staff among others).

During the COMET study, we developed and piloted an observational checklist of MBC preparation behaviors (e.g., viewed feedback), discussion of feedback report elements (e.g., trend graph or respondent comparisons),

Table 16.1 Capturing the Complexity of MBC Practice: Growing List of Feedback Practice Competencies and Developmental Capabilities

Feedback Practice Competencies	Feedback Developmental Capabilities
Able to:	*Exhibits*:
1. Explain MBC rationale and purpose	1. Motivates MBC use (e.g., rolls with resistance)
2. Operate and support others to operate MBC technology/system (e.g., navigate on computer, access paper measures)	2. Technology savvy and operational excellence
3. Interpret feedback (e.g., scores, graphs)	3. Comfort and confidence with data visualizations (e.g., graphs, percentile scores)
4. Understand feedback differences and similarities across multiple reporters	4. Holding the dialectic that multiple perspectives are informative
5. Notice feedback that is new or discrepant from existing impressions	5. Willing to acknowledge dissonant feedback as valid
6. Address MBC feedback and implementation with others	6. Collaboration with others using data-informed decision-making
7. Include feedback information in case-related documentation	7. Integrating feedback into existing workflow and tasks (e.g., case conceptualization and treatment approach)
8. Use feedback for professional development and quality improvement	8. Metacognitive ability to see and apply patterns in data to inform own and others' performance

Note: MBC = measurement-based care.

and feedback practice competencies and developmental capabilities. While the checklist was back-burnered in need of further development, recordings of 164 consultation calls that covered 294 cases were recently coded for content and consultant techniques (Casline et al., 2025). Common consultant techniques included interpretation of feedback and addressing MBC feedback with youth clients and their caregivers in past or future sessions. These correspond to competencies (3) and (6) in Table 16.1. Other less frequent topics included operation of the MBC technology, competency (2), planning how to support and increase measure completion by clients and their families, and explaining the rationale and purpose for MBC. The latter two likely correspond to competencies (1) and (2), and also capabilities (1) and (2).

Exploration of MBC From Practice- and Evidence-Based Perspectives

In the ensuing years, we have been exploring MBC and feedback from multiple perspectives and with an ever-expanding group of collaborators. We considered clinical and organizational applications of MBC in youth mental health care (Jensen-Doss et al., 2020), the utility of MBC for value-based care (Rothrock et al., 2024), and the need for an MBC professional practice guideline (Boswell et al., 2023), resulting in the development of the guideline itself. We will describe some examples of our research that have arisen from collaboration with practitioners (i.e., practice-based evidence) and compilation of available evidence by conducting several literature reviews (i.e., evidence-based practice).

When the COVID-19 pandemic began, we leveraged our experiences supporting practice partners in the disruptive shift to telehealth to collaborate with Jonathan Comer, a telehealth expert, on the rapid publication of recommendations for using MBC to enhance communication in the absence of physical proximity (Douglas et al., 2020). We later discovered supporting evidence for these theory-based recommendations in our own research. A descriptive case study of MBC implementation in a youth partial hospital program afforded a unique opportunity to explore factors associated with MBC use given that the program shift to telehealth occurred 3 months into the initial implementation process (Donelan et al., 2025). Retrospective review of MBC fidelity data showed that after an initial period of adjustment where MBC use varied substantially, implementation stabilized and remained high, with feedback report viewing by clinicians around 80%. Rates of measure completion ranged between 50% and 70% for youth clients and were somewhat lower for their caregivers. We hypothesized that clinicians supported the ongoing use of MBC, even during radical workflow changes, because they used the feedback to assess important risk factors like suicidality. We continued to explore the impact of extra-organizational factors, like the COVID-19 shift to telehealth, in a re-analysis of the INSPIRE qualitative data (Douglas et al., 2025). Using a theory-based framework to analyze the social aspects of implementing MBC, preliminary results indicate that pre-existing value and use are critical to sustaining MBC through such an extreme disruption (Douglas, Walker, et al., 2024). Themes arose that preexisting perceptions that MBC was difficult were associated with discontinuing the practice during the pandemic, while the opposite held true when MBC was considered an important part of treatment.

We are deepening our understanding of feedback as patient-centered communication that positively impacts therapeutic alliance and shared understanding in youth mental health care (Connors et al., 2025). We built on previous work defining critical characteristics for the development of MBC measures (Kelley & Bickman, 2009) to provide guidance on MBC measure selection for organizational leaders (Connors et al., 2021). We are also working with others in the broader research community to identify critical mechanisms of action in MBC treatment and implementation that could be optimized to enhance MBC's effect on treatment outcomes and organizational learning. For example, in a recently published narrative review of the literature, we summarized mechanisms of action to provide recommendations for strengthening MBC interventions and implementation (De Jong et al., 2025). We applied a clinical utility lens in a review of MBC literature to explore factors associated with usability and usefulness, including acceptability, feasibility and cost, stakeholder communication, relationships, and decision-making (McLeod et al., 2022), that could be optimized to enhance MBC's effect on outcomes.

The Elusive Goal of Sustained Successful MBC Implementation

Unfortunately, throughout this journey from the early days of MBC until now, sustained successful implementation remains elusive (Lewis et al.,

2019). Despite extensive training, ongoing coaching, and implementation monitoring as described earlier, the first Vanderbilt study found that a third of clinicians in the feedback condition never viewed a single feedback report over a two-and-a-half-year period. Yet, we found significant effects of feedback viewing on youth outcomes (Bickman et al., 2011) and decreased time to addressing problems (Douglas et al., 2015) for clinicians randomized to the session-based feedback condition compared with the 90-day feedback control condition. The second Vanderbilt study (Bickman et al., 2016) found that there is a tipping point where implementation failure negates the possibility of feedback influencing outcomes. Post-hoc analyses in both studies found a dose–response effect of feedback, where more feedback viewed correlated with better treatment outcomes. In the COMET study, clinicians administered measures for 90% of sessions and viewed feedback nearly 75% of the time, with implementation increasing as a function of how much consultation clinicians received (Woodard et al., 2025). However, when clinicians reported how they actually used the data, the picture was quite different. They indicated using it in only approximately one-fifth of sessions and focused more on current symptoms rather than reviewing longitudinal trends or incorporating feedback into treatment planning (Casline et al., 2022).

MBC Characteristics, Mechanisms, and Implementation Factors: A Series of Three Studies

Because MBC implementability and usefulness are likely intertwined (McLeod et al., 2022), we knew we wanted to proactively study MBC characteristics, mechanisms, and implementation factors. We embarked separately and together on three studies that are all intended to produce pragmatic applications that bridge that practice–research gap that influenced our early professional years.

In 2017, the first study arose from Susan's collaboration with the International Network for Psychotherapy Innovations and Research into Effectiveness (INSPIRE), a group of researchers across Europe and the United States whose work focuses on progress feedback systems in mental health. In addition to partnering on a recently published position paper (De Jong et al., 2025), the group produced an empirically derived qualitative coding scheme for MBC implementation that accounts for the dynamic nature of barriers and facilitators across multiple levels of use (Douglas et al., 2025). Based on interviews with clinical staff, managers, and leaders from nine agencies in three countries, it is hoped that the INSPIRE qualitative coding scheme can help promote a common language for MBC implementation and contribute to practice-oriented research using rapid-cycle mixed methods evaluation (Skillman et al., 2019). Additional analyses are currently underway with the application of normalization process theory coding (May et al., 2020), which focuses on the social process of implementation (Douglas, Walker, et al., 2024).

In 2022, the second study began in collaboration with Elizabeth Casline, a graduate student mentee, and Bryce McLeod, a collaborator in the area of treatment fidelity research (e.g., McLeod et al., 2023). Mandy began developing a multi-method model of assessing fidelity to MBC, combining digital usage data, clinician self-report, and observational coding of therapy sessions (Casline, 2023). They (Jensen-Doss & McLeod) have a pending award from the National Institute of Mental Health to conduct a secondary data analysis of the COMET trial utilizing these methods to identify the key MBC practices that most leverage the mechanisms and outcomes of MBC. The overall goal of this work is to develop a protocol for MBC that helps train clinicians in the key practices that optimize outcomes when using MBC in youth mental health.

Together, we received funding in 2019 from the National Institute of Mental Health for the third study, comparing unidimensional MBC (i.e., symptom feedback only) with multidimensional MBC (i.e., symptoms plus process measures). We employed an effectiveness implementation hybrid design (Curran et al., 2012), which is a test of an intervention while gathering information on fidelity and implementation. This allowed us to combine the benefits of comparative effectiveness research, where client-level outcomes are examined in clinical settings, with implementation research, where clinician- and organization-level outcomes are the focus. A study goal was to develop and pilot methods to describe MBC implementation fidelity as influenced by both challenges and the strategies used to adapt to those challenges. With extensions due to the COVID-19 pandemic, the study ended in April 2024 with feedback data from over 1,000 youth clients and their caregivers who were treated by over 100 direct care staff in outpatient, intensive outpatient, and in-home treatment settings. Primary analyses are underway.

Unpacking the Complexity With New Models, Methods, and Mindsets

Our research together and with an ever-growing network of collaborators has contributed to the development of a theory-based model of MBC that incorporates mechanisms of action for outcomes and implementation. Informed by seminal work on program theory developed by Bickman (1987) and Weiss (1995) among others, our model is called the Golden Thread Feedback Framework because it focuses on the connections or linkages that can increase visibility into potential levers of change for explaining outcomes and improving implementation. While we believe MBC mechanisms are dynamic and intertwined, we will present our model in two parts for simplicity's sake, one at the individual level and the other at the organizational level.

As shown in Figure 16.1, the first part of the model presents MBC mechanisms from the "inside-out," where the focus is on the clinician–client dyad and the bidirectional influences of individual learning and action. The second part of the model presents the "outside-in" mechanisms of organizational learning and action that influence MBC implementability and usability.

The model represents a plethora of opportunities to inform how MBC influences outcomes and how people can improve the use of MBC and add

Figure 16.1 The Golden Thread Feedback Framework: Individual and Organizational Mechanisms

Note: Two people are seated at a table facing each other, with a bidirectional arrow and words "mechanisms of individual learning and action" above. Below are the words "mechanisms of organizational learning and action" with arrows pointing in on the left and right of the figure.

value to enhance clinical work and quality at all levels. In this section we describe the Golden Thread Feedback Framework, including brief descriptions of methodological innovations and mindset shifts that resulted from its development, and how it influenced our approach to training and implementation support.

Person-Centered MBC: An "Inside-Out" View of Dynamic and Bidirectional Processes at Clinician and Client Levels

Our approach is grounded in theories of MBC mechanisms of action at both the clinician and client level. These dual and intersecting processes are illustrated in Figure 16.2.

At the clinician level, *contextual feedback intervention theory* (CFIT; Riemer & Bickman, 2011) proposes that outcomes improve when clinicians view feedback, recognize a discrepancy between treatment goals and client status, and experience cognitive dissonance. If the clinician accepts this feedback, this leads to them taking action, which could involve steps such as discussing it with a supervisor, addressing feedback in an upcoming session, or incorporating it into case conceptualization. To facilitate this clinician-level process, our training approach included materials that helped clinicians understand the MBC measures and resulting feedback, training and coaching focused on helping clinicians "get curious" about feedback rather than viewing it as critical of their work, and creating a culture of feedback where clinicians and supervisors discuss and interpret feedback together (Douglas, Woodard, et al., 2025).

At the client level, *therapeutic assessment theory* (Finn & Tonsager, 1997) posits that assessment and feedback enhances outcome by improving the client's understanding of their problems, their treatment engagement, and the therapy alliance. The *collect, share, act model* (Barber & Resnick, 2022) provides a very useful framework for laying out clinician behaviors that can operate on these mechanisms, as it describes a collaborative process that engages clients throughout the MBC process, including explaining the rationale of MBC to clients in the initial session, collaborating with them to choose measures when possible, sharing the data with clients regularly, and working collaboratively to interpret the feedback and choose a plan of action. To enhance this client-level process, training strategies included scripts and handouts for explaining MBC to clients, presentation of

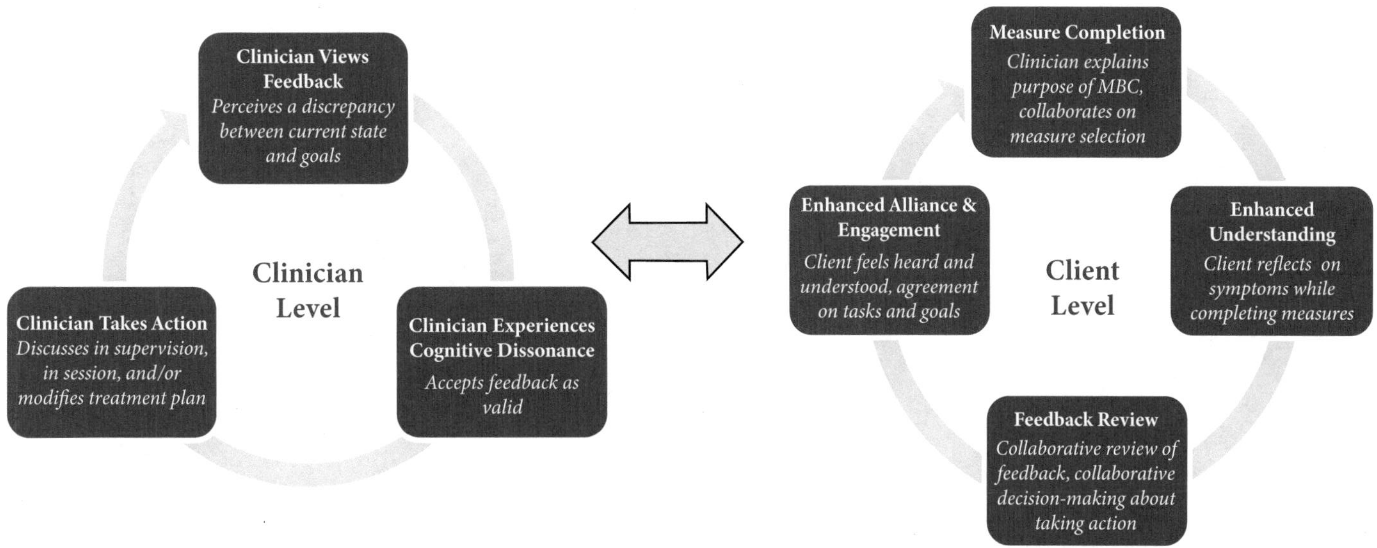

Figure 16.2 Dual and Intersecting Processes of MBC at Clinician and Client Levels

Note: Two cycles are represented with a bidirectional arrow between them, representing the clinician on the left and the client on the right. Each cycle shows a circular relationship among experiences and actions. MBC = measurement-based care.

case examples, demonstrating how feedback could be incorporated into sessions, and behavioral rehearsal (e.g., role-playing feedback discussions, role-plays where clinicians practice incorporating MBC into sessions). While we did not test our coaching model directly, promising evidence from a pilot of our coaching model, adapted for feedback-informed group therapy, found it was highly rated by clinicians (Koementas-de Vos et al., 2024). Compared with those who had not engaged in coaching, clinicians self-reported greater frequency of experimentation with using MBC feedback in treatment, and their patients reported greater frequency of feedback discussions that were considered useful.

Measuring how MBC data informs clients' and clinicians' thinking and behavior requires multiple methods across the clinical workflow. At minimum, implementation metadata available from the MBC technology provides quantitative data on session-based measure completion by clients and their caregivers and feedback viewing by clinicians. It may even be possible to tell when feedback reports were opened, and how that aligns with the timing of a treatment session to gather data on sharing of feedback visuals in session. Questions about MBC behaviors (e.g., discussing feedback with a supervisor or in session with a client) can be added to measures completed by clinicians, supervisors, and clients. Qualitative methods include dyad interviews with clients and clinicians (Brooks Holliday et al., 2021) and clinical case examples (e.g., Douglas, Woodard, et al., 2025; Jensen-Doss et al., 2020). It is also important to assess MBC practice competencies and developmental capabilities as listed above in Table 16.1, such as attitudes toward feedback, openness to feedback, and comfort with technology (De Jong et al., 2012; Jensen-Doss, Haimes, et al., 2018).

Importantly, this dynamic model of dual and intersecting processes at clinician and client levels led us to three critical shifts in our thinking. First, we would expect change may occur over time both within clinicians (as experience grows with multiple clients) and within clinician–client dyads as learning occurs. Anecdotally, it has been our experience that the more a clinician uses MBC, the more they want to use it. Because not all feedback reports have novel information, several must be viewed before there is a notable discrepancy or signal that can lead to an "aha" moment where the feedback shifts the clinician's understanding of a case (Kelley & Bickman, 2009). Thus, use of repeated measures over time is a recommended research design. Second, with a focus on explaining outcomes and improving implementation, it is important to create measurement strategies that can be used as both research instruments and as self-assessment tools. Our third mindset shift, which has substantial implications for how to support clinicians in coping with the vulnerable moment of cognitive dissonance, has been a shift from considering what feedback data *tell us* toward asking what the data *make us curious about.* Asking a question opens a window of opportunity for partnering with others (e.g., a client or supervisor) and could serve to ease the "sting" of what may be perceived as negative feedback. Asking a question can increase acceptance of feedback as valid and actionable, which CFIT states is required for feedback to have a positive effect on behavior (Riemer & Bickman, 2011).

Systemic MBC: An "Outside-In" View of Dynamic and Multidirectional Processes at All Levels of the Organization

Figure 16.3 provides a high-level overview of the levels of the system and methodological strategies we've used for both assessing and influencing MBC implementation. Culture is defined as the "why" of the organization, which is largely stable, evidenced in organizational purpose and mission, and influenced by organizational values, attitudes, and beliefs (Schein, 1985). Climate is more open to influence and consists of the "what" of an organization, which includes habits and behaviors evidenced in structures (e.g., policies, procedures, job descriptions, documentation standards) and processes (e.g., training, supervision, management practices).

We have used this figure to guide training and consultation, develop research methods, and inform ongoing implementation strategy. When used to organize change management strategy sessions with agency leaders, we've found that visuals like this contribute quickly to shared understanding about how MBC can support their business priorities. The pyramid shape is intended to draw attention to how small the MBC tool is in the context of the larger organization. The bidirectional arrow represents the "golden thread" of reinforcing feedback loops that impact how people value and use feedback in different roles and at different levels of an organization (Douglas et al., 2016; Douglas, Woodard, et al., 2025).

Olamide Olowe, a data-driven start-up founder, says to "color [the] data with culture" (Fox, 2022). Time and time again, this visual helped us to "right-size" our focus on MBC and shift our attention to the knowledge transfer processes, integration with existing structures, and alignment within

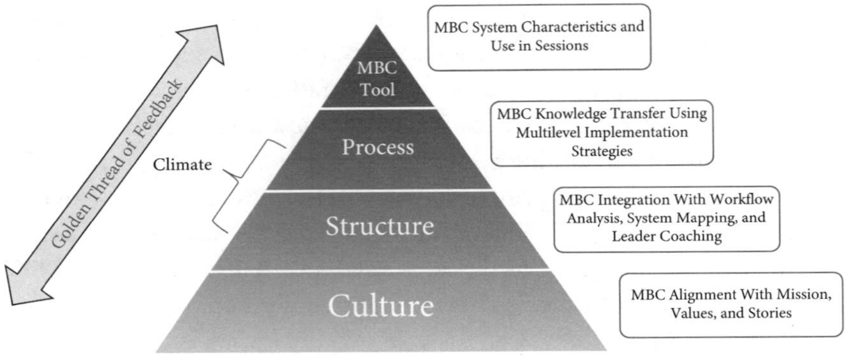

Figure 16.3 Holistic View of System Levels and Associated MBC Strategies to Leverage Knowledge Transfer for Individual and Organizational Learning
Note: A pyramid in the center shows the relationship the MBC tool has to process, structure, and culture. A bidirectional arrow to the left is titled "Golden Thread of Feedback" with explanatory text to the right. MBC = measurement-based care.

the larger organizational culture. Early in a project we begin meeting with agency leaders to better align MBC with the organizational mission, vision, and values and learn about implicit organizational norms that may influence internal communication, motivation, and accountability related to MBC use. We structure these engagements to educate leaders about MBC and its benefits, provide language for internal communication, and facilitate co-ownership in the implementation process.

We assess and address four common limiting factors that may influence receptivity to a positive feedback culture: (1) negative attitudes toward the electronic health record (EHR), (2) perceptions that the presence of data indicates a compliance issue or research, (3) the understanding that feedback is constructive criticism, and (4) agency-level key performance indicators (KPIs) that are based on reimbursable activities. For the first two factors, it's important to keep in mind that MBC is often experienced as "more data" rather than as a useful form of patient-centered communication. Consider the language and visuals used in MBC consultation and training—how might negative beliefs about the relevance of data to clinical practice be unintentionally reinforced? We suggest introducing MBC like any evidence-based practice, using stories and behavioral rehearsal to create experience rather than starting with a tutorial for operating the technology.

While feedback as constructive criticism comes with positive intentions, it's still criticism. Such a remedial approach can be a signal that feedback may be experienced more as correcting a problem, whereas a developmental approach is an iterative user-centered method to creating better solutions (Liedtka, 2020). For example, we often hear suggestions that MBC is helpful for new clinicians but not as necessary for those with more experience. Yet, doesn't every medical provider, no matter how experienced, collect common health metrics (blood pressure, temperature) at every single visit and then use the resulting information to guide the conversation when warranted?

Finally, a common change management strategy is to follow the money (i.e., assess performance and promotion practices). In healthcare systems where reimbursement is based on units of productivity, there may be a lack of existing structure and process to reward care quality. When aggregated, MBC data present an opportunity to strengthen the connection between what is measured and what is managed. Note that we are not proposing to use MBC outcome data for individual clinician performance evaluation (Casline, Douglas, et al., 2025) but, rather, shifting existing organizational performance metrics to incorporate MBC data (e.g., MBC implementation metrics become part of regular documentation auditing procedures). MBC data can be useful in bridging the care and commercialization gap to connect care quality with successful business outcomes. This can facilitate the use of data to inform performance from not just an outcomes lens but also measuring progress toward outcomes.

We also explore how data are present and used in everyday managerial decision-making, encouraging a shift to a "positive feedback culture" (Moss & Mousavizadeh, 2017; Mousavi & Kheirandish, 2017). We assess and address group dynamics like psychological safety (Edmondson, 1999) to increase culture fit for our key mindset of using feedback data to develop clinical hypotheses rather than conclusions. We incorporate agency mission, vision, and values into MBC training materials and invite leaders to co-present. Finally, we support leaders sharing critical stories of change, knowing that meaningful narratives can be powerful motivators (Douglas, Galvin, et al., 2024).

MBC and practice-oriented research share a focus on improving outcomes using evidence. We find that integrating MBC and practice-oriented research expands attention across the multiple systems in an organization. For example, a theme arising from preliminary qualitative coding of office leader and supervisor interviews was that clinician buy-in and investment in MBC depended more on local conditions than organizational level strategies (Douglas, Galvin, et al., 2024). This has informed our implementation strategy, where we use a mix of external supports and internal strategies to support integration of MBC into clinic settings. External supports included change management consultation with local and executive-level leaders, partial time (1–2 hours per week) funding for MBC champions in each office, and construction of weekly implementation benchmarks for each office. Internal strategies were co-developed together with agency staff based on findings from assessment tools like readiness assessments, system mapping, and workflow analysis to identify priority avenues for MBC integration into existing documentation procedures, supervision structures, meeting agendas, treatment intake procedures, new hire training, and so on.

MBC knowledge transfer generally followed a phased approach with increasing complexity over time: supporting MBC operations and interpretation of feedback reports, problem-solving and realignment of MBC with clinical workflow, and then broadening MBC into everyday office culture (e.g., use of aggregated implementation metrics as benchmarks for improvement). Multilevel strategies included didactic training, scripts, brief (2–3 minutes) videos for each feedback measure, operations manuals, checklists, and ongoing coaching and consultation. Just like our earlier recommendation to create measurement strategies for both research and self-assessment, we suggest viewing system-level implementation strategies as opportunities to embed evaluation to guide future iteration cycles. For example, emerging data presentations can be a vehicle for organizational leaders to integrate data into program development and iteration. We facilitated such a "data design sprint" with an agency partner's learning and development team and found that it created opportunities to model use of data for process improvement (Douglas, Cavanaugh, et al., 2024).

Call to Action and Future Directions for Practice-Oriented Research

Ultimately, we believe that improving the effectiveness of MBC on outcomes and sustaining successful implementation comes down to a shift from just using feedback data to correct problems to approaching feedback data as an opportunity to learn and grow. This requires the recognition that the generation of knowledge is a social process influenced by human values, beliefs, and culture (Weinberger, 2019). Amy Edmondson calls this the "right kind of wrong" where psychological safety reduces interpersonal barriers to failing well, and "failing well, perhaps even living well, requires us to become vigorously humble and curious—a state that does not come naturally to adults" (2023, p. 168).

Innovative methods are needed to better study and influence MBC as it happens. In a world of ever-increasing complexity, it is vital that we leverage methods from implementation science and practice-oriented research to create a learning healthcare system (Youn et al., 2024). An approach that is both human centered, with a focus on the people, and systems oriented enables us to see the connections and root causes among people and levels of the system (Douglas, Page, et al., 2024). The systemic bias that can limit receptivity to a positive feedback culture needs to be addressed from the top down, while understanding individual motivations to better influence behavior is best done from the bottom up. An iterative approach to MBC implementation that focuses on connections within and among layers of a system can increase opportunities for partnership and knowledge transfer, both key aspects of sustainability and organizational learning.

We also encourage researchers to collaborate across disciplines and partner with practice organizations and technology developers where possible. Practice-oriented researchers who incorporate MBC or routine outcome monitoring as part of their investigation of clinical routine can shed light on the broader array of feedback practice competencies and developmental capabilities that were introduced previously in Table 16.1. Irrespective of the aspect of routine clinical setting or practice that is being investigated, the inclusion of MBC and feedback can provide relevant data on treatment process and outcomes while also furthering our understanding of MBC itself. The use of dual-focus research designs, like the hybrid effectiveness-implementation design we used in our NIMH study, can allow for more complex exploration of MBC mechanisms of action associated with different levels of the system, from the intervention itself to the treatment dyad (clinician and client/caregiver) to the influence of supervision and management to contextual factors associated with culture, climate, and external healthcare setting. Ideally, we would encourage more bridge-spanning partnerships such as ours, where new perspectives may emerge from an inclusive focus on practice-based evidence and evidence-based practice.

Acknowledgments

Dr. Douglas's and Dr. Jensen-Doss's time on this manuscript was supported by R34 MH118316.

Conflict of Interest Disclosures

Vanderbilt University and Susan Douglas receive compensation related to the Peabody Treatment Progress Battery, Susan Douglas has a financial relationship with MIRAH, and both are MBC tools. The author declares a potential conflict of interest. There is a management plan in place at Vanderbilt University to monitor that this potential conflict does not jeopardize the objectivity of Dr. Douglas's research.

References

Barber, J., & Resnick, S. G. (2022). Collect, Share, Act: A transtheoretical clinical model for doing measurement-based care in mental health treatment. *Psychological Services, 20*(Suppl. 2), 150–157. https://doi.org/10.1037/ser0000629

Barlow, D. H., Farchione, T. J., Fairholme, C. P., Ellard, K. K., Boisseau, C. L., Allen, L. B., & Ehrenreich May, J. T. (2010). *Unified protocol for transdiagnostic treatment of emotional disorders: Therapist guide.* Oxford University Press. https://doi.org/10.1093/med:psych/9780199772667.001.0001

Bickman, L. (1987). Using program theory in evaluation. *New Directions for Program Evaluation, 1987*(33), 5–18. https://doi.org/10.1002/ev.1443

Bickman, L. (1996). A continuum of care. More is not always better. *American Psychologist, 51*(7), 689–701. https://doi.org/10.1037//0003-066x.51.7.689

Bickman, L., Douglas, S., De Andrade, A. R., Vides, Tomlinson, M., Gleacher, A., Olin, S., & Hoagwood, K. (2016). Implementing a measurement feedback system: A tale of two sites. *Administration and Policy in Mental Health and Mental Health Services Research, 43*(3), 410–425. https://doi.org/10.1007/s10488-015-0647-8.

Bickman, L., Kelley, S. D., Breda, C., de Andrade, A. R., & Riemer, M. (2011). Effects of routine feedback to clinicians on mental health outcomes of youths: Results of a randomized trial. *Psychiatric Services, 62*(12), 1423–1429. https://doi.org/10.1176/appi.ps.002052011

Boswell, J. F., Hepner, K. A., Lysell, K., Rothrock, N. E., Bott, N., Childs, A. W., Douglas, S., Owings-Fonner, N., Wright, C. V., Stephens, K. A., Bard, D. E., Aajmain, S., & Bobbitt, B. L. (2023). The need for a measurement-based care professional practice guideline. *Psychotherapy, 60*, 1–16. https://doi.org/10.1037/pst0000439

Brooks Holliday, S., Hepner, K. A., Farmer, C. M., Mahmud, A., Kimerling, R., Smith, B. N., & Rosen, C. (2021). Discussing measurement-based care with patients: An analysis of clinician-patient dyads. *Psychotherapy Research, 31*(2), 211–223. https://doi.org/10.1080/10503307.2020.1776413

Cannon, M., Douglas, S., & Butler, D. (2021). Developing coaching mindset and skills. *Management Teaching Review, 6*(4), 330–349. https://doi.org/10.1177/23792981211006877

Casline, E. (2023). *Measurement-based care observational coding system: Measure development and evaluation* [Doctoral dissertation]. University of Miami. https://scholarship.miami.edu/esploro/outputs/991031825217702976

Casline, E., Douglas, S., van Sonsbeek, M., Okamura, K., & Jensen-Doss, A. (2025). Measurement-based care as a tool to detect and prevent harm in youth psychotherapy. *Research on Child and Adolescent Psychopathology*, 53, 655-668. https://doi.org/10.1007/s10802-024-01262-1

Casline, E., Woodard, G. S., Lane, E., Pollowitz, S., Douglas, S., Ehrenreich-May, J., Ginsburg, G. S., & Jensen-Doss, A. (2025). Consultation content and techniques for measurement-based care implementation in youth community mental health settings. *Administration and Policy in Mental Health and Mental Health Services Research*, *52*, 401–414. https://doi.org/10.1007/s10488-024-01417-8

Casline, E., Woodard, G., Patel, Z. S., Phillips, D., Ehrenreich-May, J., Ginsburg, G. S., & Jensen-Doss, A. (2022). Characterizing measurement-based care implementation using therapist report. *Evidence-Based Practice in Child and Adolescent Mental Health*, *8*(4), 1–11. https://doi.org/10.1080/23794925.2022.2124555

Chorpita, B. F., Daleiden, E. L., & Weisz, J. R. (2005). Identifying and selecting the common elements of evidence based interventions: A distillation and matching model. *Mental Health Services Research*, *7*(1), 5–20. https://doi.org/10.1007/s11020-005-1962-6

Connors, E. H., Childs, A. W., Douglas, S., & Jensen-Doss, A. (2025). Data-informed communication: How measurement-based care can optimize child psychotherapy. *Administration and Policy in Mental Health*, *52*, 179–193. https://doi.org/10.1007/s10488-024-01372-4

Connors, E. H., Douglas, S., Jensen-Doss, A., Landes, S. J., Lewis, C. C., McLeod, B. D., Stanick, C., & Lyon, A. R. (2021). What gets measured gets done: How mental health agencies can leverage measurement-based care for better patient care, clinician supports, and organizational goals. *Administration and Policy in Mental Health and Mental Health Services Research*, *48*(2), 250–265. https://doi.org/10.1007/s10488-020-01063-w

Curran, G. M., Bauer, M., Mittman, B., Pyne, J. M., & Stetler, C. (2012). Effectiveness-implementation hybrid designs. *Medical Care*, *50*(3), 217–226. https://doi.org/10.1097/MLR.0b013e3182408812

De Jong, K., Douglas, S., Wolpert, M., Delgadillo, J., Aas, B., Bovendeerd, B., Carlier, I. V. E., Compare, A., Edbrooke-Childs, J., Janse, P. D., Lutz, W., Moltu, C., Nordberg, S., Poulsen, S., Rubel, J., Schiepek, G. K., Schilling, V., van Sonsbeek, M., & Barkham, M. (2025). Using progress feedback to enhance treatment outcomes: A narrative review. *Administration and Policy in Mental Health and Mental Health Services Research, 52*, 210–222. https://doi.org/10.1007/s10488-024-01381-3

De Jong, K., van Sluis, P., Nugter, M. A., Heiser, W. J., & Spinhoven, P. (2012). Understanding the differential impact of outcome monitoring: Therapist variables that moderate feedback effects in a randomized clinical trial. *Psychotherapy Research*, *22*(4), 464–474. https://doi.org/10.1080/10503307.2012.673023

Donelan, J., Douglas, S., Willson, A., Lester, T., & Daly, S. (2025). Implementing measurement-based care in a youth partial hospital setting: Leveraging feedback for sustainability. *Administration and Policy in Mental Health, 52*, 128–145. https://doi.org/10.1007/s10488-024-01358-2

Douglas, S. (2020). An innovator and a disruptor: Leonard Bickman on program theory, null findings, and advice to future child mental health services researchers. *Administration and Policy in Mental Health and Mental Health Services Research*, *47*, 788–794. https://doi.org/10.1007/s10488-020-01043-0

Douglas, S., Bovendeerd, B., van Sonsbeek, M., Manns, M., Milling, X. P., Tyler, K., Bala, N., Satterthwaite, T., Hovland, R. T., Amble, I., Atzil-Slonim, D., Barkham, M., de Jong, K., Kendrick, T., Nordberg, S. S., Lutz, W., Rubel, J. A., Skjulsvik, T., & Moltu, C. (2025). A clinical leadership lens on implementing progress feedback in three countries: Development of a multidimensional qualitative coding scheme. *Administration and Policy in Mental Health and Mental Health Services Research, 52*, 11–27. https://doi.org/10.1007/s10488-023-01314-6

Douglas, S., Button, S., & Casey, S. E. (2016). Implementing for sustainability: Promoting use of a measurement feedback system for innovation and quality improvement. *Administration and Policy in Mental Health and Mental Health Services Research, 43*(3), 286–291. https://doi.org/10.1007/s10488-014-0607-8

Douglas, S., Cavanaugh, P., Zahora, J., Jensen-Doss, A., Walker, E., Galvin, C., & Hines, K. (2024). *Data design sprints: Using a human-centered systems lens to build evaluation capacity and organizational learning for measurement-based care* [Unpublished manuscript]. Vanderbilt University.

Douglas, S., Galvin, C., Walker, E., & Jensen-Doss, A. (2024). *The social process of implementing measurement-based care in community mental health settings: Application of Normalization Process Theory* [Unpublished manuscript]. Vanderbilt University.

Douglas, S., Jensen-Doss, A., Ordorica, C., & Comer, J. S. (2020). Strategies to enhance communication with telemental health measurement-based care (tMBC). *Practice Innovations, 5*(2), 143–149. https://doi.org/10.1037/pri0000119

Douglas, S., Jonghyuk, B., de Andrade, A. R. V., Tomlinson, M. M., Hargraves, R. P., & Bickman, L. (2015). Feedback mechanisms of change: How problem alerts reported by youth clients and their caregivers impact clinician-reported session content. *Psychotherapy Research, 25*(6), 678–693. https://doi.org/10.1080/10503307.2015.1059966

Douglas, S., Page, A., Moltu, C., Kyron, M., & Satterthwaite, T. (2024). The connections matter: Bi-directional learning in program evaluation and practice-oriented research. *Administration and Policy in Mental Health and Mental Health Services Research, 51*, 318–335. https://doi.org/10.1007/s10488-023-01304-8

Douglas, S., Walker, E., Galvin, C., van Sonsbeek, M., Bovendeerd, B., & Moltu, C. (2024). *"It's just how we do it": The social process of implementing measurement-based care in international settings and the impact of COVID-19 restrictions* [Unpublished manuscript]. Vanderbilt University.

Douglas, S., Woodard, G., Zahora, J., Love, T., & Jensen-Doss, A. (2025). Transforming data into action: A case study on progress feedback in youth mental health. In J. Rubel & W. Lutz (Eds.), *Feedback-informed psychological therapy. CBT: Science into practice* (pp. 239–259). Springer Nature.

Edmondson, A. C. (1999). Psychological safety and learning behavior in work teams. *Administrative Science Quarterly, 44*(2), 350–383. https://doi.org/10.2307/2666999

Edmondson, A. C. (2023). *Right kind of wrong: The science of failing well.* Atria Books.

Elias, L. (2016). Using capability frameworks for career development. *Training & Development, 43*(4), 6–8.

Finn, S. E., & Tonsager, M. E. (1997). Information-gathering and therapeutic models of assessment: Complementary paradigms. *Psychological Assessment, 9*(4), 374–385. https://doi.org/10.1037/1040-3590.9.4.374

Fouad, N. A., Grus, C. L., Hatcher, R. L., Kaslow, N. J., Hutchings, P. S., Madson, M. B., Collins Jr., F. L., & Crossman, R. E. (2009). Competency benchmarks: A model for understanding and measuring competence in professional psychology across training levels. *Training and Education in Professional Psychology, 3*(4, Suppl.), S5–S26. https://doi.org/10.1037/a0015832

Fox, M. (2022, November 10). Topicals founder Olamide Olowe is youngest black woman ever to raise $10 million in funding. *Forbes.* https://www.forbes.com/sites/meimeifox/2022/11/10/topicals-founder-olamide-olowe-is-youngest-black-woman-ever-to-raise-10-million-in-funding/

Hernandez, V. R., & Douglas, S. (2022). Coaching and social work: A strategy for developing leadership and the workforce. *Advances in Social Work, 22*(2), 856–875. https://doi.org/10.18060/24949

Institute of Medicine (US) Committee on Quality of Health Care in America. (2001). *Crossing the quality chasm: A new health system for the 21st century.* National Academies Press (US). http://www.ncbi.nlm.nih.gov/books/NBK222274/

Jensen, A. L., & Weisz, J. R. (2002). Assessing match and mismatch between practitioner-generated and standardized interview-generated diagnoses for clinic-referred children and adolescents. *Journal of Consulting and Clinical Psychology, 70*(1), 158–168. https://doi.org/10.1037/0022-006x.70.1.158

Jensen-Doss, A., Douglas, S., Phillips, D. A., Gencdur, O., Zalman, A., & Gomez, N. E. (2020). Measurement-based care as a practice improvement tool: Clinical and organizational applications in youth mental health. *Evidence-Based Practice in Child and Adolescent Mental Health, 5*(3), 233–250. https://doi.org/10.1080/23794925.2020.1784062

Jensen-Doss, A., Ehrenreich-May, J., Nanda, M. M., Maxwell, C. A., LoCurto, J., Shaw, A. M., Souer, H., Rosenfield, D., & Ginsburg, G. S. (2018). Community Study of Outcome Monitoring for Emotional Disorders in Teens (COMET): A comparative effectiveness trial of a transdiagnostic treatment and a measurement feedback system. *Contemporary Clinical Trials, 74*, 18–24. https://doi.org/10.1016/j.cct.2018.09.011

Jensen-Doss, A., Haimes, E. M. B., Smith, A. M., Lyon, A. R., Lewis, C. C., Stanick, C. F., & Hawley, K. M. (2018). Monitoring treatment progress and providing feedback is viewed favorably but rarely used in practice. *Administration and Policy in Mental Health and Mental Health Services Research, 45*, 48–61. https://doi.org/10.1007/s10488-016-0763-0

Jensen-Doss, A., & Hawley, K. M. (2010). Understanding barriers to evidence-based assessment: Clinician attitudes toward standardized assessment tools. *Journal of Clinical Child & Adolescent Psychology, 39*(6), 885–896. https://doi.org/10.1080/15374416.2010.517169

Jensen-Doss, A., & Hawley, K. M. (2011). Understanding clinicians' diagnostic practices: Attitudes toward the utility of diagnosis and standardized diagnostic tools. *Administration and Policy in Mental Health and Mental Health Services Research, 38*(6), 476–485. https://doi.org/10.1007/s10488-011-0334-3

Jensen-Doss, A., & Weisz, J. R. (2008). Diagnostic agreement predicts treatment process and outcomes in youth mental health clinics. *Journal of Consulting and Clinical Psychology, 76*(5), 711–722. https://doi.org/10.1037/0022-006X.76.5.711

Jensen-Doss, A., Youngstrom, E. A., Youngstrom, J. K., Feeny, N. C., & Findling, R. L. (2014). Predictors and moderators of agreement between clinical and research diagnoses for children and adolescents. *Journal of Consulting and Clinical Psychology, 82*(6), 1151–1162. https://doi.org/10.1037/a0036657

Kelley, S. D., & Bickman, L. (2009). Beyond outcomes monitoring: Measurement feedback systems in child and adolescent clinical practice. *Current Opinion in Psychiatry, 22*(4), 363–368. https://doi.org/doi:10.1097/YCO.0b013e32832c9162

Kelley, S. D., Van Horn, M., & DeMaso, D. R. (2001). Using process evaluation to describe a hospital-based clinic for children coping with medical stressors. *Journal of Pediatric Psychology, 26*(7), 407–415. https://doi.org/10.1093/jpepsy/26.7.407

Koementas-de Vos, M. M. W., Tiemens, B., Engelsbel, F., de Jong, K., Witteman, C. L. M., & Nugter, M. A. (2024). Renewed feedback-informed group treatment for patients with anxiety and depressive disorders. *Administration and Policy in Mental Health and Mental Health Services Research.* https://doi.org/10.1007/s10488-023-01338-y

Lewis, C. C., Boyd, M., Puspitasari, A., Navarro, E., Howard, J., Kassab, H., Hoffman, M., Scott, K., Lyon, A., Douglas, S., Simon, G., & Kroenke, K. (2019). Implementing measurement-based care in behavioral health: A review. *JAMA Psychiatry, 76*(3), 324–335. https://doi.org/10.1001/jamapsychiatry.2018.3329

Liedtka, J. (2020). Putting technology in its place: Design thinking's social technology at work. *California Management Review, 62*(2), 53–83. https://doi.org/10.1177/0008125619897391

May, C., Finch, T., & Rapley, T. (2020). Normalization process theory. In P. Nilsen & S. A. Birken (Eds.), *Handbook on implementation science* (pp. 144–167). Edward Elgar Publishing.

McLeod, B. D., Jensen-Doss, A., Lyon, A. R., Douglas, S., & Beidas, R. S. (2022). To utility and beyond! Specifying and advancing the utility of measurement-based care for youth. *Journal of Clinical Child & Adolescent Psychology*, 1–14. https://doi.org/10.1080/15374416.2022.2042698

McLeod, B. D., Porter, N., Hogue, A., Becker-Haimes, E. M., & Jensen-Doss, A. (2023). What is the status of multi-informant treatment fidelity research? *Journal of Clinical Child & Adolescent Psychology, 52*(1), 74–94. https://doi.org/10.1080/15374416.2022.2151713

Moss, R. K., & Mousavizadeh, V. (2017). Implementing feedback-informed treatment: Challenges and solutions. In D. S. Prescott, C. L. Maeschalck, & S. D. Miller (Eds.), *Feedback-informed treatment in clinical practice: Reaching for excellence.* (pp. 101–121). American Psychological Association. https://doi.org/10.1037/0000039-006

Mousavi, S., & Kheirandish, R. (2017). Policy making with behavioral insight. *Journal of Behavioral Economics for Policy, 1*(1), 41–46.

Rettew, D. C., Lynch, A. D., Achenbach, T. M., Dumenci, L., & Ivanova, M. Y. (2009). Meta-analyses of agreement between diagnoses made from clinical evaluations and standardized diagnostic interviews. *International Journal of Methods in Psychiatric Research, 18*(3), 169–184. https://doi.org/10.1002/mpr.289

Riemer, M., Athay, M. M., Bickman, L., Breda, C., Douglas Kelley, S., & Vides de Andrade, A. R. (2012). The Peabody Treatment Progress Battery: History and methods for developing a comprehensive measurement battery for youth mental health. *Administration and Policy in Mental Health and Mental Health Services Research, 39*, 3–12. https://doi.org/doi:10.1007/s10488-012-0404-1

Riemer, M., & Bickman, L. (2011). Using program theory to link social psychology and program evaluation. In M. M. Mark, S. I. Donaldson, & B. Campbell (Eds.), *Social Psychology and Evaluation* (pp. 102–139). Guilford Press.

Riemer, M., Kelley, S. D., Casey, S., & Haynes, K. T. (2012). Developing effective research-practice partnerships for creating a culture of evidence-based decision making. *Administration and Policy in Mental Health and Mental Health Services Research, 39*(4), 248–257. https://doi.org/10.1007/s10488-011-0368-6

Rothrock, N. E., Bott, N., Douglas, S., McKune, E. W., Owings-Fonner, N., Ross, D., Stephens, K. A., Bard, D., Bobbitt, B. L., Childs, A. W., Doucette, A. M., Hepner, K. A., Lanca, M., Lysell, K., & Wright, C. V. (2024). Understanding and preparing for value-based care: A primer for behavioral health providers. *Professional Psychology: Research and Practice, 55*(1), 68–78. https://doi.org/10.1037/pro0000537

Schein, E. H. (1985). *Organizational culture and leadership: A dynamic view.* Jossey-Bass.

Senge, P. (1998). Sharing knowledge. *Executive Excellence, 15*(6), 11–12.

Skillman, M., Cross-Barnet, C., Singer, R. F., Rotondo, C., Ruiz, S., & Moiduddin, A. (2019). A framework for rigorous qualitative research as a component of mixed method rapid-cycle evaluation. *Qualitative Health Research, 29*(2), 279–289. https://doi.org/10.1177/1049732318795675

Weinberger, D. (2019). *Everyday chaos: Technology, complexity, and how we're thriving in a new world of possibility.* Harvard Business Review Press.

Weiss, C. H. (1995). Nothing as practical as good theory: Exploring theory-based evaluation for comprehensive community initiatives for children and families. In J. P. Connell, A. C. Kubisch, L. B. Schorr, & C. H. Weiss (Eds.), *New Approaches to Evaluating Community Initiatives: Concepts, Methods, and Contexts* (pp. 65–92). The Aspen Institute.

Weisz, J. R., Donenberg, G. R., Han, S. S., & Weiss, B. (1995). Bridging the gap between laboratory and clinic in child and adolescent psychotherapy. *Journal of Consulting and Clinical Psychology*, *65*(5), 688–701. https://doi.org/10.1037/0022-006X.63.5.688

Woodard, G. S., Casline, E., Ehrenreich-May, J., Ginsburg, G. S., & Jensen-Doss, A. (2025). Consultation as an implementation strategy to increase fidelity of measurement-based care delivery in community mental health settings: An observational study. *Administration and Policy in Mental Health and Mental Health Services Research*, *52*, 28-40. https://doi.org/10.1007/s10488-023-01321-7

Youn, S. J., Boswell, J. F., Douglas, S., Harris, B. A., Aajmain, S., Arnold, K. T., Creed, T. A., Gutner, C. A., Orengo-Aguayo, R., Oswald, J. M., & Stirman, S. W. (2024). Implementation science and practice-oriented research: Convergence and complementarity. *Administration and Policy in Mental Health and Mental Health Services Research*, *51*, 336–347. https://doi.org/10.1007/s10488-023-01296-5

CONCLUSION

17

Developing Strategic Recommendations for Prioritizing Local and National Policies to Promote Practice-Based Evidence

Michael Barkham, James F. Boswell, Dana Atzil-Slonim, Louis G. Castonguay, and Wolfgang Lutz

This final chapter comprises potential implications in four domains of influence: research, policy, professional training, and clinical practice. These implications are an amalgamation and reworking by the chapter authors of suggestions from the lead authors of the individual book chapters.[1] Understandably, the suggestions by chapter authors reflected the specific foci of their own chapters. To be transparent, in drawing up our tentative recommendations, rather than reporting the finer details of their suggestions, we have sought a level of description that is inclusive and generic to establish procedures that we hope will be applicable to all practitioners.

In line with our overall aims of influencing policy makers, we have sequenced the four domains of influence, starting with research strategies (I), from which are derived policy recommendations (II), which in turn inform clinical training (III), and lastly, impact on clinical implications (IV). But it is important to note that within a model promoting the role of practice-based evidence in delivery and improvement of mental health care, this is not the end of the sequence. Because practitioners continually collect data and evaluate their practice, the sequence naturally flows back into research and allows for adjustments and modifications in a continuous process of updating and improvements. This process is represented in Figure 17.1.

[1] Dana Atzil-Slonim, Robbie Babins-Wagner, Michael Barkham, Louis G. Castonguay, Michael J. Constantino, Susan Douglas, Paula Errázuriz, Fredrik Falkenström, Ann F. Garland, Jeffrey A. Hayes, Amanda Jenson-Doss, Wolfgang Lutz, Christian Moltu, Helene A. Nissen-Lie, Andrew C. Page, and Jacqueline B. Persons.

Michael Barkham et al., *Developing Strategic Recommendations for Prioritizing Local and National Policies to Promote Practice-Based Evidence*. In: *Practice-Based Evidence in the Psychological Therapies*. Edited by: Louis G. Castonguay et al., Oxford University Press. © Oxford University Press (2026).
DOI: 10.1093/9780197748336.003.0017

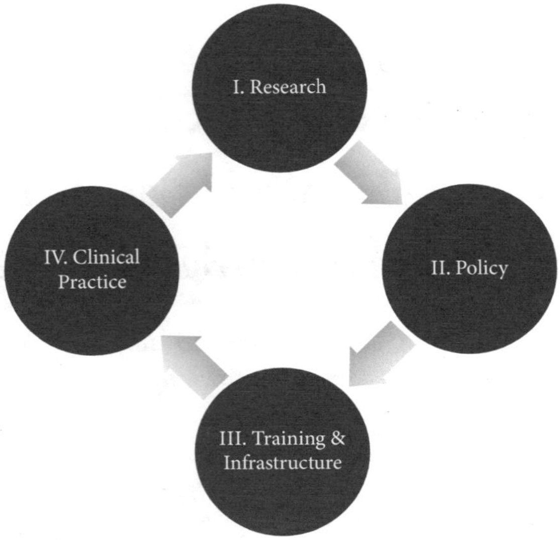

Figure 17.1 Process Model for Enhancing the Continual Relevance of Research to Local and National Policies and Their Impact on Clinical Training and Practice

Note: The figure represents four circles depicting the sequence from research, to policy, to training and supervision, and finally to clinical practice.

In terms of format, we have presented points primarily in the style of actionable statements so that readers do not have to work out what is being said: We hope this is a more direct and clear way of enabling readers to access the various take-home messages. Importantly, because there is a sequence through the 4 domains of influence, there is also a level of information flow through the 4 domains meaning there is repetition, sometimes at a general level and sometimes very specifically. We have retained this element for readers who focus in on particular sections. Also, at no point do we name any product, even if it is in the public domain. We focus on principles and heuristics, and we do not seek to promote specifically named products. The reasons, in part, are to make clear that the processes and procedures we refer to can be applied to any theoretical model of psychological therapy. As such, we do not aim to promote any one model over another.

Our recommendations are transtheoretical and underpinned by our collective view that actuarial data is a reliable source of knowledge that should inform and drive clinical judgment and action. We accept that such a perspective may be challenging for some practitioners and some models of therapy. However, the chapters in this book have shown how the paradigm of practice-based evidence builds directly from everyday practice and everyday practitioners, and it is, therefore, a paradigm of practice research for all practitioners.

Overarching Principle and Philosophy

Understandably, there is considerable potential for overlap—that is, any single point is likely to have implications in the other areas. Hence, we have attempted not to over-specify but have tried to identify more general points. Accordingly, the points made regarding each of the four domains addressed are based on an overarching principle, namely:

> Research, policy, infrastructure training, and local clinical practice are all informed, adapted, and improved by considering the systematic collection and analysis of routinely administered and assimilated local outcomes data, considered in conjunction with externally relevant research and national data, thereby emulating a learning health system.

This principle and its implied philosophy can be viewed as a current and updated version of the scientist-practitioner model, known as the Boulder model,[2] whereas now the practitioner is viewed as a person whose practice is data informed by both their own data and that of their clinical organization (i.e., practice-based evidence), together with national and international research evidence (evidence-based practice).

I. Research Strategies

In pooling the potential implications from the preceding chapters, we have drawn up a list of research recommendations that are actionable for national programs and clinical organizations involved in psychological therapies to enhance both the effectiveness of their delivery (i.e., impact of outcomes), and the equity of their reach (i.e., diversity of population needs).

[2] See Frank (1984).

A. **Adopt and implement a paradigm of practice-based evidence as an intrinsic basis for designing all subsequent research activities**

1. *Adopt routine outcome monitoring (ROM) as standard practice* by starting with either a brief condition-specific measure or brief generic measure, or with a single item—the practice needs to become the norm.
2. *Encourage ROM and practice-based research* as tools to enhance service delivery and address treatment gaps. Such activities fall under the potential arm of various national bodies.[3]
3. *Design and test interventions that match individuals to treatments* rather than fitting the individual to the practitioner's preferred intervention methods or specific theoretical models.
4. *Advocate process quality measures* (e.g., implementing a depression-screening tool at intake, or a measure of session impact) as initial steps in building databases on what practitioners do in routine practice.
5. *Address research gaps in clinical data collection, especially regarding patients who fail to engage.* For example: People who do not attend their initial sessions, and people who drop out after the initial session.[4] A disproportionate amount of research effort and activity focuses on people who are engaging in therapeutic programs rather than those who fail to engage. Attention needs to refocus on initial engagement and appropriate messaging.

B. **Establish a research strategy of designing trials *embedded* in routine practice**

1. *Adopt one form of embedded trial to maximize capacity and mimic real-world clinical decision-making. Examples include*:
   a. *Trials Within Cohorts (TWiCs):*[5] Multiple trials are embedded within a clinical organization, so they all benefit from the existing clinical infrastructure and thereby become more efficient and increase capacity.

[3] Examples of organizations include the following: in the United States, (SAMSHA), The Joint Commission, American Psychological Association, and Centers for Medicare and Medicaid Services (CMS)–approved data registries; in the United Kingdom, the National Institute for Health and Care Excellence (NICE).

[4] Historically, the modal number of therapy sessions attended is 1; See Phillips (1991).

[5] https://www.twics.global/

b. *Adaptive trials:*[6] Trials where the research design mimics clinical decision-making and can respond and adapt in view of ongoing analyses of data.

2. *Routine practice settings become the bedrock of multiple trials that benefit clinical science and patients alike.*
3. *Larger clinical trials are facilitated that are appropriately powered to lessen concerns about the generalizability of research results to routine practice.* Such trials may require funding from national agencies.[7]
4. *Encourage the establishment of crosswalk tables between well established and bona fide outcome measures.*

C. **Encourage the creation of practice-research networks as well as all avenues for mutual collaboration with practitioners nationally and internationally**

1. *Providing opportunities for diverse stakeholders* (representing different experiences and expertise in care delivery) *to actively collaborate* in the design, implementation, and dissemination of empirically rigorous and clinically helpful studies.

D. **Build in new technologies and AI into research strategies**

1. *Adopt digital technology and the judicious use of AI to support the delivery of stratified care and low-intensity interventions* aimed at the wider population.
2. *Support more preventative interventions at a population level.*
3. *Draw on diverse knowledge (qualitative, quantitative, psychometric)* to ensure technology plays a central role in delivering and adapting stakeholder-informed advancements in treatments.

E. **Increase diversity of academic disciplines within research groups and broaden diversity in target populations for research studies**

1. *Involve cognate and more diverse academic disciplines beyond psychology within research teams* (e.g., geographers, health service researchers, health economists).
2. *Emphasize culturally sensitive approaches* to ensure equitable access and effectiveness of data-informed psychological therapies across varied identity groups and diverse populations.

[6] See Bowalekar (2011).

[7] The Patient-Centered Outcomes Research Institute (PCORI) in the United States has funding mechanisms for what they label "large, pragmatic trials." https://www.pcori.org/

II. Implications for Policy Development

F. **Adopt paradigm of practice-based evidence as an equally valued and funded research paradigm to trials methodology**

1. *Promote routine clinical organizations into learning health systems* as a means for realizing the production and integration of local evidence and accumulated evidence (in the literature).[8]
2. *Fund secondary analyses of large naturalistic data sets* as a cost-efficient strategy for valuing routine data.
3. *Include quality analyses of routine data in national and local clinical practice guidelines.*
4. *Incentivize or support practices to collect ROM data* that could lead to the creation of large databases that have the potential for making important research contributions. However, such initiatives may themselves need health warnings as shown in the United States by the Centers for Medicare and Medicaid Services (CMS) initiative that started well with a "pay to collect" process for acquiring data but that subsequently generated problems and unintended consequences by overextending itself.
5. *Promote funding the development and dissemination of outcome management tools* that are free to use, can be adapted for use in diverse practice settings, and have translations available. Be wary of mandating specific outcome measures as compulsory in preference to practitioners selecting measures from a restricted basket of bona fide outcome measures to protect against freezing the field in measure development. Such activities could be carried out under the auspices of healthcare agencies and resources in specific countries.[9]
6. *Advocate process quality measures* (e.g., implementing a depression-screening tool at intake, or a measure of session impact) as initial steps in building databases on what practitioners do in routine practice.
7. *Encourage ROM and practice-based research* as tools to enhance service delivery and address treatment gaps. Such activities fall under the potential arm of various national bodies.

[8] The Agency for Healthcare Research and Quality (AHRQ) does work in this area: https://www.ahrq.gov/learning-health-systems/index.html

[9] Examples of organizations include the following: in the United States, SAMSHA, The Joint Commission, American Psychological Association, and CMS-approved data registries; in the United Kingdom, NICE.

G. **Establish relations between evidence-based (trials) and practice-based (routine) evidence based on the principle of equipoise**
  1. *Promote the paradigm of practice-based evidence and evidence-based practice in equal measure.* In addition to their complementarity, this can enhance their reciprocal influence.
  2. *Adopt embedded trials (in routine practice) and embedded measures (by routine practice)* to enable better generalizability of trial findings to routine practice.
  3. *Facilitate larger clinical trials that are appropriately powered to* lessen concerns about the generalizability of research results to routine practice. Such trials may require funding from national agencies.[10]
  4. *Extend to the adoption of smarter trials embedded in routine clinical organizations* (e.g., leapfrog trials) to accelerate the development and implementation of effective and personalized interventions.
  5. *Advocate practice-based evidence frameworks in community clinics and private practices* to reduce the research–practice gap.
  6. *Encourage the creation of practice-research networks*, providing opportunities for diverse stakeholders (representing different experiences and expertise in care delivery) to actively collaborate in the design, implementation, and dissemination of empirically rigorous and clinically helpful studies.

H. **National and international partnerships, collaboration, and infrastructure**
  1. *Promote partnerships between clinicians and research expertise* (e.g., database management, statistical analysis) through mechanisms to provide grant funding, library access, and institutional review board support.
  2. *Encourage policies supporting the integration of ROM into healthcare systems* by aligning reimbursement structures with validated care quality metrics rather than solely focusing on productivity-based measures. While this is a component of value-based care and collaborative care models, such models are still limited in practice.

[10] The Patient-Centered Outcomes Research Institute (PCORI) in the United States has funding mechanisms for what they label "large, pragmatic trials": https://www.pcori.org/

3. *Support international collaboration to standardize data collection and feedback systems across settings.* This may require navigating national and international data security and local institutional review board policies.

I. **Fund and invest in new technologies**
   1. *Adopt digital technology and judicious use of AI to support the delivery of stratified care and low-intensity interventions* aimed at the wider population.
   2. *Support more preventative interventions at a population level.*
   3. *Draw on diverse knowledge (qualitative, quantitative, psychometric)* to ensure technology plays a central role in delivering and adapting stakeholder-informed advancements in treatments.

J. **Diversity**
   1. *Emphasize culturally sensitive approaches* to ensure equitable access and effectiveness of data-informed psychological therapies across varied identity groups and diverse populations.

III. Clinical Training Infrastructure and Personal Skills Acquisition

K. **Embedding ROM principles and practices into clinical curricula and training practices**
   1. *Incorporate data-informed frameworks (i.e., ROM and associated technologies) into training programs and curricula* to encourage therapists to learn how to integrate research findings into clinical practice and develop self-reflective practice competencies.
   2. *Develop therapists' skills in interpreting and applying session-by-session feedback* to improve decision-making and treatment outcomes.
   3. *Train therapists in precision mental health approaches,* including tailoring interventions based on predictive models and patient-specific characteristics.
   4. *Use clinical problem-solving tools to train therapists in addressing challenges* like low motivation, deteriorating therapeutic alliance, and risk management.

L. **Enhanced top-up training for clinical supervisors**
   1. *Provide ongoing input and support for supervisors* regarding components of practice-based evidence.
   2. *Provide support and training to supervisors and clinic administrators* in the integration of practice-based research into clinical routines and using feedback to improve patient care.

M. **Prioritizing transtheoretical and personalized perspectives**
   1. *Encourage a reflective transtheoretical approach* where therapists combine empirical decision support with clinical judgment.
   2. *Include modules on analyzing routine outcomes data at the therapist level* and using this information to inform personalized training directions.
   3. *Create balanced focus between therapeutic techniques and common factors, including developing self-awareness*, affect regulation, and interpersonal sensitivity.

N. **Balance training on strengths and growth areas**
   1. *Personalize therapists' ongoing professional training*: Therapist performance data can be used to personalize training opportunities to fortify existing strengths and/or improve upon existing growth areas.

O. **Cross-fertilize between clinical and research postgraduates**
   1. *Provide opportunities for research trainees and clinical trainees to learn from each other* to facilitate the development of mutually respectful collaborative relationships, which help to bridge the "research–practice gap."
   2. *Provide opportunities for research trainees to learn more about the realities of practice in community-based settings* (e.g., fiscal, administrative, and clinical realities), thereby helping them enhance the ecological validity and feasibility of their research studies.

IV. Clinical Procedures and Data-Informed Practices

The clinical procedures and practices are logical extensions of the principles applied to policies and training. To reduce repetition, we have presented higher-level principles that focus on the implementation of points made under the previous headings. In effect, we have prioritized an approach to clinical practice that is data informed rather than focus on or detail aspects that emphasize specific theoretical models of psychological therapy. We have, therefore, specifically eschewed citing any clinical techniques or procedures on the basis that data-informed practice is applicable to all theoretical models.

P. **Implement routine outcome measurement and feedback systems as a key component of all clinical delivery models**
   1. *Adopt outcome measures with proven psychometric properties and endorsed by practitioners* to ensure they maximize their use to inform practice.
   2. *Use feedback procedures*, low- or high-tech, to ensure patients are responding to the assigned treatments.
   3. *Adjust the treatment decisions when there is evidence of minimal gain.*

Q. **Embrace philosophy and culture of individually implemented data-informed practice following the principle of a learning health system**
   1. *Adopt the principles of a learning health system and inform practice with evidence derived from local data collection and external (research-based) research literature.*
   2. *View the information provided by data as equivalent to continuous, patient-specific clinical supervision.*
   3. *Use routinely collected data to generate curiosity and questions, and to test clinical hypotheses, rather than seek definitive conclusions.*

R. **Build local databases**
   1. *Build local databases* to be able to determine the areas of uniqueness or differences with national data.
   2. *Understand the phenomenon of variability in data* rather than being driven by a group mean/average ("Variability is the law of life").[11]

S. **Implement stratified treatment planning and matching**
   1. *Adopt stratified care pathways for matching patients to treatments and therapists to patients* and general adoption of strategies for better matching rather than investing in "new" treatments.
   2. *Invest in strategies for addressing/improving population health* rather than a selective group of people.

[11] See Osler (1950).

3. *Target identifying patient groups for whom current treatments are less effective* and direct resources toward improving interventions for these populations.
4. *Adapt and scale up effective mental health services*, particularly in underserved populations.[12]

T. **Implement practices and procedures consistent with the principles of practice-based training. Attend and aspire to:**
1. *Utilize ROM and feedback*-informed adjustments to the delivery of therapy.
2. *Enable patients to make data-informed clinical decisions* through a collaborative decision-making process.
3. *Utilize multidimensional routine patient outcome measures* to help determine which therapists work best for whom, requiring therapists to be well informed about measures, data handling, and supporting technologies (including AI-driven models) in linking data to practice.
4. *Provide patients with therapists' historical performance information* so they can make their own data-informed referral and treatment decisions.

Conclusion

Research conducted as part of clinical routine and conducted with the goal of understanding and improving such routine has led to a rich body of practice-based evidence that should inform research policies, national and organizational guidelines for the delivery of mental health services, training programs, and day-to-day clinical practice. While randomized trials have been traditionally defined as the primary source of knowledge for the implementation of research in mental health care, the implications highlighted in this chapter demonstrate that practice-based evidence should be viewed as a complementary and equal contributor to the scientific foundations of psychological therapies.

As sophisticated technology becomes increasingly pervasive, and greater numbers of people look toward the helping professions for support, the

[12] See Fernández-Alvarez et al. (2024).

challenge for clinical practice in the coming years will be to engage in and maximize the available information to enhance the quality of patient care within all models of psychological therapy. Our hope is that the tentative recommendations documented in this chapter, together with the personal, professional, and data-informed accounts of research reported in the book chapters, help to shape and promote the principle and philosophy of practice-based evidence that provides the research, clinical, and collegial framework for all practitioners to engage in and contribute to currently and in future years.

References

Bowalekar, S. (2011). Adaptive designs in clinical trials. *Perspectives in Clinical Research*, *2*(1), 23–27. https://doi.org/10.4103/2229-3485.76286

Fernández-Alvarez, J., Molinari, G., Kilcullen, R., Delgadillo, J., Drill, R., Errázuriz, P., Falkenström, F., Firth, N., O'Shea, A., Paz, C., Youn, S. J., & Castonguay, L. G. (2024). The importance of conducting practice-oriented research with underserved populations. *Administration and Policy in Mental Health*, *51*, 358–375. https://doi.org/10.1007/s10488-023-01337-z

Frank, G. (1984). The Boulder Model: History, rationale, and critique. *Professional Psychology: Research and Practice*, *15*(3), 417–435. https://doi.org/10.1037/0735-7028.15.3.417

Osler, W. (1950). *Aphorisms from his bedside teachings and writings.* Henry Schuman.

Phillips, E. L. (1991). George Washington University's international data on psychotherapy delivery systems: Modeling new approaches to the study of psychotherapy. In L. E. Beutler & M. Crago (Eds.), *Psychotherapy research: An international review of programmatic studies* (pp. 263–273). American Psychological Association.

Index

For the benefit of digital users, indexed terms that span two pages (e.g., 52–53) may, on occasion, appear on only one of those pages.

Tables and figures are indicated by *t* and *f* following the page number.